SEXUAL ETHICS AND ISLAM

Sexual Ethics and Islam

Feminist Reflections on Qur'an, Hadith,
and Jurisprudence

Expanded & Revised Edition

Kecia Ali

ONEWORLD

SEXUAL ETHICS AND ISLAM

First published by Oneworld Publications, 2006

This edition published by Oneworld Publications, 2016
Copyright © Kecia Ali, 2006, 2016

ISBN 978-1-78074-381-3
ISBN 978-1-78074-853-5 (eBook)

Typeset by Jayvee, Trivandrum, India
Printed and bound in
Great Britain by Clays Ltd, St Ives plc

Oneworld Publications
10 Bloomsbury Street
London, WC1B 3SR
England

Study of the tradition demands an exercise of the historical imagination that is sympathetic as well as critical; sometimes what is branded as obscurantism or bigotry is simply a reflection of a climate of ideas wholly alien from that of our own time. Some of the sexual notions transmitted to us from the past are unfounded, and their effect has proved to be damaging; but while we may deplore this, we must also make the effort to understand where they originated and why they were accepted – and to realize that their advocates were rarely moved by malevolence or stupidity.

Sherwin Bailey, *Sexual Ethics: A Christian View*

Contents

Acknowledgements

This book advocates, among other things, assessing custom-ary practices and, rather than implementing them unques-tioningly, modifying them as necessary. It seems fitting, then, that as I uphold the tradition of acknowledging the numerous debts accrued in writing this volume, I alter it in one impor-tant respect: I wish to thank my family first, rather than last. My husband, Mohamad Ali, has been extraordinarily support-ive over the years I have worked on this project. Our children, Shaira, Saadia, and Tariq, continue to inspire me with their insistence on asking "why" when confronted with unfairness and injustice as well as their unwillingness to accept uncon-vincing answers. The confidence and encouragement from members of our extended family have sustained me over the years. They all have my gratitude as well as my love.

This project has its roots in my work during 2001–2003 with the Feminist Sexual Ethics Project, funded by the Ford Foundation and led by Bernadette Brooten. The first versions of several of these essays, published on its website, took shape as I worked alongside Gail Labovitz, Monique Moultrie, Raja El-Habti, and Molly Lanzarotta. I collected additional mate-rial during 2003–2004, while working on another project as a research associate at Harvard's Women's Studies in Religion Program. My colleagues at WSRP were enthusiastic; Sharon Gillerman in particular helped by translating crucial portions of an article for me on short notice. The bulk of this book was written during my time as a Florence Levy Kay postdoctoral fellow at Brandeis University. A number of its ideas were first presented and discussed in public lectures and conferences at the American Academy of Religion annual meetings, Brandeis

University, Boston University, Brown University, Clemson University, Duke University, New York University, and Princeton University.

It would be impossible to name all the individuals with whom I've enjoyed conversing and debating over the topics in this book, but a few cannot escape mention. Ebrahim Moosa and Bruce Lawrence at Duke University were particularly helpful, as was miriam cooke, who read a complete draft of the manuscript and made many helpful suggestions. Farid Esack, Jamillah Karim, Kevin Reinhart, Omid Safi, Sa'diyya Shaikh, Laury Silvers, Harvey Stark, and Amina Wadud asked perceptive questions and prompted me to clarify certain points and expand on others. Zahra Ayubi, Ariel Berman, Ayesha Siddiqua Chaudhry, Aysha Hidayatullah, Scott Kugle (who also helped with translation in a pinch), Rusmir Music, and Audrey Shore commented on chapter drafts. Anjum Ansari, Afshan Bokhari, Sepi Gilani, and Mara Worle, as well as their respective husbands Bil Ragan, Scott Chisholm, Alex Norbash, and Amr Ragy, have been part of numerous dinner conversations on the topics of this volume. Needless to say, they did not always agree with me, or each other, but their astute comments and sharp observations have made this a better book than it otherwise would be. I owe Mara special thanks for her comments on drafts of chapters 1 and 5. Though I have appreciated the advice of all of these individuals, I have not always taken it, and none of them is in any way responsible for any errors of fact or interpretation that remain.

Finally, I would like to thank Hend al-Mansour for granting permission to use her painting on the cover. It contains text drawn from Surat Yusuf, the chapter of the Qur'an that tells the story of the attempted seduction of the Prophet Joseph by his master's wife, traditionally known as Zulaykha. This "best of stories" includes passionate female desire, attempted sexual coercion, and divinely ordained standards of intimate conduct for men and women. It seemed particularly apt as an image: Muslim women are rereading and reimagining the Qur'an, in dialogue and in tension with previous approaches but still bound by certain constraints of the text itself.

Acknowledgements for the 2016 edition

I joined the faculty at Boston University in September 2006, soon after the first edition of this book appeared. BU has been a welcoming and stimulating institutional home and I am grateful for the support and interest of my colleagues in the Religion Department, Muslim Studies, and across the university. I have also had the good fortune to be involved with the American Academy of Religion and the Society for the Study of Muslim Ethics; colleagues at all stages of their careers, in numerous institutions, have connected with me, challenged me, and continually reminded me that scholarship, done right, is a conversation.

On that note, I must especially thank my conversation partners for this book, though I cannot possibly name everyone with whom I have talked about the issues discussed here. Over the years, conversations with Ayesha Chaudhry, Farid Esack, Mohammed Fadel, Juliane Hammer, Aysha Hidayatullah, Scott Kugle, Sa'diyya Shaikh, and Amina Wadud have shaped my thinking. A conference organized by Gabeba Baderoon, Fatima Seedat, Nina Hoel, and Jonathan Brockopp helped me clarify the format of this new edition. Anver Emon and Jerusha Lamptey along with her seminar students offered comments about the original edition of the book. Jessica Stern and Graeme Wood talked with me about the 'Islamic State.' Rumee Ahmed, Hina Azam, Karen Bauer, Aisha Geissinger, and Debra Majeed shared forthcoming work with me. Aisha and Debra along with Jamillah Karim, Laura P., two correspondents who wish to remain anonymous, and Laury Silvers, read drafts of one or more Codas along the way, offering suggestions, asking for clarifications, and giving pointed criticism where appropriate. Laury deserves special thanks for reading all the new material in draft at least once and giving encouragement along with critical feedback. It would not be quite true to make the usual disclaimer that none of these people is responsible for the ideas found here: in some way, they all very much are, as it was in dialogue with them that I formulated my thoughts. In their final version, however, the ideas expressed are mine, as is any blame for failures of fact or analysis.

My family was, as always, a source of strength and joy. Mohamad, Saadia, Tariq: thank you. Shaira: I miss you.

Tamam Kahn begins her *Untold: A History of the Wives of Prophet Muhammad* with the poem "who do you think you are?" It reads in part:

Who said you could do this? Who
are your ancestors, professors, godparents,
your stewards of the seen and unseen?
Locate for us your committee of yes.

This anniversary edition is dedicated to the women who comprise my committee of yes. You know who you are.

Note on texts, translation, and transliteration

Because the specific Arabic terminology and its connotations are so vital to the issues at stake, particularly where the words have legal implications, I have striven for consistency in my translation of key terms. Where I had to choose between a literal-but-awkward rendering or a more idiomatic but less precise rendering, I have generally chosen the former. Unless otherwise noted, translations of works cited in Arabic are mine and works cited in English translation are by the translator. However, because of the nuances of the terms at stake, I have often chosen to retranslate passages from Arabic text included in a parallel English/Arabic edition of a particular text. I have made clear in the Notes where I have done so.

Where I have quoted hadith works and legal texts, I have provided the titles of chapter and subsection in addition to volume and page number for the editions cited in the Bibliography, so that those working with other editions of the texts can more easily locate the relevant passages. In the case of the *Sahih*s of Bukhari and Muslim, I have usually chosen to cite the English or English/Arabic editions for ease of reference.

I have generally followed the IJMES system for transliteration but, for the sake of simplicity, I do not use diacritical marks with the exception of ' for medial hamza and ' for 'ayn. Those familiar with Arabic should not have difficulty recognizing the terms used.

Preface to the 2016 edition

In the decade since this book was first published, it has been read, cited, and discussed in a variety of settings, by Muslims and non-Muslims from a variety of backgrounds. In writing it, I imagined its primary audience as Muslim women, inside and outside the academy, engaged in critical rethinking of Islamic norms and fresh interpretations of scriptural texts. To my surprise, the book has also found a home in many classrooms, sometimes assigned in full, often in part, facilitated by its organization into topical essays. This structure emerged from the book's earliest iteration as a series of online posts and served the material well. The relatively self-contained nature of the chapters, however, partially obscures the book's main claim: genuinely transformative sexual ethics, an ethics conducive to all people's full flourishing, requires a major overhaul of who reads texts, and how they read, talk about, and implement their ideas in diverse contexts. Honesty and transparency about gendered structures of authority and power are necessary steps toward transformation.

The first edition of this book was primarily concerned with intra-Muslim debates and discussions. It focused on the theoretical and the textual, with reference to but largely abstracted from the concrete material circumstances of Muslim lives. This edition still says relatively little about lived experience, but attends more to Muslim women's reflections. It makes more of an attempt, on some topics, to connect debates occurring among Muslims to their larger discursive contexts. In part, this owes to my shift in focus. I have paid more attention in my recent scholarly projects to the ways that Muslim and non-Muslim writings about, for instance, prophetic biography have been deeply intertwined since the nineteenth century. It seems to me, though this may simply be an artifact of my attention shift, that Muslim thinking about sexuality and its regulation is increasingly entangled with non-Muslim, Western norms.

The spectrum of Muslim engagements with interlocutors both Muslim and non-Muslim is vast. There is no one Muslim perspective on anything. Even among madrasa-educated scholars, who "form a global network and ... speak a common language," one finds "a spectrum of views ranging from enlightened to obscurantist."[1] If one includes the much wider range of figures from academic, activist, and other backgrounds who participate in religious debates, one finds nearly infinite permutations of religious discourse, especially online – a forum available ten years ago, but which has far greater scope, depth, and reach today. On and offline, Muslim discourses encompass apologetic presentations of women's true status in Islam as well as unapologetically confrontational propaganda from the so-called Islamic State. Indeed, IS propaganda itself incorporates a rhetoric of liberation when recruiting Western women and girls while, in an Arabic document, celebrating women's domestic roles as an alternative to Western-style liberation.[2] In other writings, as well as in actions undertaken not just by extremist movements but also by national governments in new legislation, harsh punishments appear as defiantly resistant to Western norms: as Rafia Zakaria puts it, "Western horror represents not moral pressure to change a local practice, but rather the affirmation of its purity and rightness."[3]

This book, mainly concerned with ideas, largely ignores the concrete economic, political, and social circumstances of most Muslim women, particularly in the global south or what some call the two-thirds world. It says very little about ongoing efforts to reform "family law" in the numerous nations where putatively Islamic laws govern marriage, divorce, custody and the like. In doing so, perhaps it give the impression that these are not serious or ongoing debates. On the contrary, reform and counter-reform exist. Organizations like the long-standing Women Living Under Muslim Laws network (WLUML) and the newer Musawah, which did not exist when I wrote the first

edition of this book, differ in their methods and their philoso-
phies but are united by the goal of improving women's access
to substantive justice. Musawah's goal is to undo the seeming
"inevitability" of patriarchal versions of the law. To seriously
address the varied, complex, and shifting laws and legal debates
in one Muslim-majority nation or region, let alone all of them,
would require a massive study; that is not my task here. There
are, undoubtedly, connections as well as parallels between discourses influential in Canada and those of Jordan, Libya, or
Brunei; my emphasis, however, is primarily on Muslims in
minority contexts, especially the United States.

Though it says a bit more about American Muslim women
than about others, it is by no means an ethnographic or socio-
logical study. I remain convinced that one cannot write mean-
ingfully about lived Muslim ethics in ways that gloss over major
differences of language, location, class, education, and so forth.
The struggles over interpretation with which this book is primarily concerned do not occur in a vacuum but manifest in
a variety of ways in different locations. Still, it seemed to me
that there was justification for approaching them primarily
as abstract, textually grounded problems. As a South African
colleague remarked to me after reading the book, I seemed to
assume that difficult issues of sexual ethics could be resolved by
arriving at better readings of scripture, clearer understandings
of jurisprudence, and more cogent theological views.

I am more attentive now than I was a decade ago to the ways
in which classism, racism, and imperialism shape the production of ideas as well as lived realities. Those realities demand
our attention. Crisis stalks lands where many Muslims live.
After the hopefulness of the Arab Spring, parts of Egypt have
witnessed a mix of violent lawlessness and brutal repression.
In Syrian refugee camps, early marriage has surged as families
have sought to find protection for daughters; rape, all too common, threatens not only immediate harm but girls' future prospects – female virginity remains important. In Iraq, IS soldiers
broadcast their capture, enslavement, and sale of Yazidi girls
and women, claiming religious legitimacy for their acts, even as
they replicate the earlier secular Ba'athist regime's practice of

terrorizing opponents with sexual violence. Nigerian separatists Boko Haram have kidnapped scores of girls, forcing them into marriages, threatening to sell them as slaves; they have also begun to use women and girls to carry out bombings.

Muslim militias and armies are hardly unique in perpetrating sexual violence.[4] Yet because I – perhaps naïvely – think of religion as a resource for ethical imagination, attempts by IS and Boko Haram to justify rape as religiously sanctioned enslavement or lawful marriage seem particularly deplorable to me. By turning what has historically been a common practice of combatants regardless of religion into a signal feature of "Islamic" warfare, these militants rely on retrograde interpretations of scriptural texts and appeal to supposedly authentic religious law. At the same time, they ignore classical legal safeguards and constraints governing wartime conduct.[5] This is not to excuse or apologize for the patriarchal and misogynistic provisions of "traditional" Muslim legal thinking, which I have analyzed and critiqued extensively in this book and elsewhere.[6] Rather, it is to emphasize that these attempts to justify new brutalities with old rules instantiate novel horrors, which affect women disproportionately.

Sexual violence, by and/or against Muslims, is inseparable from other forms of violence, foreign and domestic. To focus only on sexual and sexualized violence is to ignore its imbrication with other forms of violent domination, by individuals, organizations, and states. Violence is made possible and intelligible within certain structures. To take an example not directly related to the main topic of this book, racialized violence in my homeland has been lately brought into sharp relief. The general public is increasingly aware of police killings of unarmed African American women, men, boys, girls, and, at highly disproportionate rates, trans people. The media are beginning to report the continual failure of the system to indict or convict officers who shoot, beat, or choke black people to death. There is a groundswell of outrage over systemic impunity for police brutality toward people of color. This brutality is an epiphenomenon of deeper, structural violence, including mass incarceration of African Americans, a good proportion of whom are Muslim, and militarized responses to organized dissent, including protests over black deaths.

Militarized policing in the United States is contiguous with and genealogically related to military interventions overseas and the so-called war on terror. Even setting aside the use of counter-terrorism equipment and tactics against American civilians on American soil, and the use of parallel interrogation techniques in Chicago and Guantánamo, there is the broader effect of American policy on global events – and the impact of state-authorized American deployments of violence. As the 2014 CIA Torture Report indicates, American violence includes sexualized violence. It also includes deeply impersonal, even robotic violence: drone attacks have killed thousands, including many non-combatants, during the presidency of Barack Obama alone. American drone attacks remain a terrifying fact of life in too many places, and inflame anti-American sentiments.

Geopolitics is inseparable from local Muslim (and American) realities. Acts like the invasion of Iraq contribute to regional destabilization that creates conditions for actors like IS to emerge. Sexual violence thrives in the turmoil generated in part by American military intervention in the Middle East. Creating conditions for just sexual ethics to thrive among Muslims worldwide involves curtailing American uses and abuses of political and military might.

This book, while taking cognizance of these larger questions, is primarily concerned with the assumptions underlying religious thinking and decision making. Activists insist that #BlackLivesMatter in the face of repeated demonstrations that, to many in positions of power, they do not. This book asks: Whose ideas matter? Whose voices will be taken seriously? Whose opinions will receive attention? In asking these questions, it intervenes in ongoing debates. It does not attempt to have the final word on anything but rather to make it possible for Muslims to discuss more thoughtfully crucial issues of our time. That was my hope for the first edition of this book; I hope that this updated edition will further enrich conversations.

In deciding how to update this book, I considered rewriting some of the chapters. For example, Chapter 5, on same-sex intimacy and gender identity, dodges crucial issues, including those raised by bisexuality. Scholarship, activism, and law have moved in the last decade, leaving the chapter dated, especially on transgender issues. It reflects the time in which it was written and my best thinking at that moment, though, so I have let it and the other chapters stand as originally written. Their analyses remain, I think, relevant; for every topic where conversations have proceeded in useful ways there are at least as many where they remain mired in hasty generalizations, unsupported assertions, and sloppy logic. Instead of revising earlier material, I supplement each chapter with a Coda indicating places where my thinking has changed, noting vibrant new debates, or discussing recent developments. The topics remain essentially the same, though I devote more attention to specifically American contexts and thinkers; I also discuss polygyny, mostly ignored in the first edition, in the Coda to Chapter 2. These Codas, which vary somewhat in length, are suggestive rather than exhaustive; their references to new publications are selective rather than comprehensive. The largest frustration of preparing this edition was keeping the amount of new material manageable; many of the issues raised here deserve far fuller treatments than I have given them. An afterword returns to the question of women's authority, and gestures toward work remaining to be done.

One last matter requires mention. Since, as feminists insist, all knowledge production is situated, my social location is relevant. I am a white, cisgender American woman not currently living with a disability.[7] I write from within "the 'charmed circle' of a monogamous and reproductive heterosexuality."[8] Though I draw on scholarship by and conversations with people with different identities and distinct life experiences, my work is inevitably informed by my privilege. I intend this volume as a contribution to a rethinking of gender, sexuality and ethics among Muslims; my aim is not to offer a comprehensive program of action but to encourage broader discussions among a wider range of participants. Reader, that means you.

Introduction

For the vast majority of Muslims worldwide – not only extremists or conservatives, but also those who consider themselves moderate or progressive – determining whether a particular belief or practice is acceptable largely hinges on deciding whether or not it is legitimately "Islamic." Even many of those who do not base their personal conduct or ideals on normative Islam believe, as a matter of strategy, that in order for social changes to achieve wide acceptance among Muslims they must be convincingly presented as compatible with Islam. This focus on Islamic authenticity is particularly intense on matters relating to women, gender, and the family, where complex issues are often reduced to fodder for charged debates over "women's status in Islam." The so-called woman question is central to both anti-Muslim polemic and the apologetic counter-discourse that adopts a terminology of liberation to describe the way "true" or "real" Islam respects and protects women, despite the existence of potentially oppressive "cultural" practices. The limitations of these dichotomous approaches are evident, and a rich and growing body of scholarship by Muslim women and men seeks to deepen and complicate discussions of issues relevant to women's lives as well as our understanding of the layered and intertwined nature of dominant discourses.

As a precursor to my own foray into these treacherous waters, I want to highlight the importance of questioning women's status in Islam – a phrase that can be read at least three ways. First, despite its reductionist language, the notion of "women's status in Islam" can serve as shorthand conveying the point that a number of interrelated inequities constrain the lives of many Muslim women. But this acknowledgement alone will not get

us very far. A second approach would question the usefulness
of the concept of "women's status" itself. Muslim women are
so diverse in terms of class, geography, ethnicity, age, marital
history, and education that generalizations about our "status"
are meaningless. Even if one limits the application of the term
to the realm of ideals rather than women's lived experience, the
presupposition of an idealized and uniform tradition dramatically oversimplifies a complex and heterogeneous intellectual
and textual legacy that spans nearly a millennium and a half.
Yet the tendency to cast discussions in terms of women's status persists, particularly where Muslims want to point out that
there is no necessary link between Islam and specific injustices.
Several years ago, after the September 11 attacks, I contributed
a chapter to an anthology of writings by American Muslims.[1] I
chose a title, "The Problematic Question of Women's Status in
Islam," appropriate to my essay's argument that the formulation of the question was inherently flawed. An editor returned
my proofs with the content intact, but a new and improved
title: "The True Status of Women in Islam." Although we did
reach agreement on another title (which did not mention "status" at all), the incident made clear to me that even for those
with a critical agenda, it requires vigilance to escape reliance on
clichéd and defensive modes of presentation.

The phrase "questioning women's status in Islam" can also
be read in a third way, as addressing the status of women who
question. Too often, Muslims, especially females, who challenge
certain widely accepted views are met with warnings to desist;
that way, it is said, lies heresy, blasphemy, apostasy. Those
who have appointed themselves the guardians of communal
orthodoxy are particularly vigilant on matters concerned with
women and gender – in part, because it is in these realms that
the construction of Muslim identity in self-conscious opposition to a decadent West takes place.

The terms "Islam" and the "West" are oppositional but also
interdependent; their relationship to one another is in a process of constant renegotiation, particularly now that one can
speak of "Western Muslims." The growing Muslim populations
in nations that have long exemplified the Other for Muslim

thinkers are only one reason that this dichotomy is unsatisfactory. Muslim thinkers as well as their works easily cross borders, through satellite television, Internet sites, and subsidized translations of doctrinally correct materials for distribution in European and North American mosques. Even materials produced for audiences in Muslim societies of the Middle East and South Asia are not unaffected by Western discourses; centuries of give-and-take, built on the unequal socio-economic and geopolitical foundations of European colonialism, have resulted in a palpable enmeshing of concern with the West in all facets of Muslim intellectual life and production, but none more so than women and gender.

To generalize, Western discourse from the colonial era onward portrays the basic condition of the Muslim woman as downtrodden, in contrast to the respected and (sometimes) liberated Western woman.[2] By and large, Muslim discussions of women's place, position, or status – in English and other Western languages, especially – are a reaction to these Western critiques. In quite a number of works, selective quotations from nineteenth-and twentieth-century European authorities are used either to praise Islamic norms as superior to Western ones, or to corroborate a view about female nature also held by the Muslim author. In other instances, Muslim authorities may attempt to reverse the values assigned to Muslim and Western treatment of women by criticizing lax moral standards or other elements of Western social life.

Although these works are ostensibly concerned with women, the rhetoric on both sides tends to revolve around sex and sexuality. Western media present the Muslim woman as a figure whose oppression is inextricably linked to her sexuality; her oppression is a particularly sexual one, symbolized by fanatical concern with women's bodies, "the veil," and female seclusion. Muslim critique, unwittingly echoing certain Western feminist arguments, counters that when it comes to female dress, Western societies oppress women by judging their worth as persons based on physical attractiveness. While non-Muslims judge the lot of the Muslim woman harsh because of the permissibility of polygamy, Muslim authors counter, not without some justification, that an obsessive focus on polygamy as degrading to women is hypocritical when adultery, serial remarriage, and out-of-wedlock births to men who do not take paternal responsibility are rampant in the West. In non-marital liaisons, "The man has no commitment or obligation toward the mistress or girl friend"[3] which, the argument goes, stands in contrast to the humane, honest, and realistic nature of polygamy.[4]

On matters of sexual morality in general, Muslim authors from a variety of perspectives present the Muslim model as better for women than degrading Western norms which, in allowing unrestricted sexual liberty, fail to protect women from male exploitation. A Nigerian scholar whose works on Islamic topics are circulated extensively, 'Abdul Rahman Doi captures a common sentiment when he declares, "Heart-breaking transference of love and affection, neglected wives, forsaken children, mistresses, and street girls are common features of Western life."[5] In contrast to "Western women [who] are the most unhappy creatures on earth," Muslim women are protected by breadwinning husbands who provide adequately and consistently for their dependents, a category that includes wives and children.[6] A Muslim husband is the ultimate authority within his home but does not act in a dictatorial fashion or abuse his powers of decision making, and it is his greater rationality that protects the family from the easy dissolution that would occur if women were given control over divorce.

This idealized portrait of Muslim family life clearly cannot be compared fairly to the worst abuses found in non-Muslim Western society. It is seldom acknowledged or even recognized, however, that the model of family life Doi and others idealize in this way not only does not describe reality for the majority of Muslims, but is also quite distinct from the ideals upheld in authoritative premodern texts, where sexual availability, not child-rearing or homemaking, was a wife's main duty. Of course, these texts were prescriptive rather than descriptive, and other evidence suggests that many non-elite women did perform considerable household work and were primary providers of care for their children. At the level of ideals, however, Doi's neo-traditional vision departs considerably from earlier models of Muslim sexual ethics. Although classical and medieval thinkers expressed, like Doi, strong concern for a husband's economic responsibilities toward his wife as well as his kind treatment of her, they authorized multiple wives and unlimited concubines for men with no stigma attached and accepted restrictions on women's mobility to ensure their exclusivity and availability to the men with sexual rights over them. Ninth-century jurist al-Shafi'i spoke for the majority when he declared that a husband was not bound by a stipulation in his marriage contract not to marry additional wives or take any concubines from among his female slaves, justifying his view on the ground that such a condition "would be narrowing what God made wide for [the man]."[7]

In fact, the matter-of-fact references to concubinage throughout the writings of Muslim scholars highlight the most striking difference between contemporary and classical sexual ethics: the premodern acceptance of a male owner's sexual access to his female slaves. Classical texts were not describing demographic reality, but rather participating in a discourse of advice and regulation. Nonetheless, their assumption that men would have multiple sexual partners, wives and/or concubines, stands in marked distinction to contemporary Muslim discourses on sexual relationships which, when they discuss polygamy approvingly, generally do so with justifications premised on female needs for protection rather than simple male prerogative. Although generalizations about modern sensibilities are fraught with peril, particularly given the diversity within the billion-strong Muslim populace, it is not a stretch to claim that most Muslims today would view al-Shafi'i's doctrine on permissible sexual relationships, particularly concerning slave concubines, as incompatible with fairness and justice (themselves notoriously variable concepts).[8] Yet while virtually no one advocates reviving slavery as an institution, slaveholding fundamentally shaped the contours of Islamic ethical and legal thought on sex in ways that have not been fully recognized. And although the clearly unequal model of sexual ethics enshrined in classical texts no longer makes sense to a significant number of Muslims, at least at an intuitive level, nothing new has emerged to replace it. Despite the readiness of some Muslims to discard the model inherited from the classical jurists in favor of something more egalitarian – and the desire, on the part of a subset of these, to be open to new forms of sanctioned relationships – little attention has been paid to themes such as consent, reciprocity, and coercion that are crucial to both an understanding of traditional Islamic sexual ethics and the possibilities for transformations in those ideals. My exploration of these issues in this book is a preliminary contribution to a necessary and far-ranging conversation over all aspects of sexual ethics in Muslim life and thought.

Of course, the sexual subordination of women is by no means exclusive to Muslim societies or Islamic thought. Until the very recent past there was a near universality of laws proposing a system of allocating marital rights based on an exchange of male support and protection for female "sexual, reproductive, and housekeeping services."[9] (The exact contours of such exchanges varied dramatically between and even within societies due to variables including class status and religious doctrine; in Muslim societies, the requirement of housekeeping was usually absent in theory, however prevalent in practice.) Slavery in ancient Greece and Rome, which was both widespread and legal, illustrates that the sexual use of owned persons is not unique to Islamic texts or practice; likewise, biblical texts also permit, or at least tacitly condone, the sexual use of female slaves as well as polygamy.[10] Nor are sexual slavery and sexual abuse (of both males and females) limited to ancient societies, as contemporary debates over human trafficking and sex work indicate. Specifically sexual abuse exists within a larger climate of widespread intimate violence against women and girls, from bride-burnings or "dowry deaths" in India, to "crimes of passion" in the United States and Latin America, where jealous men murder (ex-)wives or (ex-)girlfriends.

Systemic injustices call for comparative treatment of hierarchical and gendered domination across geographic, chronological, and cultural boundaries.[11] Yet although such study is necessary and fruitful, calls for comparison by those working on Islam-related topics are too often motivated not by a sincere wish to understand deeper structures of oppression but by the desire to divert attention and criticism from Islam and Muslims. It is true that Muslim norms and practices are historically consonant with those of other religions and civilizations, and that the criticisms frequently levied against Islam by non-Muslim Westerners reflect both cultural ignorance and historical amnesia. To take just one example, Americans and Europeans who decry the normative requirement of marital subordination for Muslim women seem to forget that "obedience was so fundamental to the biblical idea of a wife that it remained in Jewish and Christian wedding vows until the late twentieth century."[12] This work takes the existence of these parallels as a given, using comparative examples primarily to highlight significant variations – as, for example, between ancient Near Eastern and biblical views on illicit sex and those of classical Muslim authors. In restricting myself largely to Islamic texts and, to a lesser extent, Muslim experiences, I am aware that I run the risk of contributing to the common impression that Islam is uniquely oppressive toward women or that the problems of sexual ethics Muslims face are somehow more intractable than those confronted by adherents of other faiths. Some may view my focus on sexual matters as playing into the Western obsession with Muslim sexuality at the expense of other, more vital, areas of concern. Poverty, political repression, war, and global power dynamics are, indeed, crucial to Muslim women's lives.[13] However, even these issues cannot be entirely divorced from sex and sexuality: poverty matters differently for women, when it constrains women's inability to negotiate marriage terms or leave abusive spouses; repressive regimes may attempt to demonstrate their "Islamic" credentials by capitulating to demands for "Shari'a" in family matters or imposing putatively Islamic laws that punish women disproportionately for sexual transgressions. Nonetheless, as Jewish feminist theologian Judith Plaskow points out, "writing about sexuality unavoidably re-enacts singling it out as a special issue and problem."[14] The possible benefits of an exploration of sexual ethics seem to me worth the risks, given the frequent invocation of Islamic authenticity in those spaces where religion has a normative impact – that is, nearly everywhere.

Why, though, focus on texts when Islamic normative doctrine has never been entirely reliable as an indicator of Muslim practice? Notwithstanding British colonial official F.X. Ruxton's claim, in the preface to his translation of a fourteenth-century Maliki legal manual, that "in the case of Muhammadan countries, it is the Law that has moulded the people, and not the people the Law," in reality the effects of social circumstances on both the formulation and the implementation of the law has always been of central importance.[15] Real women's (and men's) lives do not neatly follow the patterns set out in legal manuals, and have never done so.[16] As noted above, differences between and within Muslim populations are so significant that any attempts to discuss "the Muslim woman" or "sex in Islam" must be suspect; variables of class, geography, and time period, not to mention individual characteristics which are impossible to account for in statistics, make generalizations frequently misleading. Additionally, for the sensitive subjects under discussion here, empirical evidence concerning practice is difficult to obtain. But there is a relationship between ideal and reality and there is a certain coherence to premodern prescriptive models of Muslim womanhood and sexual relations.[17] It is precisely in the arena of sexual ethics where normative Islamic texts and thought have been, and continue to be, most influential.

Before proceeding to consider these texts, it is worth asking why a Muslim who considers herself progressive (with all the caveats about the inadequacy of that term) should bother with engaging the Islamic intellectual tradition at all. Doing so, it is true, bolsters the authority of "written Islam, textual, 'men's' Islam (an Islam essentially not of the Book but of the Texts, the medieval texts)" at the expense "of the oral and ethical traditions of lived Islam."[18] As Leila Ahmed points out, "textual Islam" has historically been the province of a male elite, and does not accurately represent the understandings of Islam embedded in the experiences of many Muslims, especially women. If I do not accept the sole interpretive authority of the juristic and exegetical heritage – which is strongly patriarchal and sometimes misogynist – why not bypass it entirely, and turn to the Qur'an alone as a guide? What is to be gained from focusing energy on analysis and critique of texts that I do not consider authoritative?[19] There are several possible answers to these questions. In part, the scholars are worth studying because of their methodological sophistication, acceptance of divergent perspectives, and their diligence in the pursuit of understanding of the divine will. More obviously, they are worth analyzing because their frameworks and assumptions often undergird modern views in ways that are not fully recognized or understood.

For all of its flaws and insufficiencies, the Muslim intellectual and, especially, legal tradition provides significant ground for engagement on matters of ethics. Conventional wisdom in some circles has come to view "oral" Islam (which Ahmed equates to "women's" Islam) as more compassionate and ethical than "textual" or "official" ("men's") Islam but this is an oversimplification. As Ahmed and others show, "official" or "textual" Islam is sometimes more protective of women's rights than cultural practices that depart from the jurists' rules. It is impossible to generalize about whether popular practices are more favorable to women than strict observance of doctrine, because so much depends on which women and which doctrine. In any case, the premodern legal texts dismissed by many contemporary thinkers as hopelessly patriarchal or narrowly legalistic are attuned to ethical considerations to a considerable extent, even though, on many matters of gender and sex, their authors' ethical visions depart from those that I see as being in accordance with highest aspirations of the Qur'an. In part, this book is an attempt to demonstrate that constructive and critical engagement with the Islamic intellectual heritage can be important in providing a framework for renewed and invigorated Muslim ethical thought.

The scholarly tradition is one significant source of knowledge and wisdom; much is lost when Muslims – Qur'an-only feminists or pro-hadith Salafis – choose to bypass it for a literalist approach to source texts.[20] Careful investigation of the legal tradition, for instance, demonstrates the ways in which authorities

have, from the earliest years of Islam, used their own judgment and the customs of their societies to adapt Qur'anic and
prophetic dictates to changed circumstances. It illustrates that
some of the doctrines taken for granted as "Islamic" emerged at
a particular time and place as the result of human interpretive
endeavor and need not be binding for all time. Furthermore,
the precedent of earlier jurists can authorize a similar interpretive and adaptive process for Muslims today, including bypassing (through a variety of interpretive devices) even seemingly
clear Qur'anic statements. A legal methodology offers legitimacy for a flexible approach to the Qur'an and the Prophet's
sunnah as revelation that emerged in a historical context.[21]

How does this discussion of jurisprudence and law relate
to the issue of ethics? The word ethics does not have a precise equivalent in Arabic; *akhlaq*, the usual term, is better rendered as morals or character, and *adab*, a less frequently used
alternative, is more appropriately translated as comportment.[22]
Most of what falls under the rubric of ethics as understood in
the modern West was the purview of the Muslim jurists, who
addressed issues well beyond the scope of what is usually understood by "law." As Jonathan Brockopp states, "Islamic 'law' is
better characterized as an ethical system than a legal one. It
does not merely separate action into categories of required
and forbidden, but also includes intermediate categories of
recommended, reprehensible, and indifferent."[23] This five-
fold classification scheme (*al-ahkam al-khamsa*) became standard among Muslim thinkers, although they often disagreed
about where particular acts fell on the scale.[24] It allows for
more nuanced categorizations than the simple "lawful/forbid-
den" (*halal/haram*) dichotomy – often equated to Islamic/un-
Islamic – that informs contemporary Muslim discourses.[25] The
lawful/forbidden dyad was, of course, relevant for premodern
Muslim scholars, who warned against "making lawful what
is forbidden and forbidding what is lawful," but they generally engaged in a less categorical and more nuanced analysis of
moral and immoral behavior.

What does it mean to say that something is lawful or forbidden according to Islam (or Islamic law or *shari'a*) today? The

relationship between enforceable duties and ethical obligations has become increasingly blurred in a world where Islamic legal institutions no longer function in anything like the manner they did in the classical and medieval periods.[26] Even in the premodern Muslim world, the jurists' doctrines did not find direct expression in the courts. Given these shifts, is Islamic jurisprudence the necessary framework for resolving how to address issues of marriage, family, and sex? While some insist that the legal framework developed by Muslim jurists from approximately 900–1400 CE must govern all Muslim behavior, the reality in the contemporary world is that the vast majority of social and economic transactions engaged in by Muslims, even in majority-Muslim societies, do not strictly follow these legal precepts. Only on some matters of personal status do some majority-Muslim nations retain religiously based laws, and these differ widely from one country to another. In many cases, these postcolonial family laws also diverge sharply from the classical Islamic jurisprudence on which they are purportedly based. Among Muslim-minority populations in the nations of North America and Europe, moreover, Muslims are free to apply only those regulations that they choose, either writing them into contracts drafted to comply with applicable civil laws or entrusting compliance out of belief and conscience, just as in matters of religious practice.

As an American, I am particularly concerned with the issues facing what British scholar Abdal-Hakim Murad refers to as "Muslims living in post-traditional contexts in the West."[27] Living in a nation where Islamic law has no coercive power, regardless of its moral weight for individual believers, I write as one with the luxury of deciding whether and how to apply religious doctrine in my own life – whether to arrange my affairs to follow the dictates of one or another school of jurisprudence, or the regulations in the Qur'an, or to follow civil law. The entirely voluntary nature of all types of religious observance means that the urgent questions for Muslims living under civil laws in North America and Europe in particular are ethical or moral rather than narrowly legal. At the same time, the fact that there are no putatively Islamic civil statutes involved means that those Muslims concerned with Islamic law tend to focus on "authentic" texts, rather than national legal codes, making engagement with the tradition necessary.[28]

Even in majority-Muslim societies, there has been a dramatic shift over the past century in the role of the 'ulama, who once held a monopoly on many forms of religious authority. Although the 'ulama retain prominence in a variety of contexts, some of the most influential thinkers of the late nineteenth and especially twentieth centuries have come from outside this class, a tendency which seems likely to continue unabated in the twenty-first century. Basheer Nafi and Suha Taji-Farouki argue that reformist (*salafi*) insistence on "the primacy of the foundational Islamic texts, the Qur'an and Sunna," has been one important factor in "the rupturing of traditional Islamic authority." They suggest that "as the salafi idea of returning directly to the founding texts gradually displaced the assumption of the ulamatic traditions of learning as the necessary credentials for speaking on behalf of Islam, the Islamic cultural arena became wide open to an assortment of voices, reflecting new notions of authority."[29] In theory, the processes Taji-Farouki and Nafi identify could lead to inclusiveness. Yet as Khaled Abou El Fadl has shown, the "new notions of authority," far from opening up a democratic intellectual space, have tended toward authoritarianism, and a rigidification of debates.

Four interconnected issues recur throughout this study. First, the discourse of Islamic authenticity has had a stifling effect on intra-Muslim debates about sex and sexuality. Second, the increasing gap between classical doctrines, present-day "values," and actual sexual practices has led to questioning by some of the "don't ask, don't tell" model embedded in Islamic norms that allows for deviation in practice, provided certain ideals aren't questioned. Third, the shift in values surrounding sex brings into relief the legal tradition's systematic, though not necessarily intentional, devaluation of mutual consent as an ethico-religious value for sexual relationships and sexual acts. This classical model exists in tension with the stress on consent and mutuality in contemporary Muslim discourses on marriage and gender relations. Finally, and cutting across the

INTRODUCTION xxxiii

previous three items, I am concerned with structures of authority and the shifting and competing models of authoritativeness
invoked by participants in contemporary debates over sexual
ethics. I will address the first three items in a bit more detail,
returning to questions of authority throughout the study.

The continual framing of discussions over sex in terms of
"Islamic-ness" is part of a broader flattening of moral argument and thoughtful debate among Muslims. Kevin Reinhart
has noted the shift among Muslims to talking about "Islam" as
a source of authority rather than the Qur'an, God, the Prophet,
or the scholars.[30] On the one hand, this shift may facilitate
attention to principles; on the other hand, it allows for the
emergence of doctrinal authoritarianism. Abou El Fadl has presented a painstaking portrait of this authoritarianism, which he
views as pervasive in contemporary Muslim discourse. While
the primary targets of his critique are the numerous conservative authorities who presume to speak for Islam – or rather,
for God – his arguments are equally relevant to those who
advocate change. According to Abou El Fadl, those who would
argue against the weight of inherited tradition have an obligation to make clear that they are doing so, even as they present their case for why an alternate position has more merit.[31]
This requires acknowledging the extensive and diverse views of
previous generations of thinkers, not just citation of isolated
hadith or Qur'anic verses as if those texts were entirely disposi-
tive of a particular point.

The issue of full disclosure is particularly relevant given
the fundamental shift in conventional wisdom among many
Muslims on issues of sexual morality and gender equality,
manifested in particular in an emphasis on individual consent. Just to take one example, while the classical Muslim legal
tradition uniformly accepted a father's right to marry off his
minor daughters (and sons) without consulting them, modern statements, including a recent Saudi fatwa, gloss over this
consensus in favor of prophetic statements commanding that
they be consulted.[32] For many Muslims born and raised in
Western nations, the issue of consent emerges as well in discussions of sex outside marriage. The widespread acceptance

of sex between consenting adults in the broader culture has led some Muslims to question the rationale behind Qur'anic, hadith, and legal prohibitions of such liaisons. The confusion over the issue arises in part because of the unfamiliarity of lay Muslims with the basic concepts structuring Islamic notions of lawful sex – my third point.

There is a mismatch between views of marriage and sexual intimacy as based on mutual consent and reciprocal desire and the entire structure of classical jurisprudential doctrines surrounding lawful sexuality. These doctrines viewed *milk* – that is, ownership, dominion, or control – as the basis for licit sex, whether it was within marriage, *milk al-nikah*, or slavery, *milk al-yamin*. The general disappearance of slavery in Muslim nations has meant, of course, that only sex within marriage is now considered lawful, to the point that some Muslim apologists refuse to acknowledge that slave concubinage was considered a perfectly lawful and normal institution for well over a millennium. Because slavery is no longer legally practiced in the Muslim world, many have assumed that the regulations surrounding slavery are irrelevant to contemporary discussions of Muslim marriage and family law; thus, discussions of legal texts make little reference to the jurists' frequent treatment of questions involving slaves. Nonetheless, slavery remains conceptually central to the legal regulations surrounding marriage. The basic understanding of marriage as a relationship of ownership or control is predicated on an analogy to slavery at a fundamental level, and the discussion of wives and concubines together strengthens the conceptual relationship. These connections tend to pass unremarked, however, and the lack of active grappling with the implications of abolition can lead to irony or even absurdity. For instance, an English translator of *Sahih Muslim*, one of the two most important Sunni hadith collections, asserts that one finds "In Islam ... the absolute prohibition of every kind of extra-matrimonial connection" in his preface to a chapter (Marriage) containing several matter-of-fact references to Muslim men having sex with their female slaves.[33] His impassioned declaration seems to me less an apologetic remark tailored for Western or non-Muslim consumption than a reflection of the extent to which the entire edifice of classical thought on sex and sexuality clashes with modern expectations, including those of Muslims who are deeply committed to the relevance of the classical tradition.

It is an obvious point, but it bears stating directly: in making value judgments, people are influenced not only by religious texts and teachings but also by their own social, cultural, and religious backgrounds. The early jurists were no exception to this rule; like contemporary Muslim thinkers, they could not help but be influenced by their own sense of what was right and wrong, natural and unnatural. In engaging with Muslim texts of the past, it is important to consider the ways in which their authors' base assumptions differ from those of the present. One useful indicator of the distance separating a contemporary reader from a past audience is the hierarchy of sexual acts that twelfth-century scholar al-Ghazali, whose writings on sexuality have been frequently quoted by modern authors, presents in his magisterial work *The Revivification of the Religious Sciences*. Al-Ghazali counsels a man who cannot afford to marry a free woman that if he feels sexual urges that he needs to satisfy, marrying another's female slave is a lesser evil than masturbation, even though children born of the union will be enslaved. Neither is as bad as *zina* – in this context, fornication. Although *marriage* to someone else's slave is problematic, al-Ghazali simply assumes the permissibility of a man's sexual use of his own female slaves. Intercourse with a slave who has no opportunity to grant or withhold consent is morally better than masturbation, which cannot involve coercion, or illicit sex with a willing woman. Many Muslims today find it simply unintelligible that sex with a slave acquired for that purpose would be preferable to sex with a consenting partner to whom one had no legal tie.

I will return to the complicated subject of consent in chapter 9, but want to stress at this point that while I do not believe consent and mutuality are fundamentally incompatible with an Islamic ethics of sex, these values were not prefigured in premodern Muslim texts in a way satisfactory for the twenty-first century. Although there are important lessons to be learned from the writings of premodern Muslim scholars, a great

psychic distance separates Muslims today from the circumstances of past centuries when authoritative doctrines were
formulated. Given this very real dissonance[34] between the cultural assumptions undergirding the classical edifices of jurisprudence and exegesis and the modern notions influencing
Muslim intellectuals and ordinary people everywhere, even
those who consider themselves conservative or traditional,
there is an acute need to explore vital themes and connections
through a variety of texts.

One "modern" value that is criticized in some discussions of
the Muslim heritage concerning sex is prudery. Muslims have
often been self-congratulatory about the heritage of explicit
discussions of sex in legal and literary works, without recognizing the pervasive nature of androcentric and even misogynist
assumptions in those texts. The presence of erotica in Muslim
literature, as well as the positive valuation of sexual pleasure
in authoritative sources, does not resolve the problem of the
double standard inherent in this literature; texts focus on
men's needs and desires.[35] Even sensitive scholars can overlook
these dynamics, which are deeply ingrained in the tradition.
When the "Sex and the Umma" section of the website Muslim
WakeUp was launched in early 2004, the site editor solicited
articles from Muslim scholars in support of the endeavor.[36]
One essay quoted a ribald joke attributed by Ahmed al-Tifashi
to the Prophet's cousin and son-in-law, the fourth Sunni caliph
and first Shi'i Imam, 'Ali b. Abi Talib in a work containing "the
amusing stories, entertaining poems and flagrant incidents
involving sexual pleasure he had witnessed or heard from colleagues."[37] The joke was intended to demonstrate the "raunchy
and delightful" nature of medieval Islamic discourse in contrast to the prudery that characterizes contemporary Muslim
discussions of sex and sexuality. In it, a woman approached
'Ali to complain "that she had given away her daughter in marriage, but the husband divorced her because she was only three
feet tall. 'Three feet!' declared Ali, 'that ought to have been
enough – at most she needs to able to take nine inches!'" The
article immediately garnered comments from readers when
it was posted, with the majority aghast at the intimation that

'Ali could have possibly said such a thing. Did these replies express outrage, disgust, or even mild concern at the idea that 'Ali could have referred to a woman in such an objectified manner, reducing her to a sexual receptacle? Hardly: what shocked readers was the scandalous assertion that 'Ali could have joked in such a familiar manner with a woman who was not a close relation to himself! My point is that it is not merely contemporary prudery that Muslims concerned with sexuality have to combat; despite valuable elements in premodern texts, including a willingness to be explicit *and* have a sense of humor about sexual matters, there are deeply troubling elements that must not be ignored.

Before proceeding, I want to delineate what I am and am not attempting to accomplish in this volume. I am not a jurist, a Qur'an scholar, or an ethicist, and I certainly do not "do" jurisprudence here. Yet although this work is primarily concerned with analyzing current debates, I have tried to be forthright in stating my opinions, even when I was inclined to be more circumspect, in an effort to move discussion of issues in sexual ethics beyond critique and toward possible resolutions of difficult problems. Where I have indicated possible directions for further thought, my suggestions should be taken as tentative steps in the direction of a just ethics of sex, not as an attempt to formulate a comprehensive program of religio-legal doctrine or to have the definitive word on any of the matters under discussion here. Sherwin Bailey, writing about Christian sexual ethics, noted several decades ago that "even among those who are concerned to think and act responsibly, and to maintain high standards, there are differences of opinion as to what is right and wrong in given circumstances."[38] It is my sincere hope that this book will be taken as an invitation to conversation and fruitful debate.

1 Marriage, Money, and Sex

The husband should go to his wife once every four nights. This is fairest, because the [maximum permissible] number of wives is four. One is therefore allowed to extend the interval up to this limit. It is best that the husband should increase or decrease the amount of intercourse in accordance with his wife's need to guard her virtue, since the preservation of her virtue is a duty of the husband. If the woman's claim on intercourse has not been fixed, this is because of the difficulty of making and satisfying such a claim.
Al-Ghazali, *Book on the Etiquette of Marriage*[1]

After the first time, intercourse is his right, not her right.
Radd al-Muhtar, early nineteenth-century Hanafi legal text[2]

Muslims have practiced Islam in an enormous range of geographic, historical, and social contexts, and Muslim scholars differ, sometimes significantly, on crucial points of doctrine. Despite this diversity, virtually all agree that marriage obligates the husband to pay his wife a dower, that a Muslim husband bears the sole burden of providing for his wife and household, and that Muslim women may only marry Muslim men. Yet even Muslims who assiduously affirm these regulations do not always follow them. The gap between expressed doctrine and practice is perhaps largest in Western nations, especially the United States, my focus in this chapter. Although there are no hard figures available for American Muslim practices, anecdotal and other evidence suggests that dower continues to figure in most marriages of Muslims despite its unenforceability as a matter of civil law and the fact that it often remains unpaid.

The majority of American Muslim women contribute materially to their own support and that of their households, as many have done historically and do elsewhere, the accepted gendered allocation of marital rights and responsibilities notwithstanding. And, although "the prohibition to give Muslim women in matrimony to unbelievers ... is one of the strictest and least disputed prohibitions in Muslim law of personal status,"[3] the marriage of Muslim women to non-Muslim men occurs in the U.S. with some regularity, though not nearly as frequently as the marriage of Muslim men to non-Muslim women.[4]

With no coercive central authority or national legislative body dictating what is required for marriage between Muslims, American Muslims have adapted Islamic marriage regulations to fit prevailing legal, social, and cultural norms. These norms are not uniform even within the subset of the world's Muslims who live in the United States. African American Muslims constitute the largest single ethnic group of Muslims, followed by Asian, Arab, and African immigrants and their descendants. These larger groups are supplemented by significantly smaller numbers of white and Latina/o converts. Most are Sunnis; some are Shi'a. Marriage practices and ideals vary between and within these communities, but all must confront the relationship between civil law and religious obligation. Choices about which religio-legal precepts to observe and which should be allowed to slip into disuse are not always logical or consistent, and may have unanticipated results for individual Muslims or their communities.

This chapter considers dower, the regulations governing spousal support and sexual availability, and the prohibition of intermarriage between Muslim women and non-Muslim men. I suggest that the arguments used by Muslim thinkers, and often adopted by ordinary Muslims, to justify continued adherence to certain classical rules are incompatible with other commonly held ideas about marriage. Further, none of these regulations takes into account the vastly different context in which American Muslims live and marry. I do not attempt to construct legal arguments in opposition to standard views, but rather to critique the way in which the views are reproduced and defended. Ultimately, I suggest that reconsideration of dower, spousal support, and intermarriage provides one possible way of thinking about a new structure for egalitarian marriage that bypasses the patriarchal presumptions of these rules and avoids becoming mired in the minutiae of incremental legal reform.

"And according to what they spend from their wealth ..."[5]

Property transfer on marriage has been a common practice throughout human history, though with dramatic variation in who pays, how much they pay, and who receives the cash or goods exchanged. Sometimes gifts are reciprocal; at other times, the transfer is unidirectional, either dowry paid to the husband by the bride's family or bride price paid to the wife's family by the husband and/or his family. Marriage and dower practices in pre-Islamic Arabia have been the subject of significant speculation and little consensus.[6] Most agree that in pre-Islamic Arabia, *mahr* was compensation paid to a bride's family in exchange for considering her offspring part of the husband's tribe rather than that of her father and brothers. The Muslim dower (*mahr* or *sadaq*), paid to the wife rather than her family, is usually regarded as a modification of this practice.[7] (Numerous authors cite this shift as proof of Islam's liberatory stance toward women.[8]) There is some evidence suggesting that the *mahr* and the *sadaq*, terms used interchangeably by classical jurists, were originally distinct forms of compensation, with the latter going to the wife herself. On this view, dower payment to the bride would not be an Islamic innovation but rather an instance of the way that "Islam selectively sanctioned" certain Arabian tribal practices "while prohibiting others."[9] In any case, Islamic rules definitively allocated the money to the bride, although under certain circumstances fathers were allowed to receive it and spend it for a daughter's trousseau. Among Muslims, dower has frequently been an important part of property arrangements.[10] How significant it was or is in practice has depended on the wealth of the parties; whether the dower is in cash, in kind, or in immovable property; and whether it is paid up front, deferred to death or divorce, or split between prompt and deferred. When the deferred portion of the dower is set at a sufficient amount, it may also compensate women for some of the risk inherent in marriage when men have or have had unrestricted rights to divorce with no long-term liability for alimony; under most circumstances, a wife is only entitled to three menstrual cycles' worth of lodging and maintenance after divorce.[11]

Much modern Muslim discourse, from neo-traditional-ists and feminists alike, praises dower as a source of economic security for women and a token of a husband's willingness and ability to provide. This rhetoric is pervasive even in the United States, where most Muslims marry according to civil law. Dower persists in the vast majority of American Muslim marriages; though it is often only a symbolic amount, it differentiates Muslim marriage from that of the surrounding American society. In the United States, it is simple to set a dower amount at marriage, because religious authorities are frequently certified to perform marriages recognized by American law. However, following through on enforcement of dower obligations in the wake of divorce is much less common, in part because these same religious figures have no role in civil divorce. Other reasons include the nominal amount of dower often allocated to the bride, the informality of verbal or written dower agreements that do not meet standards for enforceable contracts, and the fact that U.S. courts have proven ambivalent in their treatment of dower obligations.[12] The practical impact of these factors belies the rhetoric about dower's importance as a safety net for women, and as an instance of the generous rights Islam "guarantees" women.

Not only are most discourses on dower irrelevant to Muslim practice in the U.S., they are also detached from the logic governing dower in Islamic jurisprudence, where dower constitutes compensation paid by the husband for exclusive legitimate sexual access to his wife. (Al-Shafi'i, among others, graphically refers to dower as "the vulva's price," *thaman al-bud'a*.[13]) Dower has a very specific purpose and is linked inextricably to other rules, such as male-initiated divorce, that are incompatible with the forms of civil marriage and divorce utilized by the majority of American Muslims. The Qur'an refers in general terms to a man's financial obligations toward his wife.[14] The hadith texts discuss a range of dower possibilities from symbolic (an iron ring) to minimal (a quarter dinar or three dirhams) to ideal (the dower paid by the Prophet to his wives or that received by his daughters) to maximum (none fixed). For the most part, these texts are silent on rationales, although the Qur'an does refer to the *ajr* (reward, compensation) paid by a man for "what he enjoys from her."[15] In the developed logic of the jurists, however, dower came to be understood as compensation in exchange for *milk al-nikah*, the husband's exclusive dominion over the wife's sexual and reproductive capacity, which also conveys his sole right to dissolve the marriage tie by unilateral divorce.

The linkage of divorce with dower may seem odd, but the husband, in the jurists' logic, is paying for a type of control. It is this control that makes sex lawful. The wife may not dissolve the marriage without a judge's approval unless specific conditions to the contrary, escape clauses of a sort, were included in the contract.[16] Given that the full dower becomes obligatory after consummation, and could represent a significant sum of money, it makes a certain kind of sense that only the husband would be able to release the wife from the marriage. Otherwise, a woman could simply marry, consummate the marriage (or rather, allow it to be consummated), and then divorce her husband while claiming the full dower amount to which she was entitled. This linkage between dower and divorce rights illustrates the interconnectedness of each element of classical legal tradition, and its attempt to achieve conceptual consistency; any attempt to modify the rules surrounding divorce but not those governing dower, as some advocates for women's rights have proposed, would alter the marital dynamic significantly.

Dower is not alone among the financial obligations associated with marriage that have been given new rationales by modern Muslim authors. Contemporary Muslim thought generally links male provision of *nafaqa*, or support, with a wife's household service: the husband/father earns a living and a wife/mother stays home and keeps the house and raises the children.[17] Yet this provider-homemaker division of labor does not reflect the actual experience of most Muslim families, where women contribute to their own support and/or that of their households and children, nor does it resonate with classical texts. Those texts, while sometimes suggesting that women have a religious obligation to manage the household, generally stress that the husband maintains his wife in exchange not for household services but for her sexual availability to him.

Sex

Current conventional wisdom among Muslims and non-Muslims alike holds that Islam is a religion with a positive view of human sexuality.[18] Medieval Christian polemics against Islam viewed its sensualism as barbaric in comparison to the purity of Christianity, but many modern commentators see Islam's world-affirming perspective as more realistic than the supposedly ascetic and world-denying stance of Christianity.[19] The comparison relies on an oversimplified view of Christianity, but the claims with regard to Islam have a basis in Muslim tradition. Key Islamic texts present marriage, and sex within it, as a natural and desirable part of human life. The Prophet Muhammad reportedly objected to religious celibacy ("No monkery in Islam")[20] and specifically claimed marriage as part of his *sunnah*, or authoritative practice. Premodern biographical treatments of his life celebrate his virility as part of his sound human nature.

Both classical and contemporary authors likewise recognize women's sexual needs and appetites, but with different emphases.[21] Classical texts note the importance of female fulfillment, but usually focus on the discord-producing effects of female dissatisfaction (the potential for social *fitna*) while stressing the wives' duty to remain sexually available to their husbands. Contemporary authors, often quoting selectively from this corpus, pay less attention to these themes.[22] Instead, they focus on women's sexual rights within marriage, attempting to prove the importance of female pleasure by highlighting the dissociation of sex from reproduction and the importance of female orgasm.

Significant texts in the Qur'an and hadith allude to the importance of female gratification and satisfaction in the sexual act. These sources, drawn on by al-Ghazali in his frequently cited writings, stress men's responsibility for making their wives' experiences pleasurable.[23] Al-Ghazali frames his discussion of the sexual act in terms of a husband's responsibility for keeping his wife satisfied; it is a matter of the husband's duty, rather than the wife's right.[24] This duty has social, as well as intimate, dimensions: a man is obligated to keep his wife satisfied in part to keep her from wreaking social havoc. Given women's generally slower trajectory of arousal and orgasm, both foreplay and prolonged stimulation are required, the former to ensure readiness for penetration, the latter to ensure attainment of climax. Foreplay, in his view, is the subject of the Qur'anic command "do some good act for your souls beforehand."[25] He also cites a statement attributed to the Prophet, counseling men not to fall upon their wives like beasts, but rather to send "a messenger" prior to the sexual act. When questioned, Muhammad is said to have clarified that this "messenger" was kisses and caresses.

Al-Ghazali insists that it is the husband's responsibility, having aroused his wife sufficiently for penetration, to see to it that she also reaches orgasm. It is likely that she will only climax after "the husband has attained his desired end"; nonetheless, "mutual estrangement" may occur "whenever the husband is too quick to ejaculate; simultaneity in the moment of orgasm is more delightful to her." This is part of his rationale for foreplay; if the wife is sufficiently close to orgasm before penetration, mutual climax is more likely. Al-Ghazali insists that the wife's dissatisfaction can damage the intimate relationship between the couple. Again, the husband is charged with ensuring this does not occur: "The husband should not be preoccupied with his own satisfaction, because the woman will often be shy."[26]

Al-Ghazali's explicit discussion of female orgasm high-lights one of the drawbacks of coitus interruptus (*'azl*), the method of birth control best known to early Muslims: a man must withdraw prior to his ejaculation to prevent concep-tion, but "coitus interruptus may diminish her pleasure." As Sa'diyya Shaikh points out, a wife is "entitled to full sexual pleasure" and has "the right to offspring if she so desires." Shaikh views this doctrine as evidence of "the priority given in Islam to mutual sexual fulfillment as well as consultative decision making between a married couple in terms of family planning."[27] Sex for non-procreative purposes was clearly per-missible: with very few exceptions, Muslim authorities accepted contraceptive measures and approved of sex with pregnant women and nursing mothers, making clear that sexual pleasure was a worthwhile aim even where pregnancy was an impossi-ble, unlikely, or undesirable outcome of intercourse. Shaikh is thus largely correct in her broad claim that "within the Islamic view of marriage, an individual has the right to sexual pleasure within marriage, which is independent of one's choice to have children."[28] Yet the mention of an ungendered "individual" who has this right ignores the context within which classical thinkers discuss marital sex. Although Hanbalis, Malikis, and Hanafis viewed the wife's permission for withdrawal as nec-essary, most Shafi'is disagreed, and the reasons behind their disagreement are instructive.[29] According to one rationale, since a wife didn't have the right to demand intercourse at any given time (a point on which the jurists largely agreed across the legal schools), her husband could prevent her from conceiving or attaining sexual pleasure by abstaining from intercourse with her entirely. Given that she therefore had no independent right to orgasm or to conception, her consent regarding withdrawal was irrelevant. This doctrine, a minority view, complicates the simple view of an "Islamic right" to female sexual pleasure.

Muslim acknowledgement of the positive aspects of female sexuality has historically coexisted with two views that chal-lenge it in different ways. First, certain elements of the clas-sical Muslim tradition treat female sexuality as dangerous, with potentially disruptive and chaotic effects on society.[30]

Historians have demonstrated how anxieties about temptation and female sexuality translated into insistence (never fully
achieved in reality) on restricting the appearance of women in
public spaces.[31] Muslim worry over *fitna* – chaos and disorder
– has often focused on the sexual temptation caused both by
women's unregulated desires and the troublesome desire that
women provoke in men. Second, and in a paradoxical relationship to this view of women as sexually insatiable and thus
prone to create social chaos, Muslim authorities have stressed
the importance of the fulfillment of male sexual needs, especially in the context of marriage. Drawing particularly on
several hadith delineating dire consequences for women who
refuse their husbands' sexual overtures, the insistence on men's
sexual needs and wives' responsibility to fulfill them has com-
peted for prominence in modern intra-Muslim discourses on
sex with the recognition of female sexual needs.

Despite the scholars' acknowledgement of the importance of
female satisfaction in the sexual act, the overwhelming weight
of the Muslim legal and exegetical tradition is on women's
obligations to make themselves sexually available to their husbands, rather than the reverse. This bias in the sources emerges
even in contemporary discussions that attempt to discuss male
and female sexual rights in parallel, highlighting the immensity
of the task for those who would redefine sex within marriage as
a fully mutual endeavor. A fatwa by conservative Saudi mufti
Ibn Jibreen[32] exemplifies the extent to which concepts of reciprocity and mutuality permeate even conservative Muslim discourses. At the same time, his strongly gendered understanding
of male and female sexuality is broadly representative of much
contemporary Muslim discourse, including that produced in
Western contexts.

Ibn Jibreen's fatwa, entitled "The Ruling on Either of
the Two Spouses Denying the Other Their Lawful Rights,"
responds to the query, "Is it permissible for either of the two
spouses to deny the natural rights of the other for a long period
of time, without any acceptable excuse?"[33] The mufti's response
exemplifies the tension between moral exhortations surrounding wives' sexual rights in marriage, and the legal logic

governing sex as part of the structure of gender-differentiated marital claims beginning with dower and carried through to divorce. Though the questioner posed the problem of "either of the two spouses [denying] the natural rights of the other" as a gender-neutral one, sex in marriage is not a gender-neutral question. Ibn Jibreen opens by accepting his questioner's premise of parity, declaring that "sexual relations" are among the "needs" of both husband and wife, but proceeds very quickly to discuss men and women in parallel, and then to differentiate them. Eschewing the view that women's desires are unmanageable, he opines that men generally have "a stronger desire" for sex than women. The rest of the fatwa considers men's sexual claims in marriage, then women's sexual claims in marriage, lastly returning to universal statements about sex in marriage.

The limited and contingent sexual rights of a wife stand in contrast to the unrestricted right of a husband to sex "whenever he desires it." With the caveat that a man may not harm her or prevent her from performing any of her religious duties, Ibn Jibreen declares that a wife has "an obligation ... to allow her husband to have sexual intercourse with her whenever he desires it." (Note the passivity here: she is to "allow" him "to have sexual intercourse with her," rather than actively having sex with him.) Ibn Jibreen accurately categorizes this as the dominant, virtually unanimous, view of the Muslim jurisprudential tradition. Like al-Ghazali, who supports the wifely obligation to be available to her husband in a passage less often quoted by modern Muslim authors,[34] Ibn Jibreen recognizes that a wife also "has rights to have her intimate needs fulfilled." However, a husband is not obligated to satisfy her "whenever" *she* "desires it"; rather the husband must "have sexual intercourse with his wife (at least) once in each third of the year, if he is able to do so."[35]

A number of hadith that make assertions about wives' sexual obligations serve as proof for this husbandly right; although Ibn Jibreen does not cite them in this fatwa, they appear in other opinions issued by the Saudi fatwa council with which he is affiliated, as well as the writings of other thinkers. Abu Huraira is the authority for five closely related narrations in had practical consequences in the legal tradition. Most jurists viewed the husband's support of his wife as an exchange for her sexual availability to him, and agreed that her sexual refusal constituted grounds for suspension of her support.[39] The dominant Hanafi view differed in a crucial way; a man had to continue to support his wife even if she refused him, so long as she remained in the marital home.[40] As an Indian author argues in 1987, in euphemistic language, in case of the wife's refusal of sex, "It is taken that she shall be in his power and [he] can be intimate with her by applying some pressure."[41] The early jurists would have considered marital rape an oxymoron; rape (*ightisab*, "usurpation") was a property crime that by definition could not be committed by the husband, who obtained a legitimate (but non-transferable) proprietary interest over his wife's sexual capacity through the marriage contract, incurring the obligation to pay dower in exchange. The Hanafi view that husbands were entitled to have sex forcibly with their wives when the latter did not have a legitimate reason to refuse sex was not widely shared outside that school. Even the majority of Hanafi thinkers who accepted this doctrine recognized a distinction between forced intercourse and more usual sexual relations between spouses; although both were equally licit, sex by force might be unethical.[42]

Unlike the clear penalties that a wife could face if she did not fulfill her husband's demand for sexual access, a sexually dissatisfied wife had few avenues for redress, despite a man's obligation to keep his wife satisfied. Those sources that do exist, beyond those cited above as encouraging foreplay, do not receive nearly as much attention as the Abu Huraira hadith cursing recalcitrant wives. In one case, Muhammad is reported to have told a man who boasted of fasting every day and praying at night that he should follow the Prophet's own example, and moderate his devotions so that he could partake of normal human activities: food, sleep, and sex. Interestingly, the terms used liken the wife in that case to almost an extension of her husband's body: "Your body has a right over you, your eyes have a right over you and your wife has a right over you."[43] This hadith is important because it moves beyond the

question of women's satisfaction in a particular act, discussed
by al-Ghazali and others, to the larger question of wives' rights
to sex itself.

What was the extent of the wife's sexual claim on her husband? With the exception of the literalist Zahiris, all legal
schools adopted the view that a marriage could be dissolved
for impotence – that is, the husband's failure to consummate the marriage. In the absence of any passage from the
Qur'an or statement from the Prophet on the topic, the jurists
based themselves on a ruling from the second caliph 'Umar.
The choice by some (such as Abu Hanifa and his disciple
Muhammad al-Shaybani) to follow this ruling while ignoring
'Umar's precedent in other cases demonstrates an exercise of
jurisprudential discretion.[44] The near unanimity on the point
suggests that there is, indeed, a strong strand of thought believing that sex is a vital element of marriage. Nonetheless, despite
the wife's right to press a claim of impotence in an unconsum-
mated marriage, the vast majority of jurists went on to declare
that she has no such right once the marriage has been consummated. One opinion quoted in the late Hanafi text *Radd
al-Muhtar* presents this sentiment particularly bluntly: "After
the first time, intercourse is his right, not her right." At best, as
in Ibn Jibreen's fatwa, she might be able to insist on intercourse
once every four months, assuming her husband was capable
of it.[45]

Sex is, by and large, a male right and female duty, according to *fiqh* texts, whatever the ethical importance of a husband's satisfying his wife and thus enabling her to keep chaste.
The repeated, though ultimately unenforceable, assertions
of some scholars as to a wife's sexual rights – or, more particularly, the husband's obligations – demonstrate an unre-
solvable tension. The modern attempt to render the spouses'
sexual rights parallel without departing from the overall
framework of gender-differentiated rights and duties set forth
by classical jurists is destined for failure; the model cannot
accommodate piecemeal modifications. The legal tradition
fundamentally views marriage as an exchange of lawful sexual access for dower, and continued sexual availability for

support. To the extent that these doctrines still inform Muslim discourses, mutuality in sexual rights cannot be a requirement, merely an ideal.

Intermarriage

As with regulations surrounding dower and sex, the issue of marriage of Muslims to "people of the Book" – *ahl al-kitab*, generally understood as Christians and Jews – demonstrates both the mutability and the limitations of existing jurisprudential approaches to intimate relationships. The Qur'an explicitly grants permission in Surah 5, verse 5 for Muslim men to marry virtuous women (*muhsanat*)[46] from among those who have received scriptures in the past. Surah 2, verse 221 prohibits marriage between Muslim men and women and those who associate partners with God (*mushrikun/mushrikat*). Surah 60, verse 10 prohibits sending female converts who have come to the Muslims back to their unbelieving husbands, who are declared to be inappropriate spouses for them. The vast majority of Muslim scholars have understood these verses, taken collectively, to forbid the marriage of Muslim women to non-Muslim men, whether "of the Book" or not, and to require the dissolution of any marriage to a non-Muslim husband when a wife converts to Islam.[47]

Their interpretations presupposed two kinds of hierarchies: Muslims were to be dominant over non-Muslims and husbands over wives. As wives were to be subordinate to their husbands, the marriage of a non-Muslim man to a Muslim woman would challenge this authority structure: "A marriage of a Muslim woman to a non-Muslim man would result in an unacceptable incongruity between the superiority which the wife should enjoy by virtue of being Muslim, and her unavoidable wifely subjection to her infidel husband."[48] The same rationale governed, although to a lesser extent, other legal discussions about socio-economic parity between spouses, particularly important in the Hanafi understanding of *kafa'a*, measuring the suitability of the groom according to whether

he was the bride's equal or better in lineage, wealth, and religious status.[49] The reverse was not true: twelfth-century Hanafi
scholar al-Marghinani's statement that "it is not necessary
that the wife be the equal of the husband, since men are not
degraded by cohabitation with women who are their inferiors"
was meant to apply with regard to suitability but applied equally
to intermarriage.[50] Though some prominent early Muslims did
object to intermarriage with Christians, in particular on theological grounds, the notion of a Muslim husband's authority
over a non-Muslim wife posed no conceptual problems.

As exegetes and jurists grappled with the issue of intermarriage, they took for granted the absolute necessity of
both Muslim political authority and male familial authority.
Classical exegetes explicitly grappled with the Qur'anic verses
mentioning intermarriage, and tried to sort out the relevant
categories (Muslims, believers, people of the Book, Jews,
Christians, non-believers, *mushrikun*). Jurists, more pragmatically inclined, attended to issues of permissibility and
conditions for interreligious marriages. For the most part,
scholars simply assumed that Muslim women couldn't marry
non-Muslim men and did not consider it necessary to elaborate
on their evidence and rationales. Ibn Rushd does not discuss
Muslim women marrying non-Muslims in his *Distinguished
Jurist's Primer* which, because it treats matters on which jurists
disagree, is often a repository for minority opinions.[51] More
tellingly, neither Ahmad b. Naqib al-Misri nor his nineteenth-
century commentator 'Umar Barakat deemed it necessary to
state that Muslim women could not marry non-Muslim men
in the classic Shafi'i manual *Reliance of the Traveller*; however,
a late twentieth-century transmitter of the text adds it as a clarification for the English translation; literally, what once went
without saying no longer does.[52]

The scholar quoted in the *Reliance* states the prohibition
without presenting a justification for it, but numerous others
have addressed the point. The increasing frequency with which
(civil) marriages between Muslim women and non-Muslim
men are occurring, or where women who convert to Islam
independently remain married to non-Muslim husbands, has

led to impassioned, but deeply flawed, arguments by Muslim thinkers intent on upholding the standard prohibition of such marriages, though in quite different terms from those provided by early and medieval thinkers, when they addressed the matter at all.[53] The rationales presented, however, are often nonsensical, as well as simplistic in their discussions of intermarriage by Muslim men. The premodern tradition demonstrates a level of complexity in discussions of intermarriage that does not carry over into contemporary discussions, suggesting the relevance of context as a factor in determining the (im)permissibility of particular types of marriages. At the same time, a reconsideration of the relevant Qur'anic passages in isolation from their traditional interpretation suggests that the text is less categorical than generally assumed; *sunnah* may also provide a model of flexibility.

Even leaving aside the dominant Shi'i view that men may not contract *nikah* with non-Muslims of any type, early Sunni discussions of intermarriage between Muslim men and Jewish or Christian women are more complex than the view, often expressed today, that while women are forbidden from intermarrying, Muslim men may marry Christian or Jewish women. Marriage of Muslim men to non-Muslim women was not as straightforward as simple permissibility. First, authorities debated who should be included in the definition of "people of the Book." Ibn 'Umar's blanket disapproval of marriage to a Christian (for who is more an idolator than someone who says that God is one of three?) is a well-known minority view, but Christian and Jewish women were agreed by Sunni scholars to be acceptable, if not ideal, as marriage partners. Instead, the debate tended to center around the categories of the Sabeans (Abu Hanifa permitted marriage to Sabean women, though his disciples did not) and Zoroastrians (not lawful, according to the Hanafis, but the inclusion of this disclaimer makes clear that some *did* hold it permissible).[54] More importantly, quite a number of thinkers held that circumstances mattered in assessing the permissibility of marriage between Muslim men and *kitabi* women. It was one thing to marry a *kitabiyya* within the safe haven of Muslim-ruled Dar al-Islam, but quite another to do it in Dar al-Harb when the possibility of the children being brought up as non-Muslims was more of a threat (assuming the husband divorced the woman and returned to his native land, which some scholars considered a strong probability). According to the view presented in the Hanafi text *Fatawa-I-Kazee Khan*, such a marriage was "valid" but "abominable" (*makruh*).[55]

The early jurists also devoted substantial discussion to the conversion of one spouse to Islam.[56] When a Christian or Jewish husband converted, he was allowed to remain married to his wife of the same faith; his conversion resulted in a permissible marriage between a Muslim man and a *kitabiyya*. On the other hand, if the wife converted while her husband retained their original religion, there was general (although not universal) agreement that their marriage could not continue, a position that has been generally upheld by scholars until the present day. However, two recent opinions by Western Muslim authorities have declared that a woman who converts to Islam is not necessarily required to divorce her *kitabi* husband. Although the positions taken in these fatwas suggests a serious challenge to the dominant view of intermarriage, an exploration of their reasoning shows that neither upsets conventional wisdom as much as might be expected.

The first fatwa, by Taha Jabir Alalwani, appears on the website of the mainstream and influential Islamic Society of North America.[57] He argues:

A questioner asks, "Is it forbidden (*haram*) for a Muslim woman to be married to a non Muslim, and what should one do?" The standard answer based on the Qur'an is that it is forbidden for a Muslim woman to be married to a non-Muslim so she should be divorced immediately. However in this particular case the circumstances are as follows: The woman has just converted to Islam and she has a husband and two young kids. The husband is very supportive, but is not at this time interested in converting. The woman was told immediately after converting that she had to divorce her husband of 20 years. Within these circumstances the question should have been: Is it worse for a Muslim woman to be married to a non-Muslim husband or for her to leave the religion? The answer is that leaving the religion is much worse, so therefore it is acceptable for her to continue with her marriage and she is responsible before Allah on Judgment Day.

Alalwani situates his response to a "questioner" asking about "a Muslim woman [being] married to a non Muslim" within a consideration of the larger issue of whether questions have been properly formulated to lead to appropriate results. The question posed was whether the situation was "forbidden" and what would be the appropriate action to take in case of such marriage. After discussing the woman's personal circumstances, Alalwani reframes the issue as a choice between the convert remaining married to a non-Muslim or leaving Islam. In asserting that the way a question is formulated affects what answer can be given, Alalwani recognizes a key facet of all intellectual endeavor, Islamic jurisprudence not excluded. However, he does not acknowledge the extent to which his own statement of what "the question should have been" predetermines its outcome: there can be no consequence worse than leaving Islam, so any alternative, even violating the prohibition on marriage between a Muslim woman and a non-Muslim man, seems reasonable.

Rather than undertaking a serious reconsideration of interreligious marriage by Muslim women, Alalwani provides a dispensation (*rukhsa*) which lightens a normal restriction to respond to an extraordinary circumstance. Indeed, he provides a truly extraordinary example: a woman married twenty years would be far more reluctant to leave her husband than one married only a few years. Further, a woman with young children would be especially hesitant to separate from their father. The fact that both these elements are present suggests contrivance: how many women married for two decades still have "two young kids"? Though the situation he describes is biologically possible, it is far more likely that a woman married for such a long time would have teenaged offspring. By depicting a situation where one is very sympathetic to the woman involved,

Alalwani increases the likelihood that readers will concur with his deliberations. But does this fatwa have relevance beyond the individual case at stake?

Although the logic of this fatwa is internally sound, its methodological premise is too superficial to be sustained or applied more broadly, as it allows for almost any manipulation of the question to result in the desired answer. Would he accept the same rationale if it were not a convert's marriage at stake but rather an unmarried Muslim woman in love with, and wanting to marry, a non-Muslim, and in danger of leaving Islam if she could not do so? What if it were two Muslim women wanting to marry each other, now permissible under civil law in certain parts of North America and Europe? Presumably, Alalwani would approach these situations differently, but this fatwa does not provide any methodological justification for doing so.

Alalwani does not suggest a broader differentiation between permitting a convert to Islam to remain married to her *kitabi* husband (where her apostasy from Islam was not feared) and cases where an unmarried Muslim woman wanted to marry a Christian or Jewish man. There is some textual support for this distinction; anecdotal evidence suggests that the first generation of Muslims viewed the preservation of an existing marriage somewhat differently than the case where no marriage yet existed.[58] The second fatwa, from the European Council for Fatwa (an all-male organization that includes North America-based Jamal Badawi among its members), does make this distinction, "affirm[ing] and repeat[ing] that it is forbidden for a Muslim female to establish marriage to a non-Muslim male" while permitting a convert to maintain her marriage under certain circumstances.[59] The fatwa acknowledges that "according to the four main schools of jurisprudence, it is forbidden for the wife to remain with her husband or indeed to allow him conjugal rights, once her period of waiting has expired." The Council bases its dissenting view on "some scholars" (those named are Ibrahim al-Nakha'i, al-Shi'bi, and Hammad ibn Abi Sulayman) who held that "it is for her to remain with him, allowing him and enjoying full conjugal rights, if he does not prevent her from exercising her religion and she has hope in

him reverting [i.e., converting] to Islam." The Council's rationale ("for women not to reject entering into Islam if they realize that they are to separate from their husbands and desert
their families by doing so") is similar to Alalwani's objective to
prevent the convert's apostasy, although the situation of one
who never becomes Muslim is less dire than that of one who
becomes Muslim only to abandon the faith.

Both fatwas acknowledge their departure from the near-
universal view on the dissolution of a female convert's marriage.
Neither, however, reconsiders the evidence on which that doctrine is based. Alalwani states simply that "the standard answer
based on the Qur'an is that it is forbidden for a Muslim woman
to be married to a non-Muslim."[60] However, his intimation that
the Qur'an explicitly forbids such marriages is misleading. The
Qur'an does not address the situation of women's marriage to
"non-Muslims" in general but rather discusses specific categories of potential spouses such as "those who associate partners
with God" (mushrikin) and "unbelievers." Although both fatwas
refer to a woman's freedom to practice her new religion, neither discusses the relation of the cases at issue to the Qur'anic
verse disapproving of Muslim women remaining married to
unbelievers (kuffar). A woman's conversion separately from her
"very supportive" husband suggests her freedom of conscience
and action. In contrast to the cases considered by these muftis,
the Qur'anic verse explicitly treats the situation of women who
had converted and left their husbands. The situation of female
converts to Islam who had come as refugees from a community engaged in conflict with the Muslims is, in several respects,
quite different from that of women who desire to remain with
their husbands, not to mention those living in a society in which
Muslims and non-Muslims coexist peacefully. The muftis could
have chosen to argue that this Qur'anic ruling is context-specific
and therefore does not apply in the dramatically altered scenario
of a Christian or Jewish woman who converts to Islam in the
United States today.

If one holds that Surah 60, verse 10 does not apply to the situation of converts in the West today, then the remaining Qur'anic
evidence against women's marriage to non-Muslims is twofold:

the prohibition in Surah 2, verse 221 on marrying women off to those who associate partners with God, and the silence surrounding women's marriage to *kitabi*s in Surah 5, verse 5. The prohibition of marriage to *mushrikin* in the former explicitly applies to both Muslim men and Muslim women. It cannot, therefore, be applicable to all "non-Muslims," as many exegetes, both classical and contemporary, have assumed in the case of women.[61] Rather, it is accepted to stand in non-contradiction to the permission for Muslim men to marry women from "those who have received the book before you" in the latter verse. To view the same command prohibiting marriage to *mushrikin* as applying more broadly to women than to men requires a significant interpretive leap, moving far beyond the verse itself. The prohibition of marrying women off to *mushrikin* in Surah 2, verse 221 does not by itself foreclose the possibility of permission for women to marry *kitabi*s. And although Surah 5, verse 5 does not explicitly grant permission for such marriages, there are numerous other instances in the Qur'an where commands addressed to men regarding women are taken to apply, *mutatis mutandis*, to women.[62]

If the Qur'an does not directly address the marriage of Muslim women to *kitabi* men, and if the presumptions about male supremacy and dominance in the home no longer hold, such that a female convert living in a majority non-Muslim nation is assured freedom to practice Islam in her home unencumbered (or to obtain a civil divorce independently if she is not), what rationale exists for continuing to prohibit marriage between Muslim women and *kitabi* men in the first place? My aim is not to construct a legal argument for the permissibility of such marriages but rather to highlight the weaknesses in most arguments against them, particularly their reliance on unspoken but fundamental assumptions about male dominance in marriage. These assumptions are no longer widely shared, or at least no longer broadly acceptable as justifications for the prohibition of intermarriage. At the same time, greater attention to the discussions surrounding men's marriage to *kitabiyya*s in both hadith and jurisprudence suggests the relevance of taking context into account in both permission for and prohibition of intermarriage. There are cogent arguments to be made for considering the permission to marry non-Muslims on the basis of factors other than gender.

Conclusion

Discussions of marriage among scholars, pundits and ordinary Muslims consist of a curious and continuously shifting mix of specific classical doctrines, isolated citations from Qur'an and hadith, and modern assumptions. Among Muslims in the United States, as in most Muslim-majority societies, classical models for marriage no longer hold sway in numerous respects. Rules that allowed for fathers to contract binding marriages for their minor children of either sex no longer persist. Apologetic discourses stress wives' sexual rights while downplaying the importance of wifely obedience. In fundamental respects, in social practice at least, the understanding of Islamic marriage has shifted. Yet there has not been a coherent alternative to the classical understanding of marriage as a fundamentally gender-differentiated institution which presumes, at least at some level, male authority and control.

Dower, which holds a central place in the legal structure of marriage and in the social practice of some Muslim communities often takes on a merely symbolic form among American Muslims. Adhering to the symbolism comes at a price, however. If dower is meant to be an economic safety net for women, then a more useful approach would depend on factors other than consummation, such as length of marriage, contribution to the household economy, wages lost and earning potential diminished during childbearing and caretaking, and so forth. Feminist assertions that women do not have any Islamic obligation to perform domestic services or childcare may have the ironic effect of devaluing those contributions. Although stress on the voluntary nature of women's performance of domestic duties can highlight their significance, this recognition that dower does not compensate for a wife's household contribution is not usually accompanied by a discussion of *precisely for what it is* that dower compensates a woman.

Discussions about dower, spousal rights, and intermarriage must occur in the context of a broader consideration of what men and women contribute to marriage and to the family, including the recognition that most American Muslims do not maintain the separate asset regime assumed by classical law and that complete male economic responsibility is more theoretical than actual. Perhaps one positive outcome of the neo-traditional vision of the wife providing homemaking and childrearing services in exchange for male providership could be the dissociation of sex from support; if sex is no longer the wife's marital duty, then it could become a fully mutual right. This does not resolve the problem of how to deal with the double-shift that emerges when women work outside the home to provide partial support for the household without the husband taking over a portion of the household duties, but it might be more reasonable to see those duties as less explicitly gendered than the others. If some Muslims want to adopt a provider/homemaker division of labor that provides some kind of economic independence for women, that ought to be negotiable. But the pretense that such a structure, and only such a structure, is religiously legitimate avoids the reality that many Muslims organize their lives differently, as well as the real incompatibility of classical definitions of male and female obligations with most contemporary understandings of spousal roles in marriage.

Coda 1

The year after *Sexual Ethics and Islam* was published, I was at a workshop with Amina Wadud and Margot Badran. Both asserted that the two most significant obstacles to Muslim women's equality were rules governing women's status within the family and women's exclusion from certain types of public ritual practice, especially leadership within it. The conjoining of patriarchy within the family and male dominance in ritual leadership led me to wonder more basically about the juxtaposition of family law and ritual law. It seems to me that today, especially but not exclusively for Muslims living in contexts where they are minorities, family law plays a role quite distinct from its function in premodern Muslim communities and societies. Marriage rules, in their earliest Muslim iterations, served as a kind of shorthand to ensure that people were essentially in right relationship to one another and that the social structure was both stable and generally just.[63] Reformists, including feminists, distinguish between rules for worship, deemed immune to change, and rules for social transactions which can, at least in theory, change with the times. Yet part of the resistance to changing rules governing, for instance, dower, arises from the fact that it has come to symbolize the religious legitimacy of the marriage, rather than merely serving as a means for regulating social recognition and property allocation.

Instead of regulating libido and lineage, property and progeny, having a *nikah* ceremony announces one's religious bona fides to a community. Isolated aspects of Islamic law are fetishized, including sometimes the *wali* (bride's guardian) and always the dower, which may or may not be enforceable in a court, and may or may not take the place of other state-generated property rules.

So-called personal status laws in Muslim-majority countries reflect multiple transformations as bureaucratic nation-states have taken over the registration, and sometimes the performance, of marriages and divorces. It is obvious to scholars but largely invisible to laypeople that civil codes typically govern family matters, even in countries with Muslim majorities, even in countries that call these laws shari'a. Governments and courts do not simply follow shari'a but rather implement jurisprudential doctrines selectively, sometimes haphazardly, and virtually always in ways that are bad for women and, especially, the poor.

There are additional factors at play when "Islamic family law" is practiced in places like the United States or United Kingdom. Today, family law in Muslim-minority contexts often interweaves religious legitimacy and civil processes, though some Muslims disdain civil law for marriage and other family matters. Instead of regulating interpersonal relations to ensure just outcomes, religious marriage and divorce practices affirm a (gendered) Muslim identity.

By contrasting the contemporary situation with earlier times, I am not implying that there was a precolonial Golden Age in which the jurists' version of Islamic law was perfectly just. My book *Marriage and Slavery in Early Islam* (2010) explores in depth the eighth- to tenth-century jurisprudence on marriage, divorce, and spousal rights. I illustrate that conceptual linkages between marriage and slavery – including dower, which parallels purchase price, and unilateral male divorce, which parallels manumission – constrain the jurists' reasoning about (free) women's rights as wives. I show that the structure of Muslim marriage in legal thinking is of a piece. Rationales for specific rules may change, with dower, for instance, coming to be understood not as the exchange-value of a woman's sex but as a provision for her financial security and a sign of the esteem in which Islam holds women, but the intertwined nature of these aspects of the legal system limits the amount of change possible, if one holds to the rules as a whole. Piecemeal change may occur, but it is doubtful whether it would be sufficiently transformative to allow egalitarian marriages to flourish.[64]

Asifa Quraishi-Landes has argued, in contrast, that though a larger transformation may be desirable, such as modeling marriage on contracts of partnership rather than contracts of sale, it remains strategically useful to work within the system of rights widely agreed to be granted by Islamic jurisprudence, including dower.[65] She recognizes that Muslims often operate in and among varied legal regimes. There are ongoing debates about how governments should treat Islamic legal provisions when a Muslim divorce comes before them. American courts remain unpredictable in their enforcement of dower and other conditions of Muslim marriage contracts. (That is, unless the contracts are written as antenuptial agreements, with provisions made according to American law.) Sometimes the provisions of the contract are better for women than standard civil property division; sometimes worse. Women sometimes benefit from strict adherence to property settlements outlined in marriage contracts and sometimes they are better off when judges toss such settlements out in favor of, for instance, community property rules.[66]

Legal pluralism is a fact of life in most countries, not only those where Muslims live as minorities. Just as there was no pristine age of egalitarian just law, there was no time in which Islamic law was implemented exclusively. In the earliest Muslim communities, Qur'anic and prophetic law merged with and diverged from Arabian custom. By the time judicial apparatuses existed and a more comprehensive legal system, so too did parallel administrative courts. There have always been multiple legal systems at play in places where Muslims live. But the idea of a religious law in contradistinction to a secular one becomes intelligible only with the rise of a privatized sphere in which religion becomes a personal activity, not one with communal weight.

In a variety of places, there have been significant debates over whether and how a parallel legal system (for example, to grant "Islamic" divorces, especially in cases of unregistered marriages) ought to operate. Take South Africa, where the government currently does not recognize Muslim marriages; as of this writing, a Muslim Marriages Bill has been languishing for years. Some feminists, including Muslims, say it makes too many capitulations to patriarchal provisions of religious law; other Muslims argue that it grants too many concessions to the secular legal system and unreasonably restricts Muslim men's religiously granted prerogatives. Muslim women's ability to claim support, inheritance, and judicial relief including divorces is hindered by their marriages' lack of formal recognition. In the UK, the recent implementation of Muslim tribunals has been hailed by some as an important step toward granting women recourse in situations where they would otherwise be stuck; others lambast them as oppression of women under the guise of multiculturalism.[67]

Discussion of unregistered Muslim marriages, forced marriages, and polygamy is often laced with Islamophobic clichés, as are criticisms of the tribunals. At the same time, there are significant theoretical and practical issues with such tribunals: Which version of Islamic law is used, and who arbitrates? As to the former, while modern nations have legal codes that are the result of negotiated processes and reform campaigns, in places like North America and Europe paradoxically it is the "authentic" classical texts along with Qur'an and sunnah that are most often invoked in debates over what is Islamic. As for the latter, who would count as a religious authority? Unlike Egypt, the American government does not appoint an official mufti. So who would serve? The imams of mosques? Muslims with degrees in civil law? What kind of knowledge would serve as the basis for making complex decisions about law and ethics in Muslim life?

It is a thorny problem to respect the desire of individuals and (some members of) communities not to rely on the apparatus of the nation-state to regulate matters of family. Informal and communally recognized mechanisms can work well, at least as a supplement to civil law. It seems naïve to claim that where tribunals do not bind they cannot coerce: if a tribunal exists, social pressures may assert that if you were a good Muslim, you would allow the tribunal to arbitrate your divorce, or your custody agreement, and so forth. Yet social pressures are not necessarily a bad thing. As Coda 2 discusses, polygyny *necessarily* exists outside the system of American law. Women with otherwise divergent perspectives on polygyny in the African American Muslim community agree that secrecy and stigma increase hardship and trauma for women with co-wives. Although criminalization makes full public recognition impossible, within communities, polygyny should not be practiced secretly; where informal marriage exists, so too must some form of alternative adjudication.

2 Lesser Evils: Divorce in Islamic Ethics

God did not make lawful anything more repugnant to Him than divorce.
Reported saying of the Prophet Muhammad, *Sunan Abi Dawud*[1]

A woman knows (that is, comes to know with certainty) that her husband has divorced her thrice; the husband denies having divorced her; and the woman has not the ability to prevent the husband from (having access to) her person: it is permissible to the woman to kill the husband; because she is helpless in preventing mischief to her person; and, therefore, it shall be allowable to her to kill him; but it is proper that she should kill him with drugs, and not with an instrument of death; because if the woman should kill him with an instrument which inflicts wound, she shall be put to death by way of *kisas* (or retaliation).
Fatawa-I-Kazee Khan, Hanafi legal text[2]

The image of a husband repudiating his wife by declaring "I divorce you, I divorce you, I divorce you" has been one of the most persistent and negative stereotypes of Muslims. And while it does not tell anything resembling a complete story, this image has a basis in reality. So-called triple divorce, while widely considered blameworthy even among the earliest Muslims, is nonetheless still practiced in many places. Recent controversies over its use have erupted in India and in Malaysia. In the former case, the All-India Muslim Personal Law Board considered whether to declare that all such triple pronouncements would be considered to effect only a single divorce; in the latter case, the issue at stake was whether such divorces were valid if delivered via text message. Both situations were complicated by the intricate and multi-layered relationship between civil and religious law, a tension that exists within every Muslim community to a greater or lesser extent.[3] Divorce is a contested issue for Muslims in nations where personal laws are ostensibly religious as well as in those places, such as the United States, where civil law alone holds formal sway. Why is a husband's unilateral, and extrajudicial, pronouncement of *talaq* so meaningful to Muslims who otherwise abide by civil laws? What are the structural considerations at stake in attempts to make divorce regulations more egalitarian? How does this treatment of divorce in the writings of the jurists relate to American Muslims? The premodern case, cited in this chapter's epigraph, of a wife whose husband has pronounced the powerful words of divorce but refuses to admit having done so, rendering the state powerless to intervene and forcing her to resort to poison to thwart his sexual advances, has surprising relevance to contemporary discussions on the relationship between individual acts, ethical practice, and enforceable law.

Untying the knot

Its religious dimensions notwithstanding, Muslim marriage is, above all, a contract. Though it will persist until death if neither spouse takes action to dissolve it, a marriage can also be ended before that time. There are both good and bad reasons for ending a marriage, according to Qur'an, *sunnah*, and the opinions of the commentators and jurists, and good and bad ways to proceed with divorce whatever the motivations behind it. It is a well-accepted principle that disharmony between spouses should not lead immediately to divorce. The Qur'an advocates reconciliation where possible, through negotiated settlements between the spouses themselves or arbiters from their families.[4] However, there will be instances when mutual good treatment is not possible; in such cases, there should be an amicable parting. This negotiated settlement may involve the wife's payment of a sum to her husband; normally, in case of *talaq*, he must not take back anything of what he gave her as dower.[5] The Qur'an contains a variety of regulations concerning these and other forms of divorce (such as the now-obscure *zihar* and *li'an*), which built on and modified pre-Islamic Arab practices.

The English term "divorce" encompasses several means of ending a marriage that are distinct in Islamic jurisprudence. The most common, *talaq* (literally, "release"), is a unilateral repudiation of the wife by the husband. This form of divorce does not require the wife's consent, and most of the classical jurists held that it was valid even without her notification. *Talaq* can be either revocable (*raj'i*) or irrevocable (*ba'in*). In a revocable divorce, the husband has the right to take back the wife during the three-menstrual-cycle waiting period (*'idda*) that follows the dissolution of all consummated marriages.[6] However, following the end of the waiting period from a revocable divorce (or after an irrevocable form of dissolution such as judicial divorce or divorce for compensation, on which see below), the couple can still remarry. This is the case even after two divorces. However, when the husband repudiates the wife for the third time, the divorce becomes "absolute." In this case, the spouses cannot remarry until the wife has married another man, and that marriage has been consummated, then ended through death or divorce. Only after this can the original spouses remarry.[7]

Triple divorce, *talaq thalatha*, occurs when a husband pronounces three repudiations at once rather than divorcing his wife once, revocably, and simply allowing the waiting period to expire without taking her back. In this way, he immediately makes his divorce of her absolute, creating a bar to remarriage between them. The Sunni jurists generally consider triple repudiation, or other similar pronouncements that lead to absolute divorces (*talaq al-batta*), to be reprehensible (*makruh*). Yet even while considering such divorces blameworthy, the vast majority of Sunni thinkers – Ibn Taymiyya is a notable exception – hold that they are effective and binding. (Shi'i jurists hold a much more restricted view of what means of divorce are legally valid, requiring, not merely preferring, the presence of witnesses, and considering only one pronouncement of divorce at a time valid. This dramatic difference illustrates quite clearly that Sunni doctrine was the result of interpretive decisions, and could have been otherwise.[8])

Just as marriage has financial implications, so does divorce; in fact, they are closely intertwined. A wife divorced by *talaq* retains the dower she received at marriage or, if it was divided into a prompt and deferred portion, the deferred portion becomes immediately due at divorce. Predictably, the prospect of receiving or having to pay a large deferred sum can serve as inducement or restraint on a spouse's actions. Some women set a large deferred dower as a disincentive for their husbands to divorce them impulsively. However, this strategy can backfire if the wife is the one to seek a divorce. In *khul'*, divorce for compensation, a wife returns her dower, waives the deferred portion, or pays some other sum to her husband in order to obtain a divorce. Almost all jurists consider his consent essential though it is not mentioned in the Qur'an or in some of the prophetic traditions that refer to it. *Khul'* is by definition irrevocable; the husband has no right to take her back during the waiting period, though the pair may remarry subsequently by mutual consent with a new contract and dower.[9]

In addition to unilateral repudiation and divorce for compensation, both of which are mentioned in the Qur'an, judicial divorce (*firaq*, *faskh* or *tatliq*) becomes permissible when the wife has cause. Judicial divorce is preferable to *khul'* for a wife who has grounds because she need not relinquish her claim to dower. Acceptable grounds for divorce vary widely among the legal schools. In the Hanafi school, which is the most restrictive, a woman has almost no grounds for obtaining a divorce provided her husband has consummated the marriage; neither failure to support her, nor life imprisonment, nor abuse is considered grounds for divorce (although she may get a separation and support if she convinces a judge). If he is declared missing, she may have the marriage dissolved (on grounds of presumed widowhood) at the time when he would have completed his natural lifespan, which could be as old as ninety. In contrast, Maliki law allows the most generous grounds for a woman to seek divorce including non-support, abandonment, and the broad charge of "injury" (*darar*), which can be physical or otherwise.

Women can use other legal strategies to obtain access to divorce without recourse to a judge. For instance, in conditional or delegated divorce the wife includes a condition in her marriage contract that allows her the right to divorce on her own initiative under certain specific circumstances, or states that she will be automatically divorced if a particular event occurs such as the husband taking another wife or moving to another town. There are possible benefits to these types of stipulations, if women have the requisite knowledge and are willing and able to convince future spouses to agree to the conditions, but they are not a panacea for inequalities in traditional divorce law. The extent to which such clauses in the marriage contract are enforceable varies widely in legal schools or contemporary national laws. Further, even clauses that were originally valid can be easily rendered ineffective through the wife's unwitting actions. More troubling still is that though these conditions can increase a woman's access to divorce, they do not restrict in any way the husband's right to repudiate her unilaterally at will. The increasingly influential view of marriage as a romantic rather than contractual institution often makes women unwilling to negotiate for or demand stipulations in their contracts, seeing them as a sign of bad faith.[10] In any case, the inclusion of such stipulations regarding divorce ratifies the notion that unilateral divorce by the husband is valid and effective, since conditional and delegated divorces function through the mechanism of *talaq*. Thus, it is contradictory to press for such stipulations regarding divorce while simultaneously arguing that a husband's right of unilateral *talaq* is not supported by the sources. If his *talaq* is not valid, then any conditional or delegated divorce right she has is equally void. (One way to avoid this conflict is to insist that the only permissible divorce is a judicial divorce; however, this raises its own set of issues surrounding the validity of civil law versus religious law.)

This sketch of legal doctrine seems to provide a fairly bleak picture for Muslim wives, but a number of historians have demonstrated that in practice women have enjoyed a good deal of flexibility in obtaining divorces on favorable terms, thanks to sympathetic judges and a variety of bargaining strategies, frequently involving claims to dower, maintenance, and custody of children. Looking at the way "Islamic family law translate[d] into the reality of medieval marriage," Yossef Rapoport finds that women's economic independence, among other factors, facilitated woman-initiated divorce, although the unrestricted nature of male oaths of repudiation contributed to the high divorce rate.[11] Twentieth-century legal reforms in nations such as India, Egypt, and Iran (both pre- and post-revolution) have sometimes dramatically improved women's access to divorce and have, to a lesser extent, penalized men's unrestricted use of *talaq*. The progress of such reforms has been hampered by continual struggles over "authenticity" and the self-aggrandizing tendencies of the modern nation-state to work to bring everything under its control. The relationship between civil and religious marriage and divorce is complex even in nations such as Pakistan, where both are ostensibly Islamic, but for Muslims in primarily non-Muslim societies the dictates of classical legal thought, as they have trickled down into conventional wisdom, remain influential.[12]

Extreme circumstances

The regulations surrounding divorce that I have just outlined do not directly account for the extreme case, mentioned in this chapter's epigraph, where Qadi Khan gives a woman permission to defend herself against her former husband's sexual advances even to the point of killing him – discreetly:

> A woman knows (that is, comes to know with certainty) that her husband has divorced her thrice; the husband denies having divorced her; and the woman has not the ability to prevent the husband from (having access to) her person: it is permissible to the woman to kill the husband; because she is helpless in preventing mischief to her person; and, therefore, it shall be allowable to her to kill him; but it is proper that she should kill him with drugs, and not with an instrument of death; because if the woman should kill him with an instrument which inflicts wound, she shall be put to death by way of *kisas* (or retaliation).[13]

This fatwa attempts to resolve an intractable problem. By divorcing his wife three times, the man has rendered her absolutely divorced from him, making sexual relations between them completely unlawful. However, his denial of the divorce is accepted as final.[14] (The legal efficacy of his declaration is taken for granted; the reponse does not even allude to it.) What, then, may his "wife" do in this case? She is certain of having been divorced and that therefore it is no more lawful to allow her husband to have sex with her than it would be for her to allow a stranger access to herself; her (former) husband is at this point legally a stranger. Failing to resist him in some fashion would be morally, if not legally, tantamount to consenting to illicit sex; she has the right (or perhaps obligation) to defend herself against such an attack, even to the point of killing her would-be rapist. What might be a mundane evidentiary dispute over whether or not a divorce has occurred becomes a life or death issue.

In allowing the woman to pursue the dictates of religious law and her conscience, Qadi Khan recognizes a distinction between the law applied by God, which grants the woman the right to defend herself against his advances, and that followed as a matter of procedure by the state, which, bound as it is by procedural rules, is only an approximation thereof. Although the man in question is trying to have sexual access to a woman over whom he no longer has any sexual rights, he cannot be brought before the authorities as a rapist, because the law as applied by the state authorities would still recognize him as her husband. The text thus differentiates between the morally permissible action – killing him – and the legally acceptable one.

This distinction between what is acceptable to God and what is acceptable to the state influences the solution arrived at by Qadi Khan, following Abu Hanifa: the woman may kill her "husband" provided she does so with "drugs," not a "weapon." Why is poisoning acceptable, while killing in some other fashion is not? Although Qadi Khan may have been influenced by the view that it was unladylike to kill using a weapon, the more salient rationale is that if she were simply to kill him by stabbing, for example, the fact of his having died an unnatural death would be obvious, and a culprit would be sought and punished. It is not fair that a woman should be subject to execution in retaliation for having defended herself against sexual assault, but she has no way of proving what transpired. Her testimony that she killed in order to avoid his attempt to have intercourse with her after he had divorced her absolutely would not be exonerating in this circumstance, just as it would not be considered adequate to prove her divorce itself. Thus, one can deduce that Qadi Khan grants permission to poison the ex-husband in order that his unnatural death escape detection. If it does not become known or cannot be proven that he has been deliberately killed (as would most likely be the case before the introduction of sophisticated forensic methodologies), then her actions will not come under scrutiny, she will not have to provide justification for them, and hence the issue of the reliability or legal worth of her testimony as to her motive for killing him – the fact of his having divorced her and denying it – will not come up.

Prominent seventeenth-century Palestinian Hanafi mufti Khayr al-Din al-Ramli's treatment of a similar case confirms this analysis. In this instance, "an evil man who harms his wife, hits her without right and rebukes her without cause" has, after swearing to divorce her "many times", finally done so. When she is able to demonstrate "that a thrice divorce had taken effect," the mufti declares that "it is permissible for her to kill him, according to many of the 'ulama', if he is not prevented [from approaching her] except by killing."[15] Because the divorce is proven, she is granted permission to kill him if he attempts to have sex with her. The juxtaposition of these two fatwas illuminates the existence of two distinct types of legal rules. Those that govern the wife's ability to kill her husband in the case addressed by Qadi Khan, where she cannot prove the divorce, can only be moral – she will be absolved of guilt in this case, and will not have to answer to the divine for a transgression. However, though her killing him is religiously licit, if she is brought before temporal authorities, she will be subject to retribution because her testimony cannot be accepted on this question. In Khayr al-Din's case, however, the divorce is proven; the woman's ex-husband is legally a stranger and she can defend herself against his advances even to the point of killing without fear of retribution.

In Qadi Khan's fatwa, the entire matter revolves around the inadmissibility of the wife's testimony. Why is it that a wife's testimony cannot be accepted regarding *talaq*? It is not, as might be supposed, an issue of women's testimony having less weight than men's but rather an issue of "plaintiff" and "defendant." Although one Qur'anic verse attributes different weight to male and female testimony, and jurists have further limited the range of cases in which women can testify, in numerous matters related to marriage the words of husband and wife are equivalent. Yet in discussing the wife's response, Qadi Khan does not even suggest that there might be any possible way for her to seek judicial recognition of his divorce of her. Allowing women's word to count with regard to their own divorces would open up the floodgates to women claiming to have been triply repudiated – likely to cause more trouble for the Hanafis in particular, given the extremely limited grounds on which women could seek divorce.[16] In Qadi Khan's implicit calculation of the relative harm in each case, to allow this man's death is acceptable in a way that tampering with the overall weight of rights granted to husbands in matters of divorce would not be.

The Hanafi solution, however, is not palatable to everyone. Moralistic traditionist-jurisprudent[17] Ibn Hanbal confronts the same question, several centuries before Qadi Khan arrives at a different ruling. First, the wife should seek to ransom herself from her husband in divorce for compensation. Though he does not say so directly, one can deduce that this is merely a strategy to get him to recognize the divorce. It will have no legal effect, since no marriage actually exists after his absolute divorce. If her husband refuses to allow this but rather compels her to remain "married" to him, "She should not adorn herself for him, nor should she come near him, and, if she possibly can, she should escape from him." Asked specifically "Should she fight him, when he desires her?" Ibn Hanbal hesitates. "I do not know," he replies. "She should not fight him. Abu Hanifa said she should fight him. She should escape from him if she can."[18] The wife here has the obligation to resist sex, but this should be accomplished by non-combative means. Ibn Hanbal's invocation of Abu Hanifa's view perhaps serves to give his listener an option beyond what he is willing to endorse.

The burden is on the woman to place herself out of reach, sexually, whether she hears the divorce pronouncement herself (according to Ibn Hanbal, "Her case is strongest" in this instance) or hears the testimony of two witnesses who can be trusted. In a case where there were witnesses, presumably she could have used their testimony to establish that her husband had in fact divorced her. Perhaps in this case her escape is a short-term measure until the witnesses can give testimony publicly to the fact of her divorce, resulting in the clarification of her marital status. If there are no witnesses, she has even stronger justification for escaping. But what exactly does it accomplish in that case? Ibn Hanbal does not say, as the text moves on to discuss an unrelated matter. If a woman escapes, presumably back to her natal kin, what happens to her marriage if her husband continues to insist that he has not divorced her? She loses her right to support and remains unable to remarry – though she avoids the collusion in illicit sexual acts, she cannot end her marriage (while her erstwhile husband is free to take another wife). Unlike in the Hanafi scenario where she kills him, she remains tied to him until and unless he acknowledges dissolving the marriage.

Cases such as those just discussed are extreme, not representative. Though judges were undoubtedly faced regularly with "claims and counterclaims" regarding the occurrence of divorce, it is impossible to know whether any particular case ever resulted in killing.[19] One of the limitations of working with legal handbooks and compilations, rather than archival documents, is that it is not possible to determine what discussions are in response to actual events and what is merely hypothetical. Particular scenarios can garner jurists' attention far out of proportion to their likelihood of occurring, simply because in resolving the legal issues at stake, challenging legal points can be illustrated or clarified. My choice of this dramatic example to discuss divorce was meant to illuminate, in a tangible way, the extensive, unilateral privilege held by husbands in the realm of divorce. Only once this is understood can contemporary discussions of *talaq* and its reform be more fully comprehended.

Prospects for reform

Reforms to divorce laws in the contemporary Muslim world have been plentiful.[20] Most of these reforms have attempted either to restrict men's unfettered exercise of their rights to *talaq* or to increase women's access to divorce for cause. Some majority-Sunni nations have accomplished the first aim by requiring some type of intervention or registration from a judge, or by declaring that three repudiations pronounced at once will count as only one divorce, as in the recent Indian debate.[21] Other nations, such as Iran, have imposed financial penalties on a husband who divorces his wife without cause. Despite these attempts to curb men's impulsive and extra-judicial use of *talaq*, almost all courts ultimately consider *talaq* pronouncements legally effective since they are recognized by religious authorities. The widely held view that a husband's pronouncement of *talaq* is religiously valid regardless of whether approved by a court, and regardless of whether or not it contravenes provisions of civil codes, constitutes a major stumbling block for efforts to reform divorce law in those nations where putatively Islamic family codes hold sway. In some ways, the codification of marriage and divorce laws has reduced the flexibility that women of the upper classes may have enjoyed in the past.[22] Though reforms have altered some of the specifics of divorce laws, they have not challenged the basic idea that divorce is a man's prerogative, while women may only obtain divorce for cause.

A more recent Egyptian law, approved by the chief jurist of Al-Azhar, the most respected institution of traditional learning in Egypt and perhaps the entire Sunni Muslim world, provides an alternate approach. As noted above, the vast majority of premodern jurists as well as contemporary national laws have considered the husband's agreement essential to *khul'*, divorce for compensation. Beginning in March 2000, Egypt granted the wife the right to obtain a *khul'* divorce from a judge without the husband's consent if she returns the dower she received at marriage.[23] Judicial *khul'* has been legal in Pakistan since the middle of the twentieth century, meaning that a wife who does not have effective grounds for divorce for cause may seek this type of divorce, returning her dower and getting out of a marriage in which she refuses to remain.[24] Similar legislation has yet to pass elsewhere, but I think it likely that eventually more reforms of this type will pass; *khul'*-on-demand is the most egalitarian reform possible without a major transformation of the legal structure of marriage. It is reasonably fair, given the role of dower, that women cannot collect dower and then proceed to divorce without any fault of the husband's. To the extent, though, that women who have grounds for judicial divorce may be induced to forgo financial rights in order to obtain *khul'* it could lead to injustice. Uncontested *khul'* has faced serious resistance wherever it has been proposed, as a violation of the husband's rights.[25] Women, it has been alleged, are too emotional to wield control of divorce.[26]

In the case of Muslims living in the United States and other nations where Islamic law is not implemented by civil courts, the relevance of modern legal reforms is minimal; and classical Islamic doctrine matters only where individuals take it into account in extrajudicial interpersonal negotiations. While it is relatively straightforward to combine an "Islamic" marriage with a civil one – religious authorities are frequently authorized by state legislatures to perform valid civil marriages – only the civil courts may pronounce divorce. A couple married both religiously and civilly can be in the awkward position of being *only* civilly divorced (if the wife insists on the necessity of a divorce pronouncement that the husband refuses to make) or only religiously divorced, if the husband pronounces *talaq* long before the civil court takes action. For the most part, American Muslim leaders have chosen to treat a divorce pronounced by the courts as the equivalent of judicial divorce in classical Islamic law, but the coexistence of civil law with an amalgam of jurisprudential doctrines and Muslim conventional wisdom makes for a confusing situation. Further, for those committed to egalitarian marriages, the existence of *talaq* as a religiously acceptable institution creates obstacles to full marital agency for women.

Talaq is so problematic because it is an entrenched right connected to the legal structure of marriage as a form of *milk*, ownership or control. A husband's power of *talaq* derived from his exclusive control over the marriage tie, just as a master's power of manumission resulted from ownership of a slave. Premodern jurists frequently drew analogies between *talaq* and manumission (*'itq*), reflecting their shared understanding that a husband, like the master of a slave, held *milk*, "ownership," over the tie joining the parties. This right was basic to the nature of marriage: the husband acquired a limited *milk* over his wife at the time of contract through payment of a dower, just as a master acquired *milk* through purchase of a slave; either could unilaterally relinquish it whenever he chose. The wife, as the one bound by the marriage tie, did not share in this power of unilateral divorce (any more than a slave could simply choose to free him- or herself). Instead, her opportunities to dissolve the marriage were limited to judicial divorce for cause, grounds for which varied greatly depending on the school; delegated divorce if authorized by her husband; and *khul'*, divorce for compensation, which was roughly analogous to a slave's negotiated purchase of his or her own freedom. Of course, the analogy can only be carried so far: a wife was not her husband's slave. But because the structure of the Islamic marriage contract presumes the husband's *milk*, control, over the continuation of the marriage, piecemeal reforms of divorce laws that do not address this basic norm will be limited in the amount of change they can ultimately effect. Long-lasting and far-reaching reform of divorce requires, more fundamentally, a reform in the basic structure of Muslim marriage itself.

Conclusion

In many countries, the primacy of civil law over "Islamic law" has been accepted in numerous realms of law, including commercial, but the repeated appeals by various actors to the authenticity of Islam with regard to rules regulating family life and sexuality have meant that in matters associated with women and family, regulations are still purportedly "Islamic." Muslims living someplace where there is a civil system of marriage and divorce with no pretensions to being based on a religious law face different challenges. In the United States, courts deal routinely with divorces among Muslims; divorces are granted to both wives and husbands on the same grounds available to any other couple. The regulation of divorce is fraught with difficulties because, aside from the interpersonal challenges, it is normally interwoven with other crucial elements of marriage structures, including who has the right to dissolve the marriage and with what financial claims. Despite claims by a number of feminist scholars and women's advocates to the contrary, inequities in divorce law – which many Muslims would agree exist – are not merely read into the Qur'anic text by misguided or even misogynist jurists. They are not anomalies that can be remedied by the simple expedient of appeals to men's better nature. The necessary shift in patterns of *talaq* must recognize that it is deeply embedded in Muslim marriage as a whole system.

Perhaps a sensible marriage and divorce structure for Muslims living in nations such as the United States, where dower is not a customary part of marriage practices among the broader population and where all divorces must go through the courts, might exclude both dower and all forms of extrajudicial divorce – claims that are closely linked in traditional jurisprudence. It would be possible to make financial arrangements as well as other household contributions the subject of a prenuptial agreement validated by the American legal system, and insist that civil marriage and divorce are the only licit forms of relationship. If marriage is structured in such a way that it can be dissolved only by a judge, whether by mutual consent or otherwise, that would eliminate much of the dual-system conflicts over the validity of unrecorded divorce pronouncements in numerous Muslim-majority countries. This is not entirely unheard of: one lesson of Qadi Khan's case, in addition to the one about the male abuse of authority, is that state authority can override certain jurisprudential doctrines, even as those doctrines guide individual life and action.

Appeals to religious sensibilities have emerged in several attempts to entice North American Muslims to participate in *shari'a* tribunals or parallel mediation/arbitration systems.[27] Such tribunals, though undoubtedly well meant, would likely be disastrous for women's rights, even leaving aside the fact that there has not been substantive discussion as to how to guarantee the qualifications of those assigned to arbitrate. At best, women might get a sympathetic interpretation of doctrines understood to be Islamic, but it is highly unlikely that they would get sophisticated modifications of legal rules. My objections to the formation of Islamic law courts in the West do not extend to individual Muslims choosing to follow particular legal doctrines in their personal affairs (what Abdullahi An-Na'im refers to as "voluntary compliance out of religious commitment"[28]) or with "independent scholars providing moral guidance to their communities on [a] private voluntary basis."[29] And it is certainly possible to write contracts that enshrine religious rights and duties for spouses – at least financial ones – in a way that makes them enforceable by Western courts.[30] Individuals should be free to negotiate those contracts, with as much information as possible about both classical and reformist interpretations of rights and obligations. However, if consenting to participate in Islamic arbitration becomes possible on a wide scale, it will also become a mark of faith, and those who choose not to will have to contend with accusations of not being good Muslims, when they may simply not believe that a *shari'a* court is capable of providing a realistic and appropriate rendering of Islamic principles into a just verdict in a context radically different from that where the law was first formulated.

Setting aside the influence of human historical factors on the development of the law, there is also the question of the contextuality of the Qur'anic revelation itself. Despite the reflexive praise for Islamic legal flexibility, there is a broad unwillingness to interfere with elements of marriage practices, such as divorce, that are explicitly referred to in the Qur'an. But are the verses on divorce meant to apply in every possible situation, or are they specific in some way to seventh-century Arabia? If they can be modified, on what basis should one do so, and how far can one go in altering specific rules? What is taken as common sense by many ordinary Muslims (the twenty-first century West is quite different from either the seventh-century West or the contemporary Muslim world and hence rules should be different) is still controversial for numerous Muslim leaders and scholars.

Coda 2

Despite its prominent place in the epigraphs to Chapter 1 and Chapter 3, I largely avoided polygamy in the original edition of this book. Why? It didn't seem to be on the agenda for most Muslims; only reporters asked me about it. Despite the centrality of polygamy – technically, polygyny – to stereotypes about Islam and Muslims, divorce directly affects far more Muslim women worldwide.[31] Like honor killings and veiling, polygyny claims a disproportionate share of attention, in ways that typically obscure rather than illuminate.[32]

So why talk about it now? Though no accurate statistics exist, the practice is more widespread among American Muslims than I had supposed; it "is becoming more visible if not growing."[33] Moreover, polygyny raises important questions about what form(s) of marriage, if any, government ought to recognize; in this way it is analogous to same-sex marriage. (As with same-sex relationships, the terms of the debate are largely set by widespread patriarchal assumptions about human nature and sexuality.) Additionally, like the topic of male providership, with which it is often intertwined, polygyny prompts thinking about how scripture is applied in varying contexts, how ideals are translated into realities, and about the diversity of women's experiences. Discourses about polygyny take certain social, political, and economic as well as ideological realities as givens. Unlike the premodern period when the acceptability – even normative status – of polygyny was taken for granted by scholars, even if only a small fraction of the population ever practiced it, in the last century it has become common to describe polygyny as a solution to female needs for provision or protection, or as a measure to protect against illicit sex.[34] Yet, as one polygyny advocate whose husband has a second wife wrote to me, it is not a matter of defending or justifying polygyny, but acknowledging it: "men having multiple women is not a strategy or a remedy but a *reality* since time immemorial."

The issue of the state is difficult to resolve but in some respects easiest to discuss. Like some forms of Muslim divorce considered in this chapter, polygyny strays beyond the bounds of the American legal system. Many states treat multiple marriages as a criminal offense; even where plural marriages are not criminalized, they are invalid. Of course, for various reasons – including a disinclination to have the bureaucratic apparatus of the nation-state intervene in their intimate affairs – some American Muslims, including African Americans, disdain formal or civil marriage altogether, even for monogamous unions.

Polygyny provides a reason for opting out. Polygynous marriages in the U.S. are by definition unregistered; it is impossible under American law for a man to be validly married to more than one woman at a time. One wife may be married civilly, but any additional marriages must be done without a civil ceremony. Particularly where the state is not involved, all forms of relationship raise tensions between utopian idealism about interpersonal projects and community norms, and the reality that the nation-state is a crucial locus for adjudication and negotiation – and, in the case of women, particularly women who have children, a guarantor of certain rights.[35]

Debra Majeed explores polygyny at length in her new monograph on the practice in the African American Muslim community of W.D. Mohammed.[36] Some of the "attractive, smart, accomplished" women she studies "unashamedly defend their partnering choices," which are driven by issues common to "life in black America," including "lack of marriageable black males" and "the desire to maintain cultural norms."[37] Majeed insists that not only can one derive knowledge about these women from studying them, but their experiences are vital for understanding "living polygyny." She frames her contribution as a study in Muslim womanism. Womanism is a Christian approach rooted in experiences of African American life that insists on the centrality of black women but not in isolation from a larger community. Majeed's Muslim womanism treats African American Muslim women's praxis as a source of norms.

Studying practices such as polygyny or divorce not from abstract doctrines but from women's experiences of living in, with, or through them is radical. Treating women as a source of knowledge about Islam means taking seriously the experiences of Muslim women who "share their husbands" or those who confront abuse, complicated divorces, or other challenges. Muslim womanism, in Majeed's view, "positions the experiences and wisdom of women at the forefront of any consideration of Muslim family life."[38]

Women's experiences, of course, differ. "The Muslim woman" (or "the Muslimwoman") is not a unified subject.[39] Even within North America – even within W.D. Mohammed's community – women have radically different experiences of polygynous marriage, to say nothing of the complicated legal, social, and economic circumstances surrounding polygyny in, for example, Pakistan, where polygyny is legal but restricted, or South Africa, where Muslim marriages have no civil standing but polygyny is recognized within customary law.[40] To be fair, women – Muslim and non-Muslim – also have radically different experiences of monogamous marriage. But structural features of polygyny, in particular its "powerful object lesson in male sexual entitlement" as one self-identified survivor puts it, and "a very concrete affirmation" that women "are expected to put up with less than optimal relationships," present additional challenges for women.[41] Consequences for women and, especially, children can be long-lasting.[42]

Despite advocating the decriminalization of polygyny, and acknowledging its liberatory effects for some, Majeed is ultimately skeptical of polygyny as a possible "pro-woman, pro-family" strategy "for the survival and empowerment of African American Muslims."[43] She observes that "encouraging examples of living polygyny ... are in the minority."[44] As she argues, "the positive examples of multiple-wife marriage are outweighed by those led by men who are financially, spiritually, and/or mentally ill-equipped for such responsibilities and involve women who feel they have no other options."[45] Although it is certainly not the case that all women married to polygynous men are unhappy with their situations, some women are steered toward polygyny with the suggestion that their marriage prospects are limited. As a colleague pointed out to me, "discourses on more/less desirable brides are raced, ethnicized, shaded, and classed, with the result that poor, dark-skinned black women, especially if they are not virgins, are disproportionately likely to be 'encouraged' to settle and accept polygamy, lest they end up being single forever."[46] The same holds for women perceived as disadvantaged by age, education, (dis)ability, or who do not conform to conventional norms of femininity or attractiveness. The larger question of sexual double standards, and the prizing of female youth, beauty, and/or virginity, is by no means exclusive to Muslims. Reflecting on polygyny in the U.S. context will require engaging a broader American culture of male sexual entitlement and patriarchal presumptions about female desirability.

Though dubious about the potential for female empowerment via shoring up male authority and responsibility, Amina Wadud explains the appeal of the idea of African American men as protectors and maintainers: slavery and post-slavery racist patriarchy gave African American women "little or no access to anything remotely resembling protection from their men, let alone maintenance."[47] Wadud points out that "this legacy frames a radically alternative perception and experience of *qiwamah*" – male authority or providership[48] – among African American Muslims. Yet this providership is often only an ideal. One hears frequently that a Muslim woman need not contribute at all toward the support of her family. Yet Wadud "never knew a single family where the woman did not also contribute to the family upkeep."[49] Many of Majeed's informants likewise work; some find themselves in financial straits when their husbands take additional wives. Polygyny, often justified as a solution to a lack of sufficient providers, may function that way in some cases but it does not always result in protection and provision for wives. Muslim women worldwide, in monogamous or polygynous marriages, tell life stories which "highlight the gaps between marriage as experienced and the normative model of gender relations and rights upheld in juristic and societal understandings" of male authority.[50]

Some insist that the problem is not polygyny but only its improper practice. After all, the Qur'an, which "offers conditional permission for men to marry up to four women simultaneously," warns against polygyny if men fear committing injustice (Q. 4:3) and a hadith threatens men who fail to treat co-wives equally with dire consequences in the afterlife.[51] However, scholars have generally understood the conditions in the Qur'anic text to be advisory rather than binding; likewise, they have defined injustice in deeply androcentric terms. For al-Shafi'i, for instance, justice between wives, on which he insists, involves only the allocation of time and perhaps money. Love and sex form no part of the equation.[52] Instead, polygyny operates seamlessly with other elements of marriage. For traditional scholars, a wife has no legal right to her husband's sexual exclusivity; most rejected contractual conditions to require it.[53] Exclusive sexual access to the wife, however, is an – perhaps *the* – essential element of the marriage contract. As with the male prerogative of unilateral extrajudicial repudiation, polygyny reflects the one-sided nature of marital authority. And for some contemporary Muslims, it is simply allowed: because God permits and the Prophet Muhammad practiced it, human beings have no right to object.[54]

The justification of polygyny as giving all women the chance to be wives and mothers also reflects the normative centering of marriage – and the idea, partially real and partially a scare tactic, that there are surplus Muslim women and not enough good men to go around. This framing commodifies and devalues women. It also takes demographic imbalance as a given. To the extent that a lack of marriageable men is real, the racist mass incarceration of African American men is one factor; another is the permission for Muslim men to marry non-Muslim women. (As the Coda to Chapter 1 noted, though Muslim women marrying non-Muslim men remains unthinkable for many, increasing numbers of lay individuals, scholars, and communities tacitly or explicitly allow it.) An additional factor is the definition of marriageable men as older, wealthier, and more educated. Within immigrant and diaspora communities, men's willingness to marry younger, less-educated women from "back home," and the unwillingness of women to do the same (or the social unacceptability of their doing so), is part of longstanding expectations, found in Muslim texts and American norms, that expect husbands to be superior to their wives in numerous respects. Mohja Kahf's spoof "The Polyandry Fatwa" represents one attempt to bring these unspoken gendered assumptions about social superiority and sexual desire to light.[55]

The appeal to masculine power and protection inflects influential African American Muslim thought, but it is broader. African American feminist theorist bell hooks suggests that "many heterosexual black men in white supremacist capitalist patriarchal culture have acted as though the primary 'evil' of racism has been the refusal of the dominant culture to allow them full access to patriarchal power, so that in sexist terms they are compelled to inhabit a sphere of powerlessness, deemed 'feminine,' hence they have perceived themselves as emasculated."[56] She argues for more collaborative and mutual forms of love and connection between (black) men and (black) women. Some Muslims are also enquiring about the damage dominant masculinity norms do to men's capacity for full flourishing.[57]

Is mutuality irreconcilable with polygyny? Must collaborative, caring relationships be egalitarian? Must they be monogamous? Must they involve civil marriage? Whatever its perils, polygyny disrupts tendencies toward unthinking idealization of the monogamous couple. American Muslims unconsciously imbibe romantic presuppositions from the U.S. context as well as from colonially inscribed Muslim thought.[58] Considering polygyny forces us to be explicit about our assumptions about male marital authority, about civil law, about fidelity (and safer sex), about partnership, about financial obligations, about emotional labor, about household labor, about the centrality of the heterosexual conjugal pair and the nuclear family. In thinking about these issues, we must foreground women's diverse experiences – those who live polygyny successfully, those who cannot do so, and those who struggle to find happiness in other forms of relationship, or none at all.[59]

3 "What your right hands possess": Slave Concubinage in Muslim Texts and Discourses

A free man may marry four free women and female slaves, not more, and he may take as many concubines as he wishes from among his female slaves. If a man has four free [wives] and a thousand concubines and wants to buy another [concubine] and a man reproaches him for that, it will be as if [that man] had committed unbelief. And if a man wants to take a concubine and his wife says to him "I will kill myself," he is not prohibited [from doing so], because it is a lawful act, but if he abstains to save her grief, he will be rewarded, because of the hadith "Whoever sympathizes with my community, God will sympathize with him."
Muhammad 'Ala al-Din Haskafi, seventeenth-century Hanafi jurist, *Al-Durr al-Mukhtar*[1]

Prior to the abolition of slavery in the nineteenth and twentieth centuries, marriage was not the exclusive mode of licit sexual relationship in most Muslim societies. Instead, throughout Islamic history, slave concubinage was practiced by those men who could afford it. Though several features of the finalized regulations governing the possession and use of female slaves were unique to Muslims, the use of female slaves as sexual partners was an accepted practice in most of the ancient Mediterranean and Near Eastern world where Islam originated. Indeed, in seeking to establish friendly relations with the Prophet Muhammad, the Byzantine commander of Alexandria sent him two enslaved sisters as a gift, along with a donkey and other goods. Medieval Muslim tradition records that the Prophet took one of these young women, Mariyya, as his concubine, eventually freeing her after she bore him a child.[2] The fact that a seventh-century Christian figure saw nothing amiss in sending a female as a gift to a powerful leader demonstrates the general acceptance of women and girls as sexual commodities in the ancient world. In pre-Islamic Arabia, as well, female captives were frequently used as sexual partners, a practice agreed by early Muslim interpreters to be sanctioned in the Qur'an's repeated references to the permissibility of men's sexual relations with women "that their/your right hands possess" (*ma malakat aymanuhum/kum*).

Ownership of slaves in general, and female slaves in particular, was referred to in non-Qur'anic texts as *milk al-yamin* ("ownership by the right hand"), and the same phrase was used to denote the slaves themselves ("property of the right hand"). Unfree women were also called *ama*[3] (female slave), *jariyya* ("slave girl"; also sometimes used for a young girl), and *suriyya*.[4] The latter term especially was used for concubines, those slaves with whom their masters maintained special sexual relationships. Concubines often received additional privileges – better quality food and clothing, and usually exemption from duties of household service – and were subject to additional restrictions, usually related to keeping them exclusively available to their masters. The status of concubine was informal, however; law and custom allowed a master to have sex with any of his (unmarried) female slaves. It was also insecure: a concubine could be freed and married by her owner, or she could be sold off, so long as he had not impregnated her.

While the Qur'an accepts the notion of men's sexual access to some unfree women – whose social, if not legal, status may have been ambiguous, according to Ingrid Mattson[5] – it does not explore the possibility of large-scale concubinage, nor was such practiced in the first Muslim community. Some modern authors have argued that only through marriage did sexual access to captive or enslaved women become permissible, but this is not the view that the medieval jurists took, nor, if one accepts the hadith sources as historically accurate, was it the practice of the first Muslim community; records show that the Prophet as well as a number of Companions and Successors had a concubine or two. However, after the Arab conquests of the seventh and eighth centuries, when the wealth of the Muslim elite increased dramatically, rulers mimicked their non-Muslim Sassanian predecessors, keeping dozens if not hundreds of female slaves, of whom many were used for pleasure.

The widespread availability of female slaves as sexual objects had dramatic implications for the development of Muslim thought on sex and marriage,[6] even if, in practice, the "harem" culture of the elite bore little resemblance to the practices of the majority of the populace. Prominent eighth-century jurist al-Shafi'i voiced the consensus legal view when he stated that a man could take as many concubines as he wished, since God did not restrict this in any way, while God forbade taking more than four wives.[7] This sentiment was conventional juristic wisdom for a millennium, as evidenced by the remarks of Hanafi Mufti of Damascus, Muhammad 'Ala al-Din Haskafi, in the late seventeenth century, to the effect that suggesting that a man with a thousand concubines should not take another was tantamount to unbelief.

Though large-scale ownership of female slaves for sexual use was an elite-only practice, slavery was a social fact in most of the Muslim world, with many slaves employed in domestic service as well as commerce, from the beginnings of Islam until abolition was decreed in the late nineteenth and twentieth centuries. Large-scale agricultural slavery, like the plantation slavery of the U.S. South, was seldom practiced in the Muslim world.[8] This was not due to any prohibition against such forms of slave labor, but rather to economic and geographical factors. This does not mean that Islamic slavery was not harsh, as some apologists have argued, or that masters were not sometimes brutal to their slaves. Paradoxically, slavery did not always equal low social status. In medieval Egypt, the Mamluk (literally, "owned") dynasty ruled for some time, with manumitted military slaves rising to govern others. The conscript slave troops (janissaries) of the Ottomans are another example. Most striking is the case of the royal concubines who wielded tremendous influence and amassed considerable wealth in the later centuries of the Ottoman empire.[9]

Slavery in Muslim societies was not merely a medieval practice; it has lingering contemporary effects, especially in certain parts of Africa and the Gulf states, regions that were the world's last to outlaw slavery, with Saudi Arabia becoming the final nation to do so in 1962. Vestigial effects of domestic slavery persist in certain Gulf nations in the failure of police and lawmakers to protect immigrant household workers against potential abuses by employers.[10] Female "guest workers" employed as maids and nannies have little recourse against sexual coercion or harsh beatings; in some cases, those who have escaped and sought refuge with the police have been forcibly returned to their abusive employers.[11] Such women are not legally enslaved, and they generally receive compensation for their work that differentiates their situation from that of those in debt bondage.[12] However, because of the acceptance of controls on their mobility (employers often take their passports), and the refusal of law enforcement officials to respond to complaints of maltreatment, they are particularly vulnerable to abuse. In some African nations such as Mauritania, actual slavery continues despite repeated declarations of abolition, the last in 1980; according to one recent report, 90,000 black Mauritanians remain essentially enslaved to Arab/Berber owners. In the Sudan, Christian captives in the ongoing civil war are often enslaved, and female prisoners used sexually, with their Muslim captors claiming that Islamic law grants them permission.[13]

Islamic law is not the only salient frame of reference in these cases, though, even if it is sometimes used as justification for enslavement and slaveholding. Although premodern jurists permitted slavery without qualms, they absolutely forbade the enslavement of other Muslims. Contrary to this principle, Muslim captives, usually from other ethnic groups, are sometimes enslaved in ongoing civil or tribal conflicts; Mende Nazer, a Sudanese Muslim, recounts her own experiences of capture and enslaved domestic labor in the Sudan and the UK, where she eventually escaped her captors, in a chilling memoir.[14] Though most common in Africa, it occurs elsewhere; one scholar has suggested that among the Taliban's "atrocities" toward Afghani Shi'a was "the enslavement of Hazara women as concubines."[15]

The existence of actual and quasi-slavery is by no means unique to the Muslim world; slavery and slavery-like practices are found in numerous nations worldwide.[16] Further, they are not found everywhere in the Muslim world; rather than "Islam" being the cause, there are specific socio-economic and political factors that help to account for their existence. Still, the claiming of religious justification for slaveholding in some of these cases makes them particularly urgent to address. Although the vast majority of contemporary Muslims agree that there is no place for slavery in the modern world, and some nineteenth- and twentieth-century reformers such as Sir Sayyid Ahmad Khan opposed the practice, the pressure to abolish slavery generally came from some combination of European colonial powers and economic and demographic shifts.[17] A few Muslim clerics, such as one writing in the mid-nineteenth-century Arabian peninsula, opposed abolition on the grounds that slavery was accepted in religious texts.[18] Similarly, one scholar argues "that slavery enjoyed a high degree of legitimacy in Ottoman society. That legitimacy derived from Islamic sanction," among other factors.[19] Although abolition did eventually occur, there was not a strong internally developed critique of slaveholding based on religious principles.

Modern Muslims, especially in the West, have devoted little attention to thinking about or discussing the religious, ethical, and legal issues associated with slavery, resorting instead to apologetic and denial.[20] Yet slavery, in norm and practice, dramatically influenced the development of laws regulating marriage, divorce, and sex that many Muslims consider binding today. The existence of slavery during Islam's early centuries resulted in a complex set of linkages between marriage and slavery in Islamic law, both being seen as forms of ownership, *milk*, that legitimized sex (in the case of slavery, only when the owner was male and the owned, female). Classical texts are replete with analogies between dower and purchase price, and divorce and manumission.[21] These seldom-acknowledged interrelationships continue to affect regulations and mindsets surrounding marriage, divorce, and sex. The once-ubiquitous conceptual vocabulary of ownership or dominion (*milk*) applied to slavery is seldom used today to discuss marriage, and the previously common parallels between husbands and masters as well as wives and slaves have largely disappeared from learned discourse. The sexual ethics forged in slaveholding contexts, however, continue to be influential in ways that are often not fully understood. Understanding the historical and legal dimensions of Muslim slavery, particularly as regards sexual access, is a necessary precursor to thinking through an ethics of sex. Reconsidering slave concubinage raises larger issues of the universality of revelation as well as substantial theological issues related to theodicy and whether justice can be historically and culturally relative.

Islam and slavery: overview of sources and history

The Qur'an makes numerous references to unfree persons – servants, captives, and slaves. These categories are not mutually exclusive, and frequently overlap.[22] Like numerous passages in the Hebrew bible and the New Testament, the Qur'an assumes the permissibility of some individuals owning or controlling others – "what their/your right hands possess" – which was an established practice in Arabia before its revelation. The Qur'an does not explicitly condemn the practice of slavery or attempt to abolish it. Nonetheless, it does provide a number of regulations designed to ameliorate the situation of those owned. It recommends freeing slaves, especially "believing" slaves,[23] a mode of classification that presumes sufficient personhood on the part of those owned to have individual faith. Manumission of a slave is required as expiation for certain misdeeds.[24] Another verse discussing emancipation involves the initiative and qualities of the enslaved person, not merely the piety or expiation of the owner, stating that masters should allow slaves who demonstrate some good to purchase their own freedom.[25] Jurists disagreed over whether this verse obliged a slave's owner to grant such a request or merely recommended such action, but clearly slavery was not always considered to be a permanent state for an enslaved individual.

The Qur'an also suggests certain means of integrating slaves, some of whom were enslaved after being captured in war, into the Muslim community, with special attention to inter-personal relationships. It allows slaves to marry other slaves or free persons[26] and prohibits owners from prostituting unwill-ing female slaves.[27] Despite this protection against one form of sexual exploitation, female slaves were not granted an abso-lute right to control sexual access to their own bodies. Rather, the text indicates that men may have lawful sexual access to "what their/your right hands possess."[28] On several occa-sions, the Qur'an mentions this category alongside "wives" or "spouses" as being those to whom sexual access is licit, thus making clear both the distinction between the two groups, who are mentioned separately, and their joint status as lawful sexual partners. (Although in some instances these references are gen-der-neutral, the possibility that such verses permitted women's, or for that matter men's, access to male captives or slaves was never seriously countenanced.)

In the first generations of Muslims, there was ambiguity and variability in status among unfree women, with less clear differentiation between the pre-Islamic category of captured wives and the Islamic category of female captives taken as war booty and subject to sexual use.[29] The hazy distinctions among those classified as "what your right hands possess" were sub-ject to refinement over time. The classical jurists elaborated significantly on the Qur'anic material concerning slavery, drawing on the practice of the Prophet and the first Muslims as well as on the customs of conquered areas, as the Muslim empire expanded and solidified under the Umayyads and subsequently the Abbasids. Legal works from that era regu-late the enslavement of war captives along with the purchase and sale of slaves. While it was decidedly forbidden to enslave other Muslims, if a non-Muslim converted to Islam after enslavement, he or she remained a slave and could be lawfully purchased and sold like any other slave. (This rule, justifi-able on the basis of the Qur'anic praise of freeing "believing" slaves – meaning, the simple fact of belief does not itself free the slave – closes a potential loophole allowing for slaves to

gain their freedom through conversion.) The jurists also prescribed penalties for slave owners who maltreated or abused
their slaves, up to and including forced manumission of the
slave without compensation to the owner.

Regulations for slave marriage and concubinage also developed over time, with special emphasis on rules to determine
the paternity and/or ownership of children born to a female
slave. A man could not simultaneously own and be married
to the same female slave.[30] The male owner of a female slave
could either marry her off to a different man, thus renouncing
his own sexual access to her, or take her as his own concubine, using her sexually himself.[31] Both situations had a specific effect on the status of any children she bore. When female
slaves were married off, any children born from the marriage
became slaves belonging to the mother's owner, though her
husband was established as their legal father. When a master
took his own female slave as a concubine, by contrast, any
children she bore would be free and legitimate, with the same
status as any children born of a free wife. The slave who bore
her master's child became an *umm walad* (literally, mother
of a child), gaining certain protections. Most importantly,
she could not be sold and she was automatically freed upon
her master's death. These guidelines for the *umm walad* were
not set forth in the Qur'an; they are frequently attributed to
the caliph 'Umar, though the Prophet's precedent in freeing
Mariyya after she bore him Ibrahim (who died in infancy) was,
no doubt, influential.[32]

Mariyya al-Qibtiyya, or Maria the Copt, appears in most
premodern sources as a slave (*ama* or *jariyya*) owned by the
Prophet. Many twentieth- and twenty-first-century works
authored by Muslims object to this portrayal, implying or outright declaring that she was his wife. Take Henry Bayman's
emphatic rejection of the view that Muhammad owned a concubine: "[T]he Prophet was *legally married* to all his wives,
even to slave girls with whom he was presented. In Islam, not
multiple marriages but illicit sex – pre- or extramarital fornication and adultery – is immoral. Islam limited the number of
female consorts to four (but recommended one), and with this

the proviso that all were brought under the protective umbrella of legal marriage."[33] Bayman's statement is circular: by definition, Muhammad was married to his wives; it is only through marriage that a woman becomes a wife. He means, presumably, that Muhammad was married to all the women with whom he had sex. Bayman thus connects the subject of concubinage to broader questions about sexual morality in Islam: by insisting that Muhammad did not simply have sex with "slave girls," and associating marriage with both lawfulness ("legal marriage") and protection ("protective umbrella"), Bayman claims Islamic superiority in matters of sex. His assertion, though, confronts major logical difficulties. He must either ignore the Sunni and Shi'i legal traditions' permission for slave concubinage and the hadith evidence showing that the Prophet's companions (if not the Prophet himself) had sex with female captives and slaves, or he must deem both legal doctrine and Muslim history to fall outside the scope of "Islam."

There is less revisionism and apology on the issue of slave concubinage in works not written or intended for consumption by Westerners – Muslim and non-Muslim. Still, it is almost unimaginable today by many Muslims that a sexual relationship between a man and a female slave bound to him only by the tie of ownership and not matrimony could be legal, much less moral. And yet, since the Prophet is the standard for morality, the exemplar of uprightness, the question of his actions – both personal and as a leader of Muslims – takes on importance.

Women, war captives, and withdrawal

Despite its intrinsic importance, in the absence of agreed criteria for approaching the matter of prophetic *sunnah* on the enslavement of war captives and the ownership of slaves, authors usually bypass the troublesome topic in silence. At times, however, such silences scream for attention, as with Ghazi Algosaibi's presentation of seven hadith with brief commentaries under the title *Revolution in the Sunnah*. Algosaibi

– a Saudi who has published in a variety of literary genres, in addition to serving in various government posts – covers topics ranging from "Integrity in Political Life" to "Prevention of Cruelty to Animals" in this volume, translated into English and published in the UK. Three of the seven deal in some significant way with women: "Women's Role in Society (and in the Military!)"; "The Rules of Proof Safeguard Rights," which has to do with witnesses to illicit sex; and, my concern here, "Family Planning." Although ostensibly concerned with the "revolutionary" words and deeds of the Prophet, in order to focus on these themes Algosaibi ignores other elements in the stories he tells that are deeply troubling for those Muslims committed to a view of Muhammad as inerrantly just and protective of the weak and defenseless.

Revolution in the Sunnah is a fitting title for his book, Algosaibi explains, because the hadith he recounts were revolutionary in their original Arabian context, and "continue to represent a real 'revolution' against the outmoded and discredited practices prevailing in these areas of life in some, if not the vast majority of, Muslim countries." By making a distinction between "Islam" and "culture," although not in so many words, Algosaibi's objective is to prove that instead of "need[ing] to import reform from abroad," Muslims can find the necessary resources for reform within Islam, "provided the opportunistic selectivity with which Islam is practised in Muslim countries is brought to an end."[34]

Algosaibi's objection to "opportunistic selectivity" is ironic, given that he displays precisely that quality in his discussion of the hadith that he chooses to illustrate his point about family planning. Quoting on the authority of "Abu Said al-Kh[u]dri":

> We went out with The Messenger of Allah (pbuh) on the expedition to the Bani al-Mustaliq and captured some concubines[35] [as part of the spoils]; and we desired them, for we were suffering from the absence of our wives, and we wished to have sexual intercourse with them, observing '*azl* (*coitus interruptus* [...]). But we said: "We are doing an

act before asking the Messenger of Allah who is amongst us?" So we asked the Messenger of Allah, and he said: "It does not matter if you do not do it, for every soul that is to be born up to the Day of Resurrection will be born."[36]

The Prophet's reported words here are sometimes reported with slight variation in other versions of this story; sometimes he affirms that no soul that God has decreed to come into existence will be thwarted. Muslim scholars debate back and forth over whether the Prophet's words mean one may practice withdrawal, but should not, or whether they grant permission without taint of disapproval, serving only as a warning that conception may occur despite the measure taken to avoid it. The moral status of withdrawal as an act was of significant enough concern to the victorious Muslim combatants that they asked the Prophet about it. The permissibility of sex with the captive women was taken for granted by all the men involved, including the Prophet himself. (There is no indication of what the captured women thought, or the wives of the men involved.) Not only do the Prophet and the soldiers ignore the question of the women's consent or lack thereof, but so does Algosaibi, focusing solely on contraception in his discussion of this hadith.[37]

The issue of female captives and their treatment cannot always be ignored in such a glaringly obvious way. When directly confronted, in a polemical context, with historical and textual permission for the sexual use of unfree women, Muslim authors sometimes respond defensively, seeking to protect Islam's reputation. It may be argued, for instance, that Islamic "slavery" bore no resemblance to harsh American chattel slavery. In this view, the Qur'anic permission for men to have sex with "what their right hands possess" was merely a way of integrating war captives into society. Sometimes, it is added that the captives would be "integrated" into the Muslim community through becoming the property of a specific man who would be responsible for them and their offspring. Whatever merit these arguments have in the context of inter-communal polemics and apologetics, however, they are insufficient for internal

Muslim reflection. In particular, the notion that women would be integrated into society by bearing offspring to their owners or captors does not apply to the case of the Bani Mustaliq: the rationale for the captors to practice withdrawal, according to other accounts, is that they did not want to impregnate the women lest they spoil their chances to ransom them.[38]

This provision of a rationale incompatible with the scenarios represented in the historical sources is one instance of a larger phenomenon of attempting to make sense of instances where Prophetic *sunnah*, classical jurisprudence, and modern notions clash. Attempting to assess an event such as the capture of women from the Bani Mustaliq (assuming one accepts the historical record as provided by Bukhari's account) by the standards even of later jurisprudence causes difficulties as "some traditions ascribe to the Prophet actions that appear to be incompatible with the opinion prevalent in later sources."[39] How can one reconcile Abu Sa'id al-Khudri's account, for example, with the later insistence of Muslim jurists that any time a man came into possession of a captive or slave, he had to wait until she had a menstrual period before having intercourse with her, in order to determine whether she was already pregnant?[40] The Prophet's reported permission for the Muslim captors to practice withdrawal with their female captives does not take any notice of this point. It has been suggested that the fact that the Prophet's reported action does not take account of the need for a waiting period is evidence that Abu Sa'id al-Khudri's account is wrong; the Prophet could not have allowed the men sexual access to the captives. This apologetic account seeking to deflect the accusation of impropriety makes the error of assuming that later legal doctrine cannot impose a requirement that was not grounded in the Prophet's actions. As a historical point, just because the jurists required something does not mean that the Prophet did it; likewise, just because the jurists allow something does not mean the Prophet did. Still, another hadith included by Abu Dawud in his Book of Marriage records the purported words of the Prophet in asserting that men must wait to have sex with captive women until they have menstruated once, and still others forbid men to have sex with women pregnant by other men. A similar issue arises regarding the religion of the captive women, who were likely to be from among the pagan Arabs. Later jurists state quite clearly that only Christian and Jewish (and perhaps Sabean or Zoroastrian) captives or slaves were permissible as sexual partners.

Nonetheless, questions about the religious affiliation and menstrual state of the female prisoners pale in comparison to the larger issue at stake: what does it mean for those who view the Prophet's actions as exemplary to accept that he tacitly allowed the rape of female captives? Is it correct to refer to the actions of the Muslim soldiers as rape, or does that term have connotations that are contextually inappropriate? Does the fact that "marriage" by capture was a common Arab custom at the time make his actions intelligible? Acceptable? Finally, assuming one accepts that the accounts in Bukhari, Muslim, and other hadith compilations are essentially accurate, what are the implications of the Prophet's action for the contemporary world? Is his precedent binding or is it to be understood as limited to the particular circumstances of his time and place?

There is general silence on these questions and their broader implications in Muslim scholarship. Algosaibi mentions the incident in passing, under the title "Family Planning," without any analysis or acknowledgement of its significance for matters beyond contraception. Other influential works treat the issues of slavery differently, but no more satisfactorily. For instance, in his 1991 translation of the classic Shafi'i work *Reliance of the Traveller*, Nuh Keller excises nearly all mention of slavery from the English text, leaving it, bracketed off, in the parallel Arabic discussions of marriage, divorce, and other social transactions.[41] The translation carries no ellipses or notation that something has been removed. As a result of this editorial sleight of hand, the importance of slavery to the medieval Middle Eastern context in which this text originated simply disappears. By way of rationale for these frequent changes, Keller affirms in his introduction that "not a single omission has been made from it" – that is, the Arabic text – "though rulings about matters now rare or non-existent have been left untranslated unless interesting for some other reason."[42] A specific reference to the missing material on slavery comes in place of a translation of the chapter on manumission: "Like previous references to slaves, the following four sections have been left untranslated because the issue is no longer current."[43] Keller thus suggests that the regulations on slavery, a now obsolete social institution, are somehow separable from the rest of the work; the other rules contained in this "Classic Manual of Islamic Sacred Law," as the translation's subtitle proclaims, are directly relevant to the lives of contemporary Muslims.

A different approach, utilized by the official Saudi fatwa council as well as some other twentieth- and twenty-first-century jurists, has been to reiterate classical doctrines as though slavery had never been abolished by national governments. In their responses to legal queries – which have influence far beyond Saudi boundaries, through online distribution and subsidized translations into European languages – they maintain references to slavery throughout, just as their medieval counterparts would have. Evaluating the conditions making polygamy permissible, the late Saudi mufti Ibn Baz stated that "if a person fears that he will not do justice [between wives], then he may only marry one wife in addition to having slaves."[44] Though seemingly the opposite of Keller's strategy of excision, this rote inclusion of material presuming the existence of slavery (even when slavery was not even mentioned in the original question) demonstrates the same unwillingness to engage with the basic problem at hand: how does one reconcile the presumption of slaveholding in Qur'an, hadith, and classical jurisprudence with the contemporary reality of the Muslim world where legal slavery no longer exists? Although the vast majority of Muslims do not consider slavery, especially slave concubinage, to be acceptable practices in the modern world, the reticence about confronting the juristic, as well as social, legacies of slavery has resulted in blindness to the hierarchical residue of its practice, to Islamic gender relations more broadly, and to marriage and sexual relations in particular.

Conclusion

I have repeatedly referred to the scriptural and legal acceptance of slavery as something troublesome to the vast majority of contemporary Muslims, when it is thought about at all.
Because of the repugnance with which slavery is viewed, arguing that other matters are linked with, or analogous to, slavery creates an opening for Muslims to think differently about
them. I claim no originality for this tactic; Fazlur Rahman
applied it to good effect at least two decades prior to this writing, when he compared slavery to polygamy.[45] Both, he argued,
were institutions that it was impossible to eradicate at once but
which were harmful and which God intended to abolish, even
if one had to follow indications of a trajectory toward abolition in the Qur'an rather than its literal words. Treating the
Qur'an as a document with some verses bound by context, but
others containing broad principles of justice that should take
precedence over specific, time-bound commands, is one essential element of feminist and other reformist interpretation of
scripture. For many ordinary Muslims, particularly those for
whom slavery is distant history, it is simple common sense.
This should not, however, be mistaken for the view that it is
"obvious" that Islam disallows slavery, and that it was always
meant to be abolished.[46] The insight is more powerful if one
acknowledges that abolition was not a foregone conclusion,
but rather the result of both non-religious historical processes
and interpretive choices by individuals. Indeed, even today
some scholars insist that although the specific circumstances
making slavery permissible may have ceased to exist – i.e., there
is no legitimate caliph to declare jihad and divide the spoils of
war, or that Muslim nations have signed international treaties
agreeing to prohibit slavery – that it is nonetheless unacceptable
to declare slavery forbidden. To do so, they argue, constitutes
a sin, because one is declaring unlawful something permitted
by God.

Muslim thinkers who reject slavery as unjust have applied
two main methods to argue that this rejection of slavery is
based on the Qur'an. First, some suggest that the abolition

of slavery is implicit in the Qur'anic message, and Muslims simply did not see it before, being blinded by their social circumstances. Mohamed Syed's stance that sex with captive or unfree women was always forbidden without marriage, and that legal permission for sex with *milk al-yamin* was the result of the jurists' misinterpretation, applies this perspective on a smaller scale.[47] Second, developing Rahman's methodology, others have argued for a trajectory from hierarchical institutions to more egalitarian ones, from acceptance of slavery to its abolition: the practical limitations of the Prophet's mission meant that acquiescence to slave ownership was necessary, though distasteful, but meant to be temporary. Fatima Mernissi makes a parallel argument that the Prophet's compromises regarding husbands' rights to control their wives were similarly necessary accommodations with patriarchal power in the interests of ensuring the success of Islam.[48] Both perspectives contain valid points: the presuppositions of interpreters matter a great deal in implementation (or lack thereof) of the Qur'an's precepts; and there is evidence that in some instances the Qur'an accommodates or gradually prohibits certain practices that God and/or Muhammad might have preferred to abolish immediately (e.g., consumption of alcohol). However, neither of these approaches is sufficient if one does not take the responsibility of individual interpreters seriously.

An approach to revelation that takes both propositions seriously allows one to interpret scripture without being bound by the assumptions of previous generations of exegetes who accepted male superiority and other social hierarchies, including slavery, without question. Additionally, one can see certain passages and Prophetic *sunnah*s as gestures in the direction of egalitarianism, capable of full realization only in a world where equality and freedom are common shared values. Yet neither of these approaches engages the critical, and critically difficult, question: where is God's justice in permitting slavery in the first place, if slavery constituted an injustice and a wrong in the seventh century, just as it would and does in the twenty-first century? And if it did not constitute an injustice and a wrong in the seventh century in God's eyes, then on what basis may anyone subsequently declare it unjust without rendering divine justice subordinate to the vagaries of human, and therefore inherently flawed, moral sensibilities?

A full consideration of questions about God, history, and justice would require delving further into philosophy and theodicy than I dare attempt; these issues have preoccupied many generations of theologians and I make no pretense of resolving them here. I raise them, though, because although generally omitted from feminist reflections on Qur'an, *sunnah*, and law, these theological questions are deeply relevant to larger issues of ethical definition.[49] How can one reconcile God's justice and goodness with the injustice of slavery, or does viewing God as just and good necessitate acceptance of slavery as part of the divine plan for humanity? To my mind, a proper response involves two propositions, each of which places a great deal of responsibility on individual Muslims. First is the view that while God is responsible for the just and the good, and guides human beings accordingly, injustice and oppression (*zulm*) come from human beings; imperfection is inevitable once one accepts the complicated possibility of human free will.[50] Second is the distinction noted by theologians between legal justice, where human beings are "commanded to observe a minimum standard of duties," and ethical justice, which "is justice in accordance with the highest virtues which establish a standard of human conduct."[51] Combined with the view that historical developments render certain specific regulations irrelevant, these notions make reform more attainable at the same time as they place a greater burden on human beings to achieve it. God clearly orders Muslims in the Qur'an to combat injustice and oppression yet simultaneously permits institutions such as slavery. Outside of accepting that slavery is a just and therefore not problematic practice (or insisting, against the clear sense of the text, that the Qur'an never actually allowed it), the only possible response is to suggest that the Qur'anic text itself requires Muslims sometimes to depart from its literal provisions in order to establish justice.

Coda 3

In the original Introduction, I wrote that "virtually no one advocates reviving slavery as an institution." I acknowledged that a few fringe thinkers accepted the theoretical permissibility of slavery, including the sexual use of female slaves, but this was a minor exception to the general state of affairs. Slavery was my go-to example of how Muslim consensus on moral and ethical norms could change over time.

Ten years later, slavery has again caught the world's attention. With exponentially more media attention than the Sudanese and Taliban soldiers' enslavement of, respectively, Christian and Hazara Shi'i women mentioned in this chapter, in 2014 Boko Haram abducted Nigerian schoolgirls, forcing some into marriages and threatening to sell others in the marketplace. The so-called Islamic State (IS) has captured and sold hundreds if not thousands of Yazidi women in Iraq and beyond.[52] The role of Western Muslim men and women, as fighters, wives, and propagandists for IS, is a source of great consternation, even panic, for observers. Though anti-Muslim propagandists insist that IS and its ilk represent, as they claim, "real" or "true" Islam, IS's doctrines and acts are rejected by the overwhelming majority of Muslims worldwide, sometimes with the claim that IS is not, in fact, Islamic.

What is a religious studies scholar to do? Not, ultimately, judge the religious bona fides of the group, but rather investigate how its adherents make authoritative claims to legitimacy within the tradition. Without glorifying the classical tradition of Muslim thought, one may say that most scholars drew the bounds of orthodoxy fairly broadly. The same can definitely not be said of IS, which is consumed with ideological purity. IS lies at the very edge of the spectrum of present or past Muslim states or mass movements, provoking comparisons to the early sectarian Kharijis.[53] Some responses to IS have been to deny that its members are Muslim. This strikes me as a dangerous tactic: contemporary progressive movements are equally distant from various doctrines and practices of Islam that have been widely historically accepted.[54] Divergence alone should not disqualify someone from participating in the Muslim tradition. IS's culture of enslavement, encompassing acts and rhetoric, functions precisely by (selective) appeal to the Muslim tradition, as well as deliberate inversion of widespread moral norms.

One might analyze IS's abduction and sexual use of female captives as an instance of rape as a weapon of war. One might treat it as a form of sex trafficking, a worldwide practice that affects far more women and girls (and others) than those sold by IS.[55] Judging by media and human rights organizations' reports, IS soldiers' patterns of sexual violation have more in common with wartime rape or sex trafficking than with classical-era practices of enslavement and slave-holding. Here, however, I focus on the rhetoric of slavery, especially "sex with slave-girls" (or abduction and rape of captives), as a window into notions of authority and interpretation.[56]

The IS online propaganda magazine *Dabiq* celebrates the taking of unbelieving slaves. It claims credit for being the first movement to do so on a wide scale. Imagining Muslim history through a reductive, distorted lens, it deems the "revival" of this authentic early practice as a sign of IS's efficacy and legitimacy. Enslavement is part of a two-pronged campaign against infidels (including Western/external and Yazidi/internal) and against neutered Muslims who have abandoned the practice of slaveholding. A female author (or an author writing under a female pseudonym) praises "the great shar'i ruling and pure prophetic Sunnah 'saby' [enslavement of captives]" and laments that "saby becomes fornication and tasarri (taking a slave-girl as a concubine) becomes rape" not in the minds of unbelievers but among "those associated with our Ummah, those whose names are Muhammad, Ibrahim, and 'Ali!"[57] She lauds the manly warrior virtues of her IS companions and disdains the "quasi men in the lands of kufr [unbelief]" who accept Western human rights norms. An earlier article, "The Revival of Slavery Before the Hour", declares not only that slavery is present in the Qur'an and sunnah, but that those Muslims who deny the legitimacy of enslavement are apostates.[58]

Elsewhere in this volume, I show how apologetic Muslim discourses, even when explicitly directed to other Muslims, often assume and respond to a presumed Western audience. IS twists this practice. Rather than seeking to assuage or rebut concerns about Muslim primitivism, IS overturns established values. Like its beheadings, its campaign of enslavement does not inadvertently scandalize right-thinking people; instead, it courts outrage.[59]

Given the "gender politics of the international idiom of Islam … characterized by images of dangerous men and vulnerable women," the Orientalized topos of oppression of women in the name of Islam is a vital weapon in IS's media-saturated savagery.[60] Although violence against women is often ignored, the salacious angle of sexual violence combined with Islamic doctrine has captivated media attention.

In December 2014, mass media in the United States and Europe made much of a "sex-slavery manual" promulgated by the IS Research and Fatwa Department. This five-page booklet with a flowery pink cover and a rhyming Arabic title reached the media by means of the Middle East Media Research Institute (MEMRI), an organization with ideological and financial links to anti-Muslim organizations.[61] Though MEMRI has been criticized for presenting a biased picture of contemporary Muslim and Middle Eastern perspectives through its selective presentation of unrepresentative examples, its translations are generally accurate. In this case, the translation omits seven of thirty-two entries, including lopping off the last five entirely, without informing readers they are receiving a truncated document.

MEMRI introduces its partial translation of *Questions and Answers on Captives and Slaves* by highlighting "that it is permissible to have sexual intercourse with non-Muslim slaves, including young girls, and that it is also permitted to beat them and trade in them."[62] It also suggests that the pamphlet "was presumably released in response to the uproar caused by the many reports this summer that ISIS had taken Yazidi girls and women as sex slaves." Since it seems likely that, as with the beheadings, at least one objective – or additional benefit – of the widespread use of enslavement and rape was to incense Westerners, the pamphlet could be understood less as response than as additional provocation. Most of the entries concern the use of slaves for sex. Some rulings quote Qur'an and hadith, while others refer to majority views of Muslim scholars. The views expressed are largely consonant with, if highly selective and simplified versions of, premodern jurisprudential doctrines.[63] Yet other elements of the pamphlet suggest specifically salvific concerns.

Based on and supportive of a grotesque and violent reality, the pamphlet nonetheless seems in part the fruit of a sincere effort to locate divine guidance for holding slaves; it attests to IS's "strange but potent new blend of utopianism and appalling carnage."[64] *Questions and Answers* connects capture, (nonconsensual) sex, and violent discipline with opportunities for Muslims to obtain religious reward through the freeing of (believing) slaves.[65] In *Dabiq*, enslavement of and reproduction through concubines is a respite from the sin of widespread illicit sex, and a vehicle for increasing the Muslim population, as well as an opportunity to advance the hour of the final battle by re-establishing abandoned practices. In *Questions and Answers*, by contrast, this polemical framing is absent; the tone is matter-of-fact.

The assumptions operative in some entries are revealing. Though disbelief is the criterion for legitimately taking captives, some queries assume slaves will convert: what must a female slave cover while she prays? There is a wild sexual imagination at play as well. One query asks whether a female slave has a right to a portion of her master's time, a share as each wife in a polygynous marriage would. The answer is that though she does not have a right to a share, he must enable her to keep chaste – so, have sex with her, marry her off, or sell her. Imagining masters as responsible for the sexual satisfaction of women they have purchased boggles the mind, unless we recall that the document contemplates the integration of slaves into a new sort of society – or rather, a very old one, harking back to (an imagined) early Muslim community.

MEMRI omits this entry from its translation and ends on a partial translation of a query about the reward for freeing a female slave. Though most entries on manumission are omitted, this one, which is explained as protecting believers from the torments of hell, helps portray Muslims as violent by emphasizing their preoccupation with "hellfire." It leaves out the immediately preceding query, a terse question about whether a female slave can buy herself from her owner. (She can.) More saliently, MEMRI's translation omits the last five entries, which pertain to freeing slaves in response to accidental killings or in expiation of obscure legal oaths. This chapter notes that Keller's translation of a medieval legal manual excises, without comment, references to slavery and the sexual use of slaves that would trouble modern readers. MEMRI's translation does the opposite, lopping off, without comment, potentially praiseworthy material.[66]

What of Muslim reactions to IS's use of enslavement? Against those Muslim extremists and anti-Muslim critics who argue that Islam is incompatible with the modern world because its scripture holds slavery permissible (and Muslims, unlike others, must supposedly read scripture literally), other Muslims have condemned (contemporary) slavery. As part of a larger rebuttal of IS, an all-male group of Sunni Muslim scholars and leaders opined that slavery was impermissible, citing changed circumstances and international treaties.[67] The argument was a mishmash of assertions of authority for a scholarly elite (IS doesn't have the proper scholarly credentials to interpret texts; we do) and historically ludicrous claims about slavery and abolition, which I have explored elsewhere.[68]

One thing these events make clear is the untenable nature of ordinary Muslims' refusal to grapple with the place of slavery in the tradition. Perhaps IS's defense of slavery as religiously legitimate, and the consequences for women and girls of their actions, will prompt further reflection by some of those who have to date maintained the theoretical permissibility of slavery while holding that the conditions for its permissibility are not met in the contemporary world.[69] From IS's perspective, these have been met. Caliphate? Check. Legitimate jihad? Check. Unbelievers? Check. Enslavement, including distribution and sale of captured women for sex? Checkmate.

4 Prohibited Acts and Forbidden Partners: Illicit Sex in Islamic Jurisprudence

Women have an Islamic right to exemption from criminalization or punishment for consensual adult intercourse.
Asra Nomani, "Islamic Bill of Rights for Women in the Bedroom," 2005[1]

> The woman who commits *zina* and the man who commits *zina*,
> lash each of them one hundred lashes.
> Do not let pity deter you in a matter ordered by God,
> if you believe in God and the Last Day
> Qur'an, Surah 24, verse 2

Sex is, paradoxically, both the most private, intimate act humans can undertake and a profoundly social activity. All societies and cultures regulate sexual activity among their members. Certain pairings are permissible, while others are not; some acts are approved, while others are disallowed. Muslims are not alone in making distinctions between what is lawful and unlawful, what is proper and improper. Nor have Muslim societies historically been unique (or uniform) in imposing consequences, including physical chastisement, on those who break the rules. However, although the particular configuration of licit and illicit sexual activities developed by classical Muslim thinkers from prescriptions in the Qur'an and *sunnah* shares certain elements with other cultures and traditions, it differs in crucial ways – in particular, in punishing men and women equally for failure to heed the limits.

The Qur'an speaks in scathing terms of sex outside lawful bounds – with a spouse or with what men's "right hands possess" – as corruption and sin, and repeatedly refers to chastity (literally, protecting one's genitals) as a virtue for both males and females.[2] *Zina*, sex between a man and a woman who is neither his wife nor his slave, was the most serious of the sexual trangressions described in the Qur'an and treated in the Prophet's *sunnah*. One critical component of *zina* as elaborated by Muslim thinkers is its consensual nature, although some thinkers categorized regular *zina* along with "*zina* by force" (*bi'l-jabr*). The free consent of two individuals to engage in sexual relations was not sufficient or even necessarily relevant to whether sex between them was licit and socially acceptable. Like ancient Near Eastern and Mediterranean codes, Muslim source texts and developed Islamic law held the view that the individual status of and legal relationship between two parties determined whether sex was licit. Were the individuals free or enslaved; married, previously married, or never married; were they male or female?

The particular configuration of lawful and unlawful acts formulated by premodern Muslim jurists does not match current laws or practices in Muslim-majority societies or among Muslims living in the West. That classical scheme, in keeping with common practice in the region at the time, accepted (non-consensual) sex with enslaved females, as well as the marriage (without consent) of male and female minors by fathers; laws today forbid both slavery and marriage of minors (although the definition of minority varies greatly).[3] The view "that consent makes a difference to whether some sexual activity is seen as immoral or not"[4] is widely shared. Most Muslims who espouse the view that consent matters do not phrase their views as categorically as American Muslim writer Asra Nomani does in stating that "consensual adult sex" should not be punishable. Rather, consent is often seen as necessary but not sufficient for sex to be lawful. Classical Muslim views about consent and its relationship, or lack thereof, to lawfulness were unremarkable in the context of broader Near Eastern and Mediterranean late antiquity, where even free women could be treated as sexual property in some sense, and familial participation in the marital arrangements of family members, especially girls, was expected. At the same time, a variety of semi-marital arrangements, including slave concubinage and temporary liaisons, were sometimes permissible, allowing some more fluid unions.

Over a thousand years later, legal concubinage no longer exists in the Muslim world, polygamy has been legally restricted in many places, and nation-state bureaucracies have become involved in marriage licensing and registration. At the same time, alternate marriage and marriage-like practices are emerging or re-emerging in various places in the Muslim-majority world. These include *mut'a*, a form of time-limited marriage approved by Shi'i law but occasionally engaged in by Sunnis in the West; *zawaj al-misyar*, "marriage in transit," a type of union which conveys more limited spousal claims than usual and has found approval from some Saudi muftis; and *zawaj 'urfi*, "customary marriage," as practiced particularly in Egypt. This last, a religious marriage not registered in accordance with civil law, is similar in numerous respects to the practice common in some European immigrant and African American communities of marrying in only religious ceremonies without seeking civil recognition. The rise in these informal marriage practices, as well as what is likely to be a rising incidence of sex outside of marriage, is attributable in part to a large and increasing gap between sexual maturity, beginning at puberty, and social maturity, the age at which it is socially reasonable to get married. This does not mean that illicit sex (premarital intercourse, extramarital liaisons, etc.) was unknown in the past or is not practiced in Muslim-majority societies today, often without discovery or punishment.[5]

The rising age of marriage for both male and female Muslims in numerous societies means that alternate forms of sexual liaisons are gaining ground de facto, notwithstanding the continuing importance of female virginity in many communities. Yet there is a general unwillingness on the part of many Muslims to confront the existence of sex outside of marriage. This reluctance is due in part to a well-integrated principle of comportment that forbids broadcasting one's own sins and requires covering up sins of others. It does not allow for serious consideration of how Muslims' sexual practices have shifted, how modern notions about the importance of consent make a flat prohibition of all non-marital sex seem less sure to some Western Muslims, and how practical matters such as the intersections between religious and civil marriage are to be addressed in modern nation-states, especially those where Muslims are a minority.

As a prelude to discussing contemporary Muslim thinking on non-marital sex, this chapter will address the classical definitions of licit and illicit behavior, and the rewards and punishments associated with each. The regulatory attention of the classical jurists was not limited to illicit activities but also encompassed even lawful sexual activity, such as between spouses.[6] In notable contrast to the hyper-attention paid to the imposition of penalties for illicit sex in some Muslim contexts today, where the enforcement of *hadd* punishments stands as a symbol of Islamic authenticity, the response of premodern jurists to unlawful sex was generally pragmatic regulation rather than dogmatic insistence on punishment for offenders. It is clear from both what is explicit and what remains unarticulated in their texts that various types of unlawful sexual activity have always been practiced in Muslim societies. Jurists and judges accepted *hadd* punishments in principle, but – at least in part because the rules of evidence made proving a charge of *zina* no small matter – frequently assumed that instances of illicit sex would go unpunished by human authorities.

Just because *zina* went unpunished did not mean, though, that there were no earthly legal consequences to intercourse outside of marriage. The effects of *zina* were regulated as part of the jurists' broader treatment of Muslims' sexual behavior, and the legal effects of lawful and unlawful sexual encounters often overlapped. The view that any sexual act merits either "payment or punishment" explains both the requirement of marriage, with dower (or purchase, in the case of a female slave), and the possibility of transmuting punishment by treating an impermissible sexual act as a mistake, for which the woman involved would receive compensation in the amount of her fair dower. Such "mistakes" also allow for the imputation of paternity, which illicit relations do not. The boundary (*hadd*) between lawful and unlawful remains unchallenged, but in practice, specific acts are not always so neatly categorized.

Protecting chastity: the classical texts

According to Qur'anic passages, hadith narratives, and the works of jurists and exegetes, lawful sex – that is, approved acts between partners who are legally permitted to one another – is good, healthy, and praiseworthy as a divinely approved form of pleasure. Unlawful sex – where the partners are forbidden to one another or, to a lesser extent, the specific acts engaged in are not approved[7] – is reprehensible, the cause of social chaos and personal sin, and deserving of earthly punishment as well as divinely wrought chastisement in the hereafter. Several hadith, found in *Sahih Muslim* among other sources, illustrate both the naturalness of sexual desire and the importance of its satisfaction only within licit contexts. Muslim presents these accounts of the Prophet's words and deeds under the heading "He who sees a woman, and his heart is affected, should come to his wife, and should have intercourse with her." The accounts, reported by Jabir b. 'Abdullah, state that Muhammad "saw a woman, and so he came to his wife, Zainab, as she was tanning a leather and had sexual intercourse with her." In the most detailed report, the Prophet subsequently advises his Companions that "when a woman fascinates any one of you and she captivates his heart, he should go to his wife and have an intercourse with her, for it would repel what he feels."[8]

From this account and other similar narrations scholars have deduced that a man is not to blame for becoming aroused by a woman to whom he has no lawful sexual access – provided he does not deliberately seek out such stimulus; another relevant piece of advice attributed to the Prophet states, translated freely, "The first look is free, but the second one will cost you."[9] Seeking satisfaction due to that arousal is not only permissible, but recommended: a man in that situation should follow the Prophet's example and return home to have intercourse with his wife. The Prophet is also reported to have said that a man will be rewarded by God for acting thus. When questioned by an incredulous companion as to why God would reward him for such a pleasurable activity, the Prophet responded by asking whether God would punish him for satisfying his desire unlawfully. Just as the illicit satisfaction of desire is punishable, Muhammad explained, so the lawful satisfaction of desire is rewarded. Female desire, it must be noted, makes no appearance in these traditions, which presume both the wife's availability and her acquiescence, not to mention her interchangeability: desire sparked by one woman could be easily satisfied with another.

Islamic definitions of lawful and unlawful sexual activity shared a double standard governing male and female sexual behavior with other ancient legal systems (Greek, Roman, and biblical). A Muslim male could have more than one licit partner – up to four wives and an unlimited number of slave concubines (and for Shiʻi men, an unlimited number of *mutʻa*, or temporary, wives) – while a Muslim female could only be sexually lawful to one man at a time, either her husband or, in the case of an unmarried female slave, her master. However, the scope of partners available to men under Islamic law was also restricted in a much more significant way than was the case in these other legal systems. Most obviously, male partners, entirely legal under Greek and Roman (though not biblical) law where the males in question were slaves or social inferiors, were prohibited under Islamic law.[10]

Muslim rules governing sex between men and women were also more stringent in key respects than those of other ancient societies, which tended to punish men for sexual contact only with virgin or married women whose sexuality was under the control of a father or husband. Under ancient Greek law, "The only officially forbidden fruit was the wife of another citizen."[11] Roman law likewise made a distinction for married men between being unfaithful and committing adultery; the more serious offense of adultery involved another man's wife.[12] Under rabbinic law, moral constraints governed the behavior of divorced or widowed women, but only offenses by or involving virgin, betrothed, or married women were punishable.[13] For a Muslim man, by contrast, any consensual sex with a woman who was neither his wife nor his *own* female slave constituted *zina*, the form of illicit sexual activity with which the classical Muslim jurists were most concerned. (There seems to have been some early tolerance for the lending of female slaves, but it was ultimately not permitted by the established legal tradition.) Although a Muslim male's partners may have been numerically unlimited in theory, for non-elite men, without the resources to own slaves or marry a second wife, monogamy would have been the norm rather than the exception.

Despite the double standard with regard to the number of lawful partners men and women could have, as well as how much say they had in the initiation, continuation, and termination of those legal ties, there was no difference with regard to punishment for sex outside those ties. The Qur'an specifies one hundred lashes each for both the male and female participants in *zina*, if free, with half as many for enslaved offenders.[14] According to precedent attributed to the Prophet Muhammad, only enslaved or never-married offenders are to be lashed; free offenders who are or have been married[15] are subject to the harsher penalty of lapidation, stoning to death – a biblical punishment for a different sexual offense.[16] Islamic law links the more severe punishment of stoning to marital status rather than gender. Thus, if a never-married woman committed *zina* with a married or previously married man, she would be flogged and he would be stoned. The reverse would be the case if the woman was or had been married and the man was a bachelor. The jurists applied these criteria unfailingly, never suggesting that women should be subjected to harsher punishment than men for the same offense, or that a man's offense was lessened if the woman he bedded was not someone else's wife or betrothed.

Though these *hadd* punishments are clearly spelled out, the imposition of either penalty for *zina* requires stringent proof, generally either by witnesses or confession. The Qur'an requires the testimony of four eyewitnesses[17] whom the jurists specify must be adult, male, Muslim, and able to testify to having seen the actual act of penetration; describing what the testimony must include, they use analogies such as a key going into a lock, or a pen dipping into an inkpot. Harsh punishment is to be meted out to those who accuse a woman of unlawful intercourse but cannot produce three additional witnesses to her crime. Such accusers become themselves guilty of the *hadd* crime of slander (*qadhf*) and are liable to flogging – eighty lashes, according to Surah 24, verse 4, almost as severe as what is specified for the crime of *zina* itself. Confession can also prove a charge of *zina*. Although the Qur'an does not mention this form of proof, a number of *hadith* report the Prophet punishing offenders on the basis of their own confessions – which, tradition makes clear, he discouraged them from making.[18] For the most part, the traditional literature and the jurists' writings demonstrate a real aversion to both accusation – at least some of which can be attributed to the Qur'anic punishment for unsupported charges – and confession.

Proof by witnessing or confession is equally applicable to men and women accused of *zina*, but one doctrine places women disproportionately in jeopardy of punishment. The dominant opinion of the Maliki school of legal thought is that pregnancy in a woman who is not currently married (or in her waiting period from divorce or widowhood) is *prima facie* evidence of *zina*. This view is not shared by the other legal schools, which hold that pregnancy does not provide the necessary degree of certainty that an unlawful act was committed. Even among the Malikis, the impact of the view that pregnancy is proof of *zina* was muted by the acceptance of a lengthy gestation period, up to four or five years, during which a pregnancy could be attributed to a previous husband. In fact, jurists and judges in premodern Muslim societies used a variety of legal maneuvers and excuses to thwart application of *hadd* penalties, even where the parties acknowledged having intercourse outside of a valid marriage. Because of the seriousness of *hadd* crimes and the severity of the penalties, it became an important legal principle that in cases of doubt, *hadd* punishments were to be dropped in favor of milder discretionary punishments. Two statements attributed to the Prophet favor this dropping of the *hadd*: "Avoid punishments so long as there is room for avoiding them" and "Keep the Muslims away from punishments wherever possible. If there is any way out for an offender to escape punishment acquit him. It is better for a judge to err in acquittal than in conviction."[19]

The jurists' strict attention to seemingly unattainable evidentiary standards also firmly placed responsibility for judgment and punishment for *zina* squarely in the hands of the public authority, rather than making it a matter for private retribution.[20] Numerous hadith found in both Bukhari and Muslim make clear that even if a man were to find his wife with another man, he could not take the law into his own hands, but rather would have to bring three additional witnesses to her act before the public authority could judge her offense. What about the case of a husband who witnesses his wife's adultery but cannot substantiate his claim with the necessary additional witnesses? In such a situation, the most he can do is deny paternity of a child his wife is carrying or has delivered, by proceeding with a series of mutual oaths, set forth in the verses directly following those on punishment for *zina*.[21] In the Qur'anic procedure known as *li'an*, he can disavow the paternity of his wife's child without being subject to the usual, nearly impossible to satisfy, requirements of proof for *zina*. However, she can defend herself against his accusations by taking four oaths that she is not guilty; then, their marriage will be dissolved and she will not be liable to punishment, but she will have sole care of the child – just as if it had been born from *zina*. Although a child born of *zina* is not himself or herself guilty of any wrongdoing, the existence of such a child is threatening to the stability of the system governing kinship and social interaction.

Marital intercourse is the paradigmatic sexual act in Islamic law. Its lawful nature does not exempt it from legal scrutiny; if anything, the opposite is the case. Sex within marriage has a variety of financial, social, and ritual consequences that require jurisprudential regulation. The first act of sexual intercourse in marriage obliges the husband to pay the wife her full dower, removes her opportunity to have the marriage dissolved on the basis of his impotence, creates kin prohibitions – that is, barriers which prevent each spouse from marrying certain close relatives of the other in the future, and obliges the wife to observe a waiting period if she is widowed or divorced. Every act of marital intercourse in which penetration occurs requires each spouse to complete a major ablution (*ghusl*) to re-establish ritual purity before he or she can pray. This list does not exhaust the legal consequences of marital sex, but it provides a starting point for considering how illicit sex compares in its legal effects.[22]

Zina differs in two crucial ways from lawful marital intercourse, aside from the issue of punishment. First, an obligation to pay dower never results from consensual unions outside of marriage. Second, any offspring of *zina* have no legal father. These twin issues of dower and paternal affiliation are the primary consequences of lawful sex between married partners (and exist, in modified form, in liaisons between owners and their concubines as well). There is one area, on the other hand, where it is uniformly agreed that *zina* does not differ from lawful marital sex: intercourse between forbidden partners makes ablutions necessary just as it does between spouses. When it comes to determining the other legal consequences of *zina*, however, the jurists disagree among themselves. Yet despite this disagreement, it is striking that they attend primarily to determining where and whether parallels between *zina* and marital intercourse exist, debating extensively over whether, for example, kin prohibitions are created by an illicit sexual encounter as they would be by marriage.

In making arguments about this issue, by and large the jurists do not discuss punishment at all, merely the question of whether kin prohibitions are established. To take one hypothetical case: does a man's wife become forbidden to him because he committed *zina* with her mother (as she would become if he consummated a marriage with her mother, even accidentally)? Since the man is married and thus, by juristic consensus, liable to be stoned to death for his offense, the issue of whether his wife becomes forbidden to him should be irrelevant. It does not matter if a man sentenced to death may or may not have intercourse with his wife, since carrying out the *hadd* punishment renders the issue moot. However, the ways in which jurists of all legal schools discussed this issue demonstrates that the *hadd* penalty was not their primary concern; in fact, the query essentially presupposes that the *hadd* will not be applied. Only if this is assumed does the question of whether the man may continue a marital relationship with his wife have any importance. This brief example shows that the jurists persisted in applying the traditional legal consequences of marital intercourse to illicit sexual acts as often as possible, in an attempt to encompass them legally, and reduce their power to cause social havoc. Even when they decided that the same consequences did not apply, it was with these ordinary effects of unlawful sex that they largely concerned themselves, rather than with punishing offenders.

It is tempting for someone who wants to minimize the importance of *hadd* punishments to emphasize the jurists' matter-of-fact treatment of illicit sexual acts, but their detail-oriented attention to the banal consequences of otherwise forbidden sexual encounters should not be mistaken for tacit approval of those acts. The jurists' approach to dealing with sexual transgressions does not mean they did not, at other times, condemn them in the strongest possible terms. The pragmatic regulation of sex did not exist only with regard to acts that some liberals might find tolerable today, such as consensual sex between unmarried adults. Rather, the same pragmatic approach extended to acts agreed to be horrific, including rape. The jurists were not giving a wink-and-a-nod approval to rape when they discussed whether a raped female needed to perform ablution after forced intercourse (the rapist, all agreed, had to do so before he could pray).[23] While the rape may have been both horrifying and deserving of punishment, the jurists had a particular concern and objective and were not distracted from it. This pragmatic, technical, legalistic approach to the issues in question does, at times, seem to lose sight of the big picture. However, it is also helpful to keep in mind the jurists' assumption that whatever sexual sin individuals might have committed, they will continue to live, and pray, as Muslims.

Paternity, legal fictions, and non-marital sex in contemporary Muslim thought

A widely cited account set during the Prophet's lifetime illuminates the continual tension between punishment and regulation as responses to unlawful sexual activity. In this narrative, two different men assert that a particular youth, born to a female slave, is of their own lineage. The son of the slave-woman's owner affirms that the young man is his brother, "born on his [father's] bed," the result of a legitimate union between owner and slave. The man who asserts this is the brother of the Prophet's wife Sawda; the slave-owner in question was her father. Another man declares that his own brother, since deceased, claimed paternity of the youth, the result of an illicit affair with the slave. The Prophet, so the story goes, attributed paternity to the slave-owner, Sawda's father, famously stating: "The child belongs to the bed, and the adulterer (*'ahir*) is to be stoned."[24] However, apparently noticing a family resemblance between the other claimant and the young man, the Prophet told Sawda to screen herself from the youth.

In part, this anecdote is a reaffirmation of basic legal norms governing sexual morality. Paternity is established by marriage or, in the case of a slave concubine, ownership. By affirming that the slave-owner was indeed the legal father of the youth borne by his female slave, the verdict rendered by the Prophet ensured the stability of this system for attributing paternity and reiterated that sexual transgressions would be severely punished.

There is another level to this tale, though, found in the Prophet's order to his wife Sawda to screen herself from the youth, despite his own verdict declaring the youth legally her brother, and therefore among those relatives in front of whom she could appear. The Prophet's command represents an acknowledgement that this particular attribution of paternity was a legal fiction. The appearance of this story in works of jurisprudence represents an acknowledgement by the jurists that their regulations also at times create legal fictions that attempt to normalize illicit sexual activity.[25]

The issue of legal fictions surrounding paternity remains a complicated issue in the present day and age, as a recent Egyptian case demonstrates. Hind al-Hinawwy bore a child, claiming that Ahmed al-Fishawy was the father and that he had married her in a widespread but largely clandestine phenomenon known as *zawaj 'urfi*, or customary marriage. *Zawaj 'urfi* is usually kept secret from parents, and remains completely outside the bureaucratic channels of the Egyptian nation-state. Nonetheless, if there are sufficient witnesses, some scholars accept that it meets the minimal requirements for a valid marriage under those interpretations of Islamic law where a bride is not required to be represented by a guardian. Al-Hinawwy's putative husband, a well-known actor, denied the marriage and rejected paternity of the child. The mother's request for DNA testing to allow her to press her claim of paternity raises a crucial question with implications far beyond her individual case: if she cannot prove the marriage, is there no valid paternity even if the test results point to the man she claims sired the child? In classical jurisprudence, there is no necessary relationship between biological paternity and legal paternity.[26] If a child were to be from *zina*, no acknowledgement from either mother or biological father can establish legal paternity for the child involved. What is at stake here is not whether or not the woman could be punished for *zina* – Egypt does not prosecute *zina*, and even if it did, whether or not the man's claim that there was no valid marriage is accepted, there are certainly grounds for a claim of mistake (*shubha*) on her part which would prevent conviction for *zina*. Rather, the issue was whether the child's alleged father could be forced to take paternal responsibility for the child, as the mother demanded.

This case would, for a variety of reasons, likely be treated as *shubha*, a mistake, which conveys paternal affiliation. But the use of DNA testing to link legal paternity with biological fatherhood raises a number of difficult questions that women who have hailed this case as a step toward sexual parity must address. In some respects, DNA as proof of paternity is analogous to physiognomy used in early Muslim communities to differentiate among various claimants (in cases of women

who remarried before observing proper waiting periods, etc.).
However, as the case of Sawda's half-brother shows, evidence
gathered in that fashion was insufficient to override a legal
claim or to establish a legal tie where none existed. Does the
shift in technology with the ready availability of DNA testing
alter this dynamic? And if so, is it a good thing?

One consideration is that if paternity testing becomes a standard practice in cases of dispute, it would substantially alter
the existing legal dynamics that set a very high bar for accusing
women of being unfaithful.[27] In the time of the Prophet and
subsequent centuries, jealous and suspicious husbands had few
avenues to pursue without irremediable consequences. Men
who called into question their wives' chastity, by imputing
illegitimacy to children they bore, either had to disavow such
children formally through the virtually defunct mechanism of
mutual cursing (li'an), thus permanently ending their marriages, or to withhold any accusations and refrain from any
defamatory speculation. If a man could order DNA testing on
his child without automatically dissolving his marriage, it would
change the balance of rights and duties in unexpected ways.

The notion of checking for compliance with paternity would
fundamentally violate the "don't ask, don't tell" principle that
is deeply influential in Muslim ethical discussions and social
practice, sometimes for better, sometimes for worse. Ebrahim
Moosa, writing about the offspring of zina, makes a point that is
more broadly valid: "juristic ethics discourages any such probing that may produce incriminating evidence that delegitimizes
the child."[28] Despite the discouraging of this probing, could a
woman be prosecuted for zina if found to have borne a child
to a man other than her husband? What about an unmarried
woman? Would DNA evidence count in place of the usually
required witnesses to the sexual act? Answers to these questions
must reflect the entire range of consequences to tinkering with
some portion of the system. If DNA were considered proof, then
one could argue that in cases where a woman is prosecuted for
zina on the basis of pregnancy, any man she names should be
tested as well, and prosecuted if DNA results show his paternity.
If evidence of the result, rather than the act, is all that is required,

then the man is just as liable to prosecution. It could be that the acceptance of DNA evidence would be of benefit, but the full range of consequences must be considered, lest the unintended effects prove far worse for women than the status quo.

The debate around this Egyptian case raises compelling issues beyond that of DNA testing. First, of course, is the complicated situation that arises from a mixed system, where classical legal models and doctrines both converge and conflict with a civil judiciary. Second is the social double standard that ascribes far more severe consequences to females than to males for breaches of chastity norms, even when the legal strictures governing their sexual contact outside of marriage are exactly the same. Third, although the dynamics of *zawaj 'urfi* are specific to Egypt, it is but one of several flourishing types of quasi-marriage through which couples seek to legitimize their sexual unions religiously while avoiding the full burden of mutual obligations – social, financial, legal, and sometimes familial – that come with fully recognized, civilly registered marriages.

Muslims who contract *zawaj 'urfi* are generally seeking to engage in sex without the expenses and complications of civil marriage while avoiding the sin of commission of *zina*. In the Egyptian case, the costs are not related to getting married per se, but rather to the social expectations of what a groom of a certain class will be able to provide for his bride at the time of marriage, the most significant being "key money" – effectively, a substantial down payment for housing. These financial expectations are one factor leading to the delay in marriages, and thus the sense of needing interim sexual outlets. The specific circumstances are different elsewhere, but in many Muslim communities later age at marriage, due in part to the increased importance of post-secondary education, has led to new challenges for Muslims who want to adhere to accepted regulations surrounding sexual conduct while at the same time having difficulties suppressing their sexual drives for a decade or more after puberty. Modern shifts in marriage patterns, however, are not the only significant change. Equally or more important is a broad shift in sensibilities to a view of sex as an activity that is primarily about the mutual consent and individual attachment of the persons involved. This perspective is particularly prevalent among Muslims living as minorities in societies such as the United States.

In her "Islamic Bill of Rights for Women in the Bedroom" (the successor to her widely circulated, and generally well-received, "Islamic Bill of Rights for Women in the Mosque"), activist, author, and self-identified single mother Asra Nomani declares, as the eighth of ten items, that "women have an Islamic right to exemption from criminalization or punishment for consensual adult intercourse."[29] Nomani claims as an "Islamic right" something that contradicts Qur'an, sunnah, and centuries of jurisprudential consensus. Yet her statement is worth considering, rather than rejecting out of hand, as it illustrates important tendencies in contemporary Muslim discourse. Those who are not 'ulama increasingly make authoritative claims about Islam. Where those who are not necessarily any better trained than Nomani make claims that their audience views as "traditional," the claims tend to be accepted without the same level of scrutiny. Nomani's strategic choice to argue on the basis of conformity to Islam is representative of much modern discussion, even if the specific claim she makes is in blatant opposition to scholarly and popular consensus.[30] Finally, Nomani's underlying assumption that the consensual nature of a sexual relationship is relevant to whether it is, or should be, subject to censure would not have been accepted by the classical jurists, but even those modern 'ulama who would disdain Nomani's characterization of the "Islamic" position on sex outside of marriage place more stress on consent than their predecessors (even if it is usually consent to marriage they are considering, rather than consent to sex outside its bounds). Nomani's statement crystallizes a widespread but largely inchoate sentiment among many contemporary Muslims: consent matters.[31]

Nomani's view on non-marital intercourse (note that it seems to be irrelevant, from her perspective, whether the parties involved are married to other individuals) reflects a broader social shift. Thus, commenting on an article that appeared on Muslim WakeUp, one self-identified American Muslim wrote:

Many Muslims at the mosque I attend believe that sex out-side of marriage is wrong. Many Muslims don't even date (not in the American way at least) in order to avoid pre-marital sex. Personally, I wouldn't be so quick to say sex outside of marriage is wrong, for two reasons. First, other than marriage, there was one other sexual relationship that was allowed in Islamic Law, and that's slave concubinage. Second, although I, personally, believe that one night stands and casual sex are wrong (not to mention rape), what about sex in committed relationships that aren't marriages? Is that *haram*? I'm sure that slave concubinage would disgust a lot of Americans, given that slave owners were allowed to have sex with their slaves with or without their consent. But if this is allowed in Islamic Law, how could sex by mutual consent in committed relationships in which both the man and the woman love and respect each other, but are not married, be *haram*? That question represents my struggle. I'm not arguing that such a rela-tionship is *halal*. My honest answer to that question is I don't know whether it's *halal* or *haram*. But I do suggest not being so quick to call it *haram*. Perhaps it's a question that requires a fatwa.[32]

This statement from a convert reflects a deference to juris-prudence combined with an assessment of how its rules (such as slave concubinage) diverge from his or her personal beliefs. The author accepts the basic validity of concepts such as *haram* and *halal*[33] and seems to respect legal author-ity when she suggests that "a fatwa" might be required. At the same time she is unaware that there is a very clear estab-lished answer to whether "sex by mutual consent in commit-ted relationships in which both the man and the woman love and respect each other but are not married" is absolutely unlawful. What this author does not do is suggest that, in light of new perspectives (e.g., finding slave concubinage disgusting), the question of lawful and permitted should be re-evaluated.

Conclusion

It is obvious that the classical model of Islamic sexual ethics no longer applies in several critical respects. Yet in order to begin to think about how a more viable and equitable ethics of sex might be developed, Muslims must grapple actively with the centrality of sex and sexuality to communal life. In the U.S. and Europe especially, but not exclusively (as the Egyptian *zawaj 'urfi* case demonstrates), Muslims are facing a crisis of sexual morality. One alternative is to push for complete adherence to classical normative standards of relating to members of the opposite sex.[34] Some communities and families manage to enforce a semblance of segregation, but it is unlikely to succeed on a large scale. Even in the medieval Muslim world, strict observance of gender segregation was practiced exclusively by an elite. Today, in societies such as Saudi Arabia, strict gender segregation is under siege; in the U.S. or the UK it exists only on the fringes of the Muslim populace. Gender segregation, of course, does not by itself prohibit all illicit sex, and gender mixing, despite some alarmist projections, does not mean that illicit sex will transpire. More than the shifting practice, it seems to me that there is a divide at the level of ideas and ideals between contemporary conventional wisdom among Muslims, especially those living in the West, and classical formulations of sexual ethics. The fear, of course, is that discarding the established legal rules for conduct will leave Muslims without any guidance. Is there a way to move past patriarchal and sexist limitations of both traditional and contemporary double standards while acknowledging that there are, and need to be, boundaries to sexual relationships?

One obstacle to frank conversation about shifting behavioral patterns is the insistence on avoiding revealing talk, a point explored further in the next chapter's treatment of same-sex intimacy. As one scholar notes, "Talk about illicit sex might be as socially destabilizing as its perpetration."[35] This is not a simple matter of prudery; the practice of avoiding potentially incriminating questions, and not sharing information about indiscretions, is woven into the fabric of

Islamic legal thought as well as embedded in Muslim social norms. Covering up one's own faults, or the faults of others, is understood as a vital duty for a believer.[36] However, the "don't ask, don't tell" model provides a tremendous obstacle to transforming ethical standards: if everyone refuses to publicly discuss the fact that, with the disappearance of early marriage, many Muslims are not waiting for marriage to have sex, the problem continues. And the social double standard (in the case of virginity, for example) means that the consequences for women are worse than those for men, even where, in legal terms, the issues are the same.

In March 2005, European scholar Tariq Ramadan alluded to this double standard in his eloquent and persuasive (but controversial) call for a moratorium on *hadd* punishments for *zina*. But in nations where "consensual adult sex" is not punished, regardless of its compliance with religious law, there are still very important matters to be discussed.[37] The Qur'anic and classical jurisprudential boundaries of what counts as licit and illicit have already been redrawn, for all practical purposes, by Muslim acceptance of the abolition of slavery and, therefore, of slave concubinage. The double standard that was operative in the past (even if, in practice, it applied only to men wealthy enough to take more than one wife or own concubines) has largely disappeared as a matter of law, with the increase in monogamy and the disappearance of slave concubinage as a legal option. *Zina* can be redefined for the twenty-first century as sex between partners not married to one another. But what element of marriage legitimizes sex and differentiates it from *zina*? Do dower payment and a unilateral right by the husband to dissolve the union at his whim (regardless of whether or not this is the usual practice) make marriage moral? Is religious marriage, a voluntary contract without civil registration, sufficient to make sex licit, without consideration of national laws that enforce certain property relationships? Ultimately, where does lawfulness rest? These are not flippant questions, but serious attempts to think about what transforms sex into something licit. What is God's stake in marriage?

Coda 4

In the decade since Tariq Ramadan appealed for a moratorium on *hadd* punishments, the contrary has happened: violent retribution for (alleged) *zina* and, more recently, apostasy
has seen an upsurge. Vigilante attackers, in Pakistan and elsewhere, take punishment into their own hands, often (though
not exclusively) targeting women. From the Sudan to Brunei,
governments have formulated new laws that they justify as
Islamic. Media attention to these "fiqhesque or quasi-fiqh
laws,"[38] many of which are horrific, prompts Muslims who
live in places where such rules do not hold sway to consider
the place of shari'a in their lives and thought. Often, they must
also contend with negative public opinion about Islam in general and Islamic law more particularly. In the United States,
orchestrated campaigns fan the flames of anti-Muslim sentiment. The oppression of Muslim women is used to highlight
Muslim savagery. Selective, and carefully packaged, accounts
from born Muslim women present "the truth" about Islamic
gender practices. White female pundits and media figures
often present this (mis)information.[39] Anti-Muslim bigotry
has reached fever pitch; assaults and murders as well as threats
and discrimination are increasing.

Poorly conceptualized and badly drafted legislative initiatives
to counter "creeping shari'a" rely on scare tactics about Islam
and Muslims.[40] The identification of shari'a with a narrow set
of repressive and barbaric laws has been a central part of a well-
funded campaign to increase animus toward Muslims.[41] Such
initiatives rely on misinformation, prejudice, and outright lies.
They also rely on the better-attested idea that law is central to
Muslim life. The notion that Islam is a predominantly legal religion holds sway as well among many Muslims and sympathetic
outsiders. Although jurisprudence has been undeniably vital to
Muslim intellectual and, to some extent, devotional life over
the centuries, its absolute centrality arises in part from colo-
nial-era portraits of Islam. European scholars held up certain
forms of Muslim life and practice as exemplary and orthodox,
while disregarding or denigrating others as mere popular

superstition. Related debates took place among Muslim thinkers, both among the traditional scholarly class and newer
professionals, some of them with Western or Western-style
educations. Intersecting and overlapping notions about Muslim
identity and the role of government shaped what came to be
valued as Islamic law in colonial bureaucracies and, eventually,
newly independent nation-states.

Over the course of the twentieth century and into the
twenty-first century, governments implemented laws with the
highest symbolic value: marriage and divorce, custody, inheritance, all under the rubric of "personal status," and then a
few symbolic harsh corporal punishments. Others have written about the modern processes through which punishments
upheld in theory and avoided in practice became emblematic
of "authentic Islam." For now, let us consider the gendered
nature of these punishments, particularly for illicit sex, as
manifested in recent legislation.

The case of Brunei fleetingly caught American attention
in 2014. Brunei's ruling Sultan indirectly owned the storied
Beverly Hills Hotel, which Hollywood stars boycotted when
they learned of a new penal code reportedly imposing the death
penalty for homosexuality. The code targets offenses including
failing to attend Friday prayers and bearing a child out of wedlock. The rules, now postponed indefinitely, also call for corporal punishments including whippings for alcohol consumption
and amputations for certain types of theft. Next comes stoning for *zina* and for male/male anal sex (no mention of lesbian
acts). The death penalty also applies to those found guilty of
insulting the Prophet.

In Brunei, as elsewhere, selective targeting of high-profile
offenses aims to prove a repressive government's Islamic credentials. Brunei mostly relies on a judicial system left over
from its days as a British protectorate. The Sultan has nonetheless insisted that Islam requires these new rules. The Sultan's
claim that "Islam" demands implementation of "shari'a"
ignores the fact that there is not now nor has there ever been
a uniform set of identifiable rules that Muslim scholars have
agreed on, much less that governments in Muslim-majority

countries have implemented over the centuries. So-called shari'a laws on the books in Brunei, Nigeria, Pakistan, Iran, Saudi Arabia, and Morocco are not directly revealed by God. They are variously imposed by decree, voted on by legislatures, signed by monarchs and subject to popular referenda. In other words, they are human products, with human histories. The pretense that these laws are straightforward implementations of God's will not only serves to justify these otherwise unjustifiable rules but also feeds the demonization and dehumanization of Muslims.

One might ask how harsh shari'a punishments – historically upheld in theory and assiduously avoided in practice – came to symbolize both a bulwark against decadent Western modernity and the establishment of an Islamic society. For centuries, Europeans viewed Muslims as sexually decadent, given to sodomy as well as more general lustful indulgences. It was only in the nineteenth century that the oppression of females came into its own as the major criticism levied against Muslims. In the xenophobic imagination, Muslim sexual puritanism coexists with horrifying sexual barbarism. In jumbled polemical assemblages, honor crimes and obsession with female virginity exist alongside polygyny, genital mutilation, pedophilia, and rape of war captives.[42]

A major theme of these Codas is the increased discursive entanglement of "Islam" and "the West." The original volume paid attention to this oppositional framing as part of the construction of an idealized Islam whose advocates hype its sexual morality as distinctive and superior. It now seems that the Western media focus on punishment is partially responsible for a feedback loop in which ever more spectacular punishments are espoused in the name of religious authenticity. As with IS's publicized brutalities, the Western audience may be part of the point and outraged responses by international human rights organizations may aid rather than hinder the cause. In a vicious cycle, violence perpetrated by Muslims with extreme views is widely portrayed as the only real Islam, delegitimizing majority-Muslim beliefs and practices.

While Western media focus on barbaric crimes and punishments, for most Muslims, whether in East L.A., Edinburgh, or Egypt, sexual mores are less about honor crimes – a category elegantly deconstructed by Lila Abu-Lughod – or *hadd* punishments and more about community expectations and marriageability.[43] Double standards remain in place in many communities, and the consequences for women of sexual involvement outside marriage remain harsher than those for men, though the particulars vary according to class and educational levels. The Egyptian case of Hind al-Hinawwy and Ahmed al-Fishawy, now resolved, presents a salutary reminder that these double standards are not purely ahistorical or religio-doctrinal. Key patriarchal rules emanate from the bureaucratic apparatus of the modern nation-state: legal paternity is linked to a child's ID card and government benefits.[44]

Patriarchy is everywhere. It involves culturally and historically specific patterns of male domination. It fuels both widespread, and largely unpunished, sexual assault on American college campuses and in the military, as well as the furor in some Muslim-majority polities to punish women who are perceived to have violated communal norms.

In mid-2014, the Sudan prosecuted and jailed Meriam Ibrahim for apostasy and illicit sex. They sentenced her to flogging and execution, deferring the sentence since she was pregnant. The charge of apostasy was based on the claim that Ibrahim was born Muslim: her religion follows that of her (Muslim) father, who left her (Christian) mother when Ibrahim was young. She was apparently raised Christian. Patriarchy allows interreligious marriage between a Muslim man and a Christian woman, but not the reverse (as discussed in Chapter 1), and supports the presumption that the child's religion follows that of its father.

The charge of illicit sex for which Ibrahim was sentenced to lashes resulted from the court deeming her marriage to a Christian man void. Since she has a Muslim father, she is considered Muslim. Since, unlike her parents' marriage between a Muslim man and a Christian, marriage between a Muslim woman and a Christian man cannot be valid, the court determined that she had sex outside marriage. Her toddler, and the child that was growing in her belly, proved her offense. Score another one for patriarchy.

According to reports, Ibrahim's case was brought to the attention of the authorities by some relatives, presumably Muslim, who objected to her marriage to a Christian. As far as the charge of illicit sex goes, a premodern court would almost certainly have exonerated her, on the grounds that any doubt – such as the fact that the woman *thought* her marriage was valid – averts the punishment. Apostasy, too, seems to have been seldom punished in practice, however strongly the rule was upheld in theory. One can make a case that, as with Brunei's new penal code, the Sudanese verdict represents a modern and profoundly problematic view of Islamic law.

Fair enough. Yet we may note the nuance and variability of traditional Islamic law while critiquing its powerful patriarchal presuppositions. However tempered they were in past practice by judicial clemency, they laid the ground for the charges against Ibrahim. Of course, context matters: we will not understand developments in the Sudan, or Brunei, or elsewhere without reference to national and global politics, economics, and – in the last case – individual family dynamics; Islamic law is only part of the picture. And yet it is a key piece of the picture. Rethinking Islamic law without questioning its basic presumptions about male dominance will not take us nearly far enough. Still, expressing outrage over cases in Brunei, Nigeria, or the Sudan, attempting to save Muslim women from their plight, while remaining impassive about brutalities inflicted on American women, is unacceptable.[45] So, too, is remaining silent about the violence Muslim women suffer not in the name of Islam but in the name of democracy.

5 Don't Ask, Don't Tell: Same-Sex Intimacy in Muslim Thought

> Illicit sex between a man and a woman (*zina*);
> anal intercourse between men (*liwat*);
> having intercourse with livestock (*ityan al-baha'im*);
> having anal intercourse with a female stranger (*ityan al-mar'a al-ajnabiyya fi dubriha*);
> tribadism (*musahaqat al-nisa'*), which is a woman doing with a woman something resembling what a man would do with her;
> and a husband having intercourse with his wife's corpse.
> From Ibn Hajar Haytami's list of *Enormities*, #338–343[1]

The excerpt above forms part of one of the many lists of major sins, or enormities (*kaba'ir*), compiled by medieval Muslim scholars.[2] Sometimes ranked in order of importance, at other times listed thematically, the entries combine theological and social sins. Sexual offenses frequently occupy prominent places in these compilations, though always below the gravest sin of associating others with God (*shirk*) and often below the sin of disrespectfulness toward one's parents. These lists are still influential today, as evidenced by Nuh Keller's inclusion of two such lists, including Ibn Hajar's sixteenth-century version, as appendices to his late twentieth-century translation of the medieval Shafi'i legal manual *Reliance of the Traveller*. Other lists, such as that of fourteenth-century hadith scholar al-Dhahabi, are readily available in print in Arabic.[3]

Al-Dhahabi's influential *Enormities* (*al-Kaba'ir*) contains seventy sins, with extensive evidence from Qur'an and hadith presented to illustrate the gravity of each act and justify its inclusion in his list. Of this number, only a handful relate to sex; of these, the most serious is *zina* (#10), illicit sex between a man and a woman, followed directly at #11 by *liwat*, or anal intercourse between men. (The term *liwat* is derived from the name of the Prophet Lot; most Qur'anic discussion of same-sex acts between men refers to the attempt by male towns-folk to molest Lot's angelic visitors.) This entry also includes a brief reference to tribadism.[4] Other relevant entries include #21, slander (*qadhf*) of a chaste woman;[5] #34, condoning or tolerating a wife's transgressions;[6] and #35, employing or acting as a *muhallil*.[7] A woman's *nushuz* (recalcitrance) toward her husband, which could involve sexual refusal or mere disobedience, is the least serious of the sex-related enormities included, at #47.[8]

Tenth-century Iraqi scholar Abu Talib Makki, whose list Keller also includes, limits his compilation "solely to sins explicitly designated as enormities by the primary texts."[9] He divides his seventeen-item list into deeds of the heart, of the tongue (including "slander of a chaste person who is a free, adult Muslim"[10]), the stomach, the genitals, the hands, the feet, and the whole body. There are "two [sins] of the genitals and they are *zina* and having anal sex in the manner of the people of Lot."[11] This joining of *zina* and *liwat* – with *zina* always mentioned first – is a common feature of the lists of al-Dhahabi, Makki, and Ibn Hajar.

Ibn Hajar's list is not selective, but rather comprehensive. While Makki itemizes seventeen enormities, and al-Dhahabi seventy, Ibn Hajar lists hundreds, divided into sections. His objective, according to Keller, "is to warn readers against any act that an Islamic scholar has classified as an enormity."[12] The sexual offenses listed in the portion of Ibn Hajar's list devoted to crimes (*jinayat*) include "*zina*; *liwat*; having intercourse with livestock; having anal intercourse with a female stranger; tribadism, which is a woman doing with a woman something resembling what a man would do with her; and a husband having intercourse with his wife's corpse."[13] This grouping begins with reference to *zina* and *liwat*, the primary sexual sins signaled by al-Dhahabi and Makki, and encompasses several other acts as well, including tribadism, which merits a brief mention in al-Dhahabi's discussion of *liwat* but does not appear in Makki's list. Aside from the exclusion of acts related to marriage, which appear in a separate section of Ibn Hajar's list, there is no easily discernible logic joining these items. The section includes both acts subject to *hadd* punishments and those subject to discretionary chastisement; acts involving two persons of the same sex, two persons of the opposite sex, and one person with an animal; acts that are forbidden because they are intrinsically sinful, as is the case with intercourse with an animal or a corpse, and those where the problem is not the act itself, but the lack of a proper legal relationship between the parties, as in the case of *zina*. While there are no circumstances under which bestiality or necrophilia can lawfully be performed,[14] in the case of *zina*, there would be no sin in the intercourse had the participants been married to each other.

What categorization applies to the same-sex[15] sexual acts described in the passage? This question itself presupposes a category that may not be relevant. Ibn Hajar deals with *liwat* and tribadism or lesbianism (*musahaqat al-nisa'*) individually and separately, not as instances of a broader sin called homosexuality. However, as I noted above, tribadism appears briefly in the section al-Dhahabi devotes to *liwat*, suggesting that they have something important in common. What, though, of the acts? In the case of anal sex, the act itself may be an enormity, regardless of who engages in it; Ibn Hajar condemns anal sex between men (*liwat*) as well as anal sex between a man and a female "stranger" – that is, a woman who is neither his wife nor his slave and over whom he has no sexual rights. In the section on marriage, Ibn Hajar also condemns a man having anal sex with his wife (though, in what is potentially an oversight, he makes no mention of a man having anal sex with his slave concubine). Tribadism is another story. Frottage is perfectly permissible between legitimate partners (a man and his wife or his concubine), so his prohibition of "a woman doing with another woman something resembling what a man would do with her" is not based on the impermissibility of the act itself. As in the case of *zina*, it is the lack of a lawful tie between the parties that renders the act illicit.

Could there be circumstances under which such a tie could legalize otherwise prohibited sexual acts between two women or two men? For the vast majority of Muslims, and certainly for Ibn Hajar and his colleagues, this is a ludicrous question; a licit same-sex relationship is a categorical impossibility. Recently, however, some self-identified queer Muslims have challenged this view, affirming the naturalness of their sexual orientation as divinely granted and seeking to consider whether it might be possible to construct a religiously valid bond between two men or two women that would legitimize sex between them. The desire on the part of some self-identified gay and lesbian Muslims to have exclusive and publicly recognized same-sex relationships, and to do so in a way that falls within an "Islamic" framework, is without precedent in Muslim history.

In describing this as a recent development, I do not mean to imply that there have not been previous instances of sexual activity, potentially including long-term affective relation-ships, between individuals of the same sex. What differs is the attempt made by some to reconcile a "homosexual" identity with a Muslim identity, and to legitimize same-sex intimate partnerships within the constraints of Islamic religious dis-course. Their desire to have sexual relationships that break conventional Islamic rules but that aspire to the highest stan-dards of Muslim ethics, as they understand them, exists in tension with vital theological and juridical principles aside from those forbidding illicit sex. The two most salient principles are that one should not expose sinful behavior, whether one's own or another's, and that it is a greater offense to deny certain rules than to break them. Taken together, these rules render any discussion of same-sex sexual intimacy a risky proposition, and make adherence to the "don't ask, don't tell" status quo appealing for many. For others, however, the tacit toleration of illicit same-sex activity, provided one does not seek public affir-mation of any intimate relationship, represents deep hypocrisy and a flagrant violation of other ethical principles.

After providing a brief survey of how the texts treat sexual activity between two men or two women, this chapter will consider the way modern Muslim thinkers from a variety of

perspectives approach the relationship between sexual orientation, sexual acts, and sexual identities. The view that exclusively
homosexual desire is innate in some individuals – a core argument of those seeking acceptance of gay and lesbian identity
– has made inroads even among some relatively conservative
Western Muslim thinkers, but the implications of this acceptance have not been fully delineated. Those who view sexual orientation as inborn but suggest that same-sex desires can never
be fulfilled lawfully confront the problem of divine injustice,
particularly where they also argue for the importance of sexual
satisfaction as a human need. On the other hand, those who
argue that innateness conveys permissibility do not satisfactorily address either the macrocosmic principles of male–female
partnership expressed in scripture or the ahistorical nature of
their claims to an innately gay orientation, claims which ignore
the diversity of historical and contemporary understandings
of sexuality. In either case, the minority Western movement
for acceptance of a gay Muslim identity, and the reaction to
it, has implications for intimate relationships in all segments
of Muslim communities, including between men and women
in marriage. For this reason, no discussion of sexual ethics can
avoid the issue of same-sex intimacy.

History

Although most Muslims would acknowledge that sexual activity between persons of the same sex takes place in Muslim-
majority societies, this concession is frequently accompanied
by an insistence that homosexuality is "Western" or "modern,"
and certainly "un-Islamic."[16] Writing in 1993, Khaled Duran
stated confidently that there were "no self-proclaimed gays in
Muslim countries" and that no movement toward the acceptance of homosexuality or gay identity was taking place among
Muslims.[17] Yet contemporary insistence on the forbiddenness
of homosexuality aside, a number of scholars have suggested
"that one might consider Islamic societies ... to provide a vivid
illustration of a 'homosexual-friendly' environment in world

history."[18] According to Scott Kugle, "when one looks through the historical and literary records of Islamic civilization, one finds a rich archive of same-sex desires and expressions, written by or reported about respected members of society: literati, educated elites, and religious scholars."[19] Another scholar states, more bluntly: "same-sex relations between men are ubiquitous in the medieval Arabo-Islamic textual universe."[20] Khaled Al-Rouhayeb, insisting on nuanced readings of texts from different genres, calls for close attention to the varieties and registers of competing discourses, allowing for some types of homoerotic desire and even activity to be celebrated, and others, including those resulting in penetration, to be condemned.[21]

Although medieval Muslim sources give the impression that homoerotic desire and sexual activity of some type between males was a normal, if religiously illicit, part of elite Muslim life, there is comparatively little on female homoeroticism in Qur'an, hadith, or interpretive texts. Although literary and, to a lesser extent, legal texts include some discussion of sexual acts between women – usually *sihaq* or *musahaqa*, "rubbing" or "pounding" – most discussion of homoerotic acts focuses on male/male sexual activity.[22] Several factors contribute to the silence surrounding female same-sex activity. Perhaps the most important is simply that many legal effects of sex depend on penetration by a penis. In the few cases where sex between women is mentioned, the legal discussion revolves around what punishment, if any, is to be imposed by the authorities as well as whether compensation equivalent to dower must be paid if hymeneal rupture has occurred. Legal discussions of male/male sex acts, by contrast, never mention dower, focusing not only on punishment but also more mundane issues such as the necessity for ablutions after penetration and the possible impediments to marriage created by same-sex liaisons.[23]

In any event, whatever textual sources reveal about the prevalence of same-sex intimate relations, the fact that some Muslims have engaged in homoerotic activities does not mean it is religiously legitimate to do so. For contemporary Muslims grappling with same-sex attractions, the key question is not: What have (some) Muslims done? But rather: what may Muslims do? Or, even more generally: what does "Islam" allow?[24] Some leave Islam entirely, while others choose to separate sexuality from religion, considering themselves Muslim but acknowledging that their sexual acts or identities are not acceptable from a religious perspective. Still others choose to actively grapple with religious precepts in order to attempt to reconcile a Muslim identity with a gay or lesbian one.

Bypassing Islamic legal thought (which, as will be seen below, does not seriously consider the possibility that any same-sex relationship could be lawful), such reconsideration usually begins with the Qur'anic discussion of male and female same-sex acts. There are numerous hadith of varying degrees of authenticity addressing *liwat* in a harshly condemnatory fashion; hadith collections also condemn lesbian acts on those rare occasions they mention them. Scholars interested in developing a framework of tolerance and acceptance for same-sex relationships usually ignore hadith entirely or address specific reports only to discredit their authenticity. The Qur'an itself becomes the basis for new interpretations, which again focus on male/male sex. There is no consensus as to whether the Qur'an even mentions female same-sex activity. It might or might not be the subject of Surah 4, verse 15, which orders that, with the incriminating testimony of four witnesses, "those (fem. pl.) among your women who approach lewdness (*al-fahisha*)" are to be "confine[d] to houses until death claims them, or God ordains for them some (other) way."[25] The precise relationship of the provisions of this verse to those on *zina* has been a topic for much debate. Does the verse "ordaining" flogging abrogate the one ordering confinement, or does this verse refer to a punishment for same-sex acts distinct from that for illicit sex between a man and a woman? This verse does not specify "two women," which would have been possible using the dual form. Immediately following, Surah 4, verse 16 also addresses illicit behavior, using the masculine/inclusive dual "two … from among you." As with all dual or plural masculine forms in Arabic, it can include both male and female, and there has been disagreement among commentators as to whether this verse refers to two men by contrast with the preceding verse, which specifies only females (though not two women), or a male–female pair, also grammatically possible.[26] Male same-sex acts, however, are mentioned on several occasions in conjunction with the story of the Prophet Lot, which is the constant referent for both classical and contemporary discussions of all same-sex sexual activity.

Contemporary scholars disagree sharply about the Qur'anic perspective on same-sex intimacy and desire as presented in the Lot story. Duran presents the conventional view when he states that the Qur'an "is very explicit in its condemnation of homosexuality, leaving scarcely any loophole for a theological accommodation of homosexuals in Islam."[27] In contrast, Kugle argues that "the Qur'an does not address homosexuality or homosexuals explicitly[.]"[28] Rather, the sacred text (like the jurists' writings) addresses particular acts, saying nothing about "identities" and very little about desires. The revisionist attempt to promote a new, more inclusive view of Qur'anic teachings on same-sex sexual acts, desires, and orientations relies on a distinction between the Qur'anic condemnation of particular same-sex acts, in this case those of the townsfolk in the Lot story, and the possibility of divine acceptance of other forms of same-sex relationships.

In order to interpret the Lot story as something besides an "explicit ... condemnation of homosexuality," scholars have used two main approaches. First, they have explored other aspects of the Lot story beyond the issue of same-sex acts. Second, they have argued that even if the acts were problematic, they were objectionable due to a factor other than those involved being of the same sex. As to the first point, the commentarial tradition and conventional wisdom have erred, Amreen Jamal shows, by placing undeserved emphasis on sexual deviancy as the particular sin of Lot's people.[29] Building on Jamal's work, by painstakingly assessing the work of several prominent premodern exegetes, Kugle demonstrates that "word-for-word replacement in classical commentaries has given rise to the dubious equation of the divine punishment of Lot's people with a condemnation of homosexuality and juridically enforceable punishments for same-sex acts."[30] The transgressions of Lot's community were far more extensive and far-reaching than sexual misconduct. Spiritual corruption has been reduced to sexual transgression, undeservedly narrowing the divine guidance contained in the stories of Lot's people.

Although these scholars make a compelling case for understanding the sexual transgressions of Lot's people in a larger context of disbelief and moral turpitude, I am less convinced by their suggestion, echoed by a number of advocacy groups, that the townsfolk's behavior was objectionable not because they sought same-sex intercourse but due to other considerations including their lack of concern for Lot's visitors' consent.[31] The argument that the Qur'an objects not because the men in question sought same-sex intimacy but rather because they intended non-consensual violation rests on an assumption that consent is necessary for an ethical or lawful sexual relationship. However, elsewhere in the Qur'anic text, as with female captives ("what your right hands possess"), consent is not always relevant to the formation of licit sexual relationships. Further, Lot offers his daughters to the marauding townsfolk without any indication that their consent mattered.[32] The daughters' lack of consent is quite striking, whether it is attributable to simple, paternally sanctioned sexual use by the would-be rapists or to marriage as a licit sexual outlet for the men. Kugle argues that this is not a case of valuing male over female, but rather guests over family members "who happen to be female."[33] One could argue that in the case of premodern patriarchal societies, only paternal consent mattered. In that case, could Lot have offered his sons to the men with equal impunity?

The more significant obstacle to reinterpretations of the Lot story is that the Qur'anic text seems to object clearly to the men's choice of sexual object: these men approach men *in preference to* those whom God created to be their mates.[34] One way of getting around this objection would be to argue that men who would otherwise choose female partners were opting to seek sex with men – this argument would be compatible with the view, expressed by some queer Muslim authors, that there are men created to take male mates, a notion I discuss below. There is strong justification for reading the Qur'an to suggest that males and females are created to mate with one another, and any *choice* to deviate from that path is blameworthy.

One cannot understand premodern Muslim scholars' interpretations of the Lot story without considering how their views on same-sex desire and sexual activity differ in crucial ways from those held by modern Westerners, including some Muslims. Their concerns were largely over actions, not orientations. That is not to accept the once-conventional view that any "homosexual" identity is a purely modern invention, and premodern thinkers knew only acts. Premodern texts, as scholarship in other contexts has shown, can present specific sexual acts as "*more* or *less* related to sexual dispositions, desires, and subjectivities."[35] Even where specific identities were associated with the performance of particular acts, these were not consistent across time and place, nor are they identical to contemporary notions of "homosexual," "gay," or "queer." The exegetes and jurists' understandings of male/male sexual activity do not take into account the possibility of a partnership where both men consider themselves "gay,"[36] but rather presuppose an age- and status-stratified asymmetrical relationship between unequal partners.

There are crucial similarities between classical Greek and Roman views on male/male sex and the norms (and practices, so far as historians can tell) of elite medieval Muslim culture. Muslims in the region generally accepted the ancient Mediterranean model, based on hierarchical notions of penetration, where no stigma except perhaps that of profligacy attaches to an adult male who penetrates, but where a free adult male who allows himself to be penetrated suffers stigma.[37] Even a preference for male youths over and above female partners, explored satirically by ninth-century littérateur al-Jahiz in his famous essay "Maids and Youths,"[38] did not make a man "homosexual" in the sense that Duran or Kugle uses the term. Male desire to penetrate desirable youths (generally, although not always, defined as "beardless," *amrad*) was perfectly normal – if never lawful – and not necessarily indicative of a deviant subjectivity, desire, or a particular sexual orientation.[39] The commonplace, not pathological, nature of such desire is illustrated by *Reliance of the Traveller*'s passing mention of the "handsome beardless youth" in its discussion of circumstances under which it is permissible or impermissible for a man to look at a female who is not his wife, slave, or kinswoman. Notably, Keller omits this portion of the text from his late twentieth-century English translation.[40]

Don't ask, don't tell

Despite the widespread medieval acceptance of same-sex desire between men and attractive male youths, Muslim thinkers took for granted that such sexual relations were neither licit nor possible to legitimize. Yet the explicit condemnation of same-sex sexual activity in medieval Islamic legal thought and by most contemporary Muslim thinkers has been tempered by tacit tolerance for its practice, provided some degree of discretion is observed. As Abdelwahab Boudhiba argues, "The fact that homosexuality" – he means same-sex acts – "was always being condemned proves only one thing: neither the religious nor the social conscience could put an end to practices that were disapproved of by Islamic ethics but to which in the last resort society closed its eyes."[41] Steven Murray, discussing both male/male and female/female sexual relations in present-day Muslim contexts, has referred to this unwillingness to acknowledge what is an open secret as "the will not to know."[42] While certainly some aspects of this logic governing same-sex encounters is specific, the overall logic of refusing to point out sins that are not crimes is not unique to same-sex sexual intimacy. Rather, it is part and parcel of a general insistence on not attempting to pursue potentially incriminating information about one's fellow Muslims or to disclose it about oneself.

The unwillingness to seek out and condemn instances of same-sex sexual activity, but rather to let them pass by, if not unnoticed then unnamed and therefore unpunished, makes sense where same-sex sexual activity, like any sexual

activity outside of marriage, is considered a criminal and therefore punishable offense. For this reason, "don't ask, don't tell"
norms make sense at a practical level, as a strategy to avoid
persecution and prosecution. In North America and Western
Europe, however, the situation is fundamentally different. In
modern Western contexts, the question emerges of the Muslim
population's reactions to the greater acceptability of same-
sex relationships in the broader society. While some Muslim
leaders have been outspoken opponents of "gay rights," a few
Muslim organizations and individuals who avoid addressing
same-sex sexual intimacy from a religious perspective have
come out in favor of tolerance and even acceptance of gays and
lesbians as a matter of civil or human rights. In doing so, they
sometimes make an analogy between discrimination against
Muslims and discrimination against sexual minorities.[43] For
example, the president of the Muslim Canadian Congress
endorsed same-sex marriage legislation in early 2005, declaring that "it is incumbent upon us, as a minority, to stand up in
solidarity with Canada's gays and lesbians despite the fact that
many in our community believe our religion does not condone
homosexuality."[44] Her remarks implicitly distinguish between
Muslims, on the one hand, and gays and lesbians, on the other:
although both are minorities, she does not acknowledge any
potential overlap between the categories. Yet she leaves a space
open for interpretation, claiming not that Islam "does not condone homosexuality," but merely "that many in our community believe" that to be the case.

Muslim discussions of "other people's homosexuality" are
less controversial than intra-Muslim dynamics when some
Muslims desire or adopt a "gay" identity (as opposed to merely
selecting a sexual partner of the same sex).[45] Moderate and
liberal Western Muslim discourses display an acceptance of
the notion of innate sexual orientation but do not question
traditional religious prohibitions of same-sex activity. The
"don't ask, don't tell" philosophy informs views such as those
presented in the Muslim Women's League position paper,
"An Islamic Perspective on Sexuality." In a subsection on
"Homosexuality," it states

Human beings are capable of many forms of sexual expression, orientation and identification. The existence of such variety again is not found in any other species and thus further demonstrates our uniqueness among God's creations. The potential for behavior, such as homosexuality, does not mean that its practice is lawful in the eyes of God. Therefore, individuals are expected to control themselves and not act on their desires if such action is contrary to the guidelines of Islam. Homosexuality, like other forms of sexual relations outside of heterosexual marriage, is thus prohibited.[46]

The statement goes on to imply that individuals should not seek to "prosecute or judge" those known to engage in "prohibited acts"; only conviction through witnessing or confession can allow for "punishment by the State." In the absence of punishment, those who engage in such acts "will then deal with the consequences of their behavior in this life and will be accountable to God on the Day of Judgment. How He ultimately judges is known only by Him." The most obvious aim of this statement is to argue against the imposition of punishments for "homosexuality," but since this is an American group, writing in the United States, the question of punishment is effectively moot. More relevantly, the exhortation not to "prosecute or judge" maintains the fiction of social harmony and adherence to rules by not exposing behavior "contrary to the guidelines of Islam."

In seeking to avoid public acknowledgement of same-sex sexual activity, the Muslim Women's League statement continues the traditional legal stance toward same-sex behavior; in other respects, however, it departs quite dramatically from the classical understanding that governed discourses surrounding same-sex attractions in acknowledging not only the possibility of an exclusively homoerotic "orientation" but also its potentially God-given nature. This view is shared by a number of Muslim groups from across the socio-political spectrum; not only Muslim gays and lesbians seeking a "theological accommodation" of their sexuality, but also some conservative Muslims who strongly oppose any such accommodation, agree on the modern idea that homosexual orientation is an inborn component of the human psyche.[47] The question of whether the innateness of desire requires an acceptance of same-sex sexual activity, however, is subject to strong disagreement.

Conceding the naturalness or God-givenness of an exclusively same-sex oriented desire puts conservative scholars into a logical bind. An essay by British Muslim Abdal-Hakim Murad, "Fall of the Family," exemplifies the perils of this approach. Murad accepts "homosexuality as an innate disposition" in some (though not all) cases, seeing a potential biological basis for it. Yet, like the Muslim Women's League, Murad stresses that there are no circumstances under which an individual with homosexual "tendencies" – which he likens to the impulses of a pyromaniac "mental patient" – can lawfully act on his or her desires. The only religiously acceptable option for someone with a homoerotic orientation is permanent chastity: Murad sees it as a test from God. His stance coincides with the Muslim Women's League statement that "individuals are expected to control themselves." However, this expectation of self-control as a defense against sexual sin runs contrary to what is prescribed not only by most medieval texts, but also by Murad elsewhere in the same essay, which focuses primarily on male–female sexual misconduct. He argues in favor of sex segregation in daily life where practical, to assist in maintaining sexual morality by suppressing opportunities for illicit sex; most individuals, he claims, are not super-moral figures who can reject temptation when freely accessible.[48] (Ironically, he does not consider the effects of sex segregation on those who are exclusively attracted to members of the same sex.) Even in a largely temptation-free society, there must be lawful outlets into which sexual desire can be channeled.[49] For heterosexuals, this lawful channel is marriage, but for those with exclusively homoerotic desires, there can be no lawful satisfaction of desire. (Most medieval Muslim authors did not confront this precise problem, at least insofar as the desire for attractive male youths was generally not considered a desire for them solely; it was the same desire as that directed toward women, and could therefore be sated with lawful partners.)

If one accepts that exclusive desire for partners of the same sex is (at least in some cases) natural and divinely originated, *and* acknowledges, as Murad does, that long-term abstinence from all sexual contact will likely fail for most individuals, then one presumes that most Muslims with orientations toward members of the same sex *will* commit transgressions. The stress on not discussing these sexual acts creates a safe space for transgression to occur without challenging the normative view that such relations are forbidden. At the same time, while such relative freedom to act has some benefits, it also puts individuals in danger from the usual concomitants of illicit liaisons (with partners of whatever sex), including not only the spread of HIV and other sexually transmissible diseases but also the unethical behavior of possibly betraying marriage vows and, indeed, one's self-respect.

The naturalness of same-sex desire for certain individuals constitutes the basic point of departure for queer-positive Muslim organizations. As the Rainbow Crescent website declares, in what is presented as an appeal to "Logic and Reason," "being Gay is not a matter of choice – but rather a divinely created reality." The exclusion of "Gay people" "from Islam ... would be excluding a whole dimension of The Creation and this would in fact undermine any claim by Islam to be The Truth (which it is)."[50] This tactically shrewd position removes the element of choice from the equation; gay (and lesbian) Muslims cannot be blamed for something innate. As intended by some gay-positive Muslim discourses, the acceptance of the view that sexual orientation is not a matter of choice but rather divine decree creates a space for queer Muslims to press for religio-legal acceptance of same-sex relationships, however unlikely widespread acceptance of this view seems as of this writing.

However, aside from the social difficulties such a strategy faces, the "just created that way"[51] discourse of sexual identity is a fundamentally ahistorical move, and requires one to ignore the complex ways in which same-sex desire and practices have operated in other times and places. What accounts for the fact that men's sexual desire for other men in the past – or in non-Western Muslim contexts today – is not viewed as "innate" in the same way? A Foucauldian approach, recognizing the historicity of desire and its representations in social and individual contexts, is attractive for historians and scholars concerned with understanding the past.[52] How does it work, though, to transform the present and shape the future, if one is concerned with determining God's stance on sexual licitness and following it? Jeffrey Weeks argues convincingly for understanding sexual identities as "necessary fictions" and "historical inventions," and themselves "sites of contestation,"[53] but how does this matter to a Muslim concerned with whether God approves of his or her partner choice and form of relationship? Is there a middle ground between essentialist and constructionist views of sexual orientation and desire, where Muslims can grapple with same-sex sexual orientation – their own or that of other Muslims? Is it possible to think that individuals are neither "created" to think and act in a particular way nor do they simply "choose" a homoerotic orientation? What does the view of "the erotic as highly socially malleable"[54] mean when one confronts the Qur'an, which is both a timeless text and a historically contextualized one?

There is broad agreement among Muslim thinkers that individuals bear moral responsibility for any sexual acts that they engage in by free choice and that illicit desires themselves do not result in any culpability before God. If one accepts the view that homoerotic desire is neither freely chosen nor inherently blameworthy, but can have no licit satisfaction, then one is left with the untenable stance that those who desire a satisfaction that cannot be obtained through licit means are, through no fault of their own, destined to choose between a celibate life devoid of sexual gratification and one of sexual release obtained through sin.[55] Both options are unpalatable. One avoids having to choose between these unacceptable alternatives if one rejects either the innateness of homoerotic orientation or the inherent sinfulness of all same-sex intimacy. If one holds that same-sex desire is not innate but rather constitutes freely chosen debauchery (as in the case of the men of Lot's story), then one does not confront the issue of divine injustice in creating individuals without providing the means for them to fulfill lawfully their basic human need for sexual expression.

Yet this notion that an exclusive same-sex sexual attraction is freely chosen is problematic for a variety of reasons, including its lack of conformity with the expressed experience of modern Western queer individuals.

The other alternative is to accept, in contrast to the near totality of Muslim thinkers, that homoerotic desire is innate *and* that its satisfaction through lawful means is possible. This view requires tricky exegetical maneuvering around the male–female dynamics of various Qur'anic verses describing creation and mating,[56] but can be reconciled with the view that same-sex acts become reprehensible or forbidden when, and only when, same-sex intimacy is freely chosen as a transgressive act by those who would ordinarily seek satisfaction with different-sex partners. It is only in this case, where same-sex desire is viewed as not sinful because it is part of a divine plan, that recognition and legitimization of intimate partnerships between same-sex couples becomes an objective.

Murad's terminology proves helpful in thinking about this new perspective. He does not identify those who have or act on same-sex desires as homosexuals, considering private behavior outside the realm of social concern. Rather, he uses the intriguing, if awkward, term "homosexualist," reserving it for those who seek to make same-sex intimacy a publicly respectable form of socio-sexual partnership. In this, he revalidates the conventional view that illicit sexual activity is a matter between an individual and God but that challenges to religio-legal regulations constitute a major transgression. Monogamous marriage between two men or two women, in its insistence that same-sex relationships can be licit, is a more disturbing prospect than multiple casual sexual relationships that, even if they constitute something of an open secret, nonetheless do not directly challenge the prohibition of same-sex intimacy.[57]

Same-sex marriage

Muhammad Abdul-Ra'uf, writing in 1977, declares that "toleration of an evil leads to other evils. First, we condone public exposure [of women's bodies]; next, dating and easy mixing; next, pre-marital 'games', extra-marital relations, and open marriages; next, the elevation of homosexuality to an acceptable moral status; and next, uni-sex marriages. Where, and when, shall we stop?"[58] In this litany of increasingly serious "evils," same-sex marriage is the worst Abdul-Ra'uf can imagine. Yet, aside from the question of what makes it an evil – divine censure being the obvious answer for Abdul-Ra'uf – the notion of relative seriousness of sinful acts is an interesting one to apply to the case of same-sex intimacy. The acts he discusses as "evils" are uniformly consensual acts; there is no mention of rape, sexual abuse of children, or any other inherently coercive practice, such as non-consensual marriage or slave concubinage – practices which would undoubtedly violate his twentieth-century sensibilities, but which were widely accepted by Muslim scholars of preceding centuries.[59] What is it about same-sex marriage that makes it so threatening that it becomes the pinnacle of all sexual sins?

When Abdul-Ra'uf was writing in the 1970s, same-sex marriage was not even on the horizon for nascent gay-rights movements in the West. A few years into the twenty-first century, marriage between persons of the same sex has gained legal standing in several places in Europe and North America, including the U.S. state of Massachusetts. The notion of marriage of a man to a man or of a woman to a woman is completely outside the frame of reference for classical Muslim jurists. Most do not even consider it a possibility in order to dismiss it. Even where it is mentioned, it is merely as a brief disqualification in terms of who can marry. The definition of *nikah* in the *Durr al-Mukhtar*, a seventeenth-century Hanafi commentary on an earlier legal manual, makes a claim regarding gender as relevant to marriage:

> [*Nikah*] according to jurists is a contract which is productive of an exclusive right of enjoyment, i.e., which validates the enjoyment by a man, of a woman, with whom marriage is not prohibited by reason of any legal impediment. Thus are excluded (from the objects of enjoyment)

a male, an idolatress, a hermaphrodite – because of the
possibility of the hermaphrodite's being a male – prohibited females,[60] a *jinnee* woman, and a watery person [*insan
al-ma'*] because of the difference of genus.[61]

This text definitively sees maleness as an impediment to marriage with another male, so much so that hermaphrodites are
forbidden as marriage partners on the grounds that they might
be male. (Note, of course, that this formulation assumes every
individual has one true sex, even if ambiguous genitalia and
secondary sex characteristics make it difficult or impossible to
determine.) Marking it as a text of its time, the text also rejects
marriage between a man and a female spirit (*jinn*) or "a watery
person." Notably, while the gender of the *jinn* is specified as
female – presumably, the prohibition against marriage to a
male applies to the *jinn* as to the human – the prohibition of
marriage to "a watery person" is gender-neutral. It is not the
lack of gender fixity but "the difference of genus" that renders
merpeople unsuitable as marriage partners, apparently.

In Muslim history, the relationship between sex, gender,
and desire is far more complex than simplistic binary regulations would suggest. Rusmir Music, writing of "an essential ambiguity" within Muslim legal categories, argues that
"Islam's jurists repeatedly allow for exceptions, though they
profess to be preserving immutable boundaries ordained by
God." While in some ways these ambiguities should open up
space for a queer project, they do not function in the jurists'
works to create such a flexible system. Rather, "the uncertain-
ties allowed by Islamic jurists, otherwise interested in neatly
ordering all aspects of life, predominantly serve to preserve
a power hierarchy benefiting men."[62] A brief discussion of
classical legal treatment of hermaphrodites and the modern
question of sex-change operations make clear both the room
for accommodations in the Islamic sex/gender system and the
limits to that ambiguity. While there is space for (temporary)
ambiguity in the realm of sex – meaning biological determinations of maleness or femaleness assigned to a particular body
– there is little tolerance for ambiguity in sexuality – that is,

with whom a person of a particular sex may have sexual contact.[63] The connection between bodily sex, socially ascribed gender, and sexual "orientation" is crucial.

Classical and medieval texts accept the existence of cases where assigning sex to a particular body, and therefore gender to a particular person, is not automatic. While a number of tests and tactics allowed for resolution of the question in most such cases, in the stubborn instance of the "problematic hermaphrodite" (*khuntha mushkil*), the jurists failed in their attempts to assign gender to what Paula Sanders calls the "ungendered body." In modern understandings, some jurists adopt a similar framework to justify sex-change operations as not correcting an indeterminacy but rather realigning body with reality – in effect, uncovering the "real" or "true" sex of the person in question. Some progressive scholarship has viewed these operations as a watershed, but the acknowledgement of the existence of transsexuals is not more of a challenge to the standard jurisprudential discourse of sex/gender than that of the hermaphrodite in classical and medieval discourses, nor is a person of ambiguous sex a challenge to the binary system once properly categorized.[64]

The danger from transgendered individuals is less about biological sex than about sexuality and its licit exercise.[65] Some of those who objected to one Egyptian surgery, where Sayyid became Sally – and to her reclassification as a woman – did so on the grounds that the relevant factor was not that of Sally's innate sense of gender but rather of sexual object choice. That is, it was not that Sayyid really was a woman, but that Sayyid wanted to have a woman's body in order to be able (lawfully) to have sex with men.[66] Specifically, she (or rather, he, because in the view of those who opposed the reclassification, there had been no change, only mutilation) "was fundamentally a *khawal*, that is, an effeminate man who is willing to play a passive, female role in sexual intercourse with other men."[67]

Returning to the subject of same-sex marriage, it becomes clear that the impermissibility of formalized same-sex relationships is only partially due to a prohibition on same-sex sexual activity. Same-sex marriage fundamentally challenges the basic structural premises of marriage as a contract. It is not just in the sex *act* that male and female are differentiated, but in the legal control over said act, in the legal right to claim it, in the legal right to form the relationship permitting it. I have shown that the boundaries of licit sex in Islamic jurisprudence – a man with his wife or his own female slave, both of whom are in some sense "owned" – require an exclusive dominion as a correlate of lawful sex. Male owners may have sex with female slaves but not (lawfully) with male slaves, and female owners may not have sexual access to their slaves of either sex. Men are the only ones permitted to be "owners" in this sense, and only women may be "owned." Ultimately, Murad and Abdul-Ra'uf are correct: same-sex marriage represents a more fundamental challenge to norms governing sexuality than does any type of illicit or clandestine union, precisely because viewing such a union as a *marriage* challenges the definition of licitness itself.

The legal structure of Islamic marriage is predicated on a gender-differentiated allocation of interdependent claims, which would be thrown into chaos by a same-sex union. In the standard contractual understanding of marriage, the husband holds *milk al-nikah*, control of the marriage tie, and the wife has a claim to dower and the obligation of sexual exclusivity and availability. Several early jurists considered the possibility of whether these rights and duties could be reallocated – whether a woman could pay a man a dower, for example, and retain control over sex and divorce – and agreed unanimously that such a reallocation is not permitted. Not only are husbands' and wives' rights distinct, but each role is fundamentally linked to the sex/gender of the person exercising it. A woman cannot wield control of the marriage tie; a man cannot be contractually bound to sexual availability to his wife. Thus, following that logic, it would not be possible for one woman to adopt the "husband" role and the other to adopt the "wife" role in the marriage of two women. The self-contained logic of the jurisprudential framework does not permit such an outcome.[68]

Conclusion

Same-sex intimacy cannot be separated from discussion of other topics in sexual ethics because the rules making a same-sex marriage unthinkable emerge not primarily, or at least not exclusively, from an explicit prohibition of same-sex activity but rather through the legal construction of marriage and sexual relationships as both gendered and hierarchical. Many of the same things that would be necessary to make marriages more gender-egalitarian would be necessary precursors to any attempt to think about same-sex partnerships. Of course, this is one reason that some will argue that such attempts to reform marriage do in fact lead inexorably down a slippery slope to same-sex marriage. The measures necessary to reformulate the nexus of marriage in the direction of egalitarian and fully mutual relations between men and women do not remove serious obstacles to the legitimization of same-sex acts, above all the notion that male and female are created to be mates for one another. However, if one sets aside macrocosmic issues, however compelling, and turns to ethical and legal reflection, one must ask whether there is some absolute standard by which same-sex intimacy can be compared to other forms of intimate partnership. Are consensual, exclusive, and long-term same-sex unions morally worse than slave concubinage, or serial marriage and remarriage? Are they worse than abusive marriages?[69] The issue of consent in weighing the ethicalness of certain acts has relevance far beyond the issue of same-sex relationships. The comment made by "an American Muslim" on the Muslim WakeUp comment boards discusses sex outside of marriage. She does not expand her point to same-sex relationships, but others do. She is unable to understand how a consensual adult relationship between a man and a woman if committed to one another could be wrong, even outside of marriage, because she is operating under a fundamentally different logic of licitness than the medieval jurists. Indeed, the jurists saw a consensual relationship between two free men as significantly worse – and deserving of *hadd* punishment for both parties – than a coerced relationship between a man and his male slave.[70] Such

sexual use was not lawful, but the master's ownership sufficiently resembled his ownership of a female slave to give rise
to a legal protection. A recent news report described a Saudi
man who has wed nearly five dozen women and girls in his lifetime (and divorced all but the last four).[71] He has clearly acted
in a legally valid, if reprehensible, manner. However, two men
or two women who live together in a lifelong pseudo-marital
union, remaining faithful, cannot be said to have acted lawfully
according to jurisprudential rules – but have they done something unethical? Is lawfulness a prerequisite, if not a sufficient
guarantor, of ethical behavior? Confronting same-sex sexual
relationships and acts challenges us to define sexual lawfulness
and ethical sex for all intimate partnerships, including those
between men and women.

Coda 5

Entangling gender identity with sexual orientation, this chapter
tries to do many – too many – complicated things. It questions
patriarchal models of marriage yet betrays occasional traces
of a yearning for a romantic affirmation of the macrocosmic
union of male and female.[72] It describes the binary gender categorization of premodern jurists, and the inextricable linkages between issues of sexual ethics in same-sex relationships
and those affecting male–female couples.[73] Even as it critiques
jurists' attempts to affix binary labels to bodies, the chapter uses
now-passé notions of fixed identity and outdated terminology. (Terminology is always in flux and provisional; it speaks
from and to shifting realities.[74]) It omits bisexuality, "a blatant
disturber of neatly gendered models," as does most of the literature published since.[75] Still, its most significant flaw, to my
mind, is that it fails to offer a principled place from which to
begin: the essential dignity and worth of each human being, and
the irrelevance of sex or gender identity to the establishment
and conduct of an ethical relationship.

A decade ago, few publications addressed same-sex desire
and relationships among Muslims. Since this book's appearance,

serious scholarly works on homosexuality, gay identity, lesbian-ism, and transsexuality have appeared. Some are ethnographic, others literary, and still others address the Muslim scriptural, interpretive, and legal tradition. Although the bulk of material still focuses on male same-sex desire and gay identity, there is a growing body of work addressing female same-sex desire and lesbian identity.

Among scholars, one of the most vigorous debates has been over the global influence of Western European and North American models of gay identity. Some argue that they are use-ful and appropriate. Others hold that compulsory homosexuality neither accounts for many Muslims' experiences nor provides a sufficiently transformative ethical ideal.[76] Some scholars suggest that work on gay and lesbian as well as transgender issues lays a foundation for further, more nuanced treatment of a range of other queer sexualities and gender identifications.[77] Perhaps. I know that my omission of bisexuality meant far more than fail-ing to account for the experience of the small fraction of Muslims who identify as bisexual. Any model that must set aside bisexuality or those who identify as gender-queer to work is fatally flawed.

Slowly, a multiplicity of trans, third-gender, and queer iden-tities and orientations is becoming part of scholarly as well as popular discussions. The repertoire of available gender-varia-tion and sexualities has shifted in both subtle and significant ways over time and according to place; one example is the *hijras* in South Asia, who are recognized as a third gender; they are not precisely trans in the way the term is used commonly in Western discourses today; similarly, South-East Asian gender orientations and gender identities are complex.[78] The Iranian government recognizes trans identities, and subsidizes surgi-cal procedures; this acceptance of certain trans identities coex-ists with harsh approaches to same-sex sexual encounters. Of course, neither religio-legal pronouncements nor government regulations exhausts the ways gender identity and same-sex desire have manifested among communities of Muslims in the past or present.[79]

The linkages between same-sex desire, gender identity pluralism, and feminism are complex and shifting. There are obvious points of connection between queer and feminist concerns: both oppose dominant heteropatriarchal norms. Yet their paths often diverge, usually when tactics inadvertently reinforce harmful ideas. Gay men, for instance, often assert or presuppose male privilege. One example is trying to use *mutʿa*, a form of time-limited marriage approved in Jaʿfari Shiʿi jurisprudence and occasionally used by diaspora Sunnis in a manner like informal/unregistered marriage, as a work-around to "traditional" marriage.[80] A few even suggest using slave-concubinage as a model. Using traditional legal rules instrumentally while ignoring their presumptions about women's subordination is, at best, insulting.

In similar fashion, straight feminists benefit from heterosexism. Feminist arguments for gender justice in (monogamous) marriage elevate companionate partnership over hierarchical, patriarchal, potentially polygynous marriage. To do so, they invoke the Prophet's monogamous marriage with Khadija and the Qur'anic version of the Adam and Eve creation story.[81] Endless repetition of narratives of male–female reproductive pairing marginalizes those with same-sex attractions and those who do not seek coupledom at all.

My reference to same-sex attractions deliberately avoids the terms gay and lesbian. This raises, again, the question of what role identity plays in partner selection. Scott Kugle, whose *Homosexuality in Islam* (2010) is the most comprehensive work on the topic to date, stresses that ethical relationships must be "within the constraints of one's internal disposition, which includes sexual orientation and gender identity."[82] Yet I wonder about this emphasis on authentic dispositions. If an ethical relationship depends on something besides the sex or gender of its participants, why the need to fix orientation and identity?

As a colleague pointed out, there are "people who at least sometimes engage in same-sex sexual acts but do not regard this as having any implications for their sexual orientation."[83] Contemporary Muslims' practices may parallel or diverge from classical Muslim assumptions that men would desire attractive male youths. The persistence of, for instance, "men who have sex with men" (a public health category meant to sidestep tricky questions about sexual orientation/identification) in numerous contexts troubles attempts to classify individuals into neat categories. At the same time, when a man exclusively attracted to and sexually involved with men chooses to marry a woman, in some cases having been counseled by religious thinkers that this is an appropriate course of action, without disclosing his same-sex attractions and involvements to his wife, his actions (and those of the pastoral figures advising him) are at the very least unethical. "Reparative" or "conversion" therapy has been disavowed by reputable organizations and many religious congregations. The notion that marriage to a woman will somehow fix a man's sexual orientation is both wrongheaded and devastating to those involved.

At the same time, pressures toward marriage are very real, and where marriage is the primary way of constituting a life-world, exclusion from marriage – same-sex or otherwise – poses barriers to human fulfillment. What does ethical mean in a world where social recognition and state recognition may or may not overlap? What does it mean when needs and desires for romance, sex, and love are intertwined in complicated ways, both ideologically and practically, with economic (inter)dependence and government benefits? Where do the individual and the familial, the personal and the social, converge and diverge? And what does it mean when the social models available for discussing identity and orientation are shifting rapidly?

Other orientations and relationship structures apart from same-sex partnership also challenge male–female monogamous pairing. I discuss polygyny in Coda 2. Another, seldom discussed, is asexuality, the absence of sexual attraction, which often involves aversion to sex and romance.[84] Lack of desire is nothing new; premodern scholars such as al-Ghazali recognized it as among those characteristics that should lead a man to abstain from marriage. (Scholars less frequently considered female desire, or its lack. Gender-differentiated expectations surrounding sex in marriage constrain asexual females more than asexual males.[85]) Some Sufis considered celibacy preferable, certainly for those whose inclinations led away from sex.[86]

Yet while lack of interest in sex has long been recognized as a characteristic of some people's natures; asexuality as an *orientation* emerges in the wake of the centrality of sexuality to human self-fashioning. Attempts to broaden discussion of mating and pairing to include same-sex couples may reinscribe romantic/ sexual coupledom as a norm, further marginalizing asexuals.[87]

To consider same-sex relationships afresh requires a historicization of heterosexuality. Though heterosexual acts are obviously as old as humanity, "heterosexual culture," especially the centrality of the (married) couple, is neither timeless nor universal.[88] Its prominence among many (though not all) Muslims, particularly educated, urban, "modern" Muslims, is an artifact partly of a shared history with the West. So is the view of male and female as "opposite" sexes who are "naturally" (and exclusively) attracted to one another.[89] Viewing sexuality as an essential part of one's identity is likewise modern. Modern doesn't mean bad, inauthentic, or unreal. It does mean that both the ubiquity of monogamous coupledom and the centrality of sexuality to one's identity are open to interrogation.

One critique raised of attempts to formulate a "sexually sensitive" or "homosexual-friendly" jurisprudence is its effort at "stabilising and 'normalising' sexual relations in the mould of modern Western tastes, as a loving relationship between two parties which is essentially monogamous."[90] Or, put differently, "The attempt to rearticulate queer sexuality in terms of heteronormative institutions ... is an effort towards conformity with the 'normal' and dominant discourse."[91] Similar critiques of marriage equality initiatives have been raised in American contexts, with critics questioning not only monogamy but also the bourgeois, patriarchal nature of marriage, as well as the way it "permits an extension of institutional power into spheres of intimacy that we reasonably might wish to keep as free as possible from intervention. Institutional recognition of intimate relations is always a double-edged sword, in that it legitimates one kind of relationship at the expense of others."[92] As with polygyny, there are crucial questions about the protective as well as invasive aspects of state regulation of sexual partnerships between adults. (As this book goes to press, the

U.S. Supreme Court has ruled that states may not ban same-sex marriage. Marriage equality is now American law.)

Farid Esack and Nadeem Mahomed argue that "to establish and endorse a concrete way of entering and maintaining same-sex sexual relations via religious law curtails the religious person's sexual conduct. It legitimises by restricting the sociality of the body, or the sexual queer self."[93] Of course it does. Law, religious or secular, "curtails ... sexual conduct," by recognizing some relations and not others as licit. To argue that there should be no regulation of sex marks a much more fundamental departure from religious law than to suggest that this law could be reformulated to accommodate same-sex marriage.

Accommodating (formal or informal) same-sex marriage among Muslims, where marriage remains the sole broadly accepted context for sexual intimacy, requires as a matter of politics a justification of same-sex relationships. Gay and lesbian Muslims continue, as a tactical necessity, to explain their sexual orientations as God-given and immutable; trans people in a variety of contexts are also likely to have to explain their innate gender identities to gain family, community, or even government support. The very need to explain how someone got to be a certain way already presumes that there is a need for explanation, that the person is second-best. No one asks a "straight" man to explain how he became attracted to women or a cisgender woman, whose biological attributes and external gender presentation are in alignment, how she decided she was female.

However pragmatically required, appeal to an ahistorical, essential gay, lesbian, or trans identity ("created that way") as a justification excludes bisexuals, who can simply "choose" only heteroerotic pairings; it also marginalizes those with more complicated or fluid queer identities, though it does not necessarily exclude those who identify as asexual or trans. (Whether the category of the *mukhannath*, or effeminate, should be understood in terms of gender identity, sexual orientation, or both remains – perhaps fittingly – ambiguous.[94])

Still, for all its shortcomings, the "created that way" notion corresponds to many individuals' "felt sense" of sexual orientation (as well as gender identity). Bridging inner conviction of an innate identity with historical and cultural variation requires a nuanced notion of social construction. Ideas about sexuality and embodiment that arise in particular cultures at particular times – or in transnational, global, Internet-mediated discourses – have effects. Gayle Salamon writes, "Social construction must not be construed oppositionally to a 'felt sense' of bodily being, for one can contend both that a body is socially constructed and that its felt sense is undeniable. What social construction offers is a way to understand *how* that felt sense arises, in all its historical and cultural variations, with all its urgency and immediacy, and to ask what it is, finally, that is delivered by that felt sense."[95] This is not only a question to be asked by people who identify as lesbian, bi, gender-fluid, or as members of other non-dominant sexual or gender groups. Rather, it is also vital to think about how heterosexual identity, maleness, and femaleness arise and come to be felt as obvious and innate.

A historical account of how certain felt senses come to be can help us to think more capaciously and creatively about the present and future. By "reading prior homoerotic systems as if they were proto-instantiations of modern homosexual ones [one loses] not only a sense of the historical distinctiveness of earlier ways of conceptualizing relations between erotic practices, self-fashionings, and classifications but also a rich feel for the instabilities of those only apparently homogenous and coherent modern sex and gender systems to which we succeed."[96] So, too, with prior heteroerotic systems in relation to modern heterosexual ones: male–female marriage in the U.S. today implies something quite different about "straight" sexuality than ancient Greek marriage did; contemporary asexuality is not the same thing as medieval monastic celibacy, even if a cloistered nun may have chosen a sex-free life. In the last decade the presumed homogeneity and coherence of "modern sex and gender systems" has become less obvious. Plurality of norms and forms, of orientations and identities, both within communities and across the globe, will likely only increase. Whatever forms of relationship Muslims engage in, the task is to ensure that long-term partnerships, erotic entanglements of shorter duration, and loving relationships both sexual and platonic contribute to, rather than detract from, human flourishing. For that flourishing to be not just worldly but afterworldly as well, those relationships must be acceptable in the sight of God; what I and others propose is that in thinking about God's guidance for human interactions, we think less about the *who* and more about the *how* of ethical relations.

6 "Reduce but do not destroy": Female "Circumcision" in Islamic Sources

"I as Imam would like, with my colleagues, to turn to the Islamic world, particularly in Africa, and inform people that female genital mutilation is prohibited. It is a matter of abuse and violation of the female body and is quite clearly forbidden according to Islam."
Swedish Muslim leader Sheikh Omar Ahmed, November 2003[1]

"Circumcision is obligatory for every male and female. [For men,] it consists of cutting the foreskin of the glans of the penis, while female circumcision consists in cutting the clitoris and is called reduction."
Reliance of the Traveller, classic Shafi'i legal manual[2]

Who determines whether a particular practice is Islamic? Is it God, via the literal words of the Qur'an? The Prophet and, secondarily, his Companions, as their statements and actions have been recorded in books of *hadith*? Should such determinations be based on the judgment of the religiously trained scholars, the 'ulama, who interpret these sources in works of exegesis and jurisprudence? Or perhaps what is Islamic might be better identified with the actual practice of Muslims rather than any normative ideal. In that case, what happens when practices vary dramatically among Muslims, or when what Muslims do contravenes the authoritative texts? When views have shifted over time, do earlier ideals or practices have more weight or does the contemporary state of affairs take precedence? Much of the confusion and imprecision in Muslim and non-Muslim discussions of controversial issues results from a lack of clarity about the scope of the claims made.

The two epigraphs to this chapter make seemingly contradictory claims about female genital cutting. The classical
legal text calls it circumcision and pronounces it "obligatory,"
while the contemporary *imam* calls it mutilation and declares
it "forbidden." This chapter will explore why these divergent
views exist, how they are expressed, and why they matter for
the majority of Muslims who are from regions where female
genital cutting, or FGC, is not practiced. I tackle this subject
with some trepidation, as I am not an expert either on FGC or
on those regions of the Muslim world where forms of excision
are most frequently practiced. Given the history of resistance
and legitimate resentment surrounding Western intervention
on this issue, I want to make clear that, while I ardently support
the ultimate eradication of all forms of female genital cutting
on a variety of grounds, I am not attempting to set myself up as
an authority as to how reform should best be achieved; women
and their male allies from regions where FGC is practiced must
be at the forefront of any movement for change.[3] I have chosen to address the topic here as a case study of how religious
sources and authority are marshalled and manipulated, and to
illustrate how the demands of scholarship and advocacy can
clash.

Although undoubtedly well meant, Shaikh Omar Ahmed's
claim to present the definitive Islamic view on what he terms
"female genital mutilation" fits into patterns of modern legal
authoritarianism, as described by Abou El Fadl. It also dove-
tails with an apologetic discourse that pervades much Muslim
English-language discussion of the subject. This stance results
in, among other things, misleading translations of key terms
and passages from legal and hadith texts even in otherwise
scholarly works. The evasion and misdirection surrounding
the textual basis for acceptance or rejection of female genital cutting is due to desire to combat negative stereotypes of
Muslims as well as to abolish the practice itself. At stake is who
has the right to decide what counts as normative for Muslims,
and what authority, if any, the determinations of the classical
jurists, who treated female circumcision approvingly, should
have today.

There are solid reasons for Muslims to reject female genital cutting without making grandiose claims about its "un-Islamic" nature, but such an approach requires a willingness to treat not only jurisprudence but also *sunnah* and hadith as products of their time, with limited currency as formal rules for contemporary application. Thorough and honest discussions of controversial practices such as female genital cutting must move beyond simplistic binaries of "Islamic" and "un-Islamic" or lawful/prohibited to a more complex scheme of ethical and moral valuation. Engaging with the complexities of the tradition is worthwhile in issues of sexual ethics far beyond the matter of excision. Nonetheless, although it is all well and good to proclaim the need for greater sophistication in methodological approaches to understanding the relationship between religious and customary practices, for those concerned with practical reforms, sweeping claims about "Islam"'s forbidding of female genital mutilation (FGM) may be more effective than detailed investigation of the layered jurisprudential treatment of the subject.

Islamic or un-Islamic?

The debate over whether or not female circumcision is "Islamic" is a specifically modern way of framing the question, although the relevance of Islamic legal categorizations to Muslim life is ages-old.[4] The "Islamic-ness" of excision is relevant to ongoing controversies because internal Muslim debates occur in a context of Western scrutiny and criticism. Externally motivated attempts to stop all female genital cutting began with European colonial officials and have continued through the efforts of Western feminists and some missionaries. (Notably, at the time Westerners were beginning to campaign against FGC in Africa, clitoridectomy was being selectively practiced in Britain and the United States as a cure for various female ailments.) The desire to combat stereotypes of Islam as uniquely misogynist is the primary motivation for many to argue that FGC is not an "Islamic" practice. Noor Kassamali, a physician with clinical expertise as well as activist credentials in the struggle against what she prefers to call female genital cutting, suggests that the "alleged association of Islam with FGC" by "the Western media" is "an even more basic issue" than whether it is "Islamic" or not. She argues that the portrayal of the practice "as a violent custom whose aim is to subjugate women and girls ... perpetuates the stereotype of Islam as a violent faith and of Muslim women as subjugated and submissive."[5] This outwardly focused critique reflects a set of power relationships that often does stand in the way of an honest scrutiny of Muslim practices.[6] At the same time, it is naïve to expect Muslims to be entirely unconcerned with dehumanizing stereotypes when the resultant Othering of Muslims contributes to the devaluation of Muslim lives and serves as justification for violence and repressive international policies.

In any case, female genital cutting is neither universal among nor exclusive to Muslims. The majority of Muslims do not practice any form of female circumcision and where it is common, it is generally performed by members of all religious groups; in Egypt, for instance, both Muslims and Christians practice female genital cutting. Kassamali notes that "Muslim groups that practice this custom often cite religious justifications ... [y]et religion is not a determining factor."[7] The severity of the practice – which varies considerably – depends on variables of locale, educational attainment, and socio-economic status, rather than religious affiliation.[8] In the majority of Muslim societies, by contrast, female circumcision is virtually unknown. In those regions where it is practiced, it almost always predates Islamization.[9] Exceptions occur in instances where immigrant groups carried the practice with them to new areas.[10] In South-East Asia, female circumcision seems to have been unknown before the coming of Islam; in Malaysia and Indonesia, only Muslims practice female circumcision. One can speculate that the transfer of the practice to this region is due to the historical pre-eminence of the Shafi'i law school there. The Shafi'is, unlike the other Sunni schools, have held that circumcision is obligatory for females as well as males, as the passage quoted at the beginning of this chapter demonstrates.

Several typologies describing female genital cutting differentiate between less and more severe procedures.[11] The least invasive procedure falling under the rubric would be the removal of the prepuce or hood of the clitoris, effectively analogous to the removal of the penile foreskin that constitutes male circumcision. This delicate operation – clitoridotomy, but sometimes erroneously called clitoridectomy – is rare, especially in Africa, and, in any event, is extremely difficult to perform on small girls where it can be difficult to distinguish between the clitoris and its prepuce. Clitoridectomy more properly refers to full or partial excision of the clitoris itself; this procedure may or may not involve removal of part or all of the labia minora. The most drastic form of genital cutting is infibulation, where not only the clitoris and labia minora but also portions of the labia majora are removed, and the vaginal orifice sewn closed, with only a small aperture left for the release of urine and menstrual fluid. Often known as the "pharonic" circumcision, it is common in certain parts of Africa such as the Sudan. The final type of "circumcision" escapes the name FGC, because in many cases it involves only a symbolic pricking, rubbing, or scraping.[12] This type seems to be most common in South-East Asia, although it has been advocated and implemented occasionally elsewhere, including in Africa, as an interim measure in the struggle toward eradication.

Beyond combating stereotypes, the desire to eradicate female genital cutting is the second, and more compelling, reason for denying it normative status. Sheikh Ahmed's statement, perhaps inadvertently, heeds an appeal issued by activist Asma A'Haleem several years earlier for "a final religious announcement clearly stating that [female circumcision] is a form of mutilation and therefore forbidden. It is not sufficient for religion to shun female circumcision. Religion should be used as a tool for condemning and preventing its occurrence."[13] A'Haleem's statement raises crucial questions about how Muslim thinkers are to engage in public discourse, and if it is ever acceptable or even ultimately productive to engage in methodologically problematic oversimplifications for strategic aims, if the alternative is not being able to affect oppressive social and cultural practices.

The instrumental use of religion promoted by A'Haleem returns us to contests over the meaning of the term "Islamic." One definition would hold that Islamic can be properly used as an adjective to describe anything that significant numbers of Muslims do. If this were the only salient definition, then FGC could reasonably be called Islamic on these grounds, at least for certain regions of the Muslim world. However, this definition lacks rigor: many Muslims do, in fact, drink alcohol despite its clear prohibition in scripture and jurisprudence. Another level of definition reserves the term for a practice that is defined by its practitioners as religious: Muslims who drink alcohol would not dream of suggesting such a practice is permitted, let alone encouraged or mandated, by their religion, but those Muslims who practice female genital cutting often justify it with reference to Islam. Opponents of the practice seek to undercut this rationale when they insist that "FGM is a practice of culture, not religion."[14]

FGC, however, is not merely a customary practice incorrectly understood as having religious authority despite its lack of sanction in authoritative scholarly sources. Rather, female circumcision of some type is either recommended or required by the dominant classical view of all Sunni schools of Islamic jurisprudence, and seems to have been generally approved by Shi'i jurists as well.[15] Jonathan Berkey surveys the legal literature, and demonstrates that although jurists' opinions "differ[ed] in nuance" they "were overwhelmingly favorable to the practice of female excision."[16] A number of modern jurists have suggested the question is open to re-examination. These include Egyptian scholars Shaikh Tantawi of al-Azhar, who has suggested that it is an appropriate question for medical doctors to decide, and Muhammad al-Ghazali, who noted that there is no account of the Prophet having his daughters circumcised.[17] Yet other members of the 'ulama support it as either *sunnah* or, in the words of Egyptian jurist Gad al-Haq 'Ali's fatwa, "a laudable practice that does honor to the women."[18] Thus, a blanket denial, such as that by Sheikh Ahmed, that "Islam" permits FGC is patently false and obscures the very real status of some type of circumcision for women as an accepted practice according to traditional jurisprudence, even if the majority of Muslims reject FGC as abhorrent and do not practice it.

A further evaluation of the Swedish leader's words leads to questions of terminology. Is he being deliberately evasive, implicitly accepting "circumcision" while explicitly condemning "mutilation"? The context in which he made his remarks, at a conference opposed to FGC, suggests otherwise. His adoption of the terminology of mutilation used by the practice's opponents makes his position very clear. Islamic legal texts, such as that by Ibn Naqib al-Misri and 'Umar Barakat quoted above, use the neutral/positive term *khitan*, circumcision, to describe the procedures carried out on both males and females, noting that *khifad*, "reduction" or "lowering," is the proper term for the latter. This terminology, along with the occasional use of "*tahara*" (purification, also used for both male and female circumcision), carries a specifically religious resonance, although the manual is devoid of explicitly religious appeals to its audience. By contrast, Sheikh Ahmed makes explicit appeals to religion, referring to his religious title ("I as Imam"), his target audience ("the Islamic world"), and the basis for his verdict ("quite clearly forbidden according to Islam").

This declaration, which demonstrates the type of authoritarianism that Abou El Fadl has so forcefully critiqued, is representative rather than unique.[19] Rather than acknowledging the traditional legal view but critiquing its bases or conclusions, those opponents of female circumcision who invoke religion as support for their position simply bypass it while claiming their own position as "Islamic." They may invoke, as evidence for the stance that Islam forbids FGC, the absence of Qur'anic statement on female circumcision and the lack of any "authentic" hadith supporting it. I will address the Qur'anic point here, and turn to the hadith sources below. A reductive definition of "Islamic," characteristic of some feminist and reformist thought, equates the Qur'an with Islam. One implication of this view is that Qur'anic silence on a particular point means that there is no valid religious authority for it. Thus, because stoning as punishment for *zina* appears only in the hadith and not in the Qur'an, stoning may be understood as an illegitimate cultural practice rather than a religiously mandated penalty. When it comes to FGC, many opponents point out that there is no Qur'anic mention of female circumcision.[20] The power for this argument is limited in the realm of circumcision, however; for one thing, the Qur'an does not make explicit mention of male circumcision either. Most who have argued against female circumcision on these grounds would not likewise present male circumcision as being un-Islamic based on the lack of Qur'anic references to it.

Other arguments speak to questions of principle rather than from Qur'anic silence. Although a number of anthropologists have recently begun to consider the ways in which some women's understanding of FGC relies on deeply ingrained notions about female beauty and gender dimorphism, most scholarship has shown that practices of, and justifications for, FGC relate to male control over female sexuality.[21] However, the linkage between FGC and female sexual interest works both ways: opponents have argued for the practice's impermissibility precisely on the grounds of wives' sexual rights; because it prevents women from achieving sexual satisfaction, "the position of these religious leaders is not only contrary to the Prophet's teaching but also the Qur'an."[22] Likewise, the Muslim Women's League position paper on Sexuality argues that "the practice of clitoridectomy ... is totally un-Islamic because it is in direct violation of both Qur'an and hadith which clearly stress the importance of sexual satisfaction for both husband and wife."[23]

Others have taken a more holistic approach, arguing for the sanctity of the body from a spiritual rather than a medical perspective. How could the jurists accept clitoral excision when they rejected "changing God's creation" (*taghyir khalq Allah*) by tattooing, plucking hairs, or filing the front teeth to create an attractive gap between them? Egyptian physician and feminist Nawal el-Saadawi argues forcefully that excision of the clitoris is a violation of the divine plan for the human body: "God does not create the organs of the body haphazardly without a plan. It is not possible that He should have created the clitoris in a woman's body only in order that it be cut off at an early stage in life."[24] The usefulness of this argument for activists, however, is significantly lessened by the fact that the same case could be made about the male foreskin, the removal of which is virtually universally accepted as a religious duty.[25] However, one can make a strong case for rejecting female circumcision based on the severity of its consequences compared to male circumcision – medical complications, including pain, infection, and secondary infertility, as well as diminished sexual response. The "changing God's creation" argument only works with those who, like Sami Aldeeb Abu-Sahlieh, also object to male circumcision. And as he acknowledges, "Male circumcision is considered to be obligatory by all Muslims. Contrary to female circumcision, it is still unimaginable, till today, that this practice could be prohibited in Muslim countries."[26] This unambiguously positive presentation of male circumcision in Muslim law and tradition can serve to highlight the persistent uncertainty and unease surrounding female circumcision, an unease manifested in the hadith sources to which I now turn.[27]

"Reduce but do not destroy"

On what sources and using what reasoning did the jurists arrive at their conclusions that female circumcision was, at the least, a meritorious act? The scant evidence concerning female circumcision centers on a few hadith found in collections other than those of Bukhari and Muslim. The most important is this report, collected by Abu Dawud:

> A woman used to perform circumcision in Medina. The Prophet (peace be upon him) said to her: "Do not cut severely as that is better for a woman and more desirable for a husband."[28]

La tunhiki, which Ahmad Hasan translates as "do not cut severely," might be more literally rendered "do not ruin" or "do not uproot." Although Abu Dawud reports this hadith, he criticizes its transmission and calls it weak. Another hadith, also classified as weak, states that *khitan*, circumcision, is a *sunnah* for men and a *makruma* (noble act) for women. Other evidence for early approval of female circumcision is less direct – unwitting rather than deliberate – and perhaps therefore more persuasive. One famous hadith declares that both partners in a sexual act must perform an ablution (to restore ritual purity before prayer) "when the two circumcised parts (*al-khitanan*) meet." It is possible to explain this away as a linguistic peculiarity of classical Arabic, according to some: the less dominant part (the female organ) is subsumed under the characterization of the more dominant part (the male organ).[29] A more likely explanation is that genital cutting was practiced on some women in seventh-century Arabia.[30] The use of "large-clitorised" as an insult (suggesting that the woman in question had not been circumcised), or reference to a man's mother as a "clitoris-cutter" assumes the existence of the phenomenon. There are also references to female circumcisers in other contexts that certainly suggest some form of clitoral excision was an accepted, if not necessarily universal, practice among some Arab tribes at the time of the Prophet.

Opponents of FGC have dealt with the circumcision hadith texts in various ways. Some scholars and activists have pointed out that the isolated hadith texts that exist on the subject are weak (e.g., *mursal* – missing a link in the chain of transmitters), and thus unreliable as evidence, a point which even supporters of the practice generally concede.[31] Alternately, or additionally, they are interpreted as recommending moderation of an existing practice, not the imposition of something unknown, a point to which I will return. In no case do the hadith convey obligation. In contemporary English-language texts, misleading summaries or translations of the Abu Dawud hadith ("Do not cut severely") often do much of the work of interpretation. To take one example, a pamphlet distributed by Minaret of Freedom and also available online quotes the hadith, explaining it as "one tradition of disputed authenticity [which] permits (but does not encourage) the removal of a miniscule segment of skin from the female prepuce, provided no harm is done."[32] The explanation of the command "do not ruin" as "removal of a miniscule segment of skin from the female prepuce" is reading a great deal into the vague words attributed to the Prophet.

Jamal Badawi, in an appendix to his well-known and frequently quoted *Gender Equity and Islam*, attempts to make similar points by interpolating several words into his own English translation suggesting specific directives that are missing from the Arabic: "Cut off only the foreskin (outer fold of skin over the clitoris; the prepuce) but do not cut off deeply (i.e. the clitoris itself), for this is brighter for the face (of the girl) and more favorable with the husband."[33] Although the Arabic text (which Badawi does not provide) does not specify what part of the anatomy is mentioned, Badawi does so himself. He defines what is to be cut ("the foreskin," "the outer fold of skin," "the prepuce") and, more importantly, what is not to be ("the clitoris itself"). As in the previous pamphlet, Badawi's objective is not to clarify for individual Muslims how they should conduct their personal affairs but rather to present Islam in a positive light to both non-Muslim and Muslim readers who may be uncomfortable with what they have heard, read, or been told about various controversial matters.

Keller's objective in his translation of *Reliance of the Traveller* is somewhat different from that of the authors just discussed, as the text is primarily a conduct manual rather than a contribution to a broader controversial literature, and he is dealing with jurisprudential doctrine rather than a Prophet statement. Nonetheless, he makes similar changes to his English rendering of the passage that I translated, in the epigraph to this chapter, as "Circumcision is obligatory for every male and female. [For men,] it consists of cutting the foreskin of the glans of the penis, while female circumcision consists in cutting the clitoris and is called reduction." For comparison, his translation (which involves several levels of elaboration of the text, utilizing coded letters and parentheses to indicate commentary) reads:

Circumcision is obligatory (O: for both men and women.
For men it consists of removing the prepuce from the
penis, and for women removing the prepuce (Ar: bazr)
of the clitoris (n: not the clitoris itself, as some mistakenly
assert). (A: Hanbalis hold that circumcision of women is
not obligatory but sunna, while Hanafis consider it a mere
courtesy to the husband.)[)]

Only the first three words of this passage ("Circumcision is
obligatory") belong to Ibn Naqib al-Misri; the words introduced by "O:" represent the commentary of 'Umar Barakat,
who is responsible for much of the content of Keller's *Reliance*.
The explanation of the less onerous requirements of the Hanbali
and Hanafi schools, introduced by "A:", is the commentary of
a modern Syrian scholar. Only rarely, with particularly sensitive matters or those on which there is striking disagreement
between the legal schools, does Keller typically include such
material. The inclusion of these qualifications here functions
to diminish the reader's perception of the place of female circumcision within religious law. The most important feature of
this translation, however, is the definition of female circumcision with Keller's own parenthetical definition (introduced by
"n") of the crucial term *bazr*.

In his translation, Keller attempts to describe the two types
of circumcision in entirely parallel ways, which requires him
to omit certain words from the discussion of male circumcision and add words to the description of female circumcision.
The Arabic text indicates that circumcision of males requires
"qata'a al-jilda alati 'ala hashfat al-dhakar," which Keller renders as "removing the prepuce from the penis." *Qata'a*, which
he renders as "removing," I have translated, above, as "cutting"
so as to preserve the potential for ambiguity in the description
of the circumcision procedure for females, although "removing" – cutting off – is the most likely meaning. The rest of the
Arabic is straightforward: *al-jilda* ("the prepuce," skin, or foreskin) which is on the glans (*hashfat*) of the penis (*al-dhakar*).
Keller's English text presents slightly less information in its
description of the male anatomy; while the Arabic refers to the

penile glans, his translation simply refers to the penis. When it comes to female circumcision, Keller departs from the text more significantly by adding a key term. He renders "qata'a al-bazr" as "removing the prepuce of the clitoris," treating *bazr* as a term specifically for the clitoral hood or prepuce. (Keller does not indicate what other term might mean clitoris, if *bazr* does not.) The vast majority of scholars, however, take for granted that *bazr* means clitoris, not clitoral prepuce.[34]

The insistence of Keller, Badawi, and others on minimizing the extent of cutting recommended or required by the Prophet's words and/or the classical legal tradition can only succeed via well-meaning but deceitful manipulation of the texts. Would it not be a better alternative, if one accepts the hadith texts, to accept that previous approval even by the Prophet, but certainly by the classical jurists, need not preclude rejection today? To some extent these sources can prove helpful, as both hadith and legal texts seek to minimize the scope of cutting performed, and not to impose a new practice or render existing custom more severe.[35]

Those activists who struggle against FGC in contexts such as Egypt and the Sudan, where some members of the 'ulama have sided with the practice's opponents, have used a variety of strategies to argue for its prohibition. Many acknowledge, as a precondition for an open and honest dialogue, that some form of female circumcision has been justified in religious terms, and attempt to discern how to present an honest, compelling argument for significant modification of the realm of what is understood to be properly Islamic. Gradualism is one vital strategy; Toubia argues that, while "the ideal goal would be total eradication" as an interim measure "recommending alternative customs is necessary." She suggests perhaps "a ritual of just nicking the clitoris or labia without excising any tissue" because "the transition from infibulation to no procedure is so drastic that few will be comfortable with it."[36] However, the extent to which this will be satisfactory is unclear; research done by Rogaia Abusharaf in the Sudan suggests that while some women are strong advocates of "sunnah" circumcision (here meaning clitoral excision, not merely a "ritual nicking") to replace the standard infibulation, others do not consider the milder cutting to be "real" circumcision.[37] In any case, in these instances scholars and activists are concerned with convincing the women who perpetuate the practice, not with affecting Western perceptions.

Conclusion

One promising avenue for change is from within the legal tradition, but there are limits to the impact the 'ulama can have on the practice of FGC. Some scholars have begun the process of attempting to shift the frame of reference and treat female circumcision as a medical procedure, as activists have suggested,[38] rather than a religious ritual and marker of Muslim identity. In doing so, they have suggested a different set of standards by which to judge associated practices. Shaykh al-Tantawi, stating that the Qur'an contains nothing on the subject and that the hadith attributing any stance to the Prophet are weak, opines that therefore one should defer to the views of doctors. On medical grounds, of course, the "surgery" fails basic qualifications for performance. Egyptian jurist Gad al-Haq, among others, however, objects to this approach on the grounds that medical knowledge is continuously changing and evolving, and it is foolish to foresake what is eternal for what is ephemeral.[39] While the 'ulama can be instrumental in struggles to eradicate FGC, there will likely always be dispute among its members. Further, relying on internal struggles within the 'ulama or even campaigns to ban FGC legally (as an Egyptian law did before it was overturned) ignores the crucial point that formal religious authority may not be the most salient ground for both practitioners and those who make decisions about following the practice, who are uniformly female, even though religious sentiment is influential.

What tactics should be employed by activists, and what role should religion play as a justification? Activist A'Haleem's appeal for a "final religious announcement" against FGC relies on a mistaken view of Islamic religious authority as something unidirectional and static. Pronouncements in this vein, such as that by Swedish Sheikh Ahmed, suppress rather than promote interpretive leeway. A historically contextualized approach – which recognizes the likelihood that the practice existed but also that it is deeply troubling in many respects – can support a process of gradual change. Although based on a tendentious presentation of the hadith text, the Minaret of Freedom's broader conclusion that the Prophet's directive as quoted in Abu Dawud "clearly forbids severity in circumcision and bases such limitation on both the potential to harm the woman and the potential to make her less desirable to her husband" seems more appropriate (though "forbids" might be replaced by "advises against"). The pamphlet argues, though, that "permitting such a ritual constitutes an act of tolerance by Islamic law for pre-Islamic practices, and may be overruled by the Islamic prohibition against harmful acts."[40] Both of these points are potentially helpful. One can think of female genital cutting as something subject to gradual change and, as Kevin Reinhart has pointed out, it can be liberating to think in terms of principles rather than specifics. Nonetheless, caution is warranted in claiming a power to "overrule" accepted practices on the basis of broad principles.

Changes in public policy and national law without concomitant changes in public opinion are futile, and potentially even counterproductive. Reform in legal thought is slow, and is not a guaranteed success. There will likely always be those, such as Egyptian scholar Gad al-Haq, who will vehemently support female circumcision. Both legal and jurisprudential reform are, I believe, necessary. But ultimately, the most crucial shift must take place in public opinion. And in order for such a shift to happen, religious language will need to be employed. However, I think that on this issue in particular – and the lesson can be applied more broadly – the simplistic invocation of "Islam" is a recipe for failure. The insistence that Islam forbids FGC is not so much false as meaningless: it depends entirely on what one intends by the term "Islam." The texts, as is frequently noted, do *not* speak for themselves, though I do think it is possible to read them in ways that yield a determination that any form of female genital cutting is reprehensible at best and that extreme forms such as infibulation must be forbidden. How does one marshal ethico-legal arguments that will be couched in terms of reprehensibility, of minimization of a customary practice? Rather than ask whether or not female circumcision is Islamic, it is more helpful to ask what legal or ethical values should be assigned to the range of practices that fall under the rubric of FGC. And indeed, if one determines that such practices are reprehensible or forbidden – verdicts for which I think there is a great deal of justification in the texts – then one must attempt to discern the best way to combat their performance. At the same time, it can be difficult to resist the temptation to make totalizing claims based on one's own sense of justice, particularly when debates are not merely theoretical but result in real injury to real women and girls.

Coda 6

This chapter raises but does not truly address questions about medicalization and ethical decision making. Medicalization refers to the ways medical professionals come to exercise authority, often over women's bodies. When it comes to female genital cutting, some have assumed that the involvement of doctors or other trained professionals, using hospitals, will improve hygiene, reduce complications, and potentially minimize the severity of any cutting. These, at least, have been rationales offered for taking the procedure out of the hands of local women. Yet, as a footnote to the chapter observes, there can be unexpected, unintended consequences of such a change. In Indonesia, having medical professionals involved has meant that instead of a ritual scraping or pricking, neonatal female "circumcision" performed in hospitals uses a cutting implement and thereby becomes a more severe operation. Additionally, whatever its practical effects, the involvement of medical professionals legitimizes the practice; in Egypt, more than three-fourths of FGC occurs in medical facilities or involves medical practitioners.[41]

At the same time as there are reasons to be skeptical of medicalization as a panacea for the worst aspects of FGC, there are benefits to medical knowledge and public health research. Doctors have been among the practice's opponents, as the chapter mentions, and some jurists have called on this knowledge as a reason to avoid FGC. Empirical data can make plain the effects of FGC on women's sexual function and health. Ethical decision making depends on understanding the tangible effects of particular practices. Knowing that infibulation causes greatly increased maternal death rates, for instance, provides grounds for appealing to the principle that avoiding harm (to women's lives and health) takes precedence over securing benefits (whatever blessing goes along with circumcision). Specialized knowledge is a vital corrective to reasoning about current social issues, including those affecting women's lives, based only on theoretical ideals. But it is a mistake to treat medical knowledge as unproblematically "objective." Medical knowledge about women's bodies is culturally constructed, and in a variety of times and places the substitution of male doctors for wise women and midwives has not been a total victory for female well-being.

Involvement of medical professionals, then, brings contradictory considerations that may illuminate the more general question of collaboration between religious scholars and other professionals for decision making about Muslim life in a vastly changed world. Tariq Ramadan has framed this as a matter of collaboration between text scholars (religious professionals) and context scholars.[42] He argues that one must bring scientists and social scientists as well as other professionals with subject-matter knowledge into conversations about Muslim ethics. Such conversations would, indeed, remedy the scenario of jurists with no knowledge of contemporary medical practice pronouncing on bioethical issues such as brain death or assisted reproductive technology. Yet in his model, contextual knowledge is treated as having no particular moral valence; it is always subject to the appropriating, hegemonic practice of the text scholars.

Is there a way out of the impasse? One vital step is to think with and theorize female experience.[43] Women's experience is – women's experiences are – diverse, multiple, plural. Any woman's story is a mix of deeply individual moments and culturally inflected, not to say determined, circumstances. Female experience is neither static nor universal. Women do not all want the same things. And yet, common concerns arise, if only from the near-universal fact of women's bodies and female sexuality being subject to greater scrutiny and surveillance than men's bodies and male sexuality. Sometimes, in Muslim contexts, female virginity and chastity are prized above women's and girls' full humanity. Yet FGC is not always only about sexual control. Women in places where genital cutting is practiced may stress beautification and sexual dimorphism, or maturity and social roles.[44] Among those who believe that religious doctrine requires FGC (a position I have sought to debunk in this chapter), questions about individual wishes are largely irrelevant.

One reason, though far from the only one, that female genital cutting is so widely reviled among Western opponents is that it stands as an intolerable assault on liberal-individualist notions of bodily autonomy. The notion of the body as one's own property has two important corollaries. First, one has the right to modify it how one chooses, including by tattooing or scarification. One may also donate one's organs and have elective plastic surgery. Notably, in the decade since this book first appeared genital surgery has risen dramatically among white American women. The ubiquity of pornography, including a preference for pubic hair removal (not previously a mainstream American practice), has raised new concerns about labial size, symmetry, and plumpness. One might also ask whether breast augmentation surgery should be considered alongside other forms of female beautification surgeries as patriarchally motivated surgical intervention on otherwise healthy women; we might call it self-inflicted rather than freely chosen. Psychoanalyst Susie Orbach has suggested that "bodily transformation is no longer linked to social ritual within the family but is part of the individual's response to wanting to produce what is an acceptable body."[45]

Second, the converse of the rule that one may modify one's own body by choice is that no one else has the right to modify it without one's consent. Thus, not only is circumcision of minor girls unacceptable in this view, but so are mutilating punishments such as amputation or lashing. (Neonatal male circumcision, once nearly universally accepted among non-Jewish American men, has become contested in recent years, but as a relatively normalized practice, it does not tend to provoke the visceral reaction that cutting associated with Others does.)

FGM, the term most opponents prefer, stands alongside honor killings and death by stoning as a symbol of Muslim barbarity. Those who would critique from within Islam are caught between the desire to oppose harmful, oppressive practices and the desire not to contribute to the further dehumanization of Muslims as imagined by non-Muslims with geopolitical power. Hence, the frequent refrain that Islam is not the problem, but Muslims who only imperfectly practice a perfect faith. This is a problematic framing for a number of reasons.

From the perspective of Religious Studies, my academic discipline, the idea is not to determine what is or is not legitimately Islamic but rather to explore contests over legitimacy and authority. How do various actors present their claims? What arguments and sources do they use? How do these differ from how other claims have been pressed in the past?[46] This book, and in particular this chapter, asks these questions. More specifically, it questions the strategies for claiming authority of those with whose objective (ending female genital cutting) I am in sympathy.

Though I view my job as a scholar as primarily one of questioning and analyzing rather than pronouncing and persuading, I *do* have normative beliefs, some stemming from religious commitment, some stemming from (to my mind compatible) feminist commitments. As someone actively engaged in confessional ethical discourses – thinking, writing, and speaking as a Muslim to try to convince other Muslims to consider certain ideas – I object to the simplistic invocation of an Islamic versus Muslim dichotomy, in which Islamic=pristinely religious, and Muslim=what Muslims actually do. Informed, no doubt, by my academic training, I am unable to perceive "Islam" as merely what a certain group of purportedly orthodox scholars say it is; given my normative beliefs, I am unable to say Islam is only what Muslims do. Juliane Hammer addresses a related problem in her discussion of work on domestic violence, Islamic studies, and normativity. As scholars, we must be committed to understanding the ways in which scriptural texts and legal thought have been invoked and contested on the question of male violence toward women. As human beings, we must object to this violence and seek to eradicate it.[47]

One thing that remains clear is the impossibility of monolithic global solutions to questions of violence against women, including FGC. Just as the etiology of genital cutting differs from place to place, and time to time, community to community, so too must movements to eradicate it. Reforms imposed from outside nearly always do more harm than good. As Norma Moruzzi suggests, "the challenge is to develop a culturally respectful, emphatically feminist approach to FGC that will foster solidarity rather than preclude it."[48] Writing on an unrelated topic, Tim Dean suggests that "a culture's right to enact consensual harm on some of its members is complicated by the question of whether one culture has the right to impose its values on another." He argues that outside "intervention commits symbolic violence in order to forestall physical violence." It is certainly overstating the case to suggest that Muslim religious life is "organized around" FGC, and unlikely in many cases that it meets the definition of "sacred ritual" that Dean uses, though in some communities it has a (diminishing) cultural centrality.[49] The question of whether physical harm is *consensual* likewise remains dubious, though when cutting is performed at or after puberty, the situation differs from when it is performed on babies or small girls. Dean acknowledges, too, that one may encounter "a clash of values ... within a culture."[50] The salient point is the trade off of physical violence and symbolic violence. This point is also raised by Farid Esack about interpretations of the Qur'an, in the chapter which follows.

7 "If you have touched women": Female Bodies and Male Agency in the Qur'an

O ye who believe! Approach not prayers with a mind befogged, until ye can understand all that ye say, – nor in a state of ceremonial impurity (Except when travelling on the road), until after washing your whole body. If ye are ill, or on a journey, or one of you cometh from offices of nature, or ye have been in contact with women, and ye find no water, then take for yourselves clean sand or earth, and rub therewith your faces and hands. For Allah doth blot out sins and forgive again and again.
Qur'an, Surah 4, verse 43[1]

Two brief sentences in a verse discussing observance of the dawn-to-dusk Ramadan fast succinctly capture much of what is essential about marriage and sex in the Qur'an: "Lawful for you on the nights of the fasts is the approach to your wives. They are garments for you and you are garments for them."[2] First, and most obviously, sex between spouses is not opposed to spiritual practice – in this case, fasting – but exists as a complement and a supplement to it. Second, and a point much remarked on by contemporary interpreters,[3] there is an undeniable reciprocity in the marital relationship; a husband is a garment for his wife just as a wife is a garment for her husband. Third, and much less often acknowledged, there is a basic asymmetry in God's speech here: God is speaking to men, about women. In this verse, as in numerous others that treat the relationship between spouses or refer to women's bodies in sexual contexts, men are the "you" and women are the "they."[4] This androcentrism is not equivalent to misogyny, but neither is it unproblematic for interpreters concerned with matters of gender and justice.[5]

Since the Qur'an is the primary mode of divine guidance to humanity as well as the basis for so much Muslim thought, any attempt to formulate an ethics of sex and intimacy must engage with the revealed text. Recent interpretations of the Qur'an have tackled many important topics related to women and gender, but few have explicitly dealt with the verses discussing sex. In this chapter, I argue that close attention to those Qur'anic verses that discuss sex can provide a new lens through which to engage in feminist exegesis. Qur'anic rules are gender-differentiated in intimate and familial matters above all, with men seemingly given greater rights and responsibilities. Recent works by a number of gender-conscious scholars have shown the extent to which standard exegetical treatments of these issues have been shaped by interpreters' presuppositions about male dominance and superiority. At the same time, feminist attempts to approach the question of male marital and familial authority have not attempted to disaggregate the issues surrounding marriage, divorce, and sex. Despite the way quite a number of verses on all topics are directed *to* men *about* women, I suggest that there is often a difference in content and tone between those focusing on marriage and divorce on the one hand, and those discussing sexual intimacy on the other. The former usually direct men to allow women particular freedoms; the latter do not contain similar directives, but rather only command men to behave in particular ways. Even those verses that posit men as having greater agency and control in intimate relationships, though, situate all human actions as being directly subject to divine scrutiny, which implies a higher ethical standard alluded to by, but not explicitly presented in, the Qur'anic text.

To whom am I speaking?

As Amina Wadud has shown, God does not always speak to a specifically male audience; indeed, such treatment is the exception rather than the rule. Yet because Arabic, like French and Hebrew, relies on gendered nouns, readers of the Qur'an must pay close attention to the content and context of each verse to determine whether particular passages are gender-specific or gender-neutral. Many Qur'anic verses address women and men together using the gender-neutral terms "human being" or "people" (*insan, nas*). These words are often poorly translated into English as "man," "mankind," or "men."[6] Part of the reason that these terms have often been rendered in this way is that these words take masculine pronouns in Arabic, but the gender of nouns is only sometimes indicative of the gender associated with the signified object. To insist that because *insan* takes a masculine pronoun it refers to a male person is untenable; logic would also then dictate that *nafs* (self or soul), which takes a feminine pronoun, would necessarily refer to a female, making the first creation female rather than male (as Muslim interpretation generally, although not universally, holds) or of unspecified gender, as some premodern commentators and a number of contemporary scholars have argued.[7]

The structure of Arabic plural forms can make it especially difficult to determine whether a gendered meaning is intended. Only exclusively female groups can be referred to with the feminine plural, while both exclusively male groups and groups including both males and females must be referred to with the masculine plural.[8] A Muslim man is a *muslim* while a Muslim woman is a *muslimah*. A group of Muslim women is *muslimat*; a group of Muslim men is *muslimun*. A group that includes both men and women is also *muslimun*.[9] Thus, when a collective noun such as *muslimun* appears in the Qur'an, it cannot be assumed that it only refers to men. In most cases, *muslimun* and similar collective plurals refer to all Muslims, male and female.

In some instances, though, a particular collective noun clearly refers specifically to males, as it is accompanied by its exclusively feminine counterpart. This tendency is most clearly illustrated in Surah 33, verse 35:

Muslim men (*muslimin*) and Muslim women (*muslimat*), believing men and believing women, devoutly obedient men and devoutly obedient women, truthful men and truthful women, patient men and patient women, humble

men and humble women, charitable men and charitable
women, men who fast and women who fast, men who
protect their chastity and women who protect their chastity, and men who remember God frequently and women
who remember God frequently, God has prepared for
them forgiveness and a great reward.

This verse describes men and women separately but in parallel fashion that makes absolutely clear their spiritual equality.
Though an equivalent meaning could have been conveyed by
the use of these terms in the masculine inclusive plural, the
separate references to men and women emphasize both the
inclusiveness of the revelation and the sameness of divine
reward to members of both sexes. The latter point is explicit in
other verses such as "And whoever does good deeds, whether
male or female, and is a believer, will enter Paradise and not be
wronged in the least."[10] The word "believer" appears here in the
male singular due to grammatical convention,[11] but the meaning is clear: God will reward males and females alike according to their deeds. Interpreters intent on proving male–female
equality in the Qur'anic message frequently quote these and
similar verses as proof of women's equality with men.[12]

On other occasions, the separate treatment of men and
women in the Qur'an indicates a lack of sameness. Regulatory
verses discussing matters such as witnessing and inheritance
explicitly differentiate between males and females. When witnessing certain types of commercial contracts, Surah 2, verse
282 declares that one can employ two men, or one man and
two women "So that if one of them errs, the other can remind
her."[13] When dividing inheritance between children of a decedent, Surah 4, verse 11 states that a male gets twice the portion
of a female, a ratio that also holds for a number of other cases.[14]
Difference, in these instances, involves obvious inequality,[15]
though whether this inequality constitutes injustice is a separate and more complicated issue.

The clear Qur'anic declarations of sameness and the equally
clear Qur'anic acceptance of inequality based upon differentiation must be understood in the context of an ever-present

tension in the Qur'an between egalitarianism and hierarchy, which exists not only with regard to the sexes but also when it comes to matters such as wealth or slavery.[16] Although the Qur'an famously insists that all people are equals before God and the only distinguishing criterion is piety, other verses acknowledge and seemingly authorize disparities in treatment based on freedom or gender.[17] Not only are some abstract rules meant to apply differently, as in the cases of witnessing and inheritance, but hierarchies of power in the interrelationships between individuals are accepted as a matter of course.[18] As Barbara Stowasser succinctly sums up, "the Qur'an does not associate its principle of equal human dignity and worthiness with notions such as absolute and individual social, political, or economic equality."[19]

Male–female relations embody both norms of ultimate sameness and earthly differentiation. One common line of argument suggests that while men and women are ontologically equal as human creations, they are not meant to be socially equal in the life of this world. Revelation is seen to justify social differentiation, either because of an assumed male superiority or, in the twentieth century, a more palatable view of male and female complementarity.[20] Asma Barlas acknowledges, but swiftly dismisses, the argument that one can "distinguish between religious and social/legal equality" in her *"Believing Women" in Islam: Unreading Patriarchal Interpretations of the Qur'an.*[21] In rejecting this division, Barlas must attempt to explain away numerous verses that suggest or command differential treatment for males and females. (She does so in part by making the sound point that difference is not always unequal.) Others have argued, persuasively, that the Qur'an does present such a distinction, but that the ontological equality of all human beings takes precedence over the earthly, temporally bound regulations that privilege men over women, as in inheritance and witnessing. Thus, specific regulations which are discriminatory toward women need not apply always, or in every context.

Feminist or gender-conscious interpretation of the Qur'an, a discipline still in its infancy despite some paradigm-altering scholarship, has tended to focus much of its attention on the issue of power as wielded in intimate relationships.[22] How, scholars have attempted to discern, can one reconcile the Qur'an's basic stance that Muslim women are first and foremost Muslims, the religious equals of men,[23] with the notion expressed in Surah 4, verse 34 that men are "*qawwamun 'ala*" ("bread-earners," "maintainers," "protectors and maintainers," "the managers of the affairs of," "in charge of," "have authority over," or "shall take full care of" women?)[24] Even within a single verse, such as Surah 2, verse 228, there can be a tension between the notion that women have rights "similar to" or "just as" or even perhaps "equal to" (*mithl*) those of men, but that "men have a degree over them." Both verses are crucial for those concerned with gender equality or equity, and the ways that they have been treated illustrate both the significant insights of feminist scholarship as well as the limitations of certain approaches to the Qur'an.

A difficult verse

Traditional scholars and contemporary Muslims from a variety of backgrounds and perspectives have interpreted Surah 4, verse 34. While classical and medieval interpretations of this verse stress female obedience and male authority, recent interpretations tend to emphasize the financial component of men's marital duties and the limits on a husband's power over his wife.[25] Many Muslims have gravitated toward the latter views, in keeping with modern discourses of complementarity rather than hierarchy, and fitting with the Qur'anic portrayal of women in other verses as full human beings and partners in the relationship of marriage. The range of ways in which this verse's key provisions have been interpreted illustrates both the presence of androcentrism and misogyny in some aspects of the Muslim tradition as well as possibilities for more egalitarian readings of scripture.

This verse presents numerous difficulties for translation, since so many of the words have contested meanings. My provisional rendering here leaves three terms in the original Arabic since they cannot be translated without taking a position on how they should be interpreted.

> Men are *qawwamun* in relation to women, according to what God has favored some over others and according to what they spend from their wealth. Righteous women are *qanitat*, guarding the unseen according to what God has guarded. Those [women] whose *nushuz* you fear, admonish them, and abandon them in bed, and strike them. If they obey you, do not pursue a strategy against them. Indeed, God is Exalted, Great.[26]

Interpreters from a variety of perspectives have addressed the key issues raised by this verse: are men "in charge" of women? What are the characteristics of righteous women? What is *nushuz* and what are its consequences? Is the command to "strike them," that is, women, to be taken literally?

This verse begins with the declaration that "men are *qawwamun* in relation to women." The word *qawwamun* (singular, *qawwam*) derives from the Arabic term for standing. It signifies one who "stands over" or "stands up for," thus potentially encompassing both authority and responsibility. These dual elements were recognized by classical commentators on this verse who attributed men's role as *qawwamun* to both divine favor of men in general over women in general ("according to what God has favored some over others") and to husbands' financial responsibility for paying dower and maintenance to their wives ("according to what they spend from their wealth"). Some commentators devoted more attention to male "perfection" and female "deficiency" than to men's financial obligations, while others acknowledged male superiority as a given but stressed a husband's duty to support his wife.

Progressive interpretations contest the notion that men are inherently superior to women. Some argue that while the verse can indeed be taken to refer to favoring men over women, this favor is only in the limited realm of the greater inheritances men receive (possibly alluded to in the immediately preceding verses). These interpreters see this connection in the next clause

of Surah 4, verse 34, which refers to men's financial responsibilities ("and according to what they spend from their wealth").
Other interpreters stress that the Qur'an only states that "God
has favored some over others" (or "one over the other") not
that men are favored over women; there is no grammatical
reason for taking men as the "some" and women as the "others." Thus, the verse might refer to some men being privileged
over other men, thereby differing in the amount of wealth they
use to maintain the women for whom they are *qawwamun*.[27]
Regardless of the specifics, the most important element in
rereadings of this verse is the focus on male support of women.
If men are *qawwamun* in part "because of what" (one possible
translation of *bi ma* along with "according to what")[28] they
spend on women, then their role is dependent on their exercise
of financial responsibility. If men no longer support women,
then they lose any resultant authority. Thus, in a family where
both husband and wife contribute to the household expenses,
the husband would not be the wife's *qawwam*.

After giving one very broad statement about men and women,
the verse turns to a specific category of women, the "righteous
women" (*al-salihat*), defining them in two ways: as *hafizat
li'l-ghayb*, women who guard or protect what is absent or
unseen, and as *qanitat*, a term that can mean obedient, subservient, or deferential. Commentators disagree on how to interpret the phrase "*hafizat li'l-ghayb*," particularly in conjunction
with *bi ma hafiza Allah*, according to, or with, or because of
what God has guarded or protected. Based on a widely quoted
hadith, most commentators suggest that these women are
those who, in the absence of their husbands, protect their own
chastity and their husbands' possessions. Progressive and feminist interpreters, however, have tended to interpret "those who
guard what is unseen" as those who fulfill their religious obligations and protect their faith, as God has guarded it.

Classical and reformist interpretations of *qanitat* also
diverge sharply. *Qanitat* is the feminine plural of *qanit*,
meaning one who is obedient, subservient, or deferential, one
who demonstrates *qunut*, from the same Arabic root (*q-n-t*).
Medieval commentators often reduce *qunut* in this context

to a woman's obedience to her husband. However, the term *qanit(at)* is used elsewhere in the Qur'an only for obedience to God and God's Messenger. 'Abdullah Yusuf Ali renders it as "devoutly obedient," in his translation of this verse, just as he does where the Qur'an applies the term to men and women alike in Surah 33, verse 35, which includes "devoutly obedient men (*qanitin*) and devoutly obedient women (*qanitat*)" among the list of those who will be rewarded by God. The Qur'an also refers to exceptional figures such as Mary and Abraham with the term *qanit*.[29] There is thus no reason for considering the use of the term in Surah 4, verse 34 to refer to anything other than women's obedience and devotion to God. In fact, interpreting *qanitat* in terms of obedience to the husband is particularly problematic, given the way that the Qur'an treats obedience to human beings and human authorities (with the exception of the Prophet) as generally significantly less worthy than obedience to God.[30]

There is, however, some type of disjunction between deference to God and the misbehavior discussed in the latter portion of the verse. The root of the word *nushuz* (*n-sh-z*) refers to rising. Most medieval Qur'an commentators understand women's *nushuz* as disobedience or rebelliousness (*isyan*) toward their husbands. Two behaviors repeatedly mentioned as forms of *nushuz* are leaving the marital home without permission and refusing the husband's sexual overtures. More rarely, disrespectfulness, "lewdness," or failure to perform religious obligations are mentioned as forms of female *nushuz*.[31] A woman who commits *nushuz* is referred to as *nashiz* or *nashiza*. Men can also commit *nushuz*, but the term is understood differently in that case.

Contemporary interpreters differ somewhat in their interpretation of *nushuz*, whether on the wife's part or the husband's. Generally, they view *nushuz* as a type of marital disharmony, arising on the part of either husband or wife, or lewd conduct, falling short of adultery, on the part of either spouse.[32] When a woman commits *nushuz*, past generations of authorities have generally agreed on measures that the husband may use. In addition to those sanctioned by the Qur'an, discussed below, jurists generally agree that a man may suspend his wife's support (*nafaqa*) if she refuses him and/or leaves home, since she has made herself unavailable to him.

Moroccan feminist Fatima Mernissi argues that *nushuz* is conceptually central to the Islamic gender system. "*Nushuz* is a Qur'anic concept; it means the rebellion of the wife against her Muslim husband's authority," she writes. "The Qur'an only refers to *nushuz* in order to describe the punishment a husband must inflict upon the wife in case she rebels."[33] Mernissi elaborates elsewhere: "*[N]ushuz* refers specifically to the wife's rebellious tendencies toward her husband in an area where female obedience is vital: sexuality. The Qur'an calls *nushuz* the wife's decision not to comply with her husband's desire to have intercourse."[34] Mernissi is mistaken in her assertion that the Qur'an explicitly defines *nushuz* in this way and in her claim that the term only appears in the Qur'an with reference to a wife's behavior, but she is substantially correct in her characterization of how the classical and medieval scholars understood the wife's *nushuz*.[35]

The Qur'an also discusses a husband's *nushuz* in Surah 4. As in verse 34, the Qur'anic passage on men's *nushuz* (verse 128) appears near other verses discussing marital discord: "If a woman fears *nushuz* or rejection (*i'rad*) from her husband, there is no blame on them if they come to a settlement, and settlement is better, even though people's souls are stingy." Interpreters generally agree on the definition of, and remedies for, men's *nushuz*. Most hold that the husband's *nushuz* is his dislike of, or aversion toward, his wife. Some accounts hold that this verse was revealed in the case of a husband who came to dislike his wife because of her advancing age or some other factor. Some state that this man was Rafi' b. Khadij, who had married a young bride and favored her over his wife of many years. Other accounts suggest that it was revealed about the Prophet and his wife Sawda. In either case, the exegetes and jurists agree that the "settlement" the Qur'an refers to consists in the wife giving up certain marital rights, as both Rafi'-'s wife and Sawda eventually did, as a means of inducing her husband not to divorce her.

While most defined the husband's *nushuz* as dislike of a wife, a minority held that the husband's *nushuz* was his maltreatment of his wife. Specifically, frequent or excessive violence, including striking her in the face, constituted *nushuz*, in this view. (This interpretation has increased in popularity in modern times.) This condemnation of a husband physically harming his wife stands in contrast to the generally accepted view that he may strike her under certain circumstances. The three measures given in Surah 4, verse 34 to be taken in cases where men fear female *nushuz* are "admonish them, and abandon them in bed, and strike them." The verb *daraba*, "to strike," is commonly translated in this context as "hit," "beat," or "scourge," though two recent translations have rendered the word as "spank."[36] The verb appears numerous times in the Qur'an with other meanings, leading some to question why it must be understood as striking in this context. One translator has proposed that *daraba* in this context does not mean strike, but rather "separate" or even "have sex with" (a metaphorical meaning attributed to the same Arabic root).[37] Commentators have broadly agreed, though, that the term is meant literally, not metaphorically, and that the verse gives permission for a husband to strike his wife for *nushuz*, although only if admonition and abandonment in bed have had no effect.

There are several layers to the problem of interpretations raised by these two verses discussing *nushuz*. It is clear that medieval interpreters were guided by certain unflattering presumptions about female nature in their discussions of righteous women and marital obedience. Further, the treatment of male and female *nushuz* as unrelated phenomena, part of the atomistic verse-by-verse approach that Fazlur Rahman criticizes, misses a vital connection between the two, something modern commentators such as Sayyid Qutb have remedied to a certain extent.[38] Yet simply noting that the Qur'an treats both male and female *nushuz* as problems does not automatically absolve the Qur'an of preferring the male over the female in this respect. That is to say, the consequences for female *nushuz* – even if *nushuz* is understood as antipathy or high-handedness, which can rightly be attributed to either spouse – do not merely differ

in the interpretations of the exegetes, but are clearly differentiated in the text of the Qur'an itself.

How, then, can one approach the Qur'an in a gender-
conscious manner, neither accepting patriarchal premises nor
falling into what Farid Esack refers to as "simplistic apologia"?
The challenges facing feminist exegetes can be clearly seen in a
comparison of two essays on Islam from the volume *What Men
Owe to Women: Voices from the World's Religions.*[39] One, by
Esack, challenges much conventional reformist wisdom about
the Qur'an's treatment of women and gender relations. The
other, by Asghar Ali Engineer, exemplifies the most common
modernist way of dealing with the issues involved, including a
significant proportion of apologetic. Their essays center largely
on Surah 2, verse 228 (the "degree" verse) and Surah 4, verse
34 ("Men are *qawwamun*"), notoriously difficult verses for
exegetes concerned with gender justice and equality. Though
women constitute the majority of contemporary scholars concerned with these problems, the similarities and differences in
this pair of essays by male scholars exemplify both the promise
and peril of particular approaches to the matters at hand.

Indicative of his unwillingness to grapple with particularly
thorny problems, Engineer omits all reference to men's "degree
over" women when he quotes from Surah 2, verse 228. He presents only the first portion of the verse, which he translates "The
rights of the wives (with regard to their husbands) are equal
to the (husbands') rights with regard to them ..."[40] A more
literal translation of this phrase would have, "To them (fem.
plural) like due from them (fem. plural) [according to what is
proper]."[41] Admittedly, this rendering is too vague to be satisfactory for those reading in English only; Engineer justifiably
adds in the notion of rights and duties (*haqq*) which, while not
present in the Arabic text, is clearly implied. Nonetheless, his
use of the term "equal" without any qualifiers or alternatives
is misleading. Still more disingenuously, Engineer substitutes
an ellipsis for the second portion of the verse which declares:
"and men have a degree over them (fem. pl.)."[42] His omission
of this clause is particularly problematic given that he uses this
verse, in tandem with Surah 33, verse 35 ("For Muslim men

and Muslim women ..."), as evidence for both justice and equality. According to Engineer, "Both of these verses leave no doubt that gender justice is highly crucial to Qur'anic teachings. These verses also make it abundantly clear that gender justice cannot be realized without gender equality."[43]

Engineer's dual assertion that gender equality is a necessary component of gender justice, and that both equality and justice are found in Surah 2, verse 228, is only rendered plausible by his manipulation of the Qur'anic text. By omitting the "degree" portion of the verse, Engineer avoids the stereotype of Muslim women as irremediably oppressed and without rights. However, to anyone familiar with the verse or who pursues the matter further, Engineer's tactic appears as a blatant attempt to hide what the Qur'an says, as if that is the only way Muslim women's rights could be affirmed. Engineer is not the only author to bypass the troublesome notion of a "degree"; non-Muslim Islamicist John Esposito, for example, gives a similarly partial quotation of the verse in *Women in Muslim Family Law*.[44] Of course, some authors – both non-Muslim polemicists and Muslims seeking to affirm male familial authority – take the opposite tack, only quoting the portion of the verse where the degree is mentioned, leaving off the description of the woman as a moral personality with both rights and obligations.[45]

More nuanced explorations of the "degree verse" by other commentators acknowledge the existence of the degree but limit its scope to the immediate Qur'anic context of divorce.[46] In granting men the additional authority to pronounce or take back divorces, "the Qur'an recognizes men as the locus of power and authority in actually existing patriarchies,"[47] but does not otherwise stipulate a husband's superiority in marriage. (Divorce is, in fact, a realm in which Qur'anic verses clearly accept or confer greater power for husbands in relation to their wives. Female responsibility to act also appears in this verse, which expresses a command regarding their action – "Divorced women shall wait concerning themselves for three [menstrual][48] cycles" – but does so in a way that makes clear women's legal passivity, referring to them as women who have been divorced.) The Qur'an's declaration in this verse that "their husbands have more right to take them back in that period if they (masc./inclusive plural) wish for reconciliation"[49] has been plausibly construed to refer to the "degree" mentioned in the verse.

The specifics of the Qur'an's regulations cannot be understood in isolation from their historical context, but how precisely that context is to serve later readers is open to debate. Engineer places himself in an ultimately untenable position: he insists, on the one hand, that the Qur'an affirms the equality of men and women, yet acknowledges, on the other, that there are "situational constraints"[50] governing the Qur'an, meaning that particular verses may not always demonstrate this equality. According to Engineer, "Scriptures both reflect the given situation and also transcend it."[51] There are both "normative" and "contextual" verses in the Qur'an.[52] *Ijtihad* – defined by Engineer as "exerting oneself to solve newly arising problems if no precise guidance was available in the Qur'an and in the Prophet's Sunnah"[53] – was to play a major role in transforming modern understandings of verses that seem unfair to women today. Ironically, Engineer blames earlier scholars for deviating from the "normative" message of the Qur'an by putting their individual interpretation on its verses, while asserting that contemporary scholars should exercise the same type of *ijtihad*.

Esack, in an article that focuses on Surah 4, verse 34, agrees with Engineer and other scholars that interpretation of the Qur'anic text has always played a significant role in determining how its verses have been understood and implemented. He notes key verses where the Qur'an advocates gender justice, including a more accurately translated but similarly truncated version of the degree verse.[54] Where he moves against the grain of Muslim feminist and reformist discourse on the Qur'an is in his assertion that it is impossible to place all blame for the difference and inequality in interpretations of the Qur'an on its interpreters. Considering himself "a Muslim with a passionate commitment to both the Qur'an and to gender justice," he recognizes that these can be "seemingly conflictual voices."[55] Esack makes the crucial point that interpreters of the Qur'an must grapple with its androcentrism in addressing certain rev-elations to men; indeed "The Qur'an's essential audience is males. ... [Women] are essentially subjects being dealt with – however kindly – rather than being directly addressed."[56]

Esack discusses Surah 4, verse 34 as a prime example of a verse presupposing male listeners; it also assumes male physical control of women. The provisions outlining measures to be taken in case of women's *nushuz* – or, more exactly, in case of men's fear of female *nushuz* – are addressed to a male audience, in sharp contrast to the way that women's different options in the face of a husband's *nushuz* are discussed in Surah 4, verse 128, where both men and women are discussed in the third person. Esack demonstrates that while classical commentaries oversimplify the matter of women's devotion to God and obedience to husbands, modern apologetics and feminist analyses frequently overlook the very clear authority delegated to men over women's bodies.

Garments for one another

In Surah 2, verse 228, positing that men have a degree over women (or that husbands have a degree over their wives), men and women are spoken of in reciprocal but unequal terms – but they are both spoken *of*. In both Surah 4, verse 34, the "striking" verse, and Surah 2, verse 187, the "garment" verse, women are spoken *of*, but men are spoken *to*.[57] This commonality between these two verses is all the more noteworthy given that the clause so frequently quoted from the latter refers to a reciprocal and mutual relationship between spouses, while the former presumes (or commands) hierarchical and gender differentiated spousal interactions. I will consider the garment verse in its entirety below, but here I want to suggest that the Qur'anic mode of address is not in itself sufficient to classify the contents of particular verses. The Qur'anic text repeatedly refers to women as a "them" who must be dealt with by men, who are its implicit or explicit addressees, with regard to matters associated with sex, women's bodies, and conduct in intimate relationships. Yet not all of these verses addressed to men about women endorse customs and rules supporting male dominance.

Verses addressed (in the second person) to men discussing women (in the third person) may or may not assume or advocate women's legal or social passivity, though the very mode of address presumes a privileged position for men as the audience for divine guidance. The extensive discussions of divorce and widowhood surrounding the "degree" verse in Surah 2 take the male as the hearer ("you") and the female as the subject or object of the revelation ("they"), but do so in order to promote women's liberty. Examples include Surah 2, verse 232 ("When you have divorced women and they [fem. plural] have reached their term"), verse 234 ("When any of you die leaving wives, they [fem. plural] are to wait on their own account"), and verse 240 ("And those of you who die leaving wives"). Though these verses are addressed to a male audience, it is not the males who are being tasked with obligations and granted agency. The women of whom God speaks are passive in the sense of *being* divorced or widowed (though one may presume a man leaving a widow did not do so intentionally), yet the crucial information conveyed in these verses is female freedom to act independently in the aftermath of a marriage's termination. Even though men, not women, are the recipients of the commands, these regulations promote women's right or duty to act – especially since, in the case of widowhood, husbands are only the addressees in a theoretical sense.

Similar injunctions in other verses, such as those stressing that the choice to remain married or to separate should be mutual, promote the relaxation of male marital and familial controls on women. The use of the dual form in relevant contexts makes clear that both spouses are intended, as in Surah 4, verse 130 ("if they [dual] separate"). A series of statements in Surah 2, verses 229–30 addresses both male and female feelings.[58] Even Surah 2, verse 230, which depicts the male action of divorce as unilateral, does not dismiss female agency entirely, presenting the woman as the active party in another marriage. (This stands in contrast to Surah 2, verse 221 where men marry and women, in the passive voice, are married.) Further, any possible reunion between two spouses after divorce appears as a mutual action, based on a mutual ability to observe God's limits.

Amina Wadud and Asma Barlas have argued that the places where the Qur'an addresses men *qua* men respond to the practical exigencies of an extant patriarchy – specifically, that of seventh-century Arabia.[59] This explanation accounts satisfactorily for discussions such as those about divorce or widowhood, and consent to marriage; commands that men fulfill obligations toward women but allow them independent action suggest a trajectory away from male familial domination and control, if not a complete rejection of patriarchy. With regard to sexual intimacy, though, this interpretation is less convincing. In a number of verses concerned with sex, women are spoken about and men are spoken to in a way that presumes male control and is unconnected with ameliorative measures intended to restrict men's scope of action or enlarge that assigned to women.

A number of considerations arise when the "garment" verse is considered in its entirety:

> Lawful for you on the nights of the fasts is the approach to your wives. They (fem. pl.) are garments for you and you are garments for them. God knows that you used to cheat yourselves, and [God] turned to you and forgave you. So now be intimate with them (*bashiruhunna*, fem. pl.) and pursue what God has written for you. And eat and drink until the white thread becomes distinct from the black thread, from the dawn, then fast completely until night. And do not be intimate with them (fem. pl.) when you are in retreat in the mosque. Those are the limits ordained by God, so do not approach them. Thus does God make signs clear to humanity, that they may be conscientious.[60]

This verse speaks to men about pursuing or abstaining from intimacy with women. Despite the address to men, there does not seem to be anything inherently gender-specific in the commands. The regulations with regard to fasting are universally taken to apply equally to male and female Muslims.[61] Perhaps, then, not only the regulations surrounding eating and drinking but also those pertaining to sex should be read as non-gender differentiated; clearly, the description of spouses as "garments" for one another is equally applicable to both sexes.[62] Moreover, there is no indication that the human consciousness of divine guidance that is counseled at the end of the verse should be limited to men. Nonetheless, the verse clearly presumes male initiation of sexual activity ("Lawful for you … is the approach") and male restraint from initiating sex when impermissible ("do not be intimate with them then").

Another passage presumes a level of male control over the intimate relationship between a couple that even more clearly assigns a dominant role to men in the sexual decision making process, with regard to both initiation of sex and sexual positions. Surah 2, verses 222–23 declares:

> They ask you about menstruation. Say, It is a hurt (*adhan*), so keep away from women during menstruation and do not approach them until they become pure. When they have purified themselves come to them in the way (*min haythu*) God has ordered you. God loves those who repent, and loves those (masc./inclusive pl.) who purify themselves. Your wives are a tilth (*harth*) for you; so come to your tilth as you wish, but do something for your souls beforehand. And be conscious of God, and know that you are going to meet God. And give good tidings to the believers.[63]

In addition to the obvious (these commands are addressed to men, about women) and the tangential (menstruation renders women impure for intercourse), these verses make two essential points. First, they presuppose male agency and female passivity with regard to the initiation of sex. Second, they place all sexual relations, like other human activity, firmly within the scope of divine regulation.

Exegetes understand Surah 2, verse 222 to be divine guidance conveyed to the Prophet in response to questions posed to him by Muslims ("They ask you about …"). It is perfectly intelligible that commands or advice about women should be directed toward men, if they were the ones doing the questioning. The content of the first verse, about sex during menstruation, clearly indicates that men bear responsibility for either keeping away from or approaching their wives for sex. It does not, for example, command men to wait for their wives to approach them after they have purified themselves from menstruation. Though women have the duty to purify themselves, it remains a male duty (or prerogative) to initiate sex once purification is complete.

The second of these verses famously declares "*nisa'ukum harthun lakum*" – "your wives are a tilth for you." The choice of metaphor seems to suggest passivity; a field, after all, is an object to be tilled, not an active partner in the decision whether or not to plow, or plant, or harvest (or to *be* plowed, etc.).[64] Barlas has argued, suggestively, that one cannot read this verse to justify the treatment of "women as men's sexual property", because "property in land" was not known in that place and time; besides, other Qur'anic verses give a different semantic scope for the term *harth*.[65] Others accept the land analogy, but stress that the likening of a woman's body, or genitals, to a tilth implies an obligation of careful cultivation, not proprietary license to act without thought for the woman's well-being.[66] Others have suggested that the passage refers to procreation and the (im)permissibility of contraception.[67] However this passage is interpreted, though, the fact remains that the Qur'an here objectifies women in the most literal sense, discussing them as matter to be acted upon not agents in their own right.

The usual account of the revelation of Surah 2, verse 223 strengthens the view that the Qur'anic text supposes male control of women's bodies; it is said to have been revealed in response to a dispute between husband and wife over the acceptability of a particular position for intercourse. The wife reportedly objected to the husband's desire to enter her from behind; this verse granted him permission to have sex with her in the position of his choosing.[68] If such is its circumstance of revelation, the verse seems to preclude a woman having any right to deny her husband sexual access (except during men-strual impurity) in the manner of his choosing. Of course, the occasion of revelation usually proposed for this verse may instead be a post facto rationalization; the Qur'anic text might merely grant freedom to married couples to determine their own sexual positions.[69] Even this analysis, however, leaves intact the presumption that husbands instigate and control sexual activity.

That said, the most important content of all of these verses is not the content related to intercourse itself but the placement of sex firmly under divine oversight – in the sense that God will call each human being, and here particularly men, to account for their deeds, even with regard to sex. As with the discussion of divorced or widowed women, these passages are anything but a license for unbridled male actions; men's access to women's bodies is controlled by divine regulation. Unlike in those cases, however, Qur'anic discussions of sexual intimacy contain no appeal for female freedom to act.[70]

Conclusion

Though the Qur'an stresses individual accountability on numerous occasions without reference to gender, men seem to have greater scope for action and moral agency, particularly with regard to marriage and sex. That is not to say that women's feelings and desires are not taken into consideration at all; discussions of verses on marriage and divorce in this chapter have shown that a woman's role in selection of a marriage partner and in regard to continuing her marriage may be necessary, if not decisive. Overall, however, the Qur'an directs men to exercise responsibility for numerous decisions in familial and intimate matters. Dominant interpretations that acknowledge this gender differentiation suggest that this arrangement reflects the natural order of things; men have both greater responsibilities and greater privileges in the divinely approved hierarchical forms of social and familial organization outlined in the Qur'an. Others, though, insist that such verses merely reflect the social norm of patriarchy, by addressing those with greater power in it. Although I am reasonably persuaded of this latter view with regard to marriage, divorce, and polygamy, I find it less convincing with regard to intimate sexual relations between husband and wife. The Qur'anic privileging of male sexual agency suggests that in some crucial sense the Qur'an is a thoroughly androcentric – though not, I would argue, misogynist – text.

Modern scholarship on the Qur'an has rightly pointed out serious oversimplifications and distortions in the commentarial tradition, where commentators' own assumptions about female inferiority and male supremacy have led to seriously flawed exegeses of particular verses. Yet, scholars intent on reform have at times committed the same error of allowing their own presuppositions to color their interpretations of the Qur'an to the extent that they fail to consider other possibly legitimate readings. It is not enough to simply posit that "the Qur'an is egalitarian and antipatriarchal,"[71] and to blame interpretations that deviate from that perspective entirely on "misreadings." Barlas, in an exercise of considerable intellectual honesty, acknowledges the role of the interpreter's beliefs in *"Believing Women" in Islam.* She writes that:

> I set out to absolve the Qur'an "itself" of culpability for what Muslims have, or have not, read into it. This does not mean that I did not consider seriously the alternative argument that the problem is not one of reading but of the very nature of some of the Qur'an's teachings. ... I wondered whether the Qur'an itself is responsible for its misreadings.[72]

Even in this attempt to query her work's presumptions, Barlas does not acknowledge the possibility that a reading of the Qur'an that arrives at different conclusions could be a legitimate reading or a faithful explication of "the Qur'an's teachings." The way she frames the issue in fact presupposes what she sets out to prove: that any patriarchy or inequality seen in the Qur'anic text is the result of a "misreading."

Barlas's work operates under the assumption that the existence of mutuality and reciprocity in intimate relationships is incompatible with hierarchy; since the former clearly exist in the Qur'an, the latter cannot. However, as David Halperin has argued with regard to ancient Greece, inequality does not preclude real and enduring affection and may, in certain circumstances, even be a condition for it; in some contexts, "personal affection and social subordination ... are two sides of the same coin."[73] It is one thing to accept this as a description of an ancient society, however, and another to view it as part of the divine plan for humanity. If the Qur'an – and, by extension, God – treats the male as the primary recipient of guidance on matters of sex, if divine revelation endorses man-on-top (figuratively, of course, as the occasion-of-revelation literature seems to suggest that position-wise, it is not the placement of the man's body but his decision about the position that matters), one must ask whether the egalitarian vision of gender justice that I and others would like to see diverges from God's understanding of essential human nature.[74]

Honesty requires me to concede the strength of some scriptural interpretations positing a privileged role for males in family and society. Still, just because these are possible – even the most straightforward – readings does not mean there cannot be equally compelling feminist interpretations of the text when historical context is considered and when critical principles of justice, kindness, and love are taken seriously. However, in order to create a body of persuasive and thorough feminist interpretation these principles will need to be defined and explored because justice, just to take one example, can mean a variety of things. One must debunk and counter aggressively patriarchal and indeed misogynist interpretations, but also justify the project of egalitarian interpretation. In the process, one must acknowledge that esteeming equality as the most important interpersonal value is a peculiarity of some modern Muslims and not something inherent in the text of the Qur'an. Feminist exegetes must take care not to be as blinded by the commitment to equality, and the presumption that equality is necessary for justice, as classical exegetes were by their assumptions about the naturalness of male superiority and dominance in family and society.

In any case, the Qur'an is not primarily a rule book but rather a revelation that captivates and engages hearts and minds. It serves not only as a source of divine guidance but also as an indicator of the divine intelligence at work in the universe; it reminds human beings of God's existence, generosity, wrath, mercy, and justice. The fact that the Qur'an has a larger purpose – and a more complicated relationship to human social and familial life than simply to provide regulations – does not excuse sloppy or apologetic readings of difficult passages. However, we do well to remember that there are limitations not only to the work of human interpretive intelligence, but to the Qur'anic text itself, at least as manifested in the earthly realm. It is, and can only ever be, a pale shadow of the ultimate Reality.

Coda 7

In the first edition of this book, I wrote that "feminist or gender-conscious interpretation of the Qur'an" was "a discipline still in its infancy." Not anymore.

As the field has matured, some once revolutionary ideas have become conventional wisdom – even if women exegetes receive no credit for these transformations.[75] Egalitarian notions of creation have come to seem commonsensical to many; even conservative scholars sometimes attend to them. To a lesser extent, ideals of companionate marriage have also spread.[76] Even as basic ideas about male–female ontological equality have percolated through Muslim thought more broadly, more sophisticated engagements with the Qur'anic text itself as well as its range of interpretations, past and present, have provided much fuller accounts of gender, justice and hierarchy in the text and in the interpretive tradition: premodern as well as contemporary, (neo)traditionalist as well as reformist.

I resist here the temptation to enumerate the myriad developments in (North American) feminist Qur'an interpretation, though two moments seem especially crucial. First was Wadud's much-explored notion of "saying 'no' to the text."[77] The other, less frequently written about but vital for highlighting the theological as well as ethical issues at stake, was Laury Silvers' exploration of the quandary posed by the "mere existence" of Q. 4:34.[78] Two recent surveys explore these and other issues more fully. Juliane Hammer's *American Muslim Women, Authority, and Activism* (2013) addresses women's *tafsir* or exegesis as part of a broader discussion of women's organizational, ritual, and scholarly efforts to achieve gender justice. Aysha Hidayatullah's *Feminist Edges of the Qur'an* (2014) addresses Muslim women's *tafsir*, again focusing mostly on American scholars.[79] Both Hidayatullah and Hammer situate women's scriptural interpretation within broader reformist and modernist currents, including male-authored Qur'an commentary. Hidayatullah, both sympathetic and critical, narrates the late twentieth-century and early twenty-first century forays of a handful of Muslim women (including me) into the field of *tafsir*; analyzes and critiques the assumptions and methodological strategies used by these scholars (including, sometimes, me); and proposes ways to move past the aporias generated by existing interpretive approaches (including, occasionally, mine).

Other recent scholarship emphasizes relationality rather than (binary) opposition, fluidity rather than fixity.[80] Jerusha Lamptey finds in Muslim women's interpretation a rich resource for thinking about religious pluralism.[81] *Never Wholly Other: A Muslima Theology of Religious Pluralism* (2014) inverts the usual practice of using men's theories to frame women's concerns. Instead, she uses women's approaches to gender to theorize religious pluralism. She finds that rather than fixed Qur'anic oppositions (Muslim, non-believer), categories of insider and outsider shift according to time and context.

Like queer theory, a body of scholarship which attends to indeterminacy, impermanence, and slippages, this scholarship is influenced by cultural movements away from triumphalist narratives. To say that these scholars are influenced by our cultural context does not mean women's commentary is merely trendy and limited while "traditional" commentary somehow transparently reflects the divine objectives in the text. Male interpreters over the centuries have been profoundly influenced by patriarchal assumptions about women, sex, and family that a great many Muslims no longer share, as richly detailed studies by Ayesha Chaudhry (*Domestic Violence in the Islamic Tradition* [2013]) and Karen Bauer (*Gender Hierarchy in the Qur'an* [2015]) illustrate. As Chaudhry and Bauer show, among contemporary interpreters, new patriarchal forms have often negotiated, partly displaced, and sometimes replicated older assumptions.[82] For feminists to acknowledge our own positionality need not mean accepting the denigration of our interpretations in contrast to decontextualized, "authoritative," "canonical" interpretations.

How, then, do we approach the Qur'an? There is a divergence between the widely shared Muslim assumption that the Qur'an constitutes verbatim divine speech and the assumption by most Christian and Jewish feminists that the Bible is a human product. These varying approaches to scripture mean that interpretive techniques used by feminist biblical scholars cannot necessarily be applied to the Qur'an.[83] Hidayatullah has suggested that in addition to thinking anew about difference, sameness, and equality we must revisit our ideas of revelation and how we conceptualize the text as divine guidance for our contemporary world. One factor keeping Muslim women from adopting controversial views on the historicity and status of the Qur'anic text such as those espoused by Abdolkarim Soroush, Nasr Hamid Abu Zayd, or others is the desire to be perceived as legitimate in the eyes of an established community. Even some women who may not think of the Qur'an as God's verbatim speech perfectly preserved through the centuries may avoid saying anything to the contrary because they are trying to win recognition of egalitarian or less patriarchal interpretations. Why rock that particular boat? Tacitly accepting the prevailing wisdom is different from insisting dogmatically on its incontrovertible truth. Skepticism and suspicion already surround feminist exegetical projects. Women accused of complicity with Western views may try especially hard to promote their views as "natural" and transparent as part of a quest for practical influence.

An alternate or complementary step offers a way out of current impasses in reading. Though we cannot entirely forgo attention to Qur'anic verses that directly address gender, power, and sexuality, what happens if we shift our attention to its stories? Qur'anic narratives both present gender binaries and undo them.[84] Recent scholarship on maternity, masculinity, and prophetic stories in the Qur'an has used literary approaches as well as theoretical work from gender and sexuality studies to showcase the complexity and heterogeneity of Qur'anic discourses about creation, reproduction, prophethood, and masculinity.[85]

This is not to suggest that the Qur'an is, for instance, supportive of trans people in a simple affirmative way. The Qur'an does not use the category transgender; to insist that it does would be to repeat the error that Hidatyullah so cogently diagnoses. On the other hand, a trans-inclusive reading has reasonable textual support. I do not mean to imply a narrative of linear progress: first gender equality, then acceptance of same-sex relationships, then inclusion of people who identify as gender-queer, and so forth. Hidayatullah critiques the idea of the trajectory beyond the Qur'an (an argument I advance in the first edition of this book, especially in Chapter 3), which presents a problem when we "trea[t] Qura'nic utterances as pointing to a trajectory beyond the speech of the Qur'an, without acknowledging that this trajectory must remove us from the Qur'an in certain ways."[86] Similarly, Omaima Abou Bakr suggests that my approach to the text leads to "the implication that the Qur'an has either failed to fulfill its role as an applied system of divine guidelines to wisdom and righteousness, or that it ought to be emptied of its content while maintaining merely the form and symbolism of its sacred ontological status."[87] I do not believe these are the only alternatives, but this framing raises vital questions about how feminists should engage the Qur'an. What might it mean to move away from the Qur'an, if we could in doing so move closer to God? Is that even a conceptual possibility? How might we turn to the Qur'an differently, not for "an applied system of divine guidelines to wisdom and righteousness" in the sense of a set of literal prescriptions, but in the sense of a font of wisdom and righteousness? Here, again, stories may be crucial.

Some of the things we associate with the forward-thinking twenty-first century were anticipated long ago. Sa'diyya Shaikh has shown the playful use of gender binaries in the writings of thirteenth-century Andalusian mystic Ibn 'Arabi.[88] He tells and retells stories in which "gender is never quite grasped definitively but is constantly shifting and opening up expansive spaces for understanding human nature."[89] Drawing from predecessors need not mean a cynical "fishing expedition" for a precedent; we need not accept that one may do something today only if classical scholars approved it. Instead, we can engage and be inspired by a rich tradition of interpretation that surpasses the dichotomous patriarchal/liberated thinking that often characterizes debates.

In Ibn 'Arabi's work, as in that of Riffat Hassan in the 1980s, creation is central. Creation is not nearly as straightforward as "God created Adam and out of Adam created Eve," as I once heard an imam say at a wedding, identifying it as "the English translation" of "Revere your Lord who created you from a single soul and from it created its mate" (Qur'an 4:1). The egalitarian nature of creation, the idea that women are not, in Hassan's words, "secondary and derivative," has been the most significant legacy of Wadud's interpretations. Among other things, it has been marshalled to support egalitarian marriage.

Egalitarian marriage advocacy rests on twin pillars: Muhammad's marriage to Khadija and Qur'an 4:1.[90] Both are discussed in ways that marginalize polygynous and/or hierarchical marriage, while emphasizing monogamous, companionate male–female partnering as the divine plan and 'true' Prophetic sunnah. Each repetition reaffirms coupled, reproductive male–female pairing as normal, natural, and divinely chosen, while marginalizing, perhaps inadvertently, lifelong celibacy and other forms of partnership. The narrative of male–female complementarity is recruitable for a narrow model of coupled family life which excludes same-sex couples, childless couples, and those who remain single by choice or otherwise. There are alternatives. Yet one might argue that male and female are incidental; it is the encounter between self and other, not dependent on gender, that creates the possibility for ethical pairings and relationships.[91]

8 The Prophet Muhammad, his Beloved Aishah, and Modern Muslim Sensibilities

Aishah narrated that the Prophet married her when she was a girl of six and he consummated the marriage when she was a girl of nine.
– *Sahih Bukhari*[1]

In 2002, Southern Baptist preacher Jerry Vines caused an uproar in the United States when he referred to the Prophet Muhammad as "a demon-possessed pedophile."[2] The accusation of demon possession hearkened back to the "Satanic Verses" controversy sparked by Salman Rushdie's 1988 novel, but Vines' remarks did not reignite that firestorm. Instead, it was his accusation of pedophilia – based on Muhammad's marriage to the young Aishah – that proved incendiary. Even in the post-9/11 climate of American hostility toward Islam, American Muslims found this attack on the Prophet particularly offensive. Outraged, many instinctively refused to accept the evidence provided by Vines and his associates for Aishah's age at marriage, though they were on solid ground as to their sources.[3] According to *Sahih Bukhari*, viewed by Sunni Muslims as the most authentic compilation of hadith reports about the Prophet and his companions, Aishah was a girl of six when her father, Abu Bakr, married her off to his close friend Muhammad. Accounts in *Sahih Muslim*, the second most respected compilation, suggest an age at marriage of either six or seven.[4] The accounts agree, however, that she was "a girl of nine" when Muhammad consummated the marriage.

American Muslim leaders and organizations found themselves at a loss as to how to deal with the issue aside from frequent repetitions of the obvious counterclaim that Vines' remarks were inflammatory. Most response focused on the sinister motivations behind, and the divisive effects of, Vines' comments, using terms such as "venomous," "bigoted," and "hate-filled." Sidestepping the substance of the allegations, Shakur Bolden, an Islamic Center president from Florida, declared: "It's outrageous that he made those comments. He should not have made those comments. Those comments do not bring people together and that's what we ought to be about – bridging communities."[5] A few spokespeople for Muslim organizations cautiously suggested that Vines' statements were inaccurate. But in one of the few attempts to refute directly the allegation about Aishah's age, Ibrahim Hooper, spokesman for the prominent Council on American-Islamic Relations, resorted to clumsily (and erroneously) suggesting that "six" and "nine" have been interpreted by many Muslim scholars to mean "sixteen" and "nineteen."[6]

There is nothing new, of course, about the Prophet's marriages being the target of non-Muslim criticism. Accusations of lust and sensuality were regular features of medieval attacks on the Prophet's character and, by extension, the authenticity of Islam as a religion.[7] This "rather abrasive criticism"[8] focused, more often than not, on the large number of Muhammad's wives or his marriage to Zaynab, the former wife of his adopted son Zayd. Aishah's age was rarely the subject of controversy in premodern discussions. In recent years, however, it has figured prominently in criticisms leveled against Islam not only by Christian polemicists but also a number of feminist, human rights, and secularist organizations. Though the controversy over Aishah's age at marriage died down fairly quickly in the national media, years later it still rages online, where it has appeared as a staple in evangelical polemics against Islam well before Rev. Vines' remarks.[9] Partially due to this added scrutiny, Muhammad's marriage to Aishah has become a topic of discussion and debate among Muslims as well.

This chapter considers contemporary Muslim treatments of Aishah's age at marriage and what they reveal about certain types of Muslim anxieties, focusing on online sources. Muslim discussions of the Prophet's personal conduct in general, and his marriage to Aishah in particular, provide a lens through which to view changed attitudes toward sex and marriage, and unresolved concerns about the appropriateness of applying medieval standards in modern life.[10] There are dangers in both historical anachronism and unchecked moral relativism, and in analyzing Muslim reflections on Muhammad's marriage to Aishah, several questions emerge about both the accuracy and relevance of historical information. The most obvious, of course, are: How old was Aishah when her marriage to the Prophet took place? And how old was she when it was consummated? I make no attempt in this chapter to assess the historical record, nor do I take a position as to Aishah's actual age at the time of consummation of her marriage. I do not think the Bukhari account of Aishah's marital history is implausible, given later legal discussions of menarche and majority, nor do I view it as infallible simply because Bukhari includes it. The cavalier treatment of this hadith by those who find its content objectionable, however, has implications that many Muslims not directly engaged in ongoing polemical struggles have not recognized. Rejecting the view that Aishah was six and nine, respectively, at marriage and consummation implies a willingness to question the reliability of Bukhari's compilation which, under other circumstances, can subject one to attack.

How to treat hadith texts is perhaps the most crucial methodological issue for contemporary Muslim reformist thinkers. Just as with the Prophet's ownership of Mariyya, or his actions in permitting Muslim soldiers sexual access to females captured in battle, if one accepts the hadith account of his marriage to Aishah, one confronts the actions of the Prophet in doing something that is unseemly, if not unthinkable, for Muslims in the West. Suggesting that he was wrong to do so raises profound theological quandaries. Yet accepting the rightness of his act raises the question: on what basis can one reject the marriage of young girls today? At stake are broader issues regarding the relevance of prophetic example to Islamic sexual ethics and the relevance of historical circumstance to the application of precedent.

Apologetics and Polemics

Contemporary Muslim discussions of the Prophet's marriages in general, and his marriage to Aishah in particular, are attentive to the broader climate of non-Muslim scrutiny and criticism of Islam. As in controversies over female circumcision, Muslim discourses on the Prophet's personal life have the dual objective of defending Islam by responding to allegations of impropriety while also engaging in intra-Muslim reflection and debate. There is a voluminous Muslim-oriented literature, in pamphlets and books, treating the Prophet's wives, and making reference to the Prophet's exemplary behavior as a husband.[11] Not surprisingly, there are also numerous discussions of these topics on a variety of Internet sites, expressing diverse perspectives, and addressed to different audiences. Muhammad's marriage to Aishah is a prominent theme in treatments of the Prophet's married life. Some articles explicitly respond to criticism of the marriage; these range from refutation to apologetic to counter-polemic, and seem to be mostly directed toward non-Muslims. Other pieces – articles, fatwas, question/answer format discussions, and postings in chat rooms and on discussion boards – are geared toward intra-Muslim dialogue. Even in Muslim-focused forums, though, the various approaches adopted by Muslim authors reflect their sense that they are engaged in an ongoing ideological struggle with "Christianity" and "the West." This oppositional stance emerges clearly in directly polemical articles but is present at least as an undercurrent in almost all discussions.

The variety of Muslim responses to the issue of Aishah's age at marriage reflects differing audiences and attitudes to the hadith sources as well as varying levels of identification with the worldwide *umma*, or Muslim community. A few groups outside the mainstream, such as the Ahmadiyya or the Submitters, flatly deny that Aishah was nine when she began marital life with the Prophet. They do so by rejecting the authority of the hadith that present this "fact." One online Ahmadi source questions the credibility of the reports about Aishah's age at marriage while attempting to defend the authenticity of the hadith literature as a whole; the article suggests that "the compilers of the books of Hadith did not apply the same stringent tests when accepting reports relating to historical matters as they did before accepting reports relating to the practical teachings and laws of Islam."[12] In making this distinction between history and law, the author attempts to deny the information in the report at hand without impugning the reliability of one core source of Muslim ritual and law. Reflecting its increased distance from Muslim orthodoxy, the Submission site, linked to the organization founded by controversial figure Rashad Khalifa, goes much further, equating hadith to Internet rumor: "All the stories circulating on the Internet and in the hadiths [sic] books about Aishah's marriage at age of 6 or 9, are no more than lies found in the corrupted books of Hadiths and completely contradict the teachings of the prophet Muhammed that came from his mouth, the Glorious Quran."[13] Despite their different attitudes to the hadith sources, both of these groups on the margins of Muslim orthodoxy agree with non-Muslim polemicists that *if* the Prophet had indeed engaged in sex with a nine-year-old girl, regardless of whether or not she was his wife, such behavior would be blameworthy. For these groups, the conflict over Aishah's age provides a chance to prove that they alone embrace "true" Islam, while other Muslims are guilty of distorting the legacy of the Prophet.

Most Muslim authors, though, are not so openly dismissive of the hadith sources, however inconvenient they may find them in this case. Those who reject the notion that the Prophet consummated his marriage with Aishah when she was nine sometimes argue or merely insinuate that the specific reports cited are inaccurate, leaving aside the question of the reliability of Bukhari or Muslim as a whole, and indeed usually refraining from even mentioning the specific location of the reports in question. For example, T.O. Shanavas, affiliated with a Kentucky-based organization called the Islamic Research Foundation International[14] simply states that "we do not know the exact age at the time of her marriage due to lack of reliable records."[15] Other accounts may attempt to discredit the reliability of Hisham b. 'Urwa as a narrator, in order to cast doubt on the particular account in question, which is related from Aishah on the authority of her nephew 'Urwa on the authority of his son Hisham.[16] Alternately, they may propose a different chronology, drawing from *sira* narratives, suggesting an earlier date of birth for Aishah based on an account declaring her to be a "girl" when a particular event occurred. Recalculating Aishah's age at marriage based on this nebulous evidence, such articles generally put her in her early to mid-teens at the time of consummation.

The attempt to revise the standard narrative of Aishah's age at marriage is not limited to online sources. In fact, the specific features of the online discussion can be better appreciated after a brief detour to evaluate how the question of Aishah's age is treated in several recently published or reprinted works aimed at Muslim audiences. The late Pakistani *'alim* Syed Suleman Nadvi writes proudly of her youth and virginal status, declaring: "Out of all the wives of the Holy Prophet [only] Hazrat Aishah had the distinction of being a virgin wife."[17] The "wedlock" occurred when Aishah was at the "tender" age of six. Three years later, "the consummation of her marriage" occurred. "Aishah was then only nine years of age," he writes.[18] The "only" in Nadvi's statement is a mark of pride, not a condemnation. Nadvi here echoes statements attributed to Aishah herself in classical sources including Ibn Sa'd, where her youth and especially virginity at marriage were a mark of honor, not a badge of shame.[19]

By contrast, in his book on the Prophet's wives British Muslim Ahmad Thompson studiously avoids any mention of consummation. Thompson presents a succinct account of events: "Soon after arriving in Madina, 'A'isha, who was now nine years old, was married to the Prophet Muhammad, who was now fifty-four years old. It was at this point that she left her family's household and joined that of the Prophet Muhammad."[20] The age Thompson provides for Muhammad in this passage coincides with the standard historical view of when consummation took place; those who dispute Aishah's age at that time do so by suggesting an earlier birthdate rather than a later date of consummation. By giving Aishah's age as nine when she "was married," Thompson thus implicitly accepts the Bukhari view of when consummation occurred. Yet by not mentioning the earlier contracting of the marriage at age six or seven, Thompson leaves the reader free to imagine that Aishah's joining of the Prophet's "household" at age nine represents a mere shift of residence, not the beginning of a marital sexual relationship.[21]

Mumtaz Moin, a Pakistani author, devotes one lengthy paragraph in her biography of Aishah to the question of her age at consummation, but refrains quite deliberately from taking a definitive position. She begins by noting that "the Muslim medieval writers generally accepted the *hadithes*, according to which the age of 'A'ishah at the time of her *nikah* with the Prophet was six or seven years, and thus she was nine years old when the marriage was consummated, three years later." Immediately following this, she declares that this view of events has "been criticized by modern historians in the light of careful research. They hold that she was fourteen or, according to some authorities, fifteen years of age at the time of the consummation of marriage." While she refers to a few of the pieces of evidence cited in support of this view, mainly two references to Ibn Sa'd (who elsewhere gives the same information as Bukhari), she does not name or cite any specific modern scholars who have purportedly upheld it.

Moin proves reluctant to advocate these revisionist views explicitly, presenting her points in detached terms, using expressions such as: "They hold," "They base their argument," "They also hold," "It has also been argued," and "It is further argued." Nonetheless, Moin structures her discussion in such a way that she leaves the reader with the impression that Aishah was fourteen or fifteen at consummation.[22] The assumption that she supports this view is strengthened by her reiteration, in the conclusion to the chapter, that "although most of the medieval Muslim historians and a number of modern writers" – and she goes on to add the "Western Orientalists" to this group, in a further move to discredit their stance – "have rather uncritically accepted the view that 'A'ishah was only nine years old when her marriage was consummated, there are valid reasons to differ from this view."[23] Moin thus impugns the reliability of the accepted narrative without directly confronting the hadith sources or explicitly affirming an alternate view.

The authors of online materials are dealing with an environment that differs in crucial ways from that of these authors. First, while Nadvi, Thompson, and Moin are addressing the question of Aishah's age at marriage in the context of larger works on, respectively, the female companions of the Prophet, the Prophet's wives, and Aishah herself, online materials are usually accessible in such a way that the question of Aishah's age appears separately from any other biographical discussions. Second, while some of the online discussions are aimed specifically at Muslims, the availability of materials to anyone with Internet access makes the actual audience significantly more diverse. Though, of course, there are no restrictions preventing non-Muslims from purchasing books from Islamic publishing houses, it is less likely that they will come across these materials without putting significant effort into obtaining them. Third, and importantly, those who gain access to online articles discussing Aishah's age at marriage will likely have located them through an Internet search engine. This means that readers have plenty of opportunity to compare and contrast various accounts, making it more important to address competing perspectives directly.

That said, quite a number of online articles simply refrain from providing specific details about the Bukhari hadith, even to question its reliability. Thus, a response to a query posted at Islam Online quotes Muzammil Siddiqi, former president of the largest American Muslim organization, the Islamic Society of North America. Siddiqi does not discuss textual evidence specifically but asserts that "historically, it is not confirmed that she was 9 years old when she came in the household of the Prophet. There are various reports from age 9 to age 24."[24] Later, he notes that "I do not agree that she was 9."[25] Such a formulation, with only vague references to "various reports," without any consideration of relative authoritativeness of the sources, sidesteps the problem of the canonical nature of the hadith included in Bukhari's *Sahih*.[26] Siddiqi treats the report on which Vines' accusation is based, and on which most polemics center, as simply an unconfirmed report with which he does not agree; he deftly dodges the larger issue of the reliability of Bukhari's accounts.

In the context of an ongoing polemical struggle, however, rejection of the narrative found in Bukhari and elsewhere would be a dangerous tactic, since it grants the premise that the most respected and widely accepted textual sources for Islam, outside of the Qur'an, are unreliable. Thus, those pieces found at the "Answering Christianity" website (engaged in an ongoing series of detailed and vigorous arguments with the "Answering Islam" site) do not ever question the premise that Aishah was nine at the time her marriage was consummated. Instead, they turn first to rational justification and then to counter-polemic.

Responding to the argument that it was morally wrong and sinful for Muhammad to have had intercourse with such a young girl, the authors at Answering Christianity and other polemical sites argue that marriage at puberty – which they assume Aishah had reached – has historically been a common human practice. The Prophet's consummation of a marriage with a nine-year-old girl was perfectly acceptable, they point out, in its socio-historical context. Puberty marked both physical and social maturity, and Muhammad's contemporaries found nothing unusual in this marriage. Even medieval critics of Islam did not object to this marriage on the basis of Aishah's youth. Thus, one author notes that "it is therefore undeniable that consummating the marriage upon puberty was also their practice and not prohibited in their religions. The age restrictions therefore only came to **certain countries** in our **current century**. It is indeed extremely hypocritical and 'self-righteous' to judge other centuries, based on new criteria."[27] Proceeding to counter-attack, the authors claim that biblical and rabbinic sources demonstrate the legitimacy of marrying very young girls. Indeed, they charge that criticism of the Prophet's marriage to Aishah is hypocrisy given the acceptability of even larger age gaps between some male figures and their female consorts.[28] One prominent line of argument distorts a

Talmudic discussion to suggest that Jewish law permits men to have sex with three-year-old girls.[29] Compared to such a rule, a nine-year-old girl seems positively mature.

It is worth pointing out, however, that despite the suggestion by some of these authors that the delay between the contracting of Aishah's marriage and its consummation was in order for her to reach puberty, I have not found explicit references in classical sources to Aishah's menarche serving as the trigger for consummation of her marriage; in a few instances, precisely the opposite claim is made.[30] Subsequent legal discussions fixing nine as an age of presumptive or potential majority if the girl claims menarche sometimes rely on a parallel to Aishah's age at consummation. However, majority and/or arrival at puberty have no necessary connection with the consummation of marriage. Though it is sometimes misleading to extrapolate back from later legal discussions, there was general agreement among later jurists that the wife's puberty was not a necessary precondition for consummation of a marriage. Premodern sources, including legal handbooks and Ottoman court archives, link a wife's readiness for consummation not to *bulugh* but rather to being physically desirable and fit for intercourse.[31]

Searching for solace

Quite a number of articles geared toward Muslims adopt and adapt arguments found in these polemics and counter-polemics, reshaping them into apologetic form, aimed at reassuring readers.[32] The issue of Aishah's age at marriage is often framed as a matter of addressing "misconceptions" held by non-Muslim Westerners, even when the author and audience are both presumably Muslim. For example, one petitioner at Islam Online requests that the mufti "help us address the misconceptions filling the mind of some people, especially the Westerners about the Prophet's marriage to Aishah, may Allah be pleased with her, as they claim it to be a sign of child abuse[.]"[33] Another query, addressed to the online mufti of the Pakistani Jamaat-e-Islami by a South African doctor, describes having read the hadith discussing Aishah's marriage as part of a Muslim study group. The writer then requests guidance as to how to answer questions from non-Muslims about the matter. The response from mufti M. Haq displays a great deal of angst over having to address the topic, noting that "I find it hard to discuss" and declaring that "I wished you had avoided this marriage or age question."[34] It is improper, he makes clear, for a Muslim to entertain doubts about any aspect of the Prophet's conduct. It seems that the mufti is picking up on the unarticulated anxieties of his questioner, who had actually only asked about strategies for responding to non-Muslims. However, there is no suggestion that this questioner had actually been asked about the issue by anyone; it seems likely that he felt discomfort at Aishah's youth and was asking about how to discuss the matter with non-Muslims as a way of asking for explanation and justification of Muhammad's conduct without suggesting that he himself harbored any doubts about its propriety. In another instance, a contributor to a Muslim discussion board makes explicit the connection between being asked about the marriage and feeling discomfort. He states that a question from his Christian friend "left me with a thorn in the heart of my faith."[35]

Clearly, whatever the context in which it is raised, Aishah's age at marriage is a difficult topic for many Muslims. To a much lesser extent than in published works directed at Muslim audiences, some online authors do present specifically "Islamic" rationales for the marriage of Muhammad to Aishah, thus contributing to a view of the marriage as serving a larger divine purpose and rendering irrelevant any discussion of Muhammad's motivations. The marriage was divinely ordained, they point out, with the angel Jibril having displayed an image of Aishah to the Prophet, declaring that she would be his wife. Further, the marriage cemented political allegiances and was therefore important to the Muslim community.[36] Most salient to the question of age, Aishah's youth enabled her to live a long time after the death of the Prophet and serve as an authority on his actions. Thus, as Sabeel Ahmed writes, "The Prophet married Aishah for the benefit of Islam and Humanity."[37] The notion of a divine purpose to the marriage is, of course, not likely to sway anyone who views the marriage as evidence for Muhammad's base instincts, or indeed anyone who does not believe in Muhammad's prophethood. The inclusion of this type of material in articles centered on Aishah's age suggests that, rather than solely addressing non-Muslim criticism, the authors recognize the need to reassure and convince Muslims of the appropriateness of this marriage.

The need to assuage Muslim doubts vies with the desire to present an Islamic critique of Western and modern cultural ideals and social practices. The author of one article from the Jamaat-e-Islami website addresses the contemporary relevance of this marriage when asked about age differences in marriage and the Prophet's marriage to Aishah specifically. He counsels that while child marriage might seem unacceptable today, and Muslims are under no compulsion to engage in it, one should be wary of criticizing it. Too strong a rejection of child marriage is tantamount to accepting a Western agenda of women's liberation and even "UN sponsored shari'ah."[38]

The anxiety over capitulation to "Western" norms is ever-present in Muslim discourses, even when texts are written by, and aimed at, Muslims living – and in some cases, born – in the West. One article that strikes a particularly defiant tone in this regard is the widely cited "The Young Marriage of 'Aishah" by AbdurRahman Robert Squires.[39] This article first appeared in 1999, three years before Vines' remarks, and it aims both at non-Muslim critics and Muslims who seek to appease them. "In the face of [non-Muslim] criticism," Squires argues, "Muslims have not always reacted well." Squires solidly backs the hadith sources, claiming that the evidence for Aishah's age in Bukhari and Muslim "is – Islamically speaking – overwhelmingly strong and Muslims who deny it do so only by sacrificing their intellectual honesty, pure faith or both." Presumably, Squires would have harsh words for former ISNA president Siddiqi, who referred to these reports as "not confirmed."

Yet "pure faith" seems insufficient for many Muslims, who must attempt to accept the Prophet's action as blameless while reconciling it with their own discomfort. Reflecting the difficult nature of such an endeavor, a contributor to a discussion on ShiaChat wrote, in response to another's suggestion to simply accept that Aishah was nine: "Like you said, there's no point trying to cover up and make excuses for what the Prophet did, because that indicates that you are ashamed of Islam and do not agree with all of the rules, which makes you being a Muslim pointless."[40] His statement reflects unresolved, and uncomfortable, questions about the relevance of historical precedent to contemporary circumstances, and the appropriateness of using contemporary criteria to evaluate authoritative religious texts in general and prophetic *sunnah* in particular. The radical variations in tone and content among the online discussions of Aishah's age at marriage suggest that many Muslims feel torn between the impossibility of uncritical acceptance of their inherited tradition and the fear that any critical stance toward that tradition will be a capitulation to those Siddiqi calls "the enemies of Islam."

Conclusion

As scholars of history will affirm, one cannot use the standards of the present to judge the past.[41] However, most Muslims are not historians and their interest in the Prophet's life and conduct is not an academic exercise but an acutely felt religious one. It is a tricky proposition to accept that the Prophet is the model of conduct for all Muslims while simultaneously believing that it would be wrong of a Muslim man to follow his example in consummating a marriage with a nine-year-old. This dissonance accounts for the substantial effort many have put into asserting or proving that Aishah had reached her teen years before her marriage was consummated. A few individuals have suggested that one can accept the Bukhari account of the marriage while considering Muhammad's marriage to the young Aishah among those matters in which the regulations governing the Prophet's actions differ from those governing that of other believing men.[42] However, though the accounts in works of *sira* and hadith treat Muhammad's marriage to Aishah as something worthy of note, in part because of several divine signs of approval, they do not suggest that it was her youth that made the marriage exceptional or noteworthy.

A more satisfactory means of grappling with the Prophet's commencement of conjugal life with a girl young by any standard, whatever her precise age, would recognize that the circumstances under which this marriage took place were radically different from those of the twenty-first century. Though in the vast majority of Muslim contexts today a nine-year-old girl would emphatically *not* be seen as an appropriate marriage partner, there was nothing shocking or socially inappropriate about such behavior in seventh-century Arabia.[43] Though most first-time brides were not nearly so young, there does not seem to have been controversy over the age difference, and some Companions of the Prophet seem to have engaged in marriages with a similar age gap.[44] Notions of childhood, as numerous historical studies have shown, vary dramatically from place to place, and imposing modern notions of adulthood as a criterion for entering into marriage validly may be inappropriate. Recognizing the vast difference between socio-historical settings can be freeing, initiating debates over the relevance of precedent, specifically *sunnah*, in radically changed contexts.

Just because one should not judge anachronistically, however, does not mean one should withhold all judgment. Just because a behavior is socially accepted does not make it good. As with slaveholding, thinking in terms of unjust social structures, rather than individual sin, can provide a helpful way of reconsidering matters of sexual ethics.[45] But while this avoids the theologically problematic notion that the Prophet did anything objectionable, what does it say about the inherent goodness of marriage between males and females of substantially different ages and levels of experience? What of such marriages today? Is it possible to argue that in any setting – tribal Afghanistan or rural India or the Arabian desert – such marriages are always unfair to the girls involved? Can one argue that different sets of standards should apply to Muslims living in different societies, without falling into the trap of extreme moral relativism masquerading as multiculturalism? In order to address these questions, Muslim discussions of *sunnah* in general, and the Prophet's marriages more particularly, need to move beyond defensiveness. Being consumed with combating negative portrayals of Islam and Muslims can lead thinkers to overlook or excuse injustices that do occur, failing in the basic duty to command the right and forbid the wrong. But how does one know right and wrong, justice and injustice?

Philosophers and ethicists, both Muslim and non-Muslim, have been engaged for centuries in debates over what constitutes "good" and what is necessary for "justice." For most premodern thinkers, slavery was morally neutral; it fell within the realm of justice – appropriate rights and obligations for those of varying statuses – provided basic parameters of good treatment were met. Likewise, equality or sameness of rights between husbands and wives in marriage was largely unthinkable. Marriage was not meant to be a setting for love between equals, but rather a particular kind of exchange by individuals fulfilling complementary roles; love was a bonus rather than a prerequisite.[46] With this set of expectations, power might come to a wife because of her youth and virginity (Aishah is reported to have boasted of the latter, which distinguished her from the Prophet's other wives, all of whom had been previously married) rather than because of wisdom and wealth.[47]

Those Muslims who strive for gender equality, considering it an essential component of justice, must address the central issue: what is justice and on what basis does one know it? Is something good because God says so? Or does God say it is good because it is, inherently, so?[48] If what God says – and indeed, what the Prophet, "a beautiful example" (Q. 30:21), does – is automatically good, then what happens when this clashes with one's own view of what is just or good? Arriving at a working resolution of this dilemma requires a consciousness of history and an acceptance of the role of the individual conscience. If one wants to consider certain moral standards as absolutes – such as the injustice of slavery – one must accept that God sometimes tolerates injustice. However, in a universe with human free will, allowing injustice is not the same as being the cause of it; God repeatedly rejects responsibility for injustice in Qur'anic passages declaring that God does not wrong or oppress people in any way, but rather people do wrong (*zulm*) "to their own selves" (or "to their own souls").[49] This assertion is freeing, in that God does not demand that Muslims act contrary to the dictates of conscience. However, it also implies a much more significant responsibility for the individual human being to make ethical judgments and take moral actions. Qur'anic regulations, in this case, must be seen as only a starting point for the ethical development of the human being, as well as for the transformation of human society.

Coda 8

Since this chapter was written, I have written more about Aishah's marriage and, through work with the secular humanitarian organization Oxfam, learned more about a range of challenges facing girls globally. These experiences pull in different directions: the former toward the varied symbolic and polemical uses of Aishah through the centuries, the latter toward practical strategies for girls' full human flourishing.

This chapter downplays the prevalence and seriousness of child marriage. Its focus on ideas rather than realities is in keeping with the basic aims of the book; still, Chapter 6, on female genital cutting, talks about the tension between activist strategies and sophisticated scholarship while this chapter leaves aside the pull of practical reform. The health and social consequences of girls being married off before maturity are real, and potentially devastating: intercourse and pregnancy ravage unready bodies; curtailed education reproduces poverty. Some Muslim-majority countries rank among the world's unhealthiest for girls, though religion need not be invoked to explain anything: impoverishment, conflict, vast social inequality (both within countries and among countries in the global capitalist system), ethnic stratification, and other factors contribute, their particular constellations depending on local contexts.

Religion is often used to explain Muslim girls' suffering.

Horror stories of underage brides in Yemen, where leaders have refused to institute a minimum marriage age, create a "common sense" about Muslim oppression of women and girls, in which white Western saviors must ride to the rescue.[50] American political figures, as widely acknowledged, justified military intervention in Afghanistan on grounds of women's oppression, in ways reminiscent of British justifications for colonial rule in Egypt.[51] Similar narratives justify some current humanitarian projects, explicitly or implicitly. Is it possible to analyze and reform unhealthy, unjust practices without sensationalizing them in a way that further dehumanizes Muslims? As Lila Abu-Lughod notes, some have begun to ask "whether humanitarianism is the new face of colonialism."[52] Ameliorating and eradicating poverty, reducing girls' suffering, and creating new possibilities are worthwhile goals; the tricky question is how to achieve them in collaboration with individuals and communities, with more listening than talking, and with more curiosity than judgment.

What does any of this have to do with Aishah's age at marriage?

If we remain with the example of child marriage, we find an array of rights discourses and religious discourses marshalled to support and oppose minimum marriage ages. One objection occasionally raised to legislating a minimum marriage age for girls is Muhammad's behavior in marrying Aishah when she was nine.[53] But this insistence on the Islamic legitimacy of marrying off minor girls is less a continuation of Muslim practice from time immemorial than a modern attempt to justify in the name of tradition a now-stigmatized practice, and in doing so to rush to the defense of a Prophet being maligned by outsiders.[54] Muhammad's behavior in marrying Aishah has become a flashpoint in these controversies.[55]

What I did not realize when I wrote this chapter a decade ago is just how recent the obsession with Aishah's age is. It owes to two developments with their roots in the nineteenth century encounter between Muslim and Western biographies of the Prophet. One development is the focus on the facts of his life story, discounting symbolism. The other is a perceived need to defend Muhammad's actions within a shared calculus of moral uprightness.

In the original chapter, I mention that one retort to polemi-cal criticism of Muhammad's marriage to Aishah despite her youth is that medieval critics found nothing amiss. My recent book *The Lives of Muhammad* (2014) explores the range of ways the Prophet's marriages have been discussed over the centuries.[56] Not only did medieval Christian critics not focus on Aishah's age, they also did not have a concept of the oppres-sion of Muslim women in general or Muhammad's wives in particular. Instead, they focused on Muhammad's debauchery and immorality, including blameworthy ambition. Concern with oppression arose in the nineteenth century. Oppression was, for European colonial thinkers, primarily manifested in Muhammad's polygyny and the practice of slavery, especially slave concubinage. It was only in the late nineteenth and early twentieth centuries that Aishah's age became a problem; and it was in the late twentieth century that it became *the* problem.

For Aishah's age to be *the* problem, her age must be taken literally. Modern biographies of Muhammad, by both Muslims and non-Muslims, are concerned with the question of histo-ricity and are uninterested in symbolic readings of factual details. For instance, it is nearly universally reported in mod-ern accounts that Muhammad married Khadija when he was twenty-five and she was forty. Most early accounts give her age as forty, but it seems unlikely that they meant it literally. Forty is a highly symbolic number, which may have only meant in her case that she was an adult in the full bloom of social matu-rity. No one thought, for instance, that it was miraculous or even worthy of comment that she reportedly bore Muhammad six or seven children despite her advanced age. Yet, by the nineteenth century, Khadija's age was being taken literally by European authors who argued that she was not sexually appeal-ing because she was old. This emphasis on her age was adopted by Muslim apologists as a defense of Muhammad against cen-turies-old accusations of lustfulness: since he married an older woman – forty now taken as Khadija's precise age – he was clearly not motivated by lust.

Should Aishah's age be taken as factual? I profess myself agnostic on that question in this chapter; I still believe we can never know for certain.[57] Neither six nor nine resonates in the way that forty does; neither is obviously symbolic. It seems to me, though, that the repetition of her age in numerous early Sunni sources must serve some purpose beyond mere recounting of fact. If consummating a marriage at the age of nine or ten (the latter given in some biographical sources[58]) were as common as apologists assert, why emphasize it? When the early biographical sources talk about Aishah, they do so in the context of her role in early Muslim history. She was a contentious figure in factional struggles for power, prestige, and legitimacy; stories told about her might denigrate or, as in the hadith sources Sunnis rely on, celebrate her merits, including her purity. The sources link youth, virginity, and purity; it is certainly possible that her youth was exaggerated to strengthen her claims to purity and, therefore, to merit.

Today, when polemicists accuse Muhammad and, by extension, Muslims of pedophilia or child abuse, Muslims and sympathetic non-Muslims have tended to respond in the two ways outlined in this chapter: they either dismiss the evidence as unreliable and recalculate Aishah's age, or they accept the numbers presented in most Muslim sources and contextualize. Analogous to women's Qur'anic exegetical strategies, this contextualizing emphasizes compromise with an existing patriarchy and gradual reform of archaic practices. Another strategy, mentioned here, is to discuss how back then or over there, girls mature earlier. What I know now that I did not know when I wrote this chapter is that this argument from climate owes to Western ways of writing about Muslims.

The Anglican preacher Humphrey Prideaux, author of an influential 1697 polemical biography of Muhammad, was titillated by the "Torrid Zone" in which girls ripen early: "Ayesha was then but six Years old, and therefore he did not bed her till two Years after, when she was full eight Years old. For it is usual in those hot Countries, as it is all India over, which is in the same Clime with Arabia, for Women to be ripe for Marriage at that Age, and also bear Children the Year following." Well into the nineteenth century, figures like novelist Washington Irving and Methodist preacher George Bush accepted that climate affected female maturation, the latter attributing Aishah's marriage "at the early age of nine" to "the surprising physical precocity peculiar to an eastern climate" and the former remarking that "the female form is wonderfully precocious in the quickening climates of the east."[59]

Today, the concern has shifted. Where earlier authors were unbothered or were even excited by the exotic East, today, they are horrified by Muslim oppression. Yet to treat child marriage as a persistent problem of exotic or debased others is to confer a timelessness at odds with its embeddedness in specific historical moments. In 2014, a reporter called to talk to me about the marriage of young teenage girls in Syrian refugee camps. She asked about the history of child marriage as a Middle Eastern practice. I acknowledged the role of patriarchy, linked to men's sexual power over women, and the existence of a set of local norms linking family honor and female sexuality. At the same time, I insisted that one cannot posit an unbroken Muslim practice of early marriage from late antiquity to the twenty-first century. To give only one example of discontinuities: among urban Arab women in the early modern era into the twentieth century, wealthier families married daughters off earlier, where more was at stake. In poorer families, women married later and had more choice of spouses.[60] Today, the reverse is the case. Poor families, without sufficient resources to care for and protect daughters, marry them off earlier. Early marriage in Syrian refugee camps reflects patriarchy to be sure, including at least partial continuity of a model that, as explained elsewhere in this book, differentiates between permitted or "licit" relations and forbidden or "illicit" ones rather than between consensual and non-consensual ones. At the same time, it is incorrect to attribute such marriages to an ahistorical, honor-bound, undifferentiated, Islamic patriarchy; instead, we must understand them in the context of a war-torn, brutal, and very modern patriarchy.

9 Toward an Islamic Ethics of Sex

It is customary to title the final section of a book "Conclusion," but I have not done so here. Far from having completed a journey, in this volume I have only attempted a first step toward defining a problem. And the problem, as I currently see it, is this: meaningful consent and mutuality, both of which I believe to be crucial for a just ethics of sexual intimacy, are structurally impossible within the constraints of lawful sexuality as defined by the classical Muslim scholars, whose views – drawing from and building on Qur'an and *sunnah* – permeate all Muslim discourses. It is possible to rethink Islamic sexual ethics to accommodate these values and there are resources within Muslim texts, both revealed and interpretive, for doing so. Nonetheless, an egalitarian sexual ethics cannot be constructed through pastiche; a methodology of picking and choosing, combining isolated elements in expedient ways, will prove insufficient to resolve the core issue at stake. We need, instead, a serious consideration of what makes sex lawful in the sight of God. The obvious response of "marriage" does not really answer the question. What type of bond does God require between spouses? Is it payment of dower that transforms an illicit liaison into a respectable union? Is it a groom's right of extrajudicial repudiation? A civil marriage license? The bride's father's consent? A public ceremony? Sincerity of commitment by the would-be spouses? All of these things? Something else entirely? Moreover, once it is decided what makes sex lawful, what makes it good? By "good" I do not primarily mean sex that is physically pleasurable, although pleasure certainly matters, but rather sex that embodies, among other virtues, kindness, fairness, compassion, and generosity.[1] These are all necessary if one is to live up to the ideal of marriage set forth in the Qur'anic declaration that God "created for you mates from among yourselves that you may find tranquility with them, and put love and mercy between you."[2]

Of course, despite this powerful and moving (and gender-neutral!) description of the divine purpose for marriage, the Qur'an also includes hierarchical and androcentric provisions for marriage and sex. The Prophet's *sunnah* as recorded in hadith contains beautiful reminders to men to consider both female pleasure and women's tender feelings, but the same sources have demeaning references to women as objects of, and subject to, male desire. The Muslim jurists who repeatedly exhorted men to treat their wives kindly, to consider women's needs for sex and companionship, and not to abuse their powers of divorce, did so within a logical framework that considered a licit sexual union impossible unless a man's exclusive control over a woman's sexual and reproductive capacity was established through marriage or slavery, which they discussed using similar terminology. Given the competing models of appropriate sex and sexual relationships between and within these complex texts, how can Muslims draw on the sources in a coherent way to make ethico-legal decisions about our intimate lives?

My way of framing the question presupposes that Muslims will undertake this process of reflection primarily as individuals, for ourselves and in dialogue with those close to us. That does not mean that religious authorities do not matter; there are thinkers whose ideas have wide currency in the West as well as in Muslim-majority societies, and for those of us lucky enough to have a respected and thoughtful *imam* or other spiritual figure at our mosque or in our community, he – or perhaps, she – may be a trusted resource. Still, while there are some formal institutions of Muslim religious learning in the United States, the majority of those who speak about Islam (or *for* Islam) have no special credentials to do so. It is often said that there is no clergy in Islam. Although that is technically true, previous generations in Muslim-majority societies have allocated a special role to the 'ulama. In the West, there is no such class of individuals to serve as an anchor or foil for Muslim public and private discussions of these complicated issues. Indeed, there has been little public discussion at all of what role religious leaders should play in Muslim life in the West, how they should be chosen and trained, and ultimately what type of authority they should wield. A limited conversation began in 2005, sparked by the controversies over female prayer leadership, but it has not yet developed into the kind of broader debate necessary for full exploration of the key questions surrounding Muslim religious authority and institutions in the United States. Still, even formal structures of religious authority will not remove the need for individual Muslims to be substantially better informed about vital issues.

Reinterpretation is not only an individual project, for application in personal lives; it must also be a collective enterprise of scholars thinking, talking, and writing jointly and in counterpoint. Muslim feminists have become part of the Islamic intellectual tradition and, in doing so, have begun to push at its boundaries and reshape its contours.[3] As we engage more deeply with the intellectual heritage of centuries of Muslim thinkers, we must neither romanticize the tradition as it stands nor be blindly optimistic about prospects for transformation within it. Most importantly, as we expose reductive and misogynist understandings of the Qur'an and hadith, refusing to see medieval interpretations as coextensive with revelation, we must not arrogate to our own readings the same absolutist conviction we criticize in others. We must accept responsibility for making particular choices – and must acknowledge that they *are* interpretive choices, not merely straightforward reiterations of "what Islam says."

In this project of interpretation, we must also recognize that on matters of sexual ethics, the Qur'an itself poses challenges for those committed to egalitarian social and intimate relationships. Progressive approaches to the Qur'anic text cannot be limited to selective presentation of egalitarian verses in isolation from their broader scriptural context. Such an approach is both fundamentally dishonest and ultimately futile; arguments about male–female equality built on the systematic avoidance of inconvenient verses will flounder at the first confrontation with something that endorses the hierarchical and gender-differentiated regulations for males and females that so many reformers would like to wish away. This is where jurisprudential methods can offer much to Muslim feminists. Not because the rulings of the jurists are themselves egalitarian – for the most part, they are not when it comes to matters of gender and sex – but because the ways in which jurists have related source texts to social contexts demonstrates that the law they constructed has "always already" been subjected to acts of interpretation. Their practice both authorizes by example human interpretive reasoning and provides a useful model for constructive dialogue between textual sources and social custom, something that has always mattered a great deal where sex and intimacy were concerned.

There are, and always have been, strong elements within Muslim norms that value sex, both as a strong human need and also as a foretaste of the delights of paradise. Sex is powerful and needs regulation, no less so for its link with the sacred. As Ze'ev Maghen points out, "Both sexuality and spirituality are largely exercises in unruliness; the *shari'a* delimits each of them and thereby makes them possible."[4] How, though, can a feminist think about sexual intimacy within the constraints of God's revelation to humanity without becoming limited by patriarchal notions that deny women's lived experience and potential as fully human, fully moral, and fully sexual beings? It is easy to find revelatory support for women being fully human and fully moral; it is more challenging, but not impossible, to see women as fully sexual in a way that recognizes their status as moral agents. One must seek out and privilege these elements in the tradition, and justify one's choices. Appealing to timeless principles rather than historical specifics is a crucial interpretive strategy. But one must be prepared to define and defend the principles chosen and promoted in this way. For instance, the necessity of equality as a component of justice must be defended, not merely asserted. Discussions among feminist, reformist, liberal, and progressive Muslims must continue increasing in philosophical and ethical complexity. Simplistic invocations of justice and equity are insufficient without consideration of the wide range of ways in which those terms have been and continue to be understood throughout Muslim history. This will mean, in part, working through the conceptual legacy of past generations of thinkers who have grappled with these questions. Although there is something to be said for a "fresh" approach to the Qur'an, there is a wealth of insightful material that directly engages critical issues for those who seek egalitarian social relations today. And there is a lot to be said for not having to reinvent the wheel.

It is important to realize, though, that if only those who are trained as religious scholars (whatever that comes to mean) are deemed capable of engaging in discussions over how Muslims should behave in their intimate lives and how Muslim families should be regulated, women will be largely excluded from the ranks of those wielding religious knowledge. Although there are no restrictions on female participation in scholarly endeavors in theory – and a number of exceptional women, past and present, have been recognized as religious authorities[5] – there are significant practical obstacles to female education in madrasa settings. Likewise, there are social considerations restricting the ascription of religious authority to women. If mastery of the classical tradition is required in order to be considered credible, women are likely to be marginalized, if not entirely excluded, from interpretive reforms. And it matters deeply that women, whose concerns and perspectives differ from men's, be among those engaging in renewed ethical thought on topics including marriage and sex.

As to the question of religious authority and influence, it is important to note that many Muslim thinkers and authors who are perceived as authorities, and who write and speak from a position of authenticity, are not themselves fully grounded in the classical tradition; they have a selective and often incoherent relationship to law and scriptural interpretation. (As Abou El Fadl points out, "the connections between the classical epistemological and hermeneutic heritage and Muslims living in the United States have been thoroughly severed."[6]) Yet because their views are congruent with conventional wisdom about what is "Islamic" – or because their maleness and ethnic background give them an air of authority – their pronouncements are not questioned. There are some scholars with a thorough grounding in the tradition who also engage with modernity in a complicated and thoughtful way but they are, sadly, relatively few compared to the broader group of those who speak in platitudes and, on issues associated with sex and sexuality in particular, make sweeping generalizations about women, gender, and Islam that do not allow for nuance, dispute, or transformation.

Part of this book's aim has been to highlight striking inconsistencies in the way that several controversial topics are approached in the work of specific authors and, more importantly, certain conventional discourses. By pointing out these inconsistencies and contradictions, it is possible to challenge and possibly dismantle certain dominant discourses. If someone insists that a wife must be continuously sexually available to her husband because Bukhari includes the Prophet's reported words to that effect, one can ask whether the questioner also accepts the authenticity of Bukhari's report that the Prophet consummated his marriage with Aishah when she was nine. If someone insists that polygamy is valid for all times and in all places because the Qur'an authorizes it, one can inquire whether the same holds true for slavery. Such juxtapositions do not replace systematic and nuanced exploration of the topics at hand; they serve, rather, to shock one's discussion partner into considering a familiar topic without the comfortable veneer of apologetic conventional wisdom. One should not stop with rough analogies on complex issues, but rather use those analogies to (re)open dormant questions about the timelessness of specific points in the Qur'an and hadith.

The freedom to treat Qur'an and hadith not as repositories of regulations to be applied literally in all times and places but as sources of guidance for Muslims in transforming their societies in the direction of fairness and justice is important. Individuals must be willing to take responsibility for acts of interpretation, rather than insisting that they are simply doing what "Islam" requires. In fact, it is a precondition for keeping Islam relevant that Muslims' understandings shift over time and place. Islam is meant to be lived in history, and human beings have, for better or worse, taken on the role of earthly vicegerents. That role cannot be fulfilled by merely carrying out orders, but must involve the exercise of initiative, judgment, and conscience. This matters not only at the level of social reform, however; the conservative view that the family is the bedrock of society deserves real attention. The values that are taught and especially lived in intimate contexts should be guided by deep ethical reflection on the overarching divine purpose for human life on earth: to command what is right, to forbid what is wrong, to do good deeds, and to be ever-conscious of God.

Afterword to the 2016 edition

If the first edition of this book was a meditation on authority and consent, this expanded edition focuses more directly
on power and experience. Two threads running through the
new material are the implications of power – financial, social,
military – and the importance of taking diverse human experiences into account when formulating ideas, norms, and policy.
Of course, power and authority are deeply intertwined, and
the relationship between power and consent is equally complicated. What sorts of consent are possible in a world of rampant inequality? What sorts of choices are really "free"? Ideas
of freedom and choice shape our notions of experience and
obscure the structural constraints on what choices are available, and to whom, even as liberal notions of the rights-bearing
self invisibly, and unevenly, chlorinate the water in which we
all swim.[1]

Contemporary Westerners, especially Americans, fetishize
choice. "Well, it's my [her] choice" is a common refrain, particularly but not only when it comes to the headscarf. Criticizing
others' choices is perceived as wrong-headed. Yet "commanding right and forbidding wrong" – roughly, the duty of
one Muslim to intervene when another is acting improperly
– has historically been a central norm of Muslim interpersonal
ethics. Giving sincere counsel (*nasiha*) is one way to carry out
the duty.[2] Though forbidding wrong is an acknowledged obligation, only some types of behavior generally generate rebukes
or reminders. I once garnered a rueful laugh when I pointed out
to Muslim chaplaincy trainees that though people may get up in

arms about a Muslim friend or relative having sex or drinking alcohol, no one stages an intervention when someone fails to pay *zakat*. Still, there is a tension between the idea that we bear responsibility for helping others do the right thing and prevailing notions that individuals ought to be able to choose freely.

In Muslim thought about forbidding wrong, the tension is between correcting someone's behavior and according them privacy. Privacy discourages investigating non-public deeds and exposing wrongdoing, one's own or that of others. Non-marital sexual conduct is, today, a prime subject of forbidding wrong. Frank discussion of consensual sexual conduct outside of marriage, including among same-sex partners, is often discouraged: one should conceal one's own sins and those of others. As I wrote in the original edition, objections to such talk make realistic assessment of practical sexual ethics for Muslims in contemporary contexts tricky, not to mention re-evaluation of what, precisely, constitutes a sin. Consent, coercion, and community recognition are all vital factors.

In some cases, the impulse to conceal sins masks abusive conduct by those in power. A new openness challenges a tendency to equate silence with honor.

Two examples suffice. In early 2015, a prominent Illinois imam was charged with criminal sexual abuse of a former employee; a civil suit, including accusations from former students at an Islamic boarding school, was also filed.[3] Some community members argued for hushing up the accusations to protect the imam's reputation and that of the community.[4] An organization formed by a Muslim woman, HEART Women and Girls, served as public advocate for survivors. The majority of leaders came down on the side of disclosure, while addressing the push from some for a cover-up. An open letter from a range of community figures distinguished between "a personal failing of a fellow believer which causes no harm or breach of public trust [and] crimes involving harm to others."[5] The former can be shielded; the latter must be publicized, not least in order to prevent further harm.

A few months later, scholar Zaynab Ansari published an online essay about "celebrity" shaykhs and a culture of flirtation, inappropriate behavior, and clandestine (polygynous) marriages among those seeking traditional learning. Unlike the Illinois case, which involved criminal charges and a lawsuit, this exploration targets no specific perpetrators. Ansari names no names, carefully navigating the competing duties of maintaining privacy and correcting wrongdoing. She notes that "misuse of power is rife" given a "toxic" blurring of boundaries made possibly by technology, and a culture of inappropriate veneration of scholars.[6] Women's vulnerability "to deception and spiritual abuse" in such climates is compounded by the lack of transparency surrounding courtship and lack of public recognition for resultant marriages – if indeed (informal) marriage does result. Of the more than 250 comments on the blog, a disappointingly large number were from men attempting to correct Ansari's perceived error in not pointing out that the first wife's consent to her husband's additional marriage is not "Islamically" required.

Stepping back from these particular cases, one reason sex is such a prominent topic of concern (as opposed to concerns of medieval scholars: music, chess-playing, and drinking alcohol) is that sex and gender norms connect to the legitimacy and authenticity of Islam writ large. A reader email a couple of years ago assumed my good intention in writing this book but encouraged me to rethink my expressed views since there are "basics that cannot be changed." I failed, in the writer's view, to understand how "Islam respects women." She failed to appreciate that these are precisely the sort of categorical claims that this book interrogates: Who determines what is basic and cannot be changed? On what basis? Are their arguments logical and consistent? What assumptions undergird them? What hierarchies and power structures do they in turn support? What does "respect" or "equality" or "justice" look like? Who decides?[7]

These are vital questions, and I am by no means the only person to ask them. But they are not asked publicly enough, often enough, with spaces for productive engagement. (I have not said "civil" since tone policing makes it too easy to dismiss women's arguments on the basis that we are not following whatever norms our interlocutors posit.) We need constructive criticism, not easy pats on the back. Feminist theorist and cultural critic bell hooks notes that many scholars are reluctant to criticize colleagues for fear that criticism will be taken as a personal attack.[8] Female solidarity does not require us to move in lock-step, though. Critical engagement is necessary for discussions to move forward.[9] Should one only critique dominant ideas? To puncture the fabric of the taken-for-granted, the thoughts that support the world-as-it-is? I do not think so. Taking ideas seriously means giving them, as Jane Austen proposes, the compliment of rational opposition. At the same time, internecine struggles between female scholars and activists must not distract from larger shared goals: to move toward greater inclusion and justice for all, and to dismantle oppressive structures of patriarchal domination. Such structures hinder efforts to create a society in which piety, as Qur'an 49:13 declares, is the key criterion for evaluating human worth.

In the past decade, women have become more prominent authorities in many contexts. From the Qubaysiyyat in Syria to Farhat Hashmi in Pakistan and Canada, women are presenting what on the surface seem conservative interpretations of religious teachings, including and perhaps especially on matters of gender roles, sometimes with direct rejections of what are deemed Western notions of liberation or feminism.[10] Although not entirely unprecedented – there are scattered examples of prominent female scholars in past centuries – their increased presence reshapes gender dynamics and rewrites the contours of individual lives; the question of how much, and in what ways, remains open.

Writing about the American Muslim community, one author suggests that "scholarship itself, and not politics, has become the cornerstone of Muslim leadership and the chosen path toward authority."[11] I would counter that what counts as scholarship is itself deeply political. Women are still largely excluded from the ranks of those who count. Men's scholarship continues to ignore contributions by women. The major premise of the first edition of this book was that much contemporary Muslim thinking about authority of texts, institutions, and especially human interpreters is deeply flawed, particularly on matters of gender and sexuality. Women's – and specifically feminist – insights remain marginalized today. A slew of recent publications by men on topics including Muhammad's legacy, theodicy, "radical reform," and "reclaiming shariʻa," all give short shrift to women's ideas. Women have written extensively on subjects from family law reform to domestic violence, from discrimination and suffering to woman-led prayer; male scholars have roundly ignored relevant publications.[12] Men pretend the debate is taking place among themselves. This is simply untrue. It was untrue ten years ago; it is even more demonstrably false today.

This neglect of women's scholarly contributions owes in part – but only in part – to the marginalization of the (secular) academy from what counts as Islamic scholarship.[13] The last decade has witnessed a steady growth in traditional/neo-traditional educational institutions, both online and bricks-and-mortar. Two prominent examples are Sunni Path and Zaytuna College, the latter now accredited as an undergraduate institution. Women's initiatives such as Al-Rawiya College, headed by shaykha Reima Yosif, represent a slow incursion of women into those arenas. Women remain underrepresented as faculty members, and unreliably included in events, conferences, debates, and discussions. Chapter 9 notes that "there are significant practical obstacles to female education in madrasa settings."[14] These obstacles are by no means limited to non-Western settings; a symposium on "The Future of the Madrasa" held at Cambridge Muslim College in May 2015 included no women among its participants.[15] Shamefully, progressive male scholars, and those writing from within academia rather than hybrid spaces, do not necessarily do better than their conservative counterparts in attending to women's ideas and publications.[16] Still, where "knowledge" only counts if it comes with a chain of transmission and a scholarly pedigree stretching back to the Prophet, women are likely to be discounted if only because they still have unequal access to teachers and educational institutions.

This book, and especially the new material in this expanded edition, is grounded in my own (largely positive) experiences of

Muslim community life in North America. There is no single American Muslim experience, of course. American Muslims are connected through our belonging to a national polity in which there is a certain climate for treating Muslims. Yet our experiences differ dramatically based on our race and socio-economic status, our family configurations, our sexual orientations, our marital statuses, our geographic locations. We confront a similar legal regime when it comes to the (in)applicability of Islamic law, yet within some communities there is precedent and support for – for example – unregistered marriages; in others, not only is civil marriage de rigueur, so too are notarized antenuptial contracts. Other differences are ideological. There is at least as much difference between me and my Salafi or neo-traditionalist countrywomen as there is between me and progressive, feminist Muslims living on the other side of the globe.

Even more so than a decade ago, American Muslims are connected to a global community of Muslims. In thinking about lived Islam and Islamic ideals, geography is not destiny. Ideas circulate globally, as do student-seekers, including women.[17] Coalition politics connect, even as they trouble appeals to a universal *umma*. Divisions as well as connections between Muslims run through this volume, though I have not explored them as fully as I might have.

This expanded edition still neglects ritual, omitting any significant treatment of ritual purity, and glossing over ritual leadership.[18] It does not discuss "the historical prevalence" – or contemporary performance – "of Muslim women's rituals that are neither performed within the mosque nor mandated by Islamic law."[19]

Three additional unexplored areas deserve further attention.

First are issues of ability and disability in the Qur'anic text and in Muslim communities. Rereading this book, I cringe at my occasional use of ableist language, particularly the use of "blind" when I meant oblivious. Metaphors and imagery that equate disability with flaws perpetuate stigmas. Blindness, deafness, and other stigmatized bodily and social characteristics intersect with gender, as sexist ideas of female bodies play out. Ideas of disability, perfection, and normalcy also play out with mental illness. Even as it is vital to combat stigma associated with disability, it is also vital not to assume that variation implies imperfection or disability. Queer and trans people are sometimes treated as defective or deviant; asexuality and same-sex sexual orientations are sometimes considered disorders. These dynamics are not exclusive to Muslims, but there has been relatively little scholarly work done on Islam and disability, and nearly nothing on the intersections of Islam, disability, and gender. Raising these questions brings to the fore assumptions about who is fully human and what sorts of communities and societies afford full flourishing to everyone.

Second, and connected to notions of whose interests deserve attention, the book says nothing about the interconnected issues of sexual ethics and animal ethics. I have argued elsewhere that there is a relationship between structures of domination of animals and of women, and that Muslim advocates for gender justice should be vegetarians.[20] Any topic that affords insight into how structures of power operate provides insight into gender dynamics.

Third, the book still says too little about race and racism, particularly as these intersect with gender and sexuality. In the United States, intra-Muslim racism remains a significant concern.[21] Additionally, racism in broader American society affects Muslims, including the many Muslims who are African American. Parallels and connections between racism against African Americans and anti-Muslim bigotry or Islamophobia require sustained, careful parsing. Questions of inclusion and authority in Muslim communities are both racial and gendered.

Rereading the book in preparing to write these new sections, I realize that I often use questions instead of declarative sentences. If anything, I have more questions now and fewer answers. bell hooks insists that criticizing the status quo does not suffice; we must offer compelling alternatives. I agree. Yet no one set of solutions, no single model of just sexual ethics will suffice for Muslims in the U.S., let alone worldwide. Not only is it easier to critique than to build, more importantly, Muslim women, Muslim families, Muslim communities are not identical. What works for some will not work for others.

Does this mean abdicating any notion of Islam as an arbiter of correct conduct? I stand by my claim that there is no Islamic ethics in isolation from the people who produce interpretations. "Islam" cannot interpret, or decree, or decide. Instead, Muslims draw from appropriate sources life-transforming guidance for personal conduct, for self-fashioning, for interpersonal relationships, and for community building.

Some hold that the answer is to turn to properly qualified scholars. Properly qualified, of course, is in the eye of the beholder. I welcome the increased participation of women in "traditional" learning but remain skeptical that this is a comprehensive answer. Rigorous methods of scholarly training can provide a brake on extreme and violent interpretations of Islam, to be sure, but too often even those who identify as scholars jettison rigor in favor of pat declarations on gender issues.[22] Moreover, by the time one has obtained the training which would allow one to be an independent scholar, not bound by the precedents of one's predecessors, one has been thoroughly inculcated in the tradition: one is not likely to question its deep assumptions.

Where does this leave us? I side with those who believe that saying "not this" is valuable even if we do not know "what next?"[23] Ideas move slowly, and have a precarious, not entirely predictable or transparent relationship to the contexts from which they emerge and which they address. People take up ideas piecemeal, and implement them idiosyncratically and without tremendous concern for overall theoretical coherence. Ideas neither emerge from nor operate in a vacuum. Economic, political, and social transformations must accompany shifts in thought – sometimes leading, sometimes following. My aim with this book, both in its original edition and in this expanded version, is to contribute to the mutually constitutive processes by which ideals and material reality move toward greater inclusivity and justice. Perhaps by the time of its twentieth-anniversary edition many concerns expressed here will be obsolete, rendered irrelevant by communal changes. I pray it will be so.

Notes

Notes to Preface

1. Moosa, *What is a Madrasa?*, p. 236.
2. Al-Khansaa Brigade, "Women of the Islamic State: A Manifesto by the Al-Khansaa Brigade," translated by the Quilliam Foundation. I thank Charlie Winter for also providing me with a copy of the original Arabic document.
3. Zakaria, "ISIS Wants You to Share This."
4. American and United Nations troops have been guilty of the same sporadically around the globe, not to mention the systematic use of rape as a weapon of war in Bosnia, Rwanda, and Columbia, or, reaching back well into the twentieth century, in Bangladesh by Pakistani troops and China by Japanese troops.
5. Of course, it is largely impossible to know how closely traditional rules were followed in classical-era wars; as I note elsewhere, one cannot fairly compare legal ideals with actual practice. Still, social historians have shown that jurisprudence concerning household slaves and slaves used for sex was often implemented in courts; the expectation was that practice would follow prescription.
6. Particularly relevant is Ali, *Marriage and Slavery in Early Islam*, the book that grew out of my doctoral dissertation, "Money, Sex, and Power."
7. Cisgender or cisgendered (or cis) refers to a person whose physical attributes or assigned sex match her or his sense of gender identity. The opposite of transgender (or trans), the term cisgender avoids making transgender the sole marked category.
8. Jakobsen and Pellegrini, *Love the Sin*, p. 144.

Notes to Introduction

1. Wolfe and Beliefnet, eds., *Taking Back Islam*.
2. On the genesis of these images, see Kahf, *Western Representations of the Muslim Woman*.
3. Al-Sheha, *Woman in the Shade of Islam*, p. 79.
4. One Indian author writing in the 1970s sums up a dominant view: "While we are by no means opposed to the granting of all legitimate

freedom to women, we cannot afford to import the characteristic evils
of Western civilization in respect of sexual liberty." Niazi, *Modern
Challenges to Muslim Families*, pp. 60–61.

5.   Doi, *Woman in Shari'ah*, p. 185.
6.   See also Wani, *Maintenance Rights of Muslim Women*, p. 9.
7.   Al-Shafiʻi, *Al-Umm*, K. al-Sadaq, "Al-shart fi'l-nikah," vol. 5, p. 108.
8.   Sheila Briggs' remarks, Feminist Sexual Ethics Project colloquium III,
     Brandeis University, September 2005.
9.   Yalom and Carstensen, "Introduction," in idem., eds., *Inside the
     American Couple*, p. 10. See also Yalom, *A History of the Wife*.
10. A number of female slaves mentioned in biblical stories bore children
     sired by their masters, who included Abraham and Jacob. On the sex-
     ual use of male slaves in the ancient world, see chapter 5.
11. Michael Sells' insistence that work on religion and violence must be
     first, comparative, and second, both critical and self-critical, applies
     equally to work on issues of religion and sexuality. Michael Sells, lec-
     ture at Brandeis University, April 21, 2005.
12. Yalom, "Biblical Models: From Adam and Eve to the Bride of Christ,"
     p. 15. Even if Yalom is generalizing here – there are some denomina-
     tions that ceased using wifely promises of obedience long before the
     time she designates – the point is well taken. See also the 1945 New
     Jersey verdict quoted by Shanely, *Just Marriage*, p. 8.
13. Haideh Moghissi, however, argues that "only individuals who have some-
     how escaped the sexual repression which dominates the lives of women
     and men in Islamic societies can deny its overriding role in defining
     women's experience. Poverty and hunger hang over women's heads
     throughout the region. But ... sexuality and sexual repression are where
     women suffer most." Moghissi, *Feminism and Islamic Fundamentalism*,
     p. 95.
14. Plaskow, "Decentering Sex," p. 30.
15. Ruxton, *Maliki Law*, p. v.
16. Historian Huda Lutfi, referring to a fourteenth-century Cairene docu-
     ment makes a more broadly applicable point: "prescriptive religious
     literature should not necessarily be taken as a reflection of reality."
     Lutfi, "Manners and Customs of Fourteenth-Century Cairene Women,"
     p. 102. See also Sonbol, "Introduction," in idem, ed., *Women, the
     Family, and Divorce Laws in Islamic History*.
17. Tucker, *Gender and Islamic History*.
18. Ahmed, *A Border Passage*, p. 128. Ahmed does recognize the value of
     this tradition, at least in comparison to "fundamentalist Islam, textual
     Islam's more narrow and more poorly informed modern descendant."
     See also Ahmed, *Women and Gender in Islam*, p. 239, where she writes
     of the dominance of the "technical, legalistic, establishment version of
     Islam, a version that largely bypasses the ethical elements in the Islamic
     message."
19. Kevin Reinhart (at the Mapping Muslim Ethics colloquium, Duke
     University, April 2005) pointed out the paradox in my project: I am
     attempting to contest the jurists' interpretive authority in part by
     focusing on them.
20. Khaled Abou El Fadl describes the selective approach to Qur'an and
     sunnah reflected in "the endless stream of dogma that one encounters

in Muslim conferences, lectures, and publications," in *The Authoritative and the Authoritarian in Islamic Discourses,* p. 17. A focus on Qur'an and "authentic" hadith to the exclusion of jurisprudential doctrines characterizes even some self-identified progressive authors, such as Syed, *The Position of Women in Islam.* Syed (p. ix) describes his approach: "I start with the relevant verses of the Quran followed by the appropriate, authentic Hadith and have supplemented where necessary with relevant remarks and comments of Islamic authorities and scholars"; additionally, he provides his "own comments in areas where there is no compelling authority to follow and yet where an urgent answer is needed."

21.   Rahman, *Islamic Methodology in History,* is the best-developed defense of this approach.

22.   Jonathan Brockopp notes that there is "a substantial literature under each of these categories," but "we would look in vain here for practical application of Islamic ideals to matters of daily life." See "Taking Life and Saving Life," in idem, ed., *Islamic Ethics of Life,* p. 10. On ethical thought broadly, see Hourani, *Reason and Tradition in Islamic Ethics.*

23.   Brockopp, "Taking Life and Saving Life," p. 10. He also notes that "sharia is far too large a category to be reduced to ethics," as it also encompasses ritual matters that are outside the purview of ethical thought (p. 11).

24.   Faruki, "Legal Implications for Today of *al-Ahkam al-Khamsa.*" Faruki mentions, but does not discuss in detail, historical developments of this scheme over several centuries.

25.   See Jackson, *Islam and the Blackamerican,* p. 160. The phenomenal success of scholar and media figure Yusuf al-Qaradawi's *The Lawful and the Prohibited in Islam,* is indicative of the desire for simple answers; a children's title by Mohammad Mazhar Hussaini likewise proclaims its relevance as *My Little Book of Halal and Haram.*

26.   Wael Hallaq argues "that the shari'a is no longer a tenable reality" and those who advocate its reapplication are "in an irredeemable state of denial." Hallaq, "Can the Shari'a be Restored?," p. 22.

27.   Murad, "Boys will be Boys: Gender Identity Issues."

28.   Zahra Ayubi points out, however, that some immigrants base their view of Islamic legal requirements (e.g., with regard to woman-initiated divorce) on modern statutory provisions of their country of origin rather than any legal school. Ayubi, "American Muslim Women Negotiating Divorce," p. 48.

29.   Taji-Farouki and Nafi, "Introduction," in idem, eds., *Islamic Thought in the Twentieth Century,* p. 10.

30.   "[O]ne of the most significant features of contemporary Muslim thought is the attachment to and even veneration of 'Islam' in controversial debate. Thus we find that [authors] accurately represent Muslim thought when they say that 'Islam requires,' or 'Islam accepts,' or some other similar locution." Reinhart, "The Past in the Future of Islamic Ethics," p. 216.

31.   Abou El Fadl, *Speaking in God's Name,* pp. 144–5, 62–3.

32.   *Al-Yawm al-Sa'udi,* "'Al-tahjiz' wa ijbar al-mar'a 'ala al-zawaj min akbar anwa' al-zulm." Antoun, "The Islamic Court," p. 464, discusses

NOTES 211

a case where a contemporary Jordanian judge concluded that al-Shafi'i
was wrong in allowing fathers to compel marriages for their children.
For references to female consent in works aimed at a general audience, in addition to the sources cited in Ali, "A Beautiful Example,"
pp. 283–4, see, e.g., Al-Sheha, *Woman in the Shade of Islam*, p. 39:
"Islam considered the opinion of the daughter in the marriage as an
essential condition for the validity of the marriage itself." Describing
"classical Islamic law" (or *Shari'a*) specifically, Khadduri, "Marriage in
Islamic Law," p. 213, declares: "Although an offer to marry is actually
made through a woman's father, the woman's consent is considered
imperative if the contract is to be binding." Fadel, "Reinterpreting the
Guardian's Role," provides a substantive re-evaluation of Maliki doctrine, and discusses its relevance to Muslim marriage in the United
States.

33. *Sahih Muslim*, trans. Siddiqi. The quote is from vol. 1–2, p. 702; hadith
discussing sex with female slaves are found in vol. 1–2, pp. 734–5 and
743–4. See also Hidayatullah, "Islamic Conceptions of Sexuality,"
p. 263, where she declares that "according to the Qur'an, the proper
vehicle for enjoying the union between sexual partners is marriage. In
fact, it is the only acceptable framework for sexual relations between
two human beings." She refers briefly to the Prophet's practice of concubinage on p. 290, n. 14. On slavery generally, and slave concubinage
specifically, see chapter 3.

34. I owe the use of the term "dissonance" in this context to Farid Esack,
personal conversation, April 2005.

35. Mohja Kahf, personal communication, March 2004.

36. Full disclosure: I was one of three scholars contributing a brief essay.

37. Kugle, "Enough with the Prudes: Bring On 'Sex and the Umma'."

38. Bailey, *Sexual Ethics: A Christian View*, p. 8.

Notes to Chapter 1

1. Al-Ghazali (Kitab Adab al-Nikah from *Ihya' 'Ulum al-Din*), trans.
Holland, *The Proper Conduct of Marriage*, p. 75.

2. Ibn 'Abidin, *Radd al-Muhtar*, vol. 4, p. 379. The text points out divergent views among earlier Hanafi authorities about the precise contours
of a husband's sexual obligations to his wife (and even his concubines),
but even those who hold that a husband may not abandon intercourse
with his wife entirely acknowledge that any failure in this regard is
not actionable before a judge once he has "exhausted her right" by
consummation.

3. Friedmann, *Tolerance and Coercion in Islam*, p. 193.

4. For one first-person account of such a marriage, see Sharif-Clark,
"Marrying a Believer."

5. This phrase, from Q. 4:34, is usually taken by exegetes to refer to both
dower and spousal support, *nafaqa*. See below.

6. Ahmed, *Women and Gender in Islam*, pp. 42–6, and sources cited
there.

7. Khadduri, "Marriage in Islamic Law," p. 213.

8. Mashhour, "Islamic Law and Gender Equality," pp. 564–5.
9. Ahmed, *Women and Gender in Islam*, p. 45; Ahmed is making a general point here, not specifically discussing *sadaq*.
10. Women's clear legal claim to dower might be vitiated in practice, with the payment either withheld by the husband or his family after marriage, divorce, or widowhood, or received and kept by the bride's family. Judges have routinely and consistently enforced female dower claims when these are brought to court. For one anecdote, see Antoun, "The Islamic Court," pp. 456–7; see also Tucker, *In the House of the Law*, pp. 53–5. On the shifting patterns of dower in Palestinian women's experiences, see Moors, *Women, Property, and Islam*. Additionally, although the legally required transfer is unidirectional, a number of Muslim societies have had informal exchanges that, in practice, transferred resources from the bride's family to the groom through trousseaus or other exchanges. See Tucker, *In the House of the Law*, pp. 55–7; Zomeño, *Dote y matrimonio en al-Andalus y el norte de Africa*; and Rapoport, *Marriage, Money, and Divorce in Medieval Islamic Society*, pp. 12–30, who discusses the function of the trousseau as a type of "gender-specific pre-mortem inheritance" (p. 30).
11. Wynn, "Marriage Contracts and Women's Rights in Saudi Arabia," and Hoodfar, "Circumventing Legal Limitation." See also Mir-Hosseini, *Marriage on Trial*, for discussion of how dower and support obligations are used as bargaining chips in divorce negotiations in Iran and Morocco.
12. Qaisi, "A Student Note."
13. See Al-Shafi'i, *Kitab Ikhtilaf Malik wa'l-Shafi'i*, in *Al-Umm*, vol. 7, p. 376; and, for similar language, Al-Shafi'i, *Al-Umm*, K. al-Sadaq, "Fi'l sadaq bi aynihi yatlafu qabla dafa'ahu," vol. 5, p. 92; K. al-Nafaqat, "Ikhtilaf al-rajul wa'l-mar'a fi'l-khul'," vol. 5, p. 300; K. al-Sadaq, "Sadaq al-shay' bi aynihi fa yujadu mu'ayban," vol. 5, p. 111; and Al-Muzani, *Mukhtasar al-Muzani*, K. al-Nikah, "Sadaq ma yazidu bi budnihi wa yanqasu," in *Al-Umm*, vol. 9, p. 194.
14. See, among other verses, Q. 4:4, 20, 24–5, and 34.
15. Q. 4:24.
16. In which case, as discussed further in chapter 2, she is using a delegated power of divorce.
17. Ali, "Progressive Muslims and Islamic Jurisprudence," pp. 169, 178–9; Mir-Hosseini, *Islam and Gender*, p. 72, for one example of where this rhetoric breaks down.
18. See Moghissi, *Feminism and Islamic Fundamentalism*, pp. 21–2; Kugle, "Sexuality, Diversity, and Ethics," pp. 192–3.
19. Schmidtke, "Homoeroticism and Homosexuality in Islam," p. 261 (although she generalizes regarding "the Judaeo-Christian tradition"). On attempts to draw a similar distinction between Judaism and Christianity, see Boyarin, *A Radical Jew*.
20. "La rahbaniyya fi'l-Islam." Although this hadith is famous, it is apparently non-canonical. See Maghen, *Virtues of the Flesh*, p. 5, n. 11.
21. For one contemporary example, see Abdul-Ra'uf, *Marriage in Islam*, pp. 49–53. Abdul-Ra'uf quotes some of the Qur'anic passages and hadith reports used by al-Ghazali, below.

22. Al-Sheha, *Woman in the Shade of Islam*, p. 49, notes this rationale for wives' sexual rights: "The husband is required and obliged by Islamic law to fulfill the sexual rights of his spouse, to ensure the satisfaction of the spouse so as to refrain one's spouse from getting involved in shameful acts, may Allah forbid."

23. Al-Ghazali died in 1111 CE. For a recent discussion of al-Ghazali, see Moosa, *Al-Ghazali and the Poetics of Imagination*. Moosa writes (p. 12) that "the Muslim tradition is saturated with Ghazali's traces." Al-Ghazali's discussion of sex in the Ihya' is one of the main sources for scholars today discussing sexuality in the classical tradition. See, for instance, Hidayatullah, "Islamic Conceptions of Sexuality," pp. 264–9, 273. Fourteenth-century jurist Ibn al-Hajj expressed similar sentiments; see Lutfi, "Manners and Customs of Fourteenth-Century Cairene Women," pp. 107–8.

24. Of course, within marriage the husband's duties are the wife's rights, and vice versa, but the choice to address the husband as the relevant actor is noteworthy.

25. Al-Ghazali, trans. Holland, *The Proper Conduct of Marriage*, p. 74. The verse is Q. 2:223 trans. 'Abdullah Yusuf Ali. For discussion of other provisions of this verse, see chapter 7.

26. Al-Ghazali, trans. Holland, *The Proper Conduct of Marriage*, p. 75.

27. Shaikh, "Family Planning, Contraception, and Abortion in Islam," p. 115.

28. Shaikh, "Family Planning, Contraception, and Abortion in Islam," p. 114; see also al-Hibri, "An Introduction," pp. 57–8.

29. Shaikh does not refer to the Shafi'i view that the wife's consent is not required. See Musallam, *Sex and Society in Islam*, p. 31; Bowen, "Muslim Juridical Opinions," pp. 325, 327–8. Also see Keller, *Reliance of the Traveller*, p. 526.

30. These points have been treated in works from Fatna Sabbah's *Woman in the Muslim Unconscious* to Geraldine Brooks' journalistic *Nine Parts of Desire: The Hidden World of Islamic Women*. Sabbah's text is problematic in numerous respects for conflating source texts with their interpretation. However, it was groundbreaking and still offers some important insights into the Islamic tradition. Fatima Mernissi's work addresses the same issues; see especially the articles collected in *Women's Rebellion and Islamic Memory*. Malti-Douglas' *Woman's Body, Woman's Word* traces these themes through a variety of medieval Arabo-Muslim literary texts.

31. See, e.g., Ahmed, *Women and Gender in Islam*, p. 27 and Lutfi, "Manners and Customs of Fourteenth-Century Cairene Women," esp. pp. 117–8.

32. Ibn Jibreen is one of the muftis associated with the Saudi fatwa organization studied by Abou El Fadl in his *Speaking in God's Name*.

33. Ibn Baz, et al., *Fatawa Islamiyah*, vol. 5, p. 391.

34. In another passage in the *Ihya'* overlooked by those who quote him in support of women's sexual rights, al-Ghazali praises the practice of female circumcision; see Berkey, "Circumcision Circumscribed," p. 32.

35. The parenthetical "at least" seems to be the translator's addition.

36. *Sahih Muslim*, K. Al-Nikah, "It is not permissible for a woman to abandon the bed of her husband," trans. Siddiqi, vol. 1–2, p. 732. A

variant ending is also mentioned with "until she comes back" instead of "until morning."

37.   *Sahih Muslim*, K. Al-Nikah, "It is not permissible for a woman to abandon the bed of her husband," trans. Siddiqi, vol. 1–2, p. 732.

38.   *Sahih Bukhari*, K. Al-Nikah, "If a woman spends the night deserting her husband's bed," trans. Khan, vol. 7, p. 93.

39.   See Ali, "Money, Sex, and Power," esp. chapter 2.

40.   *Fatawa-I-Kazee Khan*, vol. 1, p. 270 (1588, #688).

41.   Wani, *Maintenance Rights of Muslim Women*, p. 24.

42.   See Ali, "Money, Sex, and Power," chapter 2. Consent to sex within marriage is one area where comparative examples can be especially useful in sorting through the range of Muslim views. On medieval Catholic canon law, see Brundage, "Implied Consent to Intercourse." Marital rape is a fairly recent legal offense; a woman's husband "could force sexual intercourse upon her without being guilty of rape" in England until a 1991 court decision. See Doggett, *Marriage, Wife Beating, and the Law in Victorian England*, p. 46.

43.   *Sahih Bukhari*, K. al-Nikah, "Your wife has a right over you," trans. Khan, vol. 7, p. 97; see a similar anecdote in Al-Sheha, *Woman in the Shade of Islam*, pp. 49–50.

44.   See Ali, "Money, Sex, and Power," chapter 2.

45.   Ibn Taymiyya is often quoted as espousing a more categorical right to divorce for a woman whose husband does not have sex with her. See Al-Sadlaan, *Marital Discord (al-Nushooz)*, p. 33; and al-Hibri, "An Introduction," p. 70, n. 70.

46.   The term *muhsanat* is used in at least two different senses in the Qur'an. In some places, such as Q. 4:24, it means married females; in Q. 5:5 it clearly refers to unmarried women. Views differ as to whether, in this context, it means women who are chaste or those who are free. This ambiguity gave rise to juristic disagreement over whether a free Muslim man could marry an enslaved *kitabiyya* (i.e., woman from *ahl al-kitab*). The general Hanafi view was that such a marriage was permitted, but other Sunni jurists held that while concubinage with an enslaved *kitabiyya* was acceptable, and marriage with a free *kitabiyya* likewise, a free Muslim man could only marry an enslaved woman if she was Muslim. None of this discussion considers the linkage between virtue and freedom, or rather the presumption that a female slave could or would not be chaste. I borrow the translation of *muhsanat* as "virtuous" from Friedmann, *Tolerance and Coercion in Islam*, pp. 161, 179. My discussion of intermarriage touches on classical topics also covered by Friedmann's thoughtful and thorough chapter, "Interfaith Marriage," pp. 160–93, and I have cited his text as a resource for those interested in pursuing further the specific topics discussed here.

47.   They disagreed, however, as to whether that dissolution took place immediately and irrevocably or was suspended until the end of the wife's post-marital waiting period; in the latter view, if the husband converted before the waiting period expired, the marriage would continue in force.

48.   Friedmann, *Tolerance and Coercion in Islam*, p. 161.

49.   For a brief discussion of "marriage equality," see Marlow, *Hierarchy and Egalitarianism in Islamic Thought*, pp. 30–34; also see Siddiqui,

"Law and the Desire for Social Control," and Zomeño, "Kafa'a in the Maliki School."

50. Hamilton, *The Hedaya, or Guide*, vol. 1, p. 110. Hamilton's often quirky rendering ("more like a summary of al-Marghinani's views, as they appeared in the Persian translation, expressed in Hamilton's language" than a translation, according to Imran Ahsan Khan Nyazee [Ibn Rushd, *The Distinguished Jurist's Primer*, xlvi]) is the only accessible English version to date; I have retained his language here. A new translation of the *Hidaya* by Nyazee is forthcoming from Amal Press (Bristol, England), with the first volume slated for publication in 2006.

51. Rather, he provides an extended discussion of the (im)permissibility of men's marrying *kitabiyyat* and/or "idolatresses," *mushrikat*, either free or enslaved. *The Distinguished Jurist's Primer*, 2:51–3. This is not simply because he is concerned with the lawfulness of men's actions alone; the immediately preceding section discusses, if only briefly, the case of women marrying male slaves. (It is permissible, provided that the women's guardians agree and that the slaves in question do not belong to the women themselves. *The Distinguished Jurist's Primer*, 2:49, 51. However, a number of legal thinkers consider marriage between free females and enslaved males so blameworthy as to be practically forbidden.)

52. Keller, *Reliance of the Traveller*, p. 529.

53. See Friedmann, *Tolerance and Coercion in Islam*, pp. 172–3, esp. n. 72, and my discussion below.

54. *Fatawa-I-Kazee Khan*, vol. 1, p. 115 (1216 #316); see also Friedmann, *Tolerance and Coercion in Islam*, p. 180. Friedmann, pp. 185–6, identifies Ibn Hazm and Abu Thawr as holding that marriage to Zoroastrians was permissible. In other contexts where Hindus or Buddhists were the relevant minority, some Muslim scholars seem to have held that they were to be considered recipients of revelation (*ahl al-kitab*), suggesting a strong practical role for proximity in what some consider purely theological questions.

55. *Fatawa-I-Kazee Khan*, vol. 1, p. 115 (1216 #316).

56. Here, I am only treating the case of conversion by "people of the Book." In the case of other (pagan, polytheist, etc.) converts to Islam, or of apostasy from Islam, no marriage can stand, whether it is the husband or the wife who is the Muslim partner. Again, however, very early Muslim practice allows for ambiguity on this topic; there is some dispute, for instance, over whether the marriage of one of the Prophet's daughters to Abu al-'As was preserved despite his refusal to convert until her waiting period had long expired or whether a new marriage followed his conversion. Accounts taking both views are found in *Sunan al-Tirmidhi*, K. al-Nikah, "Ma ja'a fi'l-zawjayn al-mushrikayn yuslimu ihdahuma," vol. 3, pp. 447–8.

57. Alalwani, "Fiqh of Minorities (1 of 3)." I would like to thank Junaid Qadri (personal communication, November 2004) for bringing this article to my attention.

58. See Friedmann, *Tolerance and Coercion in Islam*, p. 172. Friedmann does not highlight the distinction between already being married and getting married when noting the eventual demise of the "current of opinion willing to countenance the preservation of a Muslim woman's

marriage to an unbeliever." Notably, some of these unbelievers were
non-kitabis.

59. European Council for Fatwa, Resolution 3/8, "A woman embraces
Islam and her husband does not," from the Final Statement of the 8th
Ordinary Session.

60. He thus passes the first test that Abou El Fadl sets in his discussion of
authoritarianism in Islamic thought. Syed, discussing this issue (*The
Position of Women in Islam*, pp. 44–7), also acknowledges the jurists'
prohibition and that "practice from the earliest time is against such
unions" but uses a legal maxim regarding permissibility to declare
(p. 47) that "it is an acceptable proposition that Islamic law permits
marriage between Muslim men and Muslim women with women and
men, respectively, belonging to the ahlil kitab." Syed contends that the
Qur'an and the hadith "are silent on the question of Muslim women
marrying kitabis."

61. See, for example, the fatwa from Islam Q&A (www.islam-qa.com)
"Ruling on a Muslim man marrying a non-Muslim woman and vice
versa" (Question #21380). No individual mufti is listed as the author
of the response in question, but renowned classical exegetes are quoted
as prohibiting all marriages between Muslim women and any non-
Muslim, whether *mushrik* or *kitabi*.

62. On the applicability of Qur'anic commands to men and women, see
chapter 7.

63. Stability and justice, as medieval Sunni political thinkers knew well,
could at least in the short term be opposed. Different people come
down in different places on which ought to prevail.

64. Behnam Sadeghi has argued in the context of prayer, rationales for
specific rules may change while the rules themselves continue. Sadeghi,
however, views rationales as an epiphenomenon, and rules as a sub-
stratum that is not, in and of itself, particularly meaningful or revealing. Sadeghi, *The Logic of Law Making in Islam*.

65. Quraishi-Landes, "A Meditation on *Mahr*, Modernity and Muslim
Marriage Contract Law."

66. Fournier, *Lost in Transplantation*.

67. Bowen, *Blaming Islam*.

Notes to Chapter 2

1. *Sunan Abi Dawud*, K. al-Talaq, "Bab fi karahiyyat al-talaq," vol. 1,
p. 503. Also there: "To God, Exalted and Majestic, the most repugnant
(*abghad*) of what is lawful is divorce."

2. *Fatawa-I-Kazee Khan*, vol. 2, p. 167 (2263 #1363).

3. For a survey of twentieth-century reforms in divorce laws, see An-
Na'im, ed., *Islamic Family Law in a Changing World*. For a mid-
twentieth-century discussion of Indian application of Muslim divorce
law, see Fyzee, *Outlines of Muhammadan Law*, pp. 123–62.

4. Q. 4:35, 128.

5. Barring her involvement in "clear lewdness," on which see Q. 4:19,
Q. 2:229 discusses the permissibility of compensation if both parties fear

they will not be able to adhere to appropriate limits. Ibn Rushd, *The Distinguished Jurist's Primer*, vol. 2, pp. 79–84, discusses the debates over when and whether (and how much) compensation was permitted.

6.   There are two exceptions: widows wait for four months and ten days, regardless of whether the marriage was consummated, and pregnant women's waiting periods end when they give birth. There has been dispute, however, about the case of the pregnant widow; most have settled on the view that her *'idda* ends when she gives birth and she need not observe the rest of the mourning period. Additionally, there is a different length of waiting periods for slave and free women.

7.   The jurists understand this intervening marriage to be necessary from Qur'an (2:230); they rule that this marriage to a different husband must be consummated based on a reported statement from the Prophet that it was not lawful for a woman to return to a husband who had divorced her three times "until she has tasted the sweetness [of intercourse]" with her other husband. See, among other sources, *Sahih Bukhari*, Book of Divorce, "If he divorces her triply and she marries another husband after the waiting period," trans. Khan, vol. 7, p. 182; and Tirmidhi, K. al-Nikah, "On the one for whom [she is] made lawful and the one who makes [her] lawful," vol. 3, pp. 427–9.

8.   See, for a brief summary of differences on this point, Coulson, *A History of Islamic Law*, pp. 111–13.

9.   A few early authorities including Sa'id ibn al-Musayyab held that a man could take his wife back during her waiting period from *khul'*, even without her consent, if he returned to her the compensation she had paid him.

10.   Ironically, even some members of the 'ulama turned to this type of argument in their efforts to defeat proposed Egyptian legislation for stipulations in marriage contracts. Ron Shaham summarizes the arguments of the Shaykh al-Azhar: "The Qur'an defined the required relationship between the spouses as being based on love and compassion, whereas the proposed stipulations in the marriage contract reduced this relationship to a property transaction based on bargaining." Shaham, "State, Feminists and Islamists," p. 477.

11.   Ayubi, "American Muslim Women Negotiating Divorce," pp. 128–33.

12.   Zahra Ayubi's thesis in progress, however, indicates that in some cases Muslim immigrants refer to the laws of their nations of origin as their source for authoritative Islamic law.

13.   *Fatawa-I-Kazee Khan*, vol. 2, p. 167 (2263 #1363). See also Haskafi, *The Durr-ul-Mukhtar*, pp. 230–1.

14.   The husband's ability to refute a woman's claims that he has divorced her by taking an oath seems to have been widely practiced. One case in the *Musannaf* of Ibn Abi Shayba (vol. 5, pp. 251–2) unwittingly attests to this practice when discussing a matter of inheritance in the case of "the man whose wife claimed that he had divorced her and she brought him up to the Sultan, and he had him swear that he had not divorced her, then he returned her to him." When he dies, the fact that she inherited from him implies the continued validity of the marriage.

15.   Tucker, *In the House of the Law*, p. 65; Tucker's translation.

16.   As a practical matter, premodern Hanafi judges found ways around women's access to divorce while preserving inflexibility of doctrine.

17. For the concept of "traditionist-jurisprudent," see Melchert, "Traditionist-Jurisprudents and the Framing of Islamic Law."

18. Spectorsky, *Chapters on Marriage and Divorce*, pp. 248–9.

19. Jennings, "Divorce in the Ottoman Sharia," p. 165, notes that cases of "claims and counterclaims" are common.

20. See country profiles in An-Na'im, *Islamic Family Law in a Changing World*, for specifics.

21. This can cause problems where a suspended or conditional oath of divorce working to secure the wife's option to leave the marriage if the husband does (or fails to do) a particular deed relies on the resulting divorce to be final. Given the interconnected and intricately interwoven nature of legal doctrines, tinkering with one portion of the system is likely to have significant unintended consequences elsewhere.

22. As Amira Sonbol argues, it is not always the case that codified national laws are always better than "traditional" jurisprudential doctrines. See "Introduction," in Sonbol, (ed.), *Women, the Family, and Divorce Laws in Islamic History*.

23. Esposito with DeLong-Bas, *Women in Muslim Family Law*, p. 60; see also Mashhour, "Islamic Law and Gender Equality," pp. 582–4.

24. Esposito with DeLong-Bas, *Women in Muslim Family Law*, p. 80.

25. Some have argued that the availability of *khul'* induces women who have legitimate grounds for judicial divorce without relinquishing of dower to give up their dower in exchange for ease of obtaining marital dissolution.

26. See Al-Sheha, *Woman in the Shade of Islam*, pp. 101–3, for a summary of representative views on women's initiation of divorce. Al-Sheha insists that "the most natural and logical way to this peace [mentioned in Q. 4:128] is to let the man have control of the divorce process, not the woman."

27. Eid, "Marriage, Divorce and Child Custody as Experienced by American Muslims," proposes such a system. The Canadian Council of Muslim Women has been arguing against a similar proposal at the provincial level.

28. An-Na'im, "Shari'a and Islamic Family Law," p. 3; see also p. 16.

29. An-Na'im, "Shari'a and Islamic Family Law," p. 8.

30. The use of U.S. law has been an essential element of the strategy proposed by Karamah: Muslim Women Lawyers for Human Rights (www.karamah.org) for Muslim women to safeguard their rights.

31. Polygamy, or plural marriage, encompasses both polygyny, marriage to multiple wives, and polyandry, marriage to multiple husbands. Polyandry is relatively rare, and polygamy is often used synonymously with polygyny. I use the term polygyny here as it is more precise and seems to be gaining ascendency in scholarly literature. Though legal in most Muslim-majority nations, polygyny has only ever been practiced by a small subset of the population; it is most common in places, such as sub-Saharan Africa, where it is also practiced by non-Muslims.

32. On the construction of honor crimes: Abu-Lughod, *Do Muslim Women Need Saving?*, pp. 113–42. A vast scholarly literature on veiling exists; Bucar, *Beginner's Guide to the Islamic Veil*, serves as a starting point.

33. Majeed, *Polygyny*, p. 5. Her estimate of fewer than one thousand polygynous African American Muslim households makes them not only a

tiny fraction of the African American Muslim community (less than 1/10 of 1%) but also only a small fraction of the "30,000 to 100,000 people living polygyny in the United States." (*Polygyny*, p. 2) Of these, only a minority are Muslims of any ethnicity. The wide range reflects the difficulty in accurately counting, given the widespread criminalization of polygyny.

34. These justifications are not limited to the U.S. Rafia Zakaria writes of Pakistan: "Social activists argue that multiple marriages will solve the problem of destitute women and children who are without male guardians. Clerics remind everyone that promoting what is already permitted will end illicit affairs and prostitution." Zakaria, *The Upstairs Wife*, p. 249. Interestingly, recent Islamic State propaganda juxtaposes not polygyny and prostitution but slave-concubinage and prostitution. Umm Sumayyah al-Muhajirah, "Slave-Girls or Prostitutes?"

35. At the same time, treating "the tools of liberalism … as the only worthy moral framework in which liberation and progress can be executed, has the potential of demeaning and further marginalising … some queer Muslims whose relationship with traditional Islam and/or their choice to maintain closeted sexual lives is both important and essential." Esack and Mahomed, "Sexual Diversity," p. 53.

36. Majeed, *Polygyny*. On Imam Mohammed's community, consult Karim, *American Muslim Women*; on a smaller but historically connected group, the Nation of Islam, Karim and Gibson, *Women of the Nation*.

37. Majeed, *Polygyny*, p. 14. Polygyny is framed as a way to earn God's favor in a handful of blog posts by an African American Muslim woman writing under the pseudonym Maryam Hagar. As of this writing, "At My Husband's Wedding" had last been updated in December 2013.

38. Majeed, *Polygyny*, pp. 20–1.

39. cooke, "Deploying the Muslimwoman."

40. On Pakistan, Zakaria's *The Upstairs Wife* is an excellent starting point. For South Africa, one may begin with Hoel, "Engaging Islamic sexual ethics."

41. Inhorn, *The New Arab Man*, pp. 262–9, discusses polygyny as a less-than-optimal practice in one Lebanese man's life.

42. Majeed, *Polygyny*, chapter 4, discusses children's experiences of living polygyny; blogger "Sober Second Look" offers an introspective, bitingly critical reflection in "A Call in the Night." https://sobersecondlook. wordpress.com/2014/03/15/a-call-in-the-night/ last accessed 05.14.15.

43. Majeed, *Polygyny*, p. 23.

44. Majeed, *Polygyny*, p. 20.

45. Majeed, *Polygyny*, p. 132.

46. Aisha Geissinger, personal communication, May 2015.

47. Amina Wadud, "Ethics of *Tawhid*," p. 256.

48. Chapter 7 in this volume discusses *qiwamah* (related to the word *qawwamun*).

49. Wadud, "Ethics of *Tawhid*," p. 261.

50. Musawah's project to gather Muslim women's life stories focused on this type of story. Al-Sharmani and Rumminger, "Life Stories," p. 232.

51. Majeed, *Polygyny*, pp. viii, 65.

52. Ali, *Marriage and Slavery in Early Islam*, chapter 3.
53. Ali, "Marriage in Classical Islamic Jurisprudence," discusses these conditions.
54. As chapter 9 notes, however, the same argument could be applied to slavery.
55. Originally posted on the now-defunct Muslim WakeUp site, "The Polyandry Fatwa" can be found, for now at least, at http://diasporic-discontents.blogspot.com/2007/03/polyandry-fatwa.html last accessed 05.28.15.
56. hooks, *Talking Back: Thinking Feminist, Thinking Black*, p. 147.
57. De Sondy, *Crisis of Islamic Masculinities*.
58. Ali, "Progressive Muslims and Islamic Jurisprudence" and Abugideiri, "On Gender and the Family."
59. Asexuality and aromanticism, discussed briefly in the Coda to Chapter 5, are other forms of "queer" sexuality that challenge conventional assumptions about human flourishing. Some asexuals partnered with allosexuals choose polyamorous relationships.

Notes to Chapter 3

1.   Haskafi, *The Durr-ul-Mukhtar*, p. 24. I have altered B.M. Dayal's translation of this passage in several respects.
2.   Modern apologetics, as will be seen below, frequently claim instead that she was a wife. A war captive, Rayhana, is likely to have been Muhammad's concubine, though some sources suggest that he manumitted and then married her, as he had done with Safiyya, another war prisoner he purchased from her captor. See Ibn Kathir, *The Life of the Prophet Muhammad*; and Hidayatullah, *Mariyah the Copt*.
3.   Q. 2:221, 24:32.
4.   Terms for male slaves included 'abd (also "worshipper") and both ghulam and fatah, which could refer to either male slaves or male youths.
5.   Mattson, "A Believing Slave is Better Than an Unbeliever," p. 134.
6.   Ahmed, *Women and Gender in Islam*, pp. 67, 79–101.
7.   See Q. 4:3. *Al-Umm*, K. al-Nafaqat, "Ma ja'a fi 'adad ma yahillu min al-hara'ir wa'l-imma' wa ma tahillu bihi al-furuj," 5:215.
8.   While there were frequently distinctions made between types of slaves based on race, slavery as a whole was not racialized in Muslim contexts in the way that it was in the U.S. See Lewis, *Race and Slavery in the Middle East*.
9.   Peirce, *The Imperial Harem*. Their situation was unusual, however, and some have suggested that scholarship should not treat them alongside other slaves, or perhaps even as slaves at all. See Toledano, "Representing the Slave's Body in Ottoman Society," p. 57. Davis suggests likewise that "regardless of law or theory, a slave's actual status could historically vary along a broad spectrum of rights, powers, and protections." *In the Image of God*, p. 125.
10. For one discussion, see Diederich, "Indonesians in Saudi Arabia," pp. 133–6.

11. A number of reports over the past decade from organizations including Amnesty International and Human Rights Watch have documented these abuses.

12. There is significant dispute among human rights activists today as to what constitutes an acceptable use of the term "slavery." Miers ("Contemporary Forms of Slavery," p. 239) notes that, for some servants, "in practice their condition is very like that of chattel slaves" although "it is very different in theory." Toledano (in "Representing the Slave's Body") argues for understanding slavery as a "continuum" and Davis makes a similar point: "[T]he condition of slavery itself has not always been the most abject form of servitude, and it is not necessarily so today. Some contract labor, though technically free, is more oppressive than many types of conventional bondage." *In the Image of God*, p. 123.

13. U.S. Department of State, "Slavery, Abduction and Forced Servitude in Sudan"; and iAbolish, "Spotlight on Sudan."

14. Nazer and Lewis, *Slave: My True Story*. On the past and contemporary practice of slavery in the Sudan, see Collins, "Slavery in the Sudan in History." For discussion of the historical practice of enslavement of Muslims by Muslims in Africa, with attention to racial and ethnic patterns, see Mack, "Women and Slavery in Nineteenth-Century Hausaland," esp. pp. 89–90; also Lewis, *Race and Slavery in the Middle East*, pp. 57–9.

15. Algar, *Wahabbism: A Critical Essay*, p. 57.

16. On this topic, see the Feminist Sexual Ethics Project website and the links collected there: www.brandeis.edu/projects/fse.

17. Sikainga, "Slavery and Muslim Jurisprudence in Morocco," esp. pp. 64–6 and p. 70. Lovejoy downplays the significance of European abolitionist pressure, arguing that Europe "reluctantly pursued the fight whenever compromise proved impossible." He argues, instead, that abolition resulted from the incompatibility of Africa's absorption into the modern industrial economy with "a slave-based social formation." *Transformations in Slavery*, p. 253. Likewise, Collins notes that in the Sudan, British colonial officials were largely content to focus their attention on the slave trade, and overlook the widespread practice of slavery. "Slavery in the Sudan in History," p. 80.

18. Lewis, *Race and Slavery in the Middle East*, pp. 80–81.

19. Toledano, *Slavery and Abolition*, p. 127.

20. Toledano, *Slavery and Abolition*, pp. 122–9, remarks on the Muslim view of Muslim slavery as humane and, in particular, distinct from chattel slavery as practiced in the American South. On the attention to Muslim sensibilities in Western scholarship on Muslim slavery, see Lewis, *Race and Slavery in the Middle East*, p. vi (also Toledano, *Slavery and Abolition*, pp. 138–9, on this remark by Lewis; and Davis, *In the Image of God*, pp. 137–50, for a review of Lewis' work as a whole). See also Miller, "Muslim Slavery and Slaving: A Bibliography."

21. Ali, "Money, Sex, and Power," chapters 1, 4, and 5.

22. See, in addition to other verses cited below, Q. 2:178; 16:75; and 30:28.

23. Q. 4:92.

24. Q. 4:92; 58:3.

25. Q. 24:33.

26. Q. 2:221; 4:25; 24:32.

27. Q. 24:33.

28. E.g., Q. 23:5–6; 70:29–30.

29. See Mattson, "A Believing Slave is Better Than an Unbeliever," pp. 131–41, for discussion of these issues and the suggestion that the Qur'anic verses may make a distinction between permissible sex with war captives and sex with female slaves obtained in another fashion. On the general acceptability of sexual access to captured women in the ancient Mediterranean world, see Azam, "Sexual Violence in Islamic Law."

30. Nor can a woman (who cannot have sexual access to her male slave as a "concubine") marry her own male slave.

31. On marriage to female slaves, see Ali, "Money, Sex, and Power," especially chapters 2 and 5.

32. In addition to Mattson, "A Believing Slave is Better than an Unbeliever," see Brockopp, Early Maliki Law, pp. 192–205, on the early development of regulations surrounding the umm walad.

33. Bayman, The Secret of Islam, p. 173. Emphasis in original. Note that he makes a point about the exemplariness of the Prophet, then segues into the numerical limit of four, but does not address the Prophet's exemption from that limit.

34. Algosaibi, Revolution in the Sunnah, p. 10.

35. The use of the term concubine here, in the English translation of Algosaibi's commentary, makes it seem as though the use of the "prisoners" for sexual purposes was a foregone conclusion. Khan translates the phrase that appears in Algosaibi's English essay as "captured some concubines" as "received captives from among the Arab captives." There is a similar report in Bukhari's K. al-Nikah, "Al-'Azl," trans. Khan, vol. 7, p. 103. Sahih Muslim contains similar reports in its K. al-Nikah, "Al-'Azl," trans. Siddiqi, vol. 1–2, pp. 732–3. Sachedina, "Islam, Procreation and the Law", p. 108, cites this story, as quoted in Musallam, Sex and Society in Islam, in a series of hadith, also without any comment on its implications for any matter beyond contraception.

36. Algosaibi, Revolution in the Sunnah, pp. 37–8.

37. Algosaibi, Revolution in the Sunnah, pp. 40–41.

38. See one report in Sahih Muslim, K. al-Nikah, "Al-'Azl," (trans. Siddiqi, vol. 1–2, pp. 732–3) and another in the Muwatta' of Malik ibn Anas (K. al-Talaq), which makes reference to the ransom the captors hoped to receive.

39. Friedmann, Tolerance and Coercion in Islam, p. 177 (writing on a different matter). This did not always go unrecognized by earlier jurists.

40. The exception the jurists sometimes made for those too young to menstruate implies, of course, the permissibility of having sex with them.

41. See, for example, p. 529, from the section on marriage, which contains several untranslated passages.

42. Keller, Reliance of the Traveller, ix.

43. Keller, Reliance of the Traveller, p. 459.

44. Ibn Baz, "Concerning Polygyny," in Ibn Baz et al., Islamic Fatawa Regarding Women, p. 178. He is responding to a questioner who partially quotes Q. 4:3, mentioning orphans but avoiding the portion of

the verse discussing "what your right hands possess." On the inter-connections between polygamy and slavery, see Hasan, "Polygamy, Slavery, and Qur'anic Sexual Ethics."

45. Rahman, *Major Themes of the Qur'an*, p. 48; see also Mashhour, "Islamic Law and Gender Equality," pp. 568–9.

46. See, for instance, Khadduri, "Marriage in Islamic Law"; al-Hibri, "Islam, Law and Custom," p. 26; and Mashhour, "Islamic Law and Gender Equality," p. 569. The latter argues that "what is definitely clear in the Quran is that all its texts encourage the release of slaves." Wadud expressed a similar view in *Qur'an and Woman*, p. 101, but makes a different and, I think, more persuasive argument in her later essay "Alternative Qur'anic Interpretation and the Status of Muslim Women," pp. 14–15.

47. Syed, *The Position of Women in Islam*, pp. 33–6; Syed states (p. 36) that "those jurists of Islamic law who laid down the rule that a master may have sexual relationship [sic] with his female slave without marriage are totally mistaken."

48. Mernissi, *The Veil and the Male Elite*, esp. p. 139; Khadduri, "Marriage in Islamic Law," p. 217, makes the same point a decade earlier, regarding polygamy specifically. He argues that "because he was a religious reformer who was principally interested in preaching a belief in one God – a revolutionary belief principle in pagan society – the Prophet Muhammad did not go so far as to seek a complete change in the social system. The Prophet felt that advocating radical change might adversely affect the spread of his religious teachings; therefore, he sought to effect gradual change in the law." See also Wadud, *Qur'an and Woman*, p. 9.

49. If God is all-powerful, why did God not create a better, more just world? If this is not the best world, then God is an oppressor (*muzlim*) – needless to say, a problematic view. If it is the best world, however, then it cannot be unjust (if God is just). For a more thorough exploration of these issues as they were engaged by Muslim theologians and jurists, see Ormsby, *Theodicy in Islamic Thought* and Khadduri, *The Islamic Conception of Justice*, pp. 39–77.

50. This view, linked to Hasan al-Basri (Khadduri, *The Islamic Conception of Justice*, pp. 41, 108), both reflects a repeated Qur'anic sentiment (see chapter 7) and exists in tension with views about God's omnipotence, again raising the question of why God allows *zulm* to exist in the first place, and whether doing so makes God unjust.

51. Khadduri, *The Islamic Conception of Justice*, p. 106.

52. It is difficult, perhaps impossible, to know the precise scope of their activities, since unlike other insurgent groups, rather than welcome reporting of their actions, they kidnap and kill journalists. Because my primary interest is in propaganda rather than fact, the precise details are less vital, although the extent to which the idealized image differs from reality would be revealing.

53. For parallels with the sectarian rhetoric of the Fatimid caliphate, consult Pregill, "ISIS, Eschatology, and Exegesis."

54. Though, for instance, progressive Muslims lay claim to core tenets of Islam: justice, mercy, inclusion.

55. The National Human Trafficking Resource Center hotline had 3,598 reports of intra-U.S. sex trafficking in 2014. http://www.polarisproject.

org/human-trafficking/sex-trafficking-in-the-us last accessed 05.31.15. Worldwide, figures are in the millions according to the International Labor Organization. Ashley Binetti has suggested that IS recruitment might be understood as trafficking. See Binetti, "A New Frontier: Human Trafficking and ISIS's Recruitment of Women from the West." Georgetown Institute for Women, Peace and Security, 2015. http://issuu.com/georgetownsfs/docs/i2a_-_isis_and_human_trafficking, last accessed 06.16.15.

56.   I discuss these issues further in Ali, "Redeeming Slavery."
57.   Umm Summayah al-Muhajirah, "Slave-Girls or Prostitutes?," appears in the "From Our Sisters" section.
58.   ISIS, "The Revival of Slavery Before the Hour," p. 17, states that "enslaving the families of the kuffār [unbelievers] and taking their women as concubines is a firmly established aspect of the Sharī'ah that if one were to deny or mock, he would be denying or mocking the verses of the Qur'ān and the narrations of the Prophet (sallallāhu 'alayhi wa sallam), and thereby apostatizing from Islam."
59.   Berger and Stern, ISIS: The State of Terror; Zakaria, "ISIS Wants You to Share This."
60.   The quotation is from Baderoon, Regarding Muslims, p. 118.
61.   Bail, Terrified, pp. 81–3.
62.   Al-Dawla al-Islamiyya, "Su'al wa Jawab," trans. MEMRI, "Questions and Answers." My thanks to Jessica Stern for obtaining a copy of the PDF Arabic document downloaded from the Twitter account MEMRI cites as its source for the manual.
63.   Ali, Marriage and Slavery, and works cited there.
64.   Stern and Berger, ISIS: The State of Terror, p. 3.
65.   The document makes no mention of consent; men's ability to enjoy female slaves sexually does not seem to require any consent from them (setting aside entirely the question of whether minors, who may be enjoyed without intercourse if they are unfit for intercourse, could even give such consent). According to journalist Graeme Wood, some IS supporters he has interviewed insist that a slave has the right to refuse a sexual relationship, and that sex without consent would be rape. Graeme Wood, personal communication, April 2015.
66.   If one pays close attention to the numbering of entries, one will note that the translation jumps from question 22 to 24 and from 25 to 27. No indication, however, is given that entries 28 to 32 have been removed.
67.   The "Open Letter to Baghdadi" was signed by 126 men. Since then, a few women have added themselves as signatories using the form available on the website www.lettertobaghdadi.com. The letter does not confront the "ethical problem" posed by the "mere existence" of slavery in the Qur'an, in parallel to Laury Silvers' reflection on Qur'an 4:34. Silvers, "'In the Book We Have Left Out Nothing.'"
68.   Ali, "On ISIS and Authority"; Ali, "Redeeming Slavery."
69.   A few examples can be found in Gervase-Smith, Islam and the Abolition of Slavery.

Notes to Chapter 4

1. Nomani, *Standing Alone in Mecca*, p. 295.
2. See, e.g., Q. 23:5–6. The Qur'an describes *zina* as "lewdness (*fahisha*) and an evil way," and prohibits believers from even approaching it (Q. 17:32); in Q. 33:35, parallel praises are given of Muslim men and women who embody a range of virtuous behaviors including chastity.
3. The lowest age seems to be that of nine for girls (and fourteen for boys) in post-revolutionary Iran. On nine as the age of majority for females, see chapter 8.
4. Archard, *Sexual Consent*, p. 1.
5. A variety of historical and anthropological studies demonstrate that "the norms were not always followed." However, as one ethnographer notes for Morocco, "deviation from norms was more limited in the past"; further, "there has recently been some change in the norms themselves" regarding conduct. David, "Changing Gender Relations in a Moroccan Town," p. 210. For a succinct assessment of the contemporary Moroccan situation, see Dialmy, "Moroccan Youth, Sex and Islam."
6. *Nikah*, the term used by the jurists for the marriage contract, literally refers to sexual intercourse, so closely is marriage linked to sex. The treatment of this term in a passage from Haskafi's *Durr-ul-Mukhtar* (pp. 2–3) reflects this ambiguity: according to the Hanafi view cited, in some instances the Qur'an refers to marriage when it uses *nikah*; in others, it refers to any sexual intercourse.
7. From a punishment perspective the "who" is generally more important than the "what" – a disapproved act such as anal intercourse or sex with a menstruant who is a lawful partner is much less serious than an approved act with a forbidden partner.
8. *Sahih Muslim*, K. al-Nikah, "He who sees a woman, and his heart is affected, should come to his wife, and should have intercourse with her," trans. Siddiqi, vol. 1–2, pp. 704–5. One account includes, in his subsequent advice to his Companions, the Prophet's declaration that "the woman advances and retires in the shape of a devil."
9. Translated as "The first look is yours but the second is to your loss," in Mutahari, "The Islamic Modest Dress," where it is cited to al-Hurr al-Amili, *Wasa'il al-Shi'ah* (no further publication data provided). See also "Prophet Muhammad (s.a.w) said, '... do not let a second look follow the first. The first look is allowed to you but not the second.' [Ahmad, Abu Dawood, at-Tirmidhi]" Quoted in *Islam for Today*'s article "The Girlfriend-Boyfriend Relationship."
10. For discussion of Greek and Roman attitudes toward male/male sex, see chapter 5.
11. Yalom, *A History of the Wife*, p. 22, continues: "Although heterosexual marriage was the only legally recognized form of coupledhood in ancient Greece, husbands were by no means restricted to sexual relations with their wives. They could find supplemental sex beyond the marriage bed with concubines, male and female slaves, male and female prostitutes, and male and female lovers." (See Dover, "Classical Greek Attitudes to Sexual Behavior," p. 22, for a slightly broader definition of

moikheia, including seduction of other free women under a male relation's guardianship.) Yalom notes that "wives, on the other hand, were
segregated from men other than their husbands, and severely punished
if caught with a lover." (p. 23) Yalom does not specifically address the
possibility of married women taking female lovers or making sexual
use of their female slaves. See Skinner, *Sexuality in Greek and Roman
Cultures,* pp. 139–40, on an Athenian adultery case.

12. Treggiari, *Roman Marriage,* pp. 312–3. Notably, Treggiari attributes
the later European double standard in sexual matters to the influence of Islam, not Rome. Yalom (*A History of the Wife,* pp. 31 ff.) also
addresses the issue of adulterous wives in Rome. Skinner (*Sexuality
in Greek and Roman Cultures,* pp. 206–7) uses the term adultery to
describe non-marital sex by or with a married woman without inter-
rogating the presuppositions of her definition.

13. Yalom summarizes: "[T]he ancient Hebrew law proscribing adultery
applied exclusively to women, requiring them to limit their sexual
activity to only one man. There was no such requirement for married
men, who were allowed to have sex with unattached women. ... Men
committed adultery if they had sex with another man's wife." Yalom,
"Biblical Models," p. 23. See also Davies, *The Dissenting Reader,* p. 3.

14. Q. 24:2, used in this chapter's epigraph, for the number of lashes; see
Q. 4:25 for enslaved women who commit "lewdness."

15. See discussion of the word *ihsan* as it relates to the permissibility of
marrying enslaved women from *ahl al-kitab* in chapter 1, n. 46. Note
again here the ambiguity in the term *muhsan* as it relates to the *hadd*
penalty: it refers to both freedom and marital status.

16. See Deuteronomy 22:21–7. Stoning is mentioned numerous times
elsewhere in the Hebrew bible for a variety of non-sexual offenses (e.g.,
Leviticus 20:2 and 20:27).

17. Q. 24:4.

18. In one tradition reported on the authority of Abu Huraira, the Prophet
discourages the man from persisting with his confession of *zina* by
turning his head repeatedly, until the man confessed four times, equal-
ing the testimony of four witnesses. Abu Huraira is the prime reporter
of several traditions denigrating toward women discussed in chapter 1.
Sahih Bukhari (K. al-Nikah, "A divorce given in a state of anger, under
compulsion, drunkenness, or insanity," trans. Khan, vol. 7, pp. 147–8)
reports the event on the authority of another witness as well. A similar
account appears in *Sahih Muslim.*

19. Tirmidhi, as quoted and translated by Rizvi in "Adultery and
Fornication in Islamic Jurisprudence," pp. 271–2.

20. The theoretical writings of the jurists were not always followed in
practice; courts were more willing to entertain claims regarding *zina*
and individuals concerned with family honor occasionally acted extra-
judicially when confronted with suspicious behavior. According to
Leslie Peirce, in her study of the Ottoman court of Aintab, "The law
of the jurists did not seriously envision active prosecution of illicit sex;
rather, it was concerned with maintaining social harmony in the face of
what was tacitly acknowledged as the inevitability of *zina.*" See Peirce,
Morality Tales: Law and Gender in the Ottoman Court of Aintab, for
interesting discussions about how charges of sexual misconduct might

play out in practice. The quote is from p. 354. She goes on to note, though, that though it might not be expected, based on the doctrines of the jurists, "Deliberation about *zina* in court was possible because in practice judges were able to relax the stringent rules of witness set out in juridical treatises and manuals, admitting circumstantial and hearsay evidence." (p. 355)

21. Q. 24:6–9.

22. Additionally, whether consummation has validly occurred is important in determining when a woman who needs to consummate another marriage before she can remarry a man who repudiated her three times, has "tasted the sweetness of intercourse." Occasionally, other issues arise such as whether a woman who has illicit intercourse is counted a virgin or *thayyib* (non-virgin, previously married) for the sake of determining her consent to a subsequent marriage.

23. This approach is not limited to premodern texts. Kamal, *Everyday Fiqh*, vol. 1, pp. 79–80, discusses the necessity of ablution after sex with males of any age and minor girls. The only concession to concerns about lawfulness comes in a footnote: "One should bear in mind that Islam forbids the males to insert the organ into any part of anybody except in the genital part of the wife." (p. 79)

24. *Sahih Bukhari*, K. al-Fara'id, "The child belongs to the owner of the bed," trans. Khan, vol. 8, pp. 489–90; *Sahih Muslim*, K. al-Nikah, "The child belongs to the bed and one must avoid suspicion" (my modification of Siddiqi's translation), trans. Siddiqi, vol. 1–2, pp. 744–5. See also Rubin, "'Al-walad li-l-firash'"; and Van Gelder, *Close Relationships*, p. 91, who cites this story as it appears in al-Razi.

25. Legal fictions also have limits; the story appears in Ibn Hanbal's response (see Spectorsky, ed. and trans.) *Chapters on Marriage and Divorce*, p. 102, in a context where it serves as an argument for individuals to act in accordance with the actual, not "legal," status of things. There, it refers to whether a father can marry the daughter born of an illicit union with a woman. While some – al-Shafi'i is known to hold this view – hold that there is no legal relationship between the man and his biological daughter that would prohibit such a union, Ibn Hanbal briefly alludes to the case of Sawda discussed above. See Van Gelder's summary of this debate in *Close Relationships*, pp. 90 ff.

26. The opposition to the test from some contemporary Egyptian jurists stems from precisely this distinction. On the relationship between "pater" and "genitor" in pre-Islamic Arab custom, see Van Gelder, *Close Relationships*, pp. 19–20. He makes the point that in "traditional Islam" "biological parenthood" took on a greater importance than "dominance and possession" which were key components of paternity. However, the continuing importance of the dictum that "the child belongs to the bed" suggests that he may be overstating the relevance of biology.

27. Of course, there is still the social issue of imputations surrounding honor.

28. Moosa, "The Child Belongs to the Bed," on illegitimacy in South Africa, p. 174.

29. Nomani, *Standing Alone in Mecca*, p. 295. This "Bill of Rights" was republished (pp. 155–6) along with an essay by Nomani, "Being the

Leader I Want to See," in Abdul-Ghafur, *Living Islam Out Loud*. For the mosque Bill of Rights, see *Standing Alone in Mecca*, p. 293 and "Being the Leader I Want to See," pp. 153–4.

30. See chapter 6 for discussion of another example where a self-identified religious authority makes a declaration that ignores the dominant stance of all Sunni *madhahib* even as it echoes majority-Muslim sentiment.

31. Coulson makes the point that the Islamic "law concerning sexual behavior is based upon an entirely different, almost diametrically opposite, approach" to that adopted by "most Western legal systems" which do not concern themselves "with sexual relations between consenting adults in private." ("Regulation of Sexual Behavior under Traditional Islamic Law," p. 64) Leaving aside the question of whether Coulson's characterization of "most Western legal systems" is accurate, he is certainly correct with regard to the theory: consensual relationships are a matter of divine regulation, though if they do not come to anyone's attention, they are not a matter for government intervention.

32. AmericanMuslim, in "Comments: The Fatima Incident," comments page to Mohja Kahf, "Sex and the Umma: The Fatima Incident," at http://www.muslimwakeup.com/sex/archives/2004/11/the_fatima_inci_1.php#more, last accessed 04.19.06.

33. On these categories and their use, see Abou El Fadl, *Speaking in God's Name*, p. 97.

34. Of course begging the question of how they were expected to apply across the board even in previous centuries.

35. Peirce, *Morality Tales*, p. 353.

36. Michael Cook addresses this problem, along with a number of related issues, in *Forbidding Wrong in Islam*.

37. And in any case, "legal coercion is a flawed instrument for securing moral persuasion." Sanneh, "*Shari'ah* Sanctions and State Enforcement," p. 161. Unlike Ramadan, who acknowledges discrimination in the application of *hadd* punishments, Sanneh ignores women's vulnerability and the disparities in punishment. These are highlighted by Sidahmed, "Problems in Contemporary Applications of Islamic Criminal Sanctions."

38. Azam, *Sexual Violation in Islamic Law*, p. 246.

39. Hammer, "Center Stage: Gendered Islamophobia and Muslim Women."

40. Bowen, *Blaming Islam*.

41. Bail, *Terrified*, shows "how fringe anti-Muslim organizations became mainstream" in the United States between 2001 and 2008. Consult also the reports Fear, Inc. and Fear 2.0, both available from the Center for American Progress at americanprogress.org

42. Similarly, purity pledges, clergy sex abuse scandals, sexualization of young girls, widespread rapes on college campuses and in the military, hook-up culture, companionate marriage, and ubiquitous pornography coexist in the United States. Shabana Mir's *American Muslim Women on Campus* describes how female students negotiate treacherous college sexual culture.

43. Abu-Lughod, *Do Muslim Women Need Saving?*

44. Shaham, *The Expert Witness in Islamic Courts*, pp. 154–88, esp. pp. 175–81, discusses the case in the context of DNA and other evidence for paternity.

45.   Mona Eltahawy notes that when she "is asked how best to help women in" the Middle East, she responds "help your own community's women fight misogyny. By doing so, you help the global struggle against the hatred of women." *Headscarves and Hymens*, p. 29.

Notes to Chapter 5

1.   Keller, *Reliance of the Traveller*, p. 986. This translation is mine, based on Keller's presentation of the Arabic text, and differs in several aspects from Keller's English rendering. For Keller's biographical sketch of Ibn Hajar, see p. 1054.

2.   On the genre, see Rowson, "The Categorization of Gender and Sexual Irregularity in Medieval Arabic Vice Lists."

3.   Al-Dhahabi, *Al-Kaba'ir*; for biographical information on al-Dhahabi, see *al-Kaba'ir*, pp. 9–14 and Keller, *Reliance of the Traveller*, p. 1045. Discussion of enormities occurs in mainstream modern circles as well.

4.   Al-Dhahabi, pp. 60–70.

5.   Al-Dhahabi, pp. 105–6. On *qadhf*, and the Qur'anic connection to *zina*, see chapter 4.

6.   Al-Dhahabi, pp. 155–6.

7.   Al-Dhahabi, pp. 157–9. A *muhallil* is a man who agrees to marry a woman then divorce her after consummation in order to make it possible for her to remarry a husband who has divorced her absolutely.

8.   Al-Dhahabi, *Al-Kaba'ir*, pp. 201–9. On *nushuz* more generally, see chapter 7 and works cited there.

9.   Keller's note, Keller, *Reliance of the Traveller*, p. 990. See Keller, p. 1033, for a biographical sketch of Abu Talib Makki.

10.   Keller, *Reliance of the Traveller*, p. 991. My translation.

11.   Keller, *Reliance of the Traveller*, p. 991. My translation. Keller translates as "Two are of the genitals: (12) adultery; (13) and sodomy."

12.   Keller, *Reliance of the Traveller*, p. 966.

13.   Keller, *Reliance of the Traveller*, p. 986; my translation here differs from that in the epigraph by leaving *zina* and *liwat* untranslated.

14.   Ibn Hajar specifically condemns a man having sex with his *wife's* corpse, making clear that it is the act of intercourse with a dead body that constitutes an enormity. If the text referred to any woman's corpse, one might mistakenly attribute the prohibition of intercourse to the lack of the legal tie between the parties required for any touching, let alone sex, to be licit. Of course the deceased wife is no longer really a person, and so the marriage does not actually exist after her death, but most jurists grant a man the dispensation to see and touch his dead wife's body in order to wash her corpse. If intercourse with the wife's corpse is forbidden, though touching her for purposes of final ablution is permitted, intercourse with another woman's corpse is even more strongly forbidden, given that an unrelated man may not touch a woman even to perform the pre-burial washing.

15.   I use "same-sex" as a neutrally descriptive term, sidestepping important controversies over the appropriateness of terms such as lesbian,

gay, homosexual, and queer that are largely beyond the scope of this essay. Recently, some have advocated use of the Arabic phrase *al-mithliyya al-jinsiyya* ("homosexuality" in its literal sense of sexual sameness), while others have suggested that *shudhudh jinsi* (sexual queerness) is a useful phrase. In any case, I will use the term "sex" to denote the categories male and female, while recognizing that there is a debate over whether the use of sex to denote biology and gender to denote socially and culturally determined aspects of behavior takes account of the constructed nature of seemingly natural "sex." On this, see the discussion of hermaphrodites and sex-change operations, below.

16. See, e.g., Dunne, "Power and Sexuality in the Middle East." On the attribution of "deviant" behavior to the Other, and particularly the attribution of deviant sexual practices to Muslims by Westerners, see Uebel, "Re-Orienting Desire." "The vice of sodomy," according to Crusader literature of the time, was "not only tolerated in Muslim society, but actively encouraged and openly practiced." (p. 241) Although Uebel does not ask this question, it occurs to me to wonder in what ways the current scholarship positing a "homosexual-friendly" Islamic past draws on, and contributes to, the same type of generalizations.

17. Duran, "Homosexuality and Islam," p. 183. Even more recently, none of the twenty-one chapters in Thumma and Gray's *Gay Religion* discusses Muslims, and the only mention of Islam is in passing in a footnote (p. 6, n. 1). The founding of several organizations in the 1990s and the first years of the twenty-first century (al-Fatiha, the Yoesuf Foundation, Queer Jihad) by Muslims living in the West both signaled and furthered a shift in the discussion. The emergence of the Internet as a vital educational and organizational resource has contributed to the increased social and intellectual presence of gay and lesbian (and, to a far lesser extent, bisexual and transgendered) Muslim individuals and groups. Most likely, if research on a similar volume were to begin today, at least one organization would be mentioned.

18. Kugle, "Sexuality, Diversity, and Ethics," p. 198. Of course, as Kugle goes on to argue, homosexuality is an anachronistic term.

19. Kugle, "Sexuality, Diversity, and Ethics," pp. 197–8.

20. Malti-Douglas, "Tribadism/Lesbianism," p. 124. This begs the question of who gets to be a "man" – how maleness and masculinity were constructed is a crucial issue. See also Rowson, "Gender Irregularity as Entertainment."

21. Al-Rouhayeb, *Before Homosexuality in the Arab-Islamic World, 1500–1800.*

22. The term *sihaq* is sometimes considered to be derogatory, as *liwat* clearly is. Neutral descriptive terminology adopted by some contemporary Arab activists includes masculine and feminine variants of "homosexual." Helem, "Fihrist al-'ibarat al-'arabiyya." Thanks to Ariel Berman for sharing the magazine reference with me.

23. On mundane consequences of even illicit sex, see chapter 4. However, marital prohibitions could be engendered, in some views, by sexual touching falling far short of intercourse; in such a case, the same rules could apply to same-sex contact between women, making their omission notable.

24. And this, of course, returns us to the question of how to define what is "Islamic" – discussed in chapter 6.

25. My modification of Abdullah Yusuf Ali's translation. On this matter, see Malti-Douglas, "Tribadism/Lesbianism," p. 123.

26. One may also infer that the verse addresses two men if one accepts that it addresses an exclusively male audience; Q. 4:16's "from among you" could theoretically be inclusive of women, but it stands in contrast to Q. 4:15's "from among your women."

27. Duran, "Homosexuality in Islam," p. 181.

28. Kugle, "Sexuality, Diversity, and Ethics," p. 219. See also Hidayatullah, "Islamic Conceptions of Sexuality," pp. 277–9.

29. Jamal, "The Story of Lot."

30. Kugle, "Sexuality, Diversity, and Ethics," p. 204.

31. See, for example, the website of a South African organization called "The Inner Circle." http://www.theinnercircle-za.org/index_files/page 0002.htm, last accessed 06.27.05.

32. Biblical comparisons might be fruitful, both with reference to the story of Lot and also the parallel story of the Levite's concubine in Judges, chapters 19–21. I was made aware of this latter parallel through Azam, "Sexual Violence in Islamic Law."

33. Kugle, "Sexuality, Diversity, and Ethics," p. 215. See also p. 224.

34. Q. 23:165–6.

35. Halperin, *How to do the History of Homosexuality*, p. 41; italics in original.

36. What Martha Nussbaum and Juha Sivola argue for the Greeks holds just as true for medieval Muslims: "Seeing that it was possible for the Greeks to think differently of things that many moderns have regarded as natural or even necessary helps us to remove the false sense of inevitability of our own judgments and practices." Nussbaum and Sivola, "Introduction," in idem, eds., *The Sleep of Reason*, p. 10.

37. See, e.g., Dover, *Greek Homosexuality*. As David Halperin has argued, with respect to the ancient Greeks, "The physical act of sex itself presupposed and demanded ... the assumption by the respective sexual partners of different and asymmetrical sexual roles (the roles of penetrator and penetrated), and those roles in turn were associated with social distinctions of power and gender – differences between dominance and submission as well as between masculinity and femininity." Halperin, *How to do the History of Homosexuality*, p. 147. See also Brooten, *Love Between Women*, p. 2, for the remark that "Roman-period writers presented as normative those sexual relations that represent a human social hierarchy. They saw every sexual pairing as including one active and one passive partner, regardless of gender, although culturally they correlated gender with these categories." Quoted in Halperin, p. 56. See also Walters, "Invading the Roman Body," esp. p. 31; Dover, "Classical Greek Attitudes to Sexual Behavior"; and, on Muslim discussions of male desire to be penetrated, Rowson, "Gender Irregularity," p. 53; and Rosenthal, on *ubnah*, "passive male homosexuality," (p. 45) in "Ar-Razi on the Hidden Illness."

38. Published as "The Pleasures of Girls and Boys Compared," in Colville, trans., *Sobriety and Mirth*, pp. 202–30. This essay also appears as "Boasting Match over Maids and Youths," in *Nine Essays of al-Jahiz,*

trans. Hutchins, pp. 140–66. See also, in the same volume, "The Superiority of the Belly over the Back," pp. 167–73. Hutchins' translation should be used with caution; see A.F.L. Beeston's detailed review in the *Journal of Arabic Literature*, pp. 200–9. On the genre, see also Rosenthal, "Male and Female: Described and Compared."

39.   See Rowson, "Gender Irregularity," p. 60 and, for comparison, Dover, "Classical Greek Attitudes to Sexual Behavior," p. 25. The difference between the two settings is not the naturalness of men's attraction to younger males but the illicitness of this desire in a Muslim context.

40.   Keller, *Reliance of the Traveller*, p. 512. See also Maghen, *Virtues of the Flesh*, p. 261, on ablution after touching boys.

41.   Boudhiba, *Sexuality in Islam*, p. 200.

42.   Murray, "Woman-Woman Love in Islamic Societies," p. 102.

43.   Debra Mubashshir Majeed, who describes herself as a "recovering homophobe," writes insightfully on certain parallels between same-sex marriage and polygamy in "The Battle Has Been Joined." Like others who write on this topic, Majeed drafts her categories in such a way as to assume the question of gay marriage does not apply to Muslims.

44.   Muslim Canadian Congress press release, "Human Rights for Minorities not up for Bargain: Muslim Canadian Congress endorses Same-Sex Marriage legislation."

45.   See, for a brief personal account, Saed, "On the Edge of Belonging."

46.   Muslim Women's League, "An Islamic Perspective on Sexuality."

47.   As Kugle puts it, "[C]ontemporary Muslim moralists are not insulated from modernity, even as they depict gay and lesbian Muslims as corrupted by modernity." Kugle, *Sexuality, Diversity, and Ethics*, pp. 197–8.

48.   Murad, "Fall of the Family."

49.   Rather, a desire that arises in relation to an unlawful source should be channeled in a lawful direction, as reflected in the Prophet's counsel that a man who is aroused by a woman he sees should go home and have sex with his wife.

50.   Rainbow Crescent, "Consider the Following: Logic and Reason." Capitalization in original.

51.   Jakobsen and Pellegrini, *Love the Sin*, use the phrase "born that way" to describe the essentialist position on sexual orientation and identity. I choose "just created that way" to emphasize the external, divine intentionality of the creation of a human being with a particular set of desires.

52.   "One effect of (mis)understanding the history of sexuality as a history of the discourses of sexuality has been to preserve the notion of sexuality as a timeless and ahistorical dimension of human experience, while preserving a notion of discourse as a neutral medium of representation. A second effect has been to draw a deceptively simple and very old-fashioned division between representations, conceived as socially specific and historically variable products of human culture, and realities (sexual desire, in this case, or human nature), conceived as something static and unchanging. Foucault, I argue, was up to something much more novel, a radically holistic approach that was designed to avoid such hoary metaphysical binarisms. His aim was to foreground the historicity of desire itself and of human beings as subjects of desire." Halperin, *How to do the History of Homosexuality*, p. 9.

53. Weeks, *Invented Moralities*, pp. 98–9. See, for a brief survey of modern American views as to whether same-sex or same-gender desire is innate or chosen, the essays by Jeannine Gramick and Robert Gordis, along with associated materials, under the heading "Are Homosexual and Bisexual Relations Natural and Normal?"

54. Jeffrey Weeks, "The Rights and Wrongs of Sexuality," p. 21.

55. Hidayatullah, "Islamic Conceptions of Sexuality," p. 279, points out that "the notion that Islam tolerates homosexual tendencies but not behaviors points to an inconsistency in Islamic allowances for the satiation of 'natural' sexual desire."

56. On the "macrocosmic" dimensions of sex, gender, and marriage, see Murata, *The Tao of Islam*, pp. 143–202.

57. Of course, I do not mean to imply that promiscuity is in any way characteristic of same-sex sexual activity; I am merely making the point for contrast.

58. Abdul-Ra'uf, *The Islamic View of Women and the Family*, p. 35. Quoted in Smith, "Women in Islam," p. 532, n. 14. Abdul-Ra'uf elaborates on the "inherently indisputable evil and filth of homosexuality for its own sake" in his *Marriage in Islam: A Manual*, pp. 71–2.

59. Notably, even sources that discuss non-consensual crimes such as rape seem to be virtually silent about "incest in the normal English sense, whereas the 'milk-incest' peculiar to Islam is a recurrent preoccupation." Van Gelder, *Close Relationships*, p. 83.

60. That is, women who are too closely related to be potential marriage partners.

61. Haskafi, *The Durr-ul-Mukhtar*, trans. Dayal, pp. 1–2. In the style of many commentaries, the words of the commented-upon text are incorporated into the commentary. Dayal keeps them distinct through the use of bold-faced type, but I have not retained that feature here, considering it an unnecessary distraction.

62. Music, *Queer Visions of Islam*, p. 4. While I agree with Music on this point, I am not convinced of the prospects for success of his "search for queer-affirmative Qur'anic messages that have been hidden by centuries of biased interpretations." (p. 5) Rather, I think this topic is analogous in an important way to that of male privilege and patriarchy in the Qur'an. One cannot simply blame everything on bad interpretation. See chapter 7. On hermaphrodites, see Sanders, "Gendering the Ungendered Body"; and Cilardo, "Historical Development of the Legal Doctrine."

63. On this point, see Najmabadi, "Truth of Sex." The article's summary reads: "While trans-sexuality in Iran is made legitimate, homosexuality is insistently reiterated as abnormal."

64. Skovgaard-Petersen, *Defining Islam for the Egyptian State*, pp. 319–34; Harrison, "Iran's Sex Change Operations." See Najmabadi, "Truth of Sex," for a cogent critique of this celebratory discourse. See also Music, *Queer Visions*, p. 10.

65. Skovgaard-Petersen, *Defining Islam*, p. 334. Dupret summarizes this case, presents further developments, and considers its implications in "Sexual Morality at the Egyptian Bar."

66. Skovgaard-Petersen, *Defining Islam*, p. 321.

67. Skovgaard-Petersen, *Defining Islam*, p. 326.

234   SEXUAL ETHICS AND ISLAM

68.   In a marriage between two males, would each spouse retain the right to marry three additional husbands? Imagine the chaos that would result if Husband A and Husband B each independently married Husband C. Presumably, in a lesbian marriage, both women would have to remain monogamous – but if pregnancy is not a possibility, and there would be no need for determinations as to paternity, then what would be the rationale for female monogamy? I raise these questions not to be flippant or absurd, but because thoroughly working through their implications can give insights not only about same-sex intimacy but also about expectations in male–female marriage.

69.   Kugle wonders eloquently about this at the same time he *assumes* that it goes without saying that consent is vital for good (in the sense of ethical, divinely approved) intimate relationships.

70.   Schmitt, "*Liwat* im *fiqh*."

71.   BBC News, "Saudi sets sights on 60th bride."

72.   For a critique of the gendered notions of active and passive as manifest in Murata, *The Tao of Islam*, I am indebted to Laury Silvers. Shaikh discusses Murata alongside fellow "traditionalist" Seyyed Hossein Nasr in *Sufi Narratives of Intimacy*, pp. 203–17.

73.   The imperative to sort into binary categories should not be confused with assuming male and female were "opposite" sexes. Geissinger, "Islam and Discourses of Same-Sex Desire," p. 72.

74.   On terminology: Kugle, *Living Out Islam*, pp. 16,–19; Geissinger, "Islam and Discourses of Same-Sex Desire," pp. 70–1.

75.   Sinfield, *Sexuality and Power*, p. 28.

76.   Massad, *Desiring Arabs*. Kugle, *Living Out Islam*, summarizes Massad's argument (unsympathetically): "Massad contends that gay and lesbian identity is imposed upon Arab and Middle Eastern societies as part of a 'gay international agenda' of American neoimperialism in the region," p. 4. Esack and Mahomed, "Sexual Diversity," pp. 43–45, are more sympathetic to Massad (and critical of Kugle), yet they note that Massad's critique "is complicit in a sexual and epistemological essentialism," p. 45. Samar Habib, who self-identifies as an Arab "cultural" Christian (*Arabo-Islamic Texts*, p. 9), argues for an essential lesbian identity, and posits the "familiarity" rather than "alterity" of the Arabo-Islamic past, "how very often it demanded to be understood in terms far more similar to contemporary western epistemologies of sexuality than studies of western sexuality yielded about the West's own sexual past," p. 33. She defines her *Female Homosexuality in the Middle East* as "an essentialist project" and expresses her aim of refuting "widely accepted constructionist theories of sexuality" (*Arabo-Islamic Texts*, p. 37). She is, needless to say, among Massad's detractors.

77.   Kugle, *Homosexuality in Islam*.

78.   Peletz, *Gender Pluralism*.

79.   Najmabadi, *Professing Selves*, provides a nuanced account of both transsexuality and same-sex desire.

80.   On the U.S., consult Walbridge, "Sex and the Single Shi'ite."

81.   I elaborate on the possible impact of these stories in Ali, "Muhammad and Khadija," discussed further in Coda 7.

82.   Kugle, *Homosexuality in Islam*, p. 3.

83.   Aisha Geissinger, personal communication, May 2015.

84. Decker, *The Invisible Orientation*, discusses a range of orientations including pansexual and demisexual; these mingle with various attitudes toward romance; some but not all asexuals identify as aromantic. Some asexuals desire, seek, and find relationships, romantic or otherwise. Laura P. offers a Muslim perspective on asexuality in "Integrity of Heart, Peace of Soul: Finding My Path as an Asexual Muslim." She blogs at http://ace-muslim.tumblr.com/

85. Chapter 1 in this volume and Ali, *Marriage and Slavery*, chapter 3, discuss wives' sexual refusal; neither considers asexuality or sex aversion as a motive for refusal.

86. Ali, "Virtue and Danger," p. 2.

87. Consult, e.g., Kugle, "Sexual Diversity in Islam," pp. 154 ff. and Shaikh, *Sufi Narratives of Intimacy*.

88. Tin, *The Invention of Heterosexual Culture*.

89. To generalize broadly, premodern Muslim scholars treated women as biologically, legally, and religiously defective counterparts of men rather than as "different" and "complementary." Geissinger, "Islam and Discourses of Same-Sex Desire," p. 72. Kueny, *Conceiving Identities*, writes about the medical model of female deficiency; Stowasser, "Women's Issues in Modern Islamic Thought," tracks changes in Qur'an interpretation; and Seedat, "Sex and the Legal Subject," analyzes the shift from deficiency to difference in legal theory. Katz, *Women in the Mosque*, p. 3, points out that women did not always constitute a relevant category. On a continuum of most to least masculine/empowered, male and female are only two characteristics; slave status and minority are among other potential deficiencies. Glancy, *Slavery in Early Christianity*, pp. 24–6, and Ali, *Marriage and Slavery*, discuss the complex relationship between enslavement and masculinity.

90. Esack and Mahomed, "Sexual Diversity," p. 50.

91. Esack and Mahomed, "Sexual Diversity," p. 54.

92. Dean, *Unlimited Intimacy*, p. 95. This is the rationale for some African American Muslims who do not wish to register their marriages. Majeed, *Polygyny*.

93. Esack and Mahomed, "Sexual Diversity," p. 53.

94. In addition to sources cited in the chapter, consult Kugle, *Homosexuality in Islam*, pp. 252–6.

95. Salamon, *Assuming a Body*, p. 77.

96. Jagose, *Orgasmology*, p. 45, summarizing a point made in the literature about "histories of homosexuality."

Notes to Chapter 6

1. McLoughlin, "Swedish Imam says Islam forbids female circumcision."

2. This translation is mine, from the Arabic text included in Keller, *Reliance of the Traveller*, p. 59. I will discuss Keller's translation, which differs in substantial respects, below.

3. I agree with Mahmood that "any social and political transformation is always a function of local, contingent, and emplaced struggles whose blueprint cannot be worked out or predicted in advance. And

when such an agenda of reform is imposed from above or outside, it is typically a violent imposition whose results are likely to be far worse than anything it seeks to displace." Mahmood, *Politics of Piety*, p. 36. Mahmood is not writing about FGC here, but her remarks apply.

4. Historian Jonathan Berkey has suggested that rather than focus on the seemingly endless "polemical debate as to whether female excision is or is not 'Islamic'," one can analyze the ways in which various actors understand the practice "within the broader Islamic framework." Berkey, "Circumcision Circumscribed," pp. 20–21. The polemical debate is relevant, though, to the questions about religious authority and authoritarianism that I raise in this chapter.

5. Kassamali, "When Modernity Confronts Traditional Practices," p. 40. For her explanation as to why she prefers "female genital cutting" to other terms, see n. 1, p. 58.

6. Brooks, *Nine Parts of Desire*, pp. 53–4, has criticized Muslims who "turn their wrath on the commentators criticizing the practices [of clitoridectomy and honor killings], and not on the crimes themselves. The *Progressive Muslims* volume edited by Omid Safi reflects a determination not to be silenced by the thought of giving ammunition to what Muzammil Siddiqi refers to as "the enemies of Islam" (see chapter 8, n. 24). See also miriam cooke's concept of "multiple critique," in *Women Claim Islam.*

7. Kassamali, "When Modernity Confronts Traditional Practices," p. 42.

8. However, among African Christians, Protestants seem to be more opposed to the practice than Catholics, Orthodox, or Copts. Salecl, "Cut in the Body," p. 35, n. 2, notes that "the Catholic Church never officially distanced itself from clitoridectomy; the missionaries, in Africa, for example, did not condemn this practice. Only the Anglican Church, in the 1920s, denounced this ritual and advised its missionaries to prevent it." See also Gollaher, *Circumcision*, pp. 196–7.

9. See Berkey, "Circumcision Circumscribed," pp. 21–2, for a discussion of pre-Islamic Egyptian practices.

10. According to Toubia, "The transmission route of FGM helps to clarify it as a nonreligious practice. When Islam entered Asian countries from Arabia to Iran, it did not carry FGM with it, but when it was imported to Asia through Nile Valley cultures, FGM was part of it. This was the case with the Daudi Bohra of India, whose religious beliefs are derived from an Egyptian-based sect of Islam." (Toubia, *Female Genital Mutilation*, p. 32.) Toubia does not discuss South-East Asian Muslim practices.

11. See, for instance, Little, "Female Genital Mutilation: Medical and Cultural Considerations," pp. 30–34.

12. U.S. Department of State, "Indonesia: Report on Female Genital Mutilation (FGM) or Female Genital Cutting (FGC)." The medicalization of the procedure – promoted in some African nations as an ameliorative measure – seems to be leading in South-East Asia to actual "cutting" of some type, as sharp implements such as scissors are used. Moore and Rompies, "In the Cut."

13. "Claiming Our Bodies and Ou[r] Rights: Exploring Female Circumcision as an Act of Violence," quoted in Toubia, *Female Genital Mutilation*, p. 30.

14.   Toubia, *Female Genital Mutilation*, p. 31. More recent Western scholar-
       ship tends to repeat this dismissal of any relationship between Islam and
       FGC. For example, one recent introductory text declares "Female circum-
       cision is neither an Islamic practice nor is it widespread among Muslims.
       Rather, it appears to be an African tradition that remains in practice in
       countries like the Sudan and Egypt, among Muslims and non-Muslims
       alike." Esposito, *What Everyone Needs to Know about Islam*, p. 102.

15.   Berkey discusses the Shi'a on p. 26. For one example of a matter-of-
       fact reference to female circumcision in another context, see Ruxton,
       Maliki Law, p. 155.

16.   Berkey, "Circumcision Circumscribed," p. 25.

17.   On al-Ghazali, see Roald, *Women in Islam*, p. 241, and chapter 11,
       "Female Circumcision," pp. 237–53 more broadly; see also her brief
       discussion in the conclusion, p. 299.

18.   Toubia, *Female Genital Mutilation*, p. 43.

19.   Abou El Fadl, *Speaking in God's Name*, pp. 144–5; 62–3.

20.   Even Shaikh Muhammad al-Tantawi of Al-Azhar, who has opposed
       female circumcision, makes this point. The Qur'an itself does not say
       anything about circumcision, of males or females. However, it is uni-
       versally acknowledged that male circumcision is an Islamic custom
       – virtually all Muslim males are circumcised – and it is attributed to the
       covenant between God and Abraham. According to Gollaher, "when
       a retired Libyan judge, Mustafa Kamal al-Mahdawi, published a book
       that questioned the legitimacy of the ritual [of male circumcision],
       he came under furious attacks from the clergy and the press." A swift
       response from a prominent Saudi cleric accused him of apostasy for
       rejecting the consensus view that circumcision of males was obligatory.
       Circumcision, pp. 51–2. See also Abu-Sahlieh, "Jehovah, His Cousin
       Allah, and Sexual Mutilations," p. 47. Gollaher bases his discussion of
       this case on Abu-Sahlieh's "To Mutilate in the Name of Jehovah or
       Allah." See also Barlas, *"Believing Women" in Islam*, p. 65.

21.   Berkey, "Circumcision Circumscribed," p. 30: "[T]he few medieval
       sources which discuss female excision in any detail routinely direct
       their primary attention to the question of sexuality, and in particular
       women's sexuality and its control."

22.   Kassamali, "When Modernity Confronts Traditional Practices," claims
       that Qur'an 4:1 grants Muslim women "the right to sexual satisfaction
       within the context of a marriage" as well as the right "to initiate sexual
       intercourse." (This famous verse recounting the creation of human-
       ity does not actually mention sex at all, except in its reference to the
       creation of "many men and women" from the original pair.)

23.   Muslim Women's League, "An Islamic Perspective on Sexuality." See
       also Abusharaf, "Virtuous Cuts," on women's sexual responsiveness
       after excision and/or infibulation.

24.   El-Saadawi, *The Hidden Face of Eve*, p. 42, quoted Abu-Sahlieh,
       "Jehovah, His Cousin Allah, and Sexual Mutilations," p. 46.

25.   Abu-Sahlieh ("To Mutilate in the Name of Jehovah or Allah") has
       argued that "juridical logic cannot acknowledge the distinction
       between male and female circumcision, both being the mutilation of
       healthy organs and consequently damaging the physical integrity of the
       child, whatever the religious motivations lying underneath."

26. Abu-Sahlieh, "Jehovah, His Cousin Allah, and Sexual Mutilations," p. 54.

27. In his discussion of "female genital mutilation" and male circumcision under United States law, James McBride suggests that differential treatment "may be required for equal protection of men and women," posing one potential strategy for avoiding the problems with attempts to treat the practices in the same way. McBride, "'To Make Martyrs of Their Children'," p. 235.

28. Trans. by Ahmad Hasan, as quoted in Ahmad, "Female Genital Mutilation." See *Sunan Abi Dawud*, K. al-Adab, "Ma ja'a fi'l-khitan," vol. 2, p. 657.

29. Roald, *Women in Islam*, p. 247.

30. Hoyland, *Arabia and the Arabs*, p. 129. Circumcising women appears alongside the eating of locusts as matters where tribes could differ.

31. Gollaher, *Circumcision*, p. 192; Abu-Sahlieh ("Jehovah, His Cousin Allah, and Sexual Mutilations," p. 48) extends the same criticism to hadith regarding male circumcision.

32. Ahmad, "Female Genital Mutilation."

33. Badawi, "The Issue of Female Circumcision," appendix to *Gender Equity in Islam*. In his footnote to this hadith, Badawi cites "Al-Tabarani, quoted in Al-Albani, Muhammad N., Silsilat Al-Ahadeeth Al-Sahihah, A1 Maktab Al-Islami, Beirut, Lebanon, 1983, vol. 2, Hadeeth no. 722, pp. 353–8 especially pp. 356–7" and also refers to Keller's translation of *Reliance of the Traveller*.

34. Lane's entry for "bazr" (*Arabic-English Lexicon*, Book 1, Part 1, p. 222) provides some material suggesting the term might have been understood to refer to the prepuce, but the preponderance of his material suggests it means clitoris. See also Faruqi, *Faruqi's Law Dictionary*, p. 76 (where he also gives two Arabic equivalents for "glans clitoris": *taraf* and *tarth*); and Berkey, "Circumcision Circumscribed," p. 28. Roald, *Women in Islam*, p. 243, briefly discusses Keller's translation.

35. See Berkey, "Circumcision Circumscribed," p. 28.

36. Kassamali, "When Modernity Confronts Traditional Practices," p. 51.

37. Abusharaf, "Virtuous Cuts." See also her forthcoming edited volume *Female Circumcision: Multicultural Perspectives*.

38. Kassamali, "When Modernity Confronts Traditional Practices," p. 54, suggests that FGC should "be presented as a violation of the right to good health," with particular emphasis on the consequences of infertility.

39. Abu-Sahlieh, "Jehovah, His Cousin Allah, and Sexual Mutilations," summarizes these debates on pp. 49–50.

40. Ahmad, "Female Genital Mutilation."

41. Eltahawy, *Headscarves and Hymens*, pp. 124–5; for an extended discussion, pp. 114–39.

42. Ramadan, *Radical Reform*.

43. Shaikh, "Feminism, Epistemology and Experience"; Wadud, *Inside the Gender Jihad*.

44. On the latter, consult Moruzzi, "Cutting Through Culture."

45. Orbach, *Bodies*, p. 82.

46. In early 2015, sparked by Graeme Wood's *Atlantic* article "Is ISIS Islamic," there was an interesting conversation among scholars of

Islamic Studies on precisely these questions. Bradford, "God's Pious Dictators," offers an overview with links.

47. Hammer, "Changing the World: Reflections on Islamic Studies."
48. Moruzzi, "Cutting Through Culture," p. 206.
49. Moruzzi, "Cutting Through Culture." She cites useful literature at p. 205, n. 7.
50. He continues: "Ethically, it is necessary to acknowledge that, in such circumstances, one form of violence substitutes for another – in other words, that the well-intentioned abolition of dangerous practices nonetheless perpetrates a kind of symbolic harm on cultures organized around those practices." Dean, *Unlimited Intimacy*, pp. 58–9. Dean acknowledges that one may encounter "a clash of values … within a culture."

Notes to Chapter 7

1. This translation is by 'Abdullah Yusuf Ali. See also Q. 5:6.
2. Q. 2:187; my modification of 'Abdullah Yusuf Ali's translation. The word I have translated here as "your wives" is "nisa'ikum." *Nisa'* is the Arabic word for women, but it is also used to mean wives. The Qur'an also uses the term *azwaj*, a masculine/inclusive plural of the word *zawj* (see Wadud, *Qur'an and Woman*, pp. 20–3), to mean both spouses in a general sense and also wives specifically (e.g., 33:28, with regard to the Prophet's wives); see also Barlas, *"Believing Women" in Islam*, pp. 183–4.
3. See, e.g., Syed, *The Position of Women in Islam*, p. 57: "Thus, 2:187 tells us God has given the husband and the wife a complimentary [sic] role to each other neither one dominating the other."
4. Wadud, *Qur'an and Woman*, 11. I first encountered this insight regarding the explicit audience for the text in Esack's essay "Islam and Gender Justice: Beyond Simplistic Apologia," especially pp. 195–6. Barlas makes reference to this phenomenon on a few occasions, though to very different effect.
5. Daniel Boyarin makes this distinction between androcentrism and misogyny (or gynephobia) with regard to rabbinic discourses in Boyarin, *Carnal Israel*, p. 94.
6. However, there do seem to be some places in the Qur'anic text where, despite the use of terms such as *nas*, the people addressed are male. See, e.g., Q. 3:14 which refers to "people"'s desire for women, progeny, and material wealth. The Qur'an condemns this commodity-lust, but not the implicit commodification of women. On this verse, see Wadud, *Qur'an and Woman*, pp. 53–4.
7. The most important verse discussing creation is Q. 4:1, occurring at the beginning of the Surah entitled "Women." Rethinking androcentric accounts of creation has been one vital element of Muslim women's scholarship. Even a work on modern Jordan contains a discussion of these points; see Sonbol, *Women of Jordan*, pp. 207–8, in her chapter on "Honor Crimes." Al-Sheha, *Woman in the Shade of Islam*, p. 10,

is instructive as to how far the imperatives of modern discourse have affected conservative authors; while it asserts firmly that "Islam made both the male and the female equal in terms of humanity," it translates 4:1 with parenthetical identification of "Adam" as the first creation, and "Eve" as secondary: "O mankind! Be dutiful to your Lord, Who created you from a single person (Adam), and from him (Adam) He created his wife (Eve), and from them both He created many men and women ..." For broader consideration of creation and the expulsion from the garden, see Calderini, "Woman, 'Sin' and 'Lust'."

8. The rules for plurals referring to non-humans and inanimate objects differ.

9. The same problem exists with regard to dual forms as well. The use of a masculine/inclusive dual form in Q. 4:16, describing illicit sexual activity, has given rise to disagreement among commentators as to whether the verse refers to two men or a man and a woman. See chapter 5.

10. Q. 4:124.

11. In agreement with the noun *man*, "whoever," which is grammatically masculine.

12. For example, see Badawi, *The Status of Woman in Islam*, pp. 12–13.

13. 'Abdullah Yusuf Ali translation; see also Ahmed Ali's explanatory note to his translation, p. 50. Barlas demonstrates that not all discussions of witnessing in the Qur'an privilege male testimony over female testimony. *"Believing Women" in Islam*, p. 190.

14. This verse proposes an equal division for parents of a decedent who has also left offspring, indicating that in some cases the gender of the heir is not the deciding criterion.

15. My understanding here differs from that of Barlas, who sees difference but not inequality in these regulations. *"Believing Women" in Islam*, pp. 197–200, and passim.

16. On which, in Muslim contexts more generally, see Marlow, *Hierarchy and Egalitarianism in Islamic Thought*. She puts the matter succinctly in her Introduction: "[W]hile the Qur'an frequently points out the meaninglessness of differences of rank in terms of the afterlife, it certainly does not attempt to abolish them in the present world. On the contrary, it might be observed that the Qur'an endorses several forms of worldly inequality. ... Its central point thus appears to be that such inequalities have no bearing on an individual's moral worth and ultimate fate in the next world." (p. 4) Marlow points out that the strong egalitarian trend was limited to "the equality of free Muslim males." (p. 34)

17. Q. 49:13.

18. E.g., Q. 16:71, 75. See Barlas, *"Believing Women" in Islam*, p. 5.

19. Stowasser, "Women and Citizenship in the Qur'an," p. 33.

20. Stowasser, "Women's Issues in Modern Islamic Thought," pp. 15–16, discusses this shift, which she sets in the middle of the twentieth century. Abugideiri, "On Gender and the Family," p. 242, demonstrates that "the notion of marital complementarity, as conceptualized by twentieth-century Muslim thinkers has, ironically, reified the notion of hierarchical gender difference, and thus gender inequity. Complementarity, as interpreted by this discourse, provides the Islamic pretext to duly restrict female legal rights within the family and expect the wife-mother to sacrifice those rights in the name of family cohesion."

21. Barlas, *"Believing Women" in Islam*, p. 199.
22. For an entirely different approach, focused on *taqwa*, autonomy, and pedagogy, see Barazangi, *Women's Identity and the Qur'an*.
23. E.g., Q. 33:73.
24. These are the translations of, respectively, Ahmed Ali, Shakir, 'Abdullah Yusuf Ali, Arberry, Pickthall, Dawud, and Asad.
25. Men's duties were also emphasized by jurists, who focused on the pragmatic, enforceable components of interpersonal relationships.
26. Q. 4:34, *Al-rijal qawwamun 'ala al-nisa' bi ma faddala Allahu ba'duhum 'ala ba'din wa bi ma anfaqu min amwalihim. Fa'l-salihat qanitat, hafizat li'l-ghayb bi ma hafiza Allaha. Wa allati tukhafuna nushuzahunna, fa 'izuhunna wa'hjuruhunna fi'l-madaji' wa'dribuhunna, fa in ata'nakum, fa la tabghu 'alayhinna sabilan. Inna Allah kana 'Aliyyan, Kabir.*
27. Barlas, *"Believing Women" in Islam*, pp. 185–6.
28. For discussion of the range of meanings of "bi ma," see al-Faruqi, "Women's Self-Identity in the Qur'an and Islamic Law," pp. 82–7; al-Hibri, "Islam, Law and Custom," pp. 28–33; and Wadud, *Qur'an and Woman*, p. 70.
29. For the reference to Mary, see Q. 66:12; for Abraham, see Q. 16:120. For further uses of these terms, see Q. 2:116, 238; 3:17, 43; 30:26; 33:31; 39:9; and 66:5.
30. Ali, "Women, Gender, *Ta'a* (Obedience) and *Nushuz* (Disobedience)."
31. The identification of "clear lewdness" with *nushuz* is supported by some versions of the Prophet's "Farewell Sermon" in which he outlined the measures mentioned in 4:34 as consequences for "clear lewdness" by women. His words on that occasion are also the source for the specification that any striking must be "*ghair mubarrih*," or "non-violent."
32. Abugideiri, "On Gender and the Family," p. 293, refers to Q. 4:34 as "the Qur'anic verse treating spousal lewdness," implicitly insisting on a particular definition of women's *nushuz*.
33. Mernissi, "Femininity as Subversion," p. 109.
34. Mernissi, "Morocco: The Merchant's Daughter," in *Women's Rebellion*, p. 13.
35. See Rispler-Chaim, "*Nušuz* Between Medieval and Contemporary Islamic Law"; Shaikh, "Exegetical Violence: *Nushuz* in Qur'anic Gender Ideology"; and Ali, "Women, Gender, *Ta'a* (Obedience), and *Nushuz* (Disobedience)."
36. Thomas Cleary's translation and a recent Saudi-financed version based on the translation by 'Abdullah Yusuf Ali.
37. Ahmed Ali, *Al-Qur'an: A Contemporary Translation*.
38. On Qutb's approach to *nushuz*, see Wadud, *Qur'an and Woman*, pp. 74–5.
39. Raines and Maguire, eds., Esack, "Islam and Gender Justice: Beyond Simplistic Apologia" and Engineer, "Islam, Women, and Gender Justice."
40. Engineer, "Islam, Women, and Gender Justice," p. 111. Ellipsis in original. Syed, *The Position of Women in Islam*, p. 56, calls this "complete equality" but clearly states that the "degree" portion of the verse relating to divorce is exempt from this characterization.
41. *Lahunna mithl alladhi 'alayhinna.*
42. *Wa li'l-rijal 'alayhinna daraja.*

43. Engineer, "Islam, Women, and Gender Justice," p. 111.
44. Esposito with DeLong-Bas, *Women in Muslim Family Law*, p. 134; see also Niazi, *Modern Challenges*, p. 11.
45. Nasr, "Manhood in the Qur'an and Sunnah."
46. Wadud makes this point (*Qur'an and Woman*, p. 68), while situating her discussion of Q. 2:228 within a larger discussion of "degrees" elsewhere in the Qur'an (ibid., pp. 66–9). See also Barlas, *"Believing Women" in Islam*, pp. 192–7; Syed, *The Position of Women in Islam*, p. 56. Syed does stress "equality", however, which he views as being reinforced by 2:187, the garment verse.
47. Barlas, *"Believing Women" in Islam*, p. 6.
48. My modification of 'Abdullah Yusuf Ali's translation.
49. My modification of 'Abdullah Yusuf Ali's translation. Note that the "they" is in the masculine/inclusive plural, so it could mean if the husbands want to reconcile, or if *both* the husbands and wives want to reconcile. However, the former interpretation is more likely since the husbands are the ones said to have "more right."
50. Engineer, "Islam, Women, and Gender Justice," p. 112.
51. Engineer, "Islam, Women, and Gender Justice," p. 112.
52. Engineer, "Islam, Women, and Gender Justice," p. 118. He elaborates: "The normative pronouncements of the Qur'an are eternal and while rethinking issues in Islamic Shari'ah, particularly pertaining to women's rights, the normative pronouncements will have precedence over the contextual. But during the early centuries contextual often had precedence over normative and it was quite 'normal' then. And hence these formulations became widely acceptable in that society. These laws were thought to be normative then and hence struck deep roots in society as well as in the hearts and minds of the people. They came to acquire the status of immutability with the passage of time."
53. Engineer, "Islam, Women, and Gender Justice," p. 121.
54. Esack "Islam and Gender Justice," p. 190, quoting Q. 2:228 (mistakenly cited as 2:118): "And women shall have rights similar to the rights against them, according to what is equitable." He also quotes Q. 9:71: "Believers, men and women, are protectors, one of another: they enjoin what is just and forbid what is evil."
55. Esack, "Islam and Gender Justice," p. 188.
56. Esack, "Islam and Gender Justice," p. 195.
57. Q. 4:34 begins with references to both men and women in the third person ("Men are *qawwamuna 'ala* women"), but switches to second-person address to men when discussing female *nushuz*.
58. For example, if "they both fear that they will not observe God's limits." Q. 2:229
59. Barlas, *Believing Women in Islam*, p. 198, specifically with regard to Q. 4:34; Wadud, *Qur'an and Woman*, pp. 80–82.
60. My translation, drawing on Cleary.
61. Aisha Geissinger addresses the issue of how the Qur'an treats gender in this verse and others that discuss fasting in an as-yet unpublished paper, "Gendering the Communal Body: Fasting in the Qur'an and the Hadith."
62. One can thus understand Qur'anic injunction to perform ablution "if you have touched women"; see this chapter's epigraph as well as

Q. 5:6. The addressees ("you") are in the masculine/inclusive plural, but consensus holds that ablution is not merited by women touching women, as it would be if the command applied to both men and women. Rather, it is men touching women that generates the obligation of ablution, making men the addressees. There is disagreement as to what type of touching generates the requirement of ablution (whether mere skin contact is meant or specifically sexual touching) as well as whether the same requirements apply to women who touch men. See discussion in Maghen, *Virtues of the Flesh*, pp. 247–50. Maghen (p. 250) quotes Ibn Hazm's statement in the *Muhalla* that the Qur'anic provision "is binding for men if they touch women and for women if they touch men." (My translation, from the Arabic text presented by Maghen.)

63. My translation, drawing on Cleary and 'Abdullah Yusuf Ali.

64. The importance of this metaphor appears in a hadith where, with regard to the permissibility of performing coitus interruptus, someone says: "She is your field, if you wish, water it; if you wish, leave it thirsty."

65. Barlas, *"Believing Women" in Islam*, pp. 160–64. The summary by Kassis, *A Concordance of the Qur'an*, p. 548, shows a number of instances in which *harth* refers specifically to agricultural use (in addition to the verbal form in Q. 56:63, see 2:71, 205; 3:14; 3:117; 6:136, 138; 21:78; 68:22) and one verse, 42:20, where the term appears three times referring to the *harth* of this world or that of the hereafter.

66. The connotations of fertility also implicit in this reference to a woman as a tilth have also been used to argue that *harth* implies productivity, and so it is vaginal intercourse that is meant, not anal intercourse. See, e.g., Ibn Taymiyya, *Al-Fatawa al-Kubra*, K. al-Nikah, "Fi rajul yankihu zawjatahu fi dubriha," vol. 2, pp. 74–5.

67. Sachedina, "Islam, Procreation and the Law," p. 109.

68. In *Sahih Muslim*, the source of the conflict is reported as a Jewish objection to intercourse from behind. K. al-Nikah, "Permissibility of having sexual intercourse with one's wife from the front or from behind avoiding the anus," trans. Siddiqi, vol. 1–2, pp. 731–2.

69. For an interesting parallel discussion of sexual positions in rabbinic law, see Boyarin, *Carnal Israel*, pp. 110–11, 116–20.

70. The one relevant verse possibly suggesting that a woman could reject male sexual control is in the command not to force female slaves into prostitution against their wills; see chapter 3.

71. Barlas, *"Believing Women" in Islam*, p. 5.

72. Barlas, *"Believing Women" in Islam*, p. 205.

73. Halperin, *How To Do the History of Homosexuality*, p. 153.

74. For a useful reflection on related questions, see Plaskow, "The Right Question is Theological."

75. Ali, "The Omnipresent Male Scholar." Ahmed, "Islamic Law and Theology," argues that feminist thought underlies the pragmatic approach to Islamic law.

76. Bauer, *Gender Hierarchy in the Qur'an*, p. 4.

77. Wadud, *Inside the Gender Jihad*, p. 192, in dialogue with Khaled Abou El Fadl's notion of the "conscientious pause" (*Speaking in God's Name*,

pp. 94, 213). These ideas are discussed in Hammer, *American Muslim Women*, pp. 68–69, and Hidayatullah, *Feminist Edges of the Qur'an*, pp. 138–40. I discuss Wadud briefly in Ali, "Just Say Yes," p. 123, contrasting her "no" and Abou El Fadl's "conscientious pause" with al-Shafi'i's practice: he sometimes explicitly affirms scriptural texts while presenting interpretations which effectively negate the texts, or render them inoperative.

78.   Silvers proposes drawing on the writings of thirteenth-century Andalusian mystic Ibn 'Arabi as a way of approaching the fearsome task of interpreting the text, or perhaps the task of interpreting the fearsome text. Silvers, "In the Book We Have Left Out Nothing."

79.   Rhouni, *Secular and Islamic Critiques in the Work of Fatima Mernissi*, touches on similar topics.

80.   Hidayatullah, *Feminist Edges of the Qur'an*, pp. 186–92. Though scholars including Asma Barlas have made similar points, Hidayatullah argues that earlier women's thinking has sometimes been mired in binary oppositions despite its explicit affirmation of the importance of relationality: "While exegetes of feminist tafsir have understood gender as a dynamic social performance ... of sexual difference, they have inadvertently – often contrary to their stated intentions – remained attached to essentialized conceptions of sex and sexual difference," p. 186. She suggests that "a more productive understanding of equality will require a different view of sexual difference and sex," p. 189.

81.   Lamptey, *Never Wholly Other*; consult, also, the contributions to Aslan, Hermansen, and Medeni, eds, *Muslima Theology*.

82.   Chaudhry, *Domestic Violence in the Islamic Tradition*, and Bauer, *Gender Hierarchy in the Qur'an*, both attend to premodern thinkers and contemporary ones. For another approach to gender in Qur'anic interpretation, consult Geissinger, *Gender and Muslim Constructions of Exegetical Authority*.

83.   On this point, Hidayatullah, *Feminist Edges*, pp. 59–60. Raja Rhouni does advocate a new perspective on the Qur'anic text (Hidayatullah, pp. 144–5).

84.   I explore these issues in the Qur'anic stories of Mary in an article in progress; an early attempt to think through some of these issues appears in Birkel, *Qur'an in Conversation*.

85.   For instance, Kueny, *Conceiving Identities*, and De Sondy, *The Crisis of Islamic Masculinities*.

86.   Hidayatullah, *Feminist Edges*, p. 176.

87.   Omaima Abou-Bakr, "The Interpretive Legacy of Qiwama as an Exegetical Construct," p. 61.

88.   Shaikh, *Sufi Narratives of Intimacy*.

89.   Shaikh, *Sufi Narratives of Intimacy*, p. 150.

90.   Ali, "Muhammad and Khadija."

91.   I owe my thinking on this point to conversations with Amina Wadud, Laury Silvers, and Sa'diyya Shaikh. Also Dean, *Unlimited Intimacy*, pp. 180–1.

Notes to Chapter 8

1. *Sahih Bukhari*, Book of Marriage, "A man marrying off his minor children," no. 64 and nearly identical content with a different chain of transmitters under the next item, "The marrying of a daughter by her father to the ruler," no. 65 (trans. Khan, vol. 7, p. 50). See also "Who consummated a marriage with his wife when she was a girl of nine years," no. 88 reported on the authority of 'Urwa by his son Hisham. All three versions mention that "she remained with him for nine years" – that is, until his death.

2. See, for example, Sachs, "Baptist Pastor Attacks Islam"; Cooperman, "Anti-Muslim Remarks Stir Tempest"; and Jones, "Baptist pastor's words shock Muslim leaders."

3. This point is made by Rev. Jerry Falwell in his comment on the matter, "Muhammad, a 'demon-possessed pedophile'?" The sources cited by Vines can be found in Caner and Caner, *Unveiling Islam*, pp. 41, 56, 59–60, 135, 141, n. 4. The statement provoked additional comment in the Baptist press. Sources are more fully explored in Starnes, "Southern Baptist leaders affirm Vines in the wake of national attacks," and Wingfield, "What are the facts behind Vines' words?"

4. *Sahih Muslim*, K. al-Nikah, "It is permissible for the father to give the hand of his daughter in marriage even when she is not fully grown up" (trans. Siddiqi, vol. 1–2, pp. 715–16; the translator's extended apologetic in the notes to these hadith is noteworthy on its own). Al-Nasa'i's *Sunan* includes one cluster of reports positing ages at marriage of six, seven, and nine; each of the three specifies that consummation occurred at age nine. Another adjacent report puts marriage at nine, but does not mention consummation. (K. al-Nikah, "Inkah al-rajul ibnatahu al-saghira," vol. 6, pp. 82–3.) Two other reports in al-Nasa'i, found in a section entitled "Consummation with a girl of nine," both provide an age of six at marriage and nine at consummation. (K. al-Nikah, "Al-bina'a bi ibnat tis'a," vol. 6, p. 131.) Ibn Hanbal provides a report in which Aishah was six or seven at marriage, nine at consummation, and eighteen at Muhammad's death. (*Chapters on Marriage and Divorce*, p. 97.) On al-Shafi'i's and Ibn Hanbal's treatment of this marriage, see Ali, "A Beautiful Example," pp. 280–82. Her age was not the only noteworthy information about Aishah's marriage; other reports in various hadith texts point out that her marriage and consummation took place during the month of Shawwal, previously considered inauspicious for such events.

5. *First Coast News*, June 13, 2002, http://www.firstcoastnews.com/news/2002-06-13/islam_vines.asp, last accessed 11.26.04.

6. Cooperman, "Anti-Muslim Remarks Stir Tempest." This is apparently a possible feature of Arabic. However, it has not been a common interpretation. Furthermore, while the reports in Bukhari's Book of Marriage include only the additional information that she was with him for nine years (until his death, as all accounts are clear that she was his wife until that time); other accounts, including one in *Sahih Muslim* and one in Al-Nasa'i's *Sunan* state specifically that she was eighteen when Muhammad died; it is not possible to suggest that this

meant twenty-eight. (This point was made eloquently by Christopher Melchert in an email to the Islam section of the American Academy of Religion after this was first drafted.) Notably, a press release from CAIR does not include any specific information about Aishah's age. See Islam-Infonet, "Baptists Call Prophet Muhammad Demon-Possessed Pedophile." Other less direct attempts to rebut the claim are quoted by Jones: "Syad Ahsani of Arlington, Southwest regional chairman of the American Muslim Alliance, said Muhammad was betrothed to the child, which was a common practice; however, such marriages weren't consummated until children reached adolescence. [Hodan] Hassan [a spokeswoman for the Washington-based Council for American-Islamic Relations,] said it is not known when Muhammad's marriage was consummated." Jones, "Baptist pastor's words shock Muslim leaders." For the Council on American-Islamic Relations, see CAIR, "President Bush asked to repudiate anti-Muslim remarks."

7. On these accusations, see Reeves, *Muhammad in Europe*, pp. 215–16, 236–40.

8. Malik, *Islam and Modernity*, p. 69.

9. For one example of an anti-Islam site making claims about Aishah's age at marriage, see Ex-Muslim.com, "Evidence that Aisha was 9 when her marriage to Muhammad was consummated."

10. On age of sexual consent, see Archard, *Sexual Consent*, pp. 116–29. Archard's discussion is helpful in what it says, and illuminating in what it does not. As is to be expected from a work concerned with sexual consent in the modern Western world, he does not discuss children and sex in the context of marriage, except to note (p. 117) that in contemporary Europe "all jurisdictions set the age at which persons can marry some years higher" than the age of sexual "majority" – i.e., permissible sexual activity. See pp. 126–8 for a brief discussion of inter-generational sexual activity.

11. See Stowasser, *Women in the Qur'an, Tradition, and Interpretations*.

12. Aziz, "Age of Aisha (*ra*) at time of marriage," from the website of Ahmadiyya Anjuman Isha'at Islam Lahore Inc. U.S.A.

13. Submission.org, "Prophet Muhammed's Marriage to Aisha." Note that there is no explicit mention of Muhammad's marriage to Aishah in the Qur'an.

14. He is identified as its vice-president in various online materials, but its website (http://www.irfiweb.org/) is not available as of 11.25.05.

15. Shanavas, "Ayesha's Age: The Myth of a Proverbial Wedding Exposed." Shanavas frames his comments as an "answer to [his] Christian friend." He argues that "based on the evidences presented above, the marriage of fifty-two-year-old Prophet (pbuh) with Ayesha (ra) at nine year of age is only a proverbial myth. On the contrary, Ayesha (ra) was an intel-lectually and physically mature Bikr (virgin = adult unmarried woman with no sexual experience) when she married Prophet (pbuh)."

16. On one scholarly attempt to assess this corpus of material, see Schoeler, "Foundations for a New Biography of Muhammad."

17. Nadvi, *Women Companions of the Holy Prophet and Their Sacred Lives*, p. 34.

18. Nadvi, *Women Companions of the Holy Prophet and Their Sacred Lives*, p. 35.

19.   Spellberg, *Politics, Gender, and the Islamic Past*, p. 31.

20.   Thompson, *The Wives of the Prophet Muhammad*, p. 15. Thompson includes parenthetical Arabic honorifics after the mentions of the Prophet and Aishah which are not reproduced here.

21.   Syed explicitly declares, without citing any sources, what Thompson only implies: "The Prophet's (pbuh) own marriage to Ayesha when she was nine years old was performed in Mecca long before the Islamic laws of marriage were revealed at Medina by the Qur'anic verses. However as the consummation of the said marriage of Ayesha and the Prophet (pbuh) was postponed for five years (some say seven years) to allow Ayesha to attain majority, in reality the marriage of Ayesha took place when she was either 14 or 16 years old." *The Position of Women in Islam*, p. 40.

22.   Moin, *Umm al-Mu'minin 'A'ishah Siddiqah*, pp. 4–5.

23.   Moin, *Umm al-Mu'minin 'A'ishah Siddiqah*, p. 8.

24.   Identified in the article as "Dr. Muzammil H. Siddiqi, former President of the Islamic Society of North America and Director of the Islamic Society of Orange County, Garden Grove, California." He continues: "Her maturity, knowledge, intelligence, and contributions during the life of the Prophet and afterwards all indicate that she was either an exceptional nine-year-old or must have been older than that. Whatever the case may be about her age, one thing is certain: she was a most compatible spouse of Prophet Muhammad. None of the contemporaries of the Prophet, his friends or foes, are reported to be surprised by this marriage or made objections to it." Siddiqi, "Would a 50-year-old 'Prophet of God' Have Sex with a 9-year-old Girl?"

25.   Likewise, in one of three question-and-answer exchanges about Aishah's age posted at the Jamaat-e-Islami site, the respondent gives, without any textual citation, his own personal opinion that "consummation [occurred] at the age of 9 to 11."

26.   Even a Jamaat-e-Islami response to a question as to whether Aishah was seven at her marriage is answered in the following way: "There are different reports and traditions regarding Umm-ul-Mo'mineen Aishah's age when she was betrothed. What every one agrees to is that while the promise/*nikah* happened in Makkah, she was delivered to the house of the Prophet (s.a.w.) (meaning her '*Rukhsati*') about *four* years later in Medina. Thus even according to the age you have quoted, she was about 11 years old when she entered the Prophet's *haram* in Madina. Some believe that she was above 13; some others reports say much older (17, 19). The generally quoted age is 9 years." Haq, "Marriage of Ayesha (RA) with Prophet Muhammad (p.b.u.h.)" In reponse to an earlier query, the same author makes clear that while "Some scholars do insist that she was older ... most agree she was either 6 or 7 when betrothed." He gives his "personal opinion" that "consummation [took place] at the age of 9 to 11."

27.   Muhaddith.org, "Answers to Attacks Against Islam: Morality of marrying Aishah at an early age," emphasis in original.

28.   See, for example, Osama Abdullah's "My response to the 'Child Molester' lie against our beloved Prophet, Muhammad peace be upon him," from answering-christianity.com, which contains sections from Talmud and references to biblical prophets. Similar materials

are included under the heading "The Bible on marriage of young girls with much older men," in the Aziz, "Age of Aisha (*ra*) at time of marriage."

29.   For a thorough discussion of the rabbinic issue at stake, see Meacham, "Marriage of Minor Girls in Jewish Law."

30.   There are references to nine as the age of presumptive majority in some texts such as Ibn Hanbal's, but I have not come across any explicit reference to Aishah's menarche as trigger for consummation. Bukhari's chapter heading prefacing one of his reports on Aishah's marriage includes a discussion of the '*idda* (post-marital waiting period) for pre-pubescent girls, which presumes consummation of a marriage before menarche. K. al-Nikah, "A man marrying off his minor children," trans. Khan, vol. 7, p. 49; possibly also "A woman looking at Ethiopians and the like if it does not lead to bad consequences," trans. Khan, vol. 7, p. 119. In one fifteenth-century Cairo court case, the Prophet's marriage to Aishah was used as evidence for the permissibility of marrying off minor girls. Petry, "Conjugal Rights versus Class Prerogatives," p. 233.

31.   See, e.g., Tucker, *In the House of the Law*, pp. 155–6; and Motzki, "Child Marriage in Seventeenth-Century Palestine."

32.   See the entry on "Ayesha" in *The American Muslim*, "Answers to Questions Non Muslims Ask," an alphabetical list from "Abrahamic Faiths" to "Women's Issues." Interestingly, the compilers of this list make much the same distinction between articles aimed at dialogue and those aimed at polemic.

33.   Islam Online.net, "Addressing Misconceptions about Prophet's Marriage to 'Aisha."

34.   Haq, "Marriage of Ayesha (RA) with Prophet Muhammad (p.b.u.h.)."

35.   Shanavas, "Ayesha's Age: The Myth of a Proverbial Wedding Exposed."

36.   Haq writes, "So in this marriage with A'isha there was a desire to cement the bonds of friendship with Abu Bakr as well as the desire for propagating the teachings of Islam, particularly delicate matters relating to women folk." "Marriage of Ayesha (RA) with Prophet Muhammad (p.b.u.h.)." See also Sabeel Ahmed, "Why Did Prophet Muhammad (pbuh) Married [sic] Young Aisha Siddiqa (r.a.)?," the first of which is "To reinforce the friendly relations already existing with Abu Bakr (his closest companion)." Interestingly, the notion that the marriage was a calculated strategic move is one point raised by polemicists as well; here, though, it has been given a different valuation and serves to deflect accusations of lechery.

37.   Ahmed, "Why Did Prophet Muhammad (pbuh) Married [sic] Young Aisha Siddiqa (r.a.)?" The article identifies Ahmed as a student of famous polemicist Ahmed Deedat, and notes – without any apparent sense of irony – that "his main interest is in comparative religion."

38.   Haq, "Marriage of Ayesha (RA) with Prophet Muhammad (p.b.u.h.)." The passage deserves to be quoted at length: "The issue of child marriage has come via West and is part of a whole 'package' that intends to dismantle Islam as a social code and state philosophy. Try to look at the components in that whole context. Let me give you a few tips:

'child marriage', 'gender equality', 'women empowerment', 'sex education', 'reproductive control', 'contraception', 'sustainable growth', — are among the few terms used in the gender context. Can you please tell me that you know enough about this 'UN sposored shari'ah', that is being thrust as alternative to the Shari'ah of Islam? If you are not well aware, then kindly be careful about pushing too hard even some seemingly 'reasonable' issues like child marriage. The real intention (seems) not to stop this practice today (which is more a Hindu issue) but lead to the erroneous conclusion that Islam permitted a 'wrong' thing."

39. Squires, "The Young Marriage of 'Aishah."
40. http://www.shiachat.com/forum/index.php?showtopic=42999&pid=538017&st=0&#entry538017, last accessed 11.04.04. For an extended discussion with a number of Sunni perspectives, see also http://www.ummah.org.uk/forum/showthread.php?t=7838, last accessed 11.04.04, which takes off from Understanding-Islam.com's article "What was Ayesha's (ra) Age at the Time of Her Marriage to the Prophet (pbuh)?"
41. On this point, see Moosa, "The Debts and Burdens of Critical Islam," pp. 21–3.
42. These rules mostly relate to the greater number of his wives, restrictions on his ability to marry new ones, and his freedom from a strict schedule of turn-taking between them. See Ali, "A Beautiful Example," pp. 274–5.
43. I have heard anecdotal evidence, however, that marriages of girls of that age have continued into the modern era; one Saudi woman reported her grandmother's marriage at this age. Similarly, after the Iranian revolution of 1979, the age of marriage for girls (with parental consent) was lowered to nine, though it has since been raised.
44. Various sources report, for example, that 'Umar b. al-Khattab, the second caliph and father of the Prophet's wife Hafsa, later married the Prophet's granddaughter, born to 'Ali and Fatima.
45. Plaskow, "Decentering Sex."
46. After this was written, I came across a strikingly similar sentiment expressed by Stephanie Coontz (*Marriage, a History*, p. 19). She writes: "I don't believe that people of the past had more control over their hearts than we do today or that they were incapable of the deep love so many individuals now hope to achieve in marriage. But love in marriage was seen as a bonus, not a necessity."
47. Not that either wealth or wisdom was trivial, either in the Prophet's own marital history or Islamic history more broadly.
48. This is a radically oversimplified view of the medieval 'Ashari/Mu'tazili debate. Anderson provides a summary of the basic views of the Asharites and the Mutazilites in *Islamic Law and the Modern World*, pp. 9–10. This question is not just a Muslim one; C.S. Lewis sums up the Christian debate in strikingly similar terms, as "whether God commands certain things because they are right, or whether certain things are right because God commands them." *The Problem of Pain*, p. 99. These issues still have currency today, even if the debate remains largely unspoken. See Squires, "The Young Marriage of Aishah," for the claim that "according to Judaism, Christianity,

and Islam, right and wrong are ordained by Almighty God. As such, morality does not change over time based on our whims, desires, or cultural sensitivities."

49.   Q. 3:117, 9:70, 11:101, 16:33, 29:40, and 30:9. Rahman, *Major Themes of the Qur'an*, p. 25, states that "all injustice [*zulm*] is basically reflexive."

50.   Abu-Lughod, *Do Muslim Women Need Saving?*, especially chapters 2 and 3. Eltahawy, *Headscarves and Hymens*, 169–73, focuses on the abuses and not their media deployment in ways similar to the material Abu-Lughod critiques, though Eltahawy rejects the need for Western intervention and elsewhere counsels Westerners to fight patriarchy in their own contexts.

51.   The classic account of Lord Cromer's calculated defense of women appears in Ahmed, *Women and Gender in Islam*.

52.   Abu-Lughod, *Do Muslim Women Need Saving?*, p. 175.

53.   According to standard biographical and hadith sources, the marriage took place when she was six or seven. Today, when marriage equates to sex, writings often discuss the contract as a betrothal, elide consummation, and treat nine as simply the age of marriage. Ali, *Lives of Muhammad*, pp. 178–9.

54.   Chaudhry, "Forging an Egalitarian Theology: Advocating for Minimum Age of Marriage in Light of Muhammad's Marriage to 'A'isha," unpublished paper presented at Pennsylvania State University, December 2014.

55.   Ali, *Lives of Muhammad*, pp. 190–2.

56.   In addition to Ali, *The Lives of Muhammad*, this afterword draws from http://islamicommentary.org/2014/10/aisha-mother-of-the-faithful/ and http://www.bu.edu/today/2015/kecia-ali/ http://islamicommentary. org/2014/10/kecia-ali-on-the-lives-of-muhammad-book-q-a/

57.   Still, as I argue in the chapter, it is disingenuous simply to highlight variation without any attempt to account for the relative authoritativeness of disparate accounts. Eltahaway, *Headscarves and Hymens*, p. 172: "Aisha's age has been disputed, with varying accounts putting it at nine and others at nineteen."

58.   Ali, *Lives of Muhammad*, chapter 5, gives references to these sources and discusses them at some length.

59.   References are included in Ali, *Lives of Muhammad*.

60.   Tucker, "The Arab Family in History," pp. 200, 203.

Notes to Chapter 9

1.   Sheila Briggs' remarks, Feminist Sexual Ethics Project colloquium II, Brandeis University, September 2004. See also Judith Plaskow, "Decentering Sex," "Authority, Resistance, and Transformation," and *The Coming of Lilith*.

2.   Q. 30:21.

3.   Working off Alasdair MacIntyre's discussion of tradition, Edward Curtis proffers a helpful definition: "tradition is not an historical product so much as an historical process in which human beings, interacting with each other in discrete social contexts, invent, embrace, and inherit

something that they care about and argue over, whether explicitly or
not." Curtis, *Islam in Black America*, p. 4.

4. Maghen, *Virtues of the Flesh*, p. 282.
5. See, e.g., Roded, *Women in Islamic Biographical Collections*, pp. 63–89.
6. Abou El Fadl, *The Authoritative and the Authoritarian in Islamic Discourses*, p. 13.

Notes to Afterword

1. Abu-Lughod, *Do Muslim Women Need Saving?*, illustrates the multiple registers of rights-talk.
2. Cook, *Forbidding Wrong in Islam*, discusses the (gendered) duty of commanding right and forbidding wrong.
3. Matt Apuzio, "Sexual Abuse Allegations Against Imam Stir Rifts in Insular Illinois Community." February 14, 2015. http://www.nytimes.com/2015/02/16/us/sexual-assault-suit-against-illinois-imam-highlights-a-communitys-divisions.html?ref=todayspaper&_r=2 last accessed 06.29.15. The article repeatedly turns to the theme of taboos surrounding sex and the possible damage to women's reputations of making accusations.
4. Azizah al-Hibri, "Silence v. Justice: The Case of the Abused Muslim Women in Elgin." February 24, 2015. http://www.huffingtonpost.com/azizah-alhibri/silence-v-justice-the-cas_b_6739202.html last accessed 06.29.15.
5. http://www.patheos.com/blogs/altmuslim/2015/03/sexual-abuse-case-in-illinois-open-letter-from-ulema-regarding-rights-of-media-and-public-discussion/ last accessed 06.29.15.
6. Zaynab Ansari, "Blurred Lines: Women, 'Celebrity' Shaykhs, and Spiritual Abuse." May 27, 2015. http://muslimmatters.org/2015/05/27/blurred-lines-women-celebrity-shaykhs-spiritual-abuse/ last accessed 06.29.15.
7. I wrote about this email in a blog post. Ali, "Religion is Good Counsel."
8. hooks, *Art on My Mind*, p. 114.
9. In *Feminist Edges of the Qur'an*, Hidayatullah presciently anticipates that her book might give ammunition to those who would disparage the project of feminist Qur'an interpretation. Yet the book attacks neither feminism nor the female scholars who have contributed so much to the contemporary climate of ideas.
10. Spielhaus and Hammer, eds, "Muslim Women and the Challenge of Authority," special issue of *The Muslim World*; its articles cite many additional sources.
11. Korb, *Light Without Fire*, p. 57.
12. Ali, "The Omnipresent Male Scholar." Women scholars tend to do better than men at including female voices without marginalizing men. Still, the original edition of this book contained nearly twice as many individual men in its index as women.
13. On Muslim women's studies: Wadud, *Inside the Gender Jihad*; Hammer, *American Muslim Women*, pp. 114–20.

14. Moosa, *What is a Madrasa?*, primarily addresses the dominant male-centric tradition but includes a brief discussion of female madrasas, pp. 159–63.

15. Consult http://www.cambridgemuslimcollege.org/the-future-of-the-madrasa/, published 05.05.15; last accessed 05.31.15.

16. Ali, "The Omnipresent Male Scholar." To take a more recent example, Khaled Abou El Fadl, whose *Speaking in God's Name* is an excellent exploration of gender in contemporary neo-traditionalist Muslim thought, gave a ringing endorsement to the edited volume *Men in Charge? Rethinking Authority in the Islamic Legal Tradition*, calling it "the best treatment of women and Islamic law that I have read in the past twenty years ... profound, eye-opening and even exhilarating." He continues: "It is difficult for me to take seriously any student or scholar dealing with the subject of guardianship of men over women in Islam unless, or until, they have read and digested this book." Yet his own most recent book, *Reasoning with God: Reclaiming Shari'ah in the Modern Age*, published only a few months prior to *Men in Charge?*, fails to cite a single one of the book's contributors, some of whom have been publishing on Islam and Islamic law for two decades.

17. Grewal, *Islam is a Foreign Country*, explores these transnational patterns of study and learning and the ideas about authority embedded in them.

18. Lizzio, "Gendering Ritual," discusses menstruation; there is more work to be done on embodiment. On ritual leadership, including the 2005 Friday prayer led by Amina Wadud, good sources include Hammer, *American Muslim Women*, and Elewa and Silvers, "'I am one of the people'." I address the ways in which the five pillars are gendered in a work in progress.

19. Katz, *Women in the Mosque*, p. 4. As Katz notes, "The meaning of women's ritual activities is not exhausted by their failure to conform to standards constructed by (some) male scholars." (p. 10.) One may debate whether emphasis on certain normative rituals, such as Friday prayers, represents a curtailing of women's spiritual and religious agency.

20. Ali, "Muslims and Meat-Eating."

21. The newly established Muslim Anti-Racism Collaborative (www.muslimarc.org) addresses these issues.

22. Take, for instance, the assertions about slavery found in the "Open Letter to Baghdadi."

23. Povinelli, *Economies of Abandonment*, pp. 189, 191.

Bibliography

Classical and Legal Texts in Arabic and translation

Note: In alphabetizing entries, both the Arabic prefix *al-* and the letter *'ayn* are disregarded.

Abu Dawud Sulayman b. al-Ash'ath al-Sijistani. *Sunan Abi Dawud.* 2 vols. Cairo: n.p., 1952.

Bukhari, [Muhammad b. Isma'il]. *The Translation of the Meanings of Sahih Al-Bukhari,* Arabic-English. 8 vols. Trans. Muhammad Muhsin Khan. Revised edition. New Delhi: Kitab Bhavan, 1987.

Al-Dhahabi, Shams al-Din Abi 'Abd Allah Muhammad ibn Ahmad ibn 'Uthman. *Al-Kaba'ir.* Cairo: Dar al-Bayan al-Haditha, 2001.

Al-Dawla al-Islamiyya. *Su'al wa Jawab 'an al-Sabi wa'l-Riqab.* (Questions and Answers on Captives and Slaves) Al-Himma Library, 2014. Partial English translation, MEMRI, http://www.memrijttm.org/islamic-state-isis-releases-pamphlet-on-female-slaves.html (last accessed 12.05.14).

Al-Ghazali, Abu Hamid. *The Proper Conduct of Marriage in Islam (Adab an-Nikah). Book Twelve of Ihya' Ulum ad-Din.* Trans. Muhtar Holland. Fort Lauderdale (FL): Al-Baz Publishing, 1998.

—— *Marriage and Sexuality in Islam: A Translation of Al-Ghazali's Book on the Etiquette of Marriage from the Ihya'.* Ed. and trans. Madelain Farah. Salt Lake City: University of Utah Press, 1984.

—— *Ihya' 'Ulum al-Din.* Beirut: Dar al-Arqam, 1998.

Haskafi, Muhammad Ala-ud-din. *The Durr-ul-Mukhtar, Being the Commentary of the Tanvirul Absar of Muhammad Bin Abdullah Tamartashi.* Trans. B.M. Dayal. (English trans. with Arabic text.) New Delhi: Kitab Bhavan, 1992 [1913].

Ibn 'Abidin, Muhammad Amin ibn 'Umar. *Radd al-Muhtar 'ala al-Durr al-Mukhtar Sharh Tanwir al-Absar.* Beirut: Dar al-Kutub al-'Ilmiyyah, 1994.

Ibn Abi Shayba, Abu Bakr 'Abd Allah b. Muhammad. *Al-Kitab al-Musannaf fi'l-Ahadith wa'l-Athar.* 9 vols. Beirut: Dar al-Kutub al-'Ilmiyyah, 1995.

Ibn Baz, Abd al-Aziz ibn Abd Allah, et al. *Islamic Fatawa Regarding Women: Shariah Rulings Given by the Grand Mufti of Saudi Arabia Sheikh Ibn Baz, Sheikh Ibn Uthaimin, Sheikh Ibn Jibreen and Others on Matters Pertaining to Women.* Compiled by Muhammad bin Abdul-Aziz al-Musnad. Trans. Jamaal Al-Din M. Zarabozo. Riyadh, Saudi Arabia: Darussalam, 1996.

—— Ibn Baz, Shaykh 'Abdul-'Aziz bin 'Abdullah, et al. *Fatawa Islamiyah: Islamic Verdicts,* vol. 5. Collected by Muhammad bin 'Abdul-'Aziz Al-Musnad. Riyadh: Darussalam, 2002.

Ibn Hanbal. See Spectorsky.

Ibn Kathir. *The Life of the Prophet Muhammad* (Al-Sirah al-Nabawiyyah). 4 vols. Trans. Trevor Le Gassick. Reading (UK): Centre for Muslim Contribution to Civilization, Garnet Publishing, 2000.

Ibn Majah, Abu 'Abd Allah Muhammad ibn Yazid al-Qazwini. *Sunan Ibn Majah*. Ed. Muhammad Fu'ad 'Abd al-Baqi. Cairo: Dar Ihya' al-Kutub al-'Arabiyya, 1952.

Ibn Naqib al-Misri. See Keller.

Ibn Rushd. *The Distinguished Jurist's Primer: A translation of* Bidayat al-Mujtahid. 2 vols. Trans. Imran Ahsan Khan Nyazee. Reading (UK): Centre for Muslim Contribution to Civilization, Garnet Publishing, 1994–6.

Ibn Taymiyya, Ahmad b. 'Abd al-Halim. *Al-Fatawa al-Kubra*. Cairo: Kurdistan al-'Ilmiyyah, 1948.

Al-Jahiz. *Sobriety and Mirth: A Selection of the Shorter Writings of al-Jahiz*. Trans. Jim Colville. London: Kegan Paul, 2002.

—— *Nine Essays of al-Jahiz*, University Studies, Series VII: Theology and Religion. Trans. William M. Hutchins. New York: Peter Lang, 1989.

Kazee Khan (Qadi Khan). *Fatawa-I-Kazee Khan, with Arabic Text, Relating to Mahomedan Law of Marriage, Dower, Divorce, Legitimacy and Guardianship of Minors, according to the Soonnees*. (Tagore Law Lectures) Fakhruddin Hassan bin Mansur al-Uzjandi al Farghani (Kazee Khan). Trans. and ed. Mahomed Yusoof Khan Bahadur and Wilayat Hussain. New Delhi: Kitab Bhavan, 1994 [1977].

Keller, Nuh Ha Mim (trans. and ed.). Ahmad ibn Naqib al-Misri, *Reliance of the Traveller: A Classic Manual of Islamic Sacred Law*. Beltsville (MD): Amana Publications, 1994 [1991].

Laoust, Henri. *Le Precis de Droit d'Ibn Qudama*. Beirut: Institut Français de Damas, 1950.

Malik ibn Anas. *Al-Muwatta*. Trans. Aisha Abdurrahman At-Tarjumana and Yaqub Johnson. Ed. Idris Mears. Norwich (UK): Diwan, 1982.

Marghinani, 'Ali ibn Abi Bakr. *The Hedaya, or Guide: A Commentary on the Mussulman Laws*. 2nd edn. Trans. Charles Hamilton. Pref. and Index Standish Grove Grady. Lahore: Premier Book House, 1975 [1957].

Muslim [b. al-Hajjaj al-Qushayri]. *Sahih Muslim, Being Traditions of the Sayings and Doings of the Prophet Muhammad as Narrated by His Companions and Compiled under the title Al-Jami'-us-Sahih*. 4 vols. Trans. 'Abdul Hamid Siddiqi. New Delhi: Kitab Bhavan, 1995 [1977].

—— *Sahih Muslim*. 8 vols. in 2. Egypt: Maktabah wa Matbu'ah Muhammad 'Ali Sabih wa awlad, n.d. [1963?].

Al-Muzani, Isma'il b. Yahya. *Mukhtasar al-Muzani 'ala al-Umm*. Published as vol. 9 of al-Shafi'i, *al-Umm*.

Al-Nasa'i, Ahmad b. Shu'ayb. *Sunan al-Nasa'i, bi sharh al-Hafiz Jalal al-Din al-Suyuti wa Hashiyah al-Imam al-Sindi*. 8 vols. in 4. Ed. Hasan Muhammad al-Mas'udi. Beirut: Dar Ihya' al-Turath al-'Arabi, n.d. [1930?].

Al-Shafi'i, Muhammad b. Idris. *Al-Umm*. 9 vols. Beirut: Dar al-Kutub al-'Ilmiyya, 1993.

—— *Kitab Ikhtilaf Malik wa'l-Shafi'i*. In idem, *Al-Umm*, vol. 7.

Spectorsky, Susan A. (ed. and trans.). *Chapters on Marriage and Divorce: Responses of Ibn Hanbal and Ibn Rahwayh*. Austin: University of Texas Press, 1992.

Al-Tirmidhi, Abu 'Isa Muhammad b. 'Isa. *Al-Jami' al-Sahih, wa huwa Sunan al-Tirmidhi*. Ed. Ahmad Muhammad Shakir. Cairo: Matbu'ah Mustafa al-Babi, 1937.

Qur'an Translations

Abdel Haleem, M.A.S. *The Qur'an: A New Translation*. Oxford: Oxford University Press, 2004.

Ali, 'Abdullah Yusuf. *The Holy Qur'an: Text, Translation and Commentary*. Revised edn. Brentwood (MD): Amana Corporation, 1989.

Ali, Ahmed. *Al-Qur'an: A Contemporary Translation*. Princeton (NJ): Princeton University Press, 1988.

Arberry, Arthur J. *The Koran Interpreted*. London: Allen & Unwin; New York: Macmillan, 1955.

Asad, Muhammad. *The Message of the Qur'an*. Bitton, nr. Bristol (UK): The Book Foundation, 2003 [1980].

Cleary, Thomas. *The Qur'an: A New Translation*. Chicago: Starlatch Press, 2004.

Dawood, N.J. *The Koran*. 5th rev. edn. London and New York: Penguin, 1990.

Pickthall, Marmaduke. *The Glorious Koran*. Albany (NY): State University of New York Press, 1976.

Shakir, M.H. *The Qur'an*. 8th U.S. edn. Elmhurst (NY): Tahrike Tarsile Qur'an, Inc., 1993.

Other Sources

Note: In alphabetizing entries, both the Arabic prefix *al-* and the letter *'ayn* are disregarded.

Abdallah, Osama. "My response to the 'Child Molester' lie against our beloved Prophet, Muhammad peace be upon him." http://www.answering-christianity. com/aisha.htm (last accessed 04.17.06).

Abdul-Ghafur, Saleemah (ed.). *Living Islam Out Loud: American Muslim Women Speak*. Boston: Beacon Press, 2005.

Abdul-Ra'uf, Muhammad. *Marriage in Islam: A Manual*. Alexandria (VA): Al-Saadawi Publications, 2000 [1972].

—— *The Islamic View of Women and the Family*. New York: Robert Speller and Sons, 1977.

Abu-Lughod, Lila. *Do Muslim Women Need Saving?* Cambridge (MA): Harvard University Press, 2014.

Abou El Fadl, Khaled. *The Great Theft: Wrestling Islam from the Extremists*. San Francisco: Harper San Francisco, 2005.

—— *The Authoritative and the Authoritarian in Islamic Discourses: A Contemporary Case Study*. 3rd edn. Alexandria (VA): Al-Saadawi Publications, 2002.

—— *And God Knows the Soldiers: The Authoritative and the Authoritarian in Islamic Discourses*. Lanham (MD): University Press of America, 2001.

—— *Conference of the Books: The Search for Beauty in Islam*. Lanham (MD): University Press of America, 2001.

—— *Reasoning with God: Reclaiming Shari'ah in the Modern Age*. London: Rowman and Littlefield, 2014.

—— *Speaking in God's Name: Islamic Law, Authority, and Women*. Oxford: Oneworld Publications, 2001.

Abugideiri, Hibba. "On Gender and the Family." In *Islamic Thought in the Twentieth Century*. Ed. Taji-Farouki and Nafi. London: I.B. Tauris, 2004 223–59.

Abusharaf, Rogaia Mustafa. "Virtuous Cuts: Female Genital Circumcision in an African Ontology." *Differences: A Journal of Feminist Cultural Studies* 12.1 (2001): 112–40.

—— (ed.). *Female Circumcision: Multicultural Perspectives.* Philadelphia: University of Pennsylvania Press, 2006.

Abu-Sahlieh, Sami A. Aldeeb. "To Mutilate in the Name of Jehovah or Allah: Legitimization of Male and Female Circumcision." *Medicine and Law* 13.7–8 (1994): 575–622. Also available online at www.cirp.org/library/cultural/aldeeb1/ (last accessed 03.21.04).

—— "Jehovah, His Cousin Allah, and Sexual Mutilations." In *Sexual Mutilations: A Human Tragedy.* Ed. George C. Denniston and Marilyn Fayre Milos. New York and London: Plenum Press, 1997. 41–62.

Ahmad, Imad-ad-Dean. "Female Genital Mutilation: An Islamic Perspective." Minaret of Freedom Institute Pamphlet #1. http://www.minaret.org/fgm-p.htm (last accessed 01.15.04).

Ahmed, Leila. *A Border Passage: From Cairo to America–A Woman's Journey.* New York: Farrar, Straus and Giroux, 1999.

—— *Women and Gender in Islam: Historical Roots of a Modern Debate.* New Haven (CT): Yale University Press, 1992.

Ahmed, Sabeel. "Why Did Prophet Muhammad (pbuh) Married [sic] Young Aisha Siddiqa (r.a.)?" April 29, 1998. http://www.iol.ie/~afifi/BICNews/Sabeel/sabeel6.htm (last accessed 09.14.03).

Alalwani, Taha Jabir. "Fiqh of Minorities (1 of 3)." Web summary by Omar Tarazi. http://www.isna.net/services/library/papers/fiqh/FiqhofMinorities1.html (last accessed 04.06.06).

Algar, Hamid. *Wahabbism: A Critical Essay.* Oneonta (NY): Islamic Publications International, 2002.

Algosaibi, Ghazi A. *Revolution in the Sunnah.* Trans. Leslie McLoughlin. London: Saqi Books, 2004 [1988].

Ali, Kecia. "'A Beautiful Example': The Prophet Muhammad as a Model for Muslim Husbands." *Islamic Studies* 43.2 (2004): 273–91.

—— "Brunei's Horrific New Penal Code – And Why It Matters." May 9, 2014. last accessed April 18, 2015. http://cognoscenti.wbur.org/2014/05/09/sultan-of-brunei-sharia-law-beverly-hills-hotel-kecia-ali (last accessed 04.18.15).

—— "Just Say Yes: Law, Consent, and Muslim Feminist Ethics." In *A Jihad for Justice: Honoring the Life and Work of Amina Wadud.* Ed. Kecia Ali, Juliane Hammer, and Laury Silvers. E-book: 48HourBooks, 2012. 121–34. Available for free download at http://www.bu.edu/religion/people/faculty/bios/kecia-ali/.

—— *The Lives of Muhammad.* Cambridge (MA): Harvard University Press, 2014.

—— *Marriage and Slavery in Early Islam.* Cambridge (MA): Harvard University Press, 2010.

—— "Marriage in Classical Islamic Jurisprudence: A Survey of Doctrines." In *The Islamic Marriage Contract.* Ed. Frank Vogel and Asifa Quraishi. Cambridge, (MA): Harvard University Press, 2009. 11–45.

—— "Money, Sex, and Power: The Contractual Nature of Marriage in Islamic Jurisprudence of the Formative Period." Duke University Ph.D. dissertation, 2002.

—— "Muhammad and Khadija." *Critical Muslim* 14 (April 2015): 53–63.

—— "Muslims and Meat-Eating: Vegetarianism, Gender, and Ethical Pluralism." *Journal of Religious Ethics* 43.2 (June 2015): 268–88.

—— "The Omnipresent Male Scholar." *Critical Muslim* 8 (September 2013): 61–73.

—— "Progressive Muslims and Islamic Jurisprudence: The Necessity for Critical Engagement with Marriage and Divorce Law." In *Progressive Muslims*. Ed. O. Safi. Oxford: Oneworld Publications, 2003. 163–89.

—— "Redeeming Slavery: The 'Islamic State' and the Quest for Islamic Morality." *Mizan: Journal of Interdisciplinary Approaches to Muslim Societies and Civilizations* 1 (forthcoming).

—— "Religion is Good Counsel." September 11, 2013. http://feminismandreligion.com/2013/09/11/religion-is-good-counsel-by-kecia-ali/ (last accessed 04.19.15).

—— "Whose Shari'a Is It?" May 27, 2014. http://feminismandreligion.com/2014/05/27/whose-sharia-is-it-by-kecia-ali/ (last accessed 04.18.15).

—— "Women, Gender, *Ta'a* (Obedience), and *Nushuz* (Disobedience) in Islamic Discourses." In *Encyclopedia of Women and Islamic Cultures*. Ed. Suad Joseph. Leiden: Brill, 2007. Vol. 5: 309–13.

Ammar, Nawal H. "In the Shadow of the Pyramids: Domestic Violence in Egypt." *International Review of Victimology* 7.1–3 (2000): 29–46.

Anderson, J.N.D. *Islamic Law in the Modern World*. New York: New York University Press, 1959.

Antoun, Richard T. "The Islamic Court, the Islamic Judge, and the Accommodation of Traditions; A Jordanian Case Study." *International Journal of Middle East Studies* 12.4 (1980): 455–67.

Archard, David. *Sexual Consent*. Boulder (CO): Westview Press, 1998.

Aslan, Ednan, Marcia Hermansen, and Elif Medeni, eds. *Muslima Theology: The Voices of Muslim Women Theologians*. Frankfurt: Peter Lang, 2013.

Ayubi, Zahra. "American Muslim Women Negotiating Divorce." Brandeis University undergraduate honors thesis, 2006.

Azam, Hina. *Sexual Violation in Islamic Law: Substance, Evidence, and Procedure*. New York: Cambridge University Press, 2015.

—— "Sexual Violence in Islamic Law: From Discursive Foundations to Classical Maliki Articulation." Duke University Ph.D. dissertation, in progress.

Aziz, Zahid, comp. "Age of Aisha (*ra*) at time of marriage." Website of Ahmadiyya Anjuman Isha'at Islam Lahore Inc. U.S.A., http://www.muslim.org/islam/aisha-age.html (last accessed 01.26.04).

BBC News. "Saudi sets sights on 60th bride." March 17, 2004. http://news.bbc.co.uk/ 2/hi/middle_east/3520362.stm (last accessed 04.07.06).

Babayan, Kathryn and Afsaneh Najmabadi, eds. *Islamicate Sexualities*. Cambridge (MA): Harvard University Press, 2008.

Badawi, Jamal. "Appendix: The Issue of Female Circumcision." Excerpted from *Gender Equity in Islam*. Reproduced at http://www.soundvision.com/info/gender/femalecircumcision.asp (last accessed 07.17.04).

—— *The Status of Woman in Islam*. Plainfield (IN): MSA of U.S. and Canada, n.d. [1971].

Baderoon, Gabeba. *Regarding Muslims: From Slavery to Post-Apartheid*. Johannesburg: Wits University Press, 2014.

Bail, Christopher. *Terrified: How Anti-Muslim Fringe Organizations Became Mainstream*. Princeton (NJ): Princeton University Press, 2015.

Bailey, Sherwin. *Sexual Ethics: A Christian View*. New York: Macmillan, 1963.

Barazangi, Nimat Hafez. *Women's Identity and the Qur'an*. Gainesville: University Press of Florida, 2005.

Barlas, Asma. "Amina Wadud's Hermeneutics of the Qur'an: Women Rereading Sacred Texts." In *Modern Muslim Intellectuals and the Qur'an*. Ed. S. Taji-Farouki. London: Oxford University Press/The Institute of Ismaili Studies 2004. 97–123.

—— "*Believing Women*" *in Islam: Unreading Patriarchal Interpretations of the Qur'an*. Austin: University of Texas Press, 2002.

Bauer, Karen. *Gender Hierarchy in the Qur'ān: Medieval Interpretations, Modern Responses*. Cambridge: Cambridge University Press, 2015.

Bayman, Henry. *The Secret of Islam: Love and Law in the Religion of Ethics*. Berkeley (CA): North Atlantic Books, 2003.

Beeston, A.F.L. Review of *Nine Essays of al-Jahiz*. *Journal of Arabic Literature* 20 (1989): 200–9.

Berkey, Jonathan P. "Circumcision Circumscribed: Female Excision and Cultural Accommodation in the Medieval Near East." *International Journal of Middle East Studies* 28.1 (1996): 19–38.

Bernstein, Elizabeth and Laurie Schaffner (eds.). *Regulating Sex: The Politics of Intimacy and Identity*. New York: Routledge, 2005.

Binetti, Ashley. "A New Frontier: Human Trafficking and ISIS's Recruitment of Women from the West." Georgetown Institute for Women, Peace and Security, 2015. http//issuu.com/georgetownsfs/docs/i2a – isis and human trafficking (last accessed 06.16.15).

Blackburn, Simon. *Lust*. Oxford: Oxford University Press, 2004.

Boudhiba, Abdelwahab. *Sexuality in Islam*. Trans. Alan Sheridan. Boston: Kegan Paul, 1985.

Bowen, Donna Lee. "Muslim Juridical Opinions Concerning the Status of Women as Demonstrated by the Case of '*Azl*." *Journal of Near Eastern Studies* 40.4 (1981): 323–8.

Bowen, John. *Blaming Islam*. Cambridge (MA): MIT Press, 2012.

Boyarin, Daniel. *A Radical Jew: Paul and the Politics of Identity*. Berkeley: University of California Press, 1994.

—— *Carnal Israel: Reading Sex in Talmudic Culture*. Berkeley: University of California Press, 1993.

Bradford, Joe. "God's Pious Dictators-or-Is ISIS Islamic? Depends who you ask." February 24, 2015. http://www.joebradford.net/gods-pious-dictators-or-is-isis-islamic-depends-who-you-ask/ (last accessed 06.04.15).

Brockopp, Jonathan E. (ed.). *Islamic Ethics of Life: Abortion, War, and Euthanasia*. Columbia: University of South Carolina Press, 2003.

Brockopp, Jonathan E. "Taking Life and Saving Life." In *Islamic Ethics of Life*. Ed. idem. 1–19 (2003).

—— *Early Maliki Law: Ibn 'Abd al-Hakam and his Major Compendium of Jurisprudence*. Leiden: Brill, 2000.

Brooks, Geraldine. *Nine Parts of Desire: The Hidden World of Islamic Women*. New York: Anchor Books, 1995.

Brooten, Bernadette J. *Love Between Women: Early Christian Responses to Female Homoeroticism*. Chicago: University of Chicago Press, 1998.

Brown, Daniel. "The Triumph of Scripturalism: The Doctrine of Naskh and its Modern Critics." In *The Shaping of an American Islamic Discourse: A Memorial to Fazlur Rahman*. Ed. Earle H. Waugh and Frederick M. Denny. Atlanta: Scholars Press, 1998. 49–66.

—— *Rethinking Tradition in Modern Islamic Thought*. Cambridge: Cambridge University Press, 1996.

Brundage, James A. "Implied Consent to Intercourse." In *Consent and Coercion to Sex and Marriage*. Ed. A. Laiou. Cambridge, Massachusetts: Harvard University Press, 1998. 245–56.

Bucar, Elizabeth. *A Beginner's Guide to the Islamic Veil*. Oxford: Oneworld Publications, 2012.

—— "Bodies at the Margins: The Case of Transsexuality in Catholic and Shi'i Ethics." *Journal of Religious Ethics* 38.4 (2010): 601–15.

CAIR (Council on American-Islamic Relations). "President Bush asked to repudiate anti-Muslim remarks." http://cair-net.org/default.asp?Page=articleView&id=838&theType=NR (last accessed 04.06.06).

Calder, Norman. "Hinth, Birr, Tabarrur, Tahannuth: An Inquiry into the Arabic Vocabulary of Vows." *Journal of the School of Oriental and African Studies* 51.22 (1998): 214–39.

Calderini, Simonetta. "Woman, 'Sin' and 'Lust': The Fall of Adam and Eve According to Classical and Modern Muslim Exegesis." In *Religion and Sexuality*. Ed. Michael A. Hayes, et al. Roehampton Institute London Papers 4. Sheffield (UK): Sheffield Academic Press, 1998. 49–63.

Caner, Ergun Mehmet and Emir Fethi Caner. *Unveiling Islam: An Insider's Look at Muslim Life and Beliefs*. Grand Rapids (MI): Kregel Publications, 2002.

Chaudhry, Ayesha. *Domestic Violence in the Islamic Tradition*. Oxford: Oxford University Press, 2013.

Cilardo, Agostino. "Historical Development of the Legal Doctrine Relative to the Position of the Hermaphrodite in the Islamic Law." *The Search* 2.7 (1986): 128–70.

Collins, Robert O. "Slavery in the Sudan in History." *Slavery and Abolition* 20.3 (1999): 69–95.

Cook, Michael. *Forbidding Wrong in Islam*. Cambridge: Cambridge University Press, 2003.

Cooke, Miriam. "Deploying the Muslimwoman." In miriam cooke, Fawzia Ahmad, Margot Badran, Minoo Moallem, and Jasmin Zine, "Roundtable Discussion: Religion, Gender, and the Muslimwoman." *Journal of Feminist Studies in Religion* 24.1 (Spring, 2008): 91–9.

—— *Women Claim Islam: Creating Islamic Feminism through Literature*. New York: Routledge, 2000.

Coontz, Stephanie. *Marriage, A History: From Obedience to Intimacy or How Love Conquered Marriage*. New York: Viking Penguin, 2005.

Cooperman, Alan. "Anti-Muslim Remarks Stir Tempest." *Washington Post*; http://www.washingtonpost.com/ac2/wp-dyn/A14499-2002Jun19?language =printer; (last accessed 11.26.04).

Coulson, Noel. "Regulation of Sexual Behavior under Traditional Islamic Law." In *Society and the Sexes in Medieval Islam*. Ed. Afaf Lutfi al-Sayyid-Marsot. Malibu (CA): Undena Publications, 1979. 64–8.

—— *A History of Islamic Law*. Edinburgh: Edinburgh University Press, 1964.

Curtis, Edward E., IV. *Islam in Black America: Identity, Liberation, and Difference in African-American Muslim Thought*. Albany: State University of New York Press, 2002.

Dabiq, Umm Sumayya al-Muhajirah. "Slave-Girls or Prostitutes?" *Dabiq*, May 9, 2015: 44–9.

—— "The Revival of Slavery before the Hour." *Dabiq*, November 4, 2014: 14–17.

David, Susan Schaefer. "Changing Gender Relations in a Moroccan Town."

In *Arab Women: Old Boundaries, New Frontiers.* Ed. Judith E. Tucker. Bloomington: Indiana University Press, 1993. 208–23.

Davies, Eryl W. *The Dissenting Reader: Feminist Approaches to the Hebrew Bible.* Aldershot (UK): Ashgate, 2003.

Davis, David Brion. *In the Image of God: Religion, Moral Values, and Our Heritage of Slavery.* New Haven (CT): Yale University Press, 2001.

Davison, Julia O'Connell and Jacqueline Sánchez Taylor. "Travel and Taboo: Heterosexual Sex Tourism to the Caribbean." In *Regulating Sex.* Ed. Bernstein and Schaffner. London: Routledge, 2004. 83–99.

De Sondy, Amanullah. *The Crisis of Islamic Masculinities.* London: Bloomsbury, 2014.

Dean, Tim. *Unlimited Intimacy: Reflections on the Subculture of Barebacking.* Chicago: University of Chicago Press, 2009.

Decker, Julie Sondra. *The Invisible Orientation: An Introduction to Asexuality.* New York: Carrel Books, 2014.

Dialmy, Abdessamad. "Moroccan Youth, Sex and Islam." *Middle East Report* 206 (Spring 1998): 16–17.

Diederich, Mathias. "Indonesians in Saudi Arabia: Religious and Economic Connections." In *Transnational Connections and the Arab Gulf.* Ed. Madawi Al-Rasheed. London: Routledge, 2005. 128–46.

Doggett, Maeve E. *Marriage, Wife Beating, and the Law in Victorian England.* Columbia (SC): University of South Carolina Press, 1993.

Doi, 'Abdul Rahman. *Woman in Shari'ah (Islamic Law).* London: Ta-Ha Publishers, 1994 [1989].

Dover, K.J. "Classical Greek Attitudes to Sexual Behavior." In *Women in the Ancient World: The Arethusa Papers.* Ed. J. Peradotto and J.P. Sullivan. Albany: State University of New York Press, 1984. Republished in Laura K. McClure (ed.). *Sexuality in the Classical World: Readings and Sources.* Malden (MA): Blackwell Publishing, 2002. 19–33.

—— *Greek Homosexuality.* Cambridge (MA): Harvard University Press, 1977.

Dunne, Bruce. "Power and Sexuality in the Middle East." *Middle East Report* 206 (Spring 1998): 8–11, 37.

Dupret, Baudouin. "Sexual Morality at the Egyptian Bar: Female Circumcision, Sex Change Operations, and Motives for Suing." *Islamic Law and Society* 9.1 (2001): 42–69.

Duran, Khalid. "Homosexuality in Islam." In *Homosexuality and World Religions.* Ed. Arlene Swidler. Valley Forge (PA): Trinity Press International. 1993. 181–97.

Eickelman, Dale F. "Compromised Contexts: Changing Ideas of Texts in the Islamic Tradition." In *Text and Context in Islamic Societies.* Ed. Irene A. Bierman. Reading (UK): Ithaca Press, 2004. 155–70.

Eid, Talal. "Marriage, Divorce and Child Custody as Experienced by American Muslims." Harvard University Divinity School Th.D. dissertation, 2005.

Elewa, Ahmed and Laury Silvers. "'I am one of the people': A Survey and Analysis of Legal Arguments on Woman-Led Prayer in Islam." In *Journal of Law and Religion* 26.1 (2010–11): 141–71

Eltahawy, Mona. *Headscarves and Hymens.* New York: Farrar, Straus and Giroux, 2015.

Engineer, Asghar Ali. "Islam, Women, and Gender Justice." In *What Men Owe to Women: Men's Voices from World Religions.* Ed. Raines and Maguire. 109–28.

Esack, Farid. "Islam and Gender Justice: Beyond Simplistic Apologia." In *What*

Men Owe to Women: Men's Voices from World Religions. Ed. Raines and Maguire. New York: State University of New York Press, 2001. 187–210.

Esack, Farid and Nadeem Mahomed. "Sexual Diversity, Islamic Jurisprudence and Sociality." *Journal of Gender and Religion in Africa* 17.2 (December 2011): 41–57.

Esposito, John. *What Everyone Needs to Know about Islam.* Oxford: Oxford University Press, 2002.

Esposito, John L. with Natana J. DeLong-Bas. *Women in Muslim Family Law.* 2nd edn. Syracuse (NY): Syracuse University Press, 2001.

European Council for Fatwa. Resolution 3/8, "A woman embraces Islam and her husband does not." From the Final Statement of the 8th Ordinary Session of the European Council for Fatwa, http://www.e-cfr/eng/article/php?sid=35 (last accessed 02.07.06).

Ex-Muslim.com. "Evidence that Aisha was 9 when her marriage to Muhammad was consummated." http://www.exmuslim.com/com/evidence.htm (last accessed 11.04.04).

Fadel, Mohammed. "Reinterpreting the Guardian's Role in the Islamic Contract of Marriage: The Case of the Maliki School." *The Journal of Islamic Law* 3.1 (1998): 1–26.

Falwell, Jerry. "Muhammad, a 'demon-possessed pedophile'?" Published 06.15.02, http://www.worldnetdaily.com/news/article.asp?ARTICLE_ID=27975 (last accessed 11.26.04).

Faruki, Kemal. "Legal Implications for Today of *al-Ahkam al-Khamsa* (The Five Values)." In *Ethics in Islam.* Ed. R.G. Hovannisian. Malibu: Undenda Publications, 1985. 65–72.

Faruqi, Harith Suleiman. *Faruqi's Law Dictionary, Arabic-English.* 3rd edn. Beirut: Librairie du Liban, 1986.

Al-Faruqi, Lamya'. *Women, Muslim Society, and Islam.* Plainfield (IN): American Trust Publications, 1994 [1988].

Al-Faruqi, Maysam J. "Women's Self-Identity in the Qur'an and Islamic Law." In *Windows of Faith: Muslim Women Scholar-Activists in North America.* Ed. G. Webb. Syracuse: Syracuse University Press, 2000.

First Coast News. http://www.firstcoastnews.com/news/2002-06-13/islam_vines. asp (last accessed 11.26.04).

Friedmann, Yohanan. *Tolerance and Coercion in Islam: Interfaith Relations in the Muslim Tradition.* Cambridge: Cambridge University Press, 2003.

Fournier, Pascale. *Lost in Transplantation: Muslim Marriage in Western Courts.* Surrey, UK: Ashgate, 2010.

Fyzee, Asaf A.A. *Outlines of Muhammadan Law.* London: Oxford University Press, 1955.

Geissinger, Aisha. *Gender and Muslim Constructions of Exegetical Authority: A Rereading of the Classical Genre of Qur'an Commentary.* Leiden: Brill, 2015.

—— "Gendering the Communal Body: Fasting in the Qur'an and the Hadith." Unpublished paper presented at the American Academy of Religion Annual Meeting, Philadelphia, November 2005.

—— "Islam and Discourses of Same-Sex Desire." In *Queer Religion: Homosexuality in Modern Religious History.* Ed. Donald L. Boisvert and Jay Emerson Johnson. Santa Barbara, CA: Praeger, 2012, pp. 69–90.

Gibson, Dawn-Marie and Jamillah Karim. *Women of the Nation: Between Black Protest and Sunni Islam.* New York: New York University Press, 2014.

Glancy, Jennifer A. *Slavery in Early Christianity*. Minneapolis, (MN): Fortress Press, 2006.

Gollaher, David L. *Circumcision: A History of the World's Most Controversial Surgery*. New York: Basic Books, 2000.

Graff, E.J. *What is Marriage For? The Strange History of Our Most Intimate Institution*. Boston: Beacon Press, 2004 [1999].

Gramick, Jeannine and Robert Gordis. "Are Homosexual and Bisexual Relations Natural and Normal?" In *Taking Sides: Clashing Views on Controversial Issues in Human Sexuality*. 2nd edn. Ed. Robert T. Francoeur. Guilford (CT): The Dushkin Publishing Group, 1989. 34–53.

Habib, Samar. *Arabo-Islamic Texts on Female Homosexuality, 850–1780 A.D.* Youngstown, New York: Teneo Press, 2009.

——— *Female Homosexuality in the Middle East: Histories and Representations*. New York: Routledge, 2007.

Habib, Samar, ed. *Islam and Homosexuality*. Vols. 1–2. Santa Barbara (CA): Praeger, 2010.

Hadassah-Brandeis Institute. "Loyal Daughters and Liberated Women: An Interfaith Discussion." Conference on Choosing Limits, Limiting Choices: Women's Status and Religious Life, presented by the Hadassah-Brandeis Institute and JOFA: The Jewish Orthodox Feminist Alliance, March 13, 2005, Brandeis University. Transcript at www.brandeis.edu/hbi/pubs/Loyal_Daughters-edited.doc (last accessed 03.04.06).

Haeri, Shahla. "The Politics of Dishonor: Rape and Power in Pakistan." In *Faith and Freedom: Women's Human Rights in the Muslim World*. Ed. Mahnaz Afkhami. Syracuse (NY): Syracuse University Press, 1995. 161–74.

Hallaq, Wael. "Can the Shari'a be Restored?" In *Islamic Law and the Challenges of Modernity*. Ed. Yvonne Yazbeck Haddad and Barbara Freyer Stowasser. Walnut Creek (CA): AltaMira Press, 2004. 21–53.

Halperin, David M. "Forgetting Foucault: Acts, Identities, and the History of Sexuality." In *The Sleep of Reason: Erotic Experience and Sexual Ethics in Ancient Greece and Rome*. Ed. Martha C. Nussbaum and Juha Sivola. Chicago: University of Chicago Press, 2002. 21–54.

——— *How to do the History of Homosexuality*. Chicago: University of Chicago Press, 2002.

Hammer, Juliane and Riem Spielhaus, eds, *The Muslim World*, Special Issue: Muslim Women and the Challenge of Authority. 103.3 (July 2013): 287–431.

Hammer, Juliane. *American Muslim Women, Authority, and Activism: More Than a Prayer* Austin (TX): University of Texas Press, 2014.

——— "Center Stage: Gendered Islamophobia and Muslim Women." In *Islamophobia in America: The Anatomy of Intolerance*. Ed. Carl W. Ernst. New York: Palgrave Macmillan, 2013. 107–44.

——— "Changing the World: Reflections on Islamic Studies," http://www.equinoxpub.com/blog/2014/06/changing-the-world-reflections-on-islamic-studies/ (last accessed 04.19.15).

Haq, M. "Marriage of Ayesha (RA) with Prophet Muhammad (p.b.u.h.)." http://www.jamaat.org/qa/ayeshara.html (last accessed 04.16.06).

Harrison, Frances. "Iran's sex-change operations." http://news.bbc.co.uk/2/hi/programmes/newsnight/4115535.stm (last accessed 05.25.05).

Hasan, Zeeshan. "Polygamy, Slavery and Qur'anic Sexual Ethics, 1994." First published in Bangladesh in the August 30, 1996 issue of *Star Weekend* magazine. Republished at http://www.liberalislam.net/polygamy-1 (last accessed 05.06.06).

Hassan, Riffat. "Muslim Women and Post-Patriarchal Islam." In *After Patriarchy: Feminist Transformations of the World Religions*. Ed. Paula M. Cooey, et al. Maryknoll (NY): Orbis Books, 1991.

Helem. "Fihrist al-'ibarat al-'arabiyya," *Barra Magazine* (www.helem.net, Lebanon), no. 0, 2005: 17.

Al-Hibri, Azizah Y. "An Introduction to Muslim Women's Rights." In *Windows of Faith: Muslim Women Scholar-Activists in North America*. Ed. G. Webb. Syracuse: Syracuse University Press, 2000. 51–71.

—— "Islamic Law and Muslim Women in America." In *One Nation Under God?: Religion and American Culture*. Ed. Marjorie B. Garber and Rebecca L. Walkowitz. New York: Routledge, 1999. 128–42.

—— "Islam, Law, and Custom: Redefining Muslim Women's Rights." In *American University Journal of International Law and Policy* 12.1 (1997): 1–44.

—— "Family Planning and Islamic Jurisprudence." In *Religious and Ethical Perspectives on Population Issues*. Ed. Azizah Y. al-Hibri, Daniel C. Maguire, and James Martin-Schramm. Washington DC: The Religious Consultation on Population, Reproductive Health and Ethics, 1993. 2–11.

Hidayatullah, Aysha. *Feminist Edges of the Qur'an*, New York: Oxford University Press, 2014.

—— "Islamic Conceptions of Sexuality." In *Sexuality and the World's Religions*. Ed. David W. Machacek and Melissa M. Wilcox. Santa Barbara (CA): ABC-Clio, 2003. 255–92.

—— *Mariyah the Copt: Gender, Sex, and Heritage in the Legacy of Muhammad's Umm Walad*. University of California, Santa Barbara M.A. thesis, 2005.

Hoel, Nina. "Engaging Islamic sexual ethics: Intimacy, pleasure and sacrality," *Sexualities* 18. 1–2 (2015): 80–99.

Hoodfar, Homa. "Circumventing Legal Limitation: Mahr and Marriage Negotiation in Egyptian Low-Income Communities." In idem, ed. *Shifting Boundaries in Marriage and Divorce in Muslim Communities*, vol. 1 (Women Living Under Muslim Laws Special Dossier). Montpellier, France: Women Living Under Muslim Laws, 1996. 121–41.

hooks, bell. *Art on My Mind: Visual Politics*. New York: The New Press, 1995.

—— *Feminism is for Everybody*. Boston (MA): South End Press, 2000.

—— *Talking Back: Thinking Feminist, Thinking Black*. Boston (MA): South End Press, 1989.

Hourani, George F. *Reason and Tradition in Islamic Ethics*. Cambridge: Cambridge University Press, 1985.

Hovannisian, Richard G. (ed.). *Ethics in Islam*. Malibu (CA): Undena Publications, 1985.

Hoyland, Robert G. *Arabia and the Arabs: From the Bronze Age to the coming of Islam*. London: Routledge, 2001.

Humphreys, R. Steven. "Borrowed Lives: The Reproduction of Texts in Islamic Cultures." In *Text and Context in Islamic Societies*. Ed. Irene A. Bierman. Reading (UK): Ithaca Press, 2004. 69–86.

Hussaini, Mohammad Mazhar. *My Little Book of Halal and Haram*. Chicago (IL): Iqra' International Educational Foundation, 1987.

iAbolish. "Spotlight on Sudan." http://www.iabolish.com/slavery_today/sudan/index.html (last accessed 05.06.06).

Ilkkaracan, Pinar. "Islam and Women's Sexuality: A Research Report from

Turkey." In *Good Sex: Feminist Perspectives from the World's Religions*. Ed. Patricia Beattie Jung, et al. New Brunswick (NJ): Rutgers University Press, 2002. 61–76.

Imam, Ayesha M. "The Muslim Religious Right ('Fundamentalists') and Sexuality." In *Good Sex: Feminist Perspectives from the World's Religions*. Ed. Patricia Beattie Jung, et al. New Brunswick (NJ): Rutgers University Press, 2002. 15–30.

Inhorn, Marcia. *The New Arab Man: Emergent Masculinities, Technologies, and Islam in the Middle East*. Princeton (NJ): Princeton University Press, 2012.

Islam for Today. "The Girlfriend-Boyfriend Relationship." http://www.islam-fortoday.com/girlfriend.htm (last accessed 02.07.06).

Islam Online (www.islamonline.net). "Addressing Misconceptions about Prophet's Marriage to 'Aisha" (dated February 2003). http://www.islamon-line.net/fatwa/english/FatwaDisplay. asp?hFatwaID=63495 (last accessed 11.04.04).

Islam Q&A (www.islam-qa.com). "Ruling on a Muslim man marrying a non-Muslim woman and vice versa" (Question #21380). http://63.175.194.25/index.php?ln= eng&QR=21380 (last accessed 01.12.06).

Jackson, Sherman A. *Islam and the Blackamerican: Looking toward the Third Resurrection*. New York: Oxford University Press, 2005.

Jagose, Annamarie. *Orgasmology*. Durham (NC): Duke University Press, 2013.

Jakobsen, Janet R. and Ann Pellegrini. *Love the Sin: Sexual Regulation and the Limits of Religious Tolerance*. New York: New York University Press, 2003.

Jamal, Amreen. "The Story of Lot and the Qur'an's Perception of the Morality of Same-Sex Sexuality." *Journal of Homosexuality* 41.1 (2001): 1–88.

Jennings, Ronald C. "Divorce in the Ottoman Sharia Court of Cyprus, 1580–1640." In *Studia Islamica* 78 (1994): 155–67.

Johansen, Baber. "Commercial Exchange and Social Order in Hanafite Law." In *Law and the Islamic World: Past and Present*. Royal Danish Academy of Sciences and Letters monograph series Historisk-filosofiske Meddelser, vol. 68. Ed. Christopher Toll and Jakob Skovgaard-Petersen. Copenhagen: Munksgaard, 1995. 81–95.

—— "Secular and Religious Elements in Hanafite Law. Function and Limits of the Absolute Character of Government Authority." In *Contingency in a Sacred Law: Legal and Ethical Norms in the Muslim Fiqh*. Ed. Baber Johansen. Leiden: Brill, 1999. 189–218 (originally published in E. Gellner and J.C. Vatin. *Islam et Politique au Maghreb*. Paris: Editions du CNRS, 1981. 218–303).

—— "The Valorization of the Body in Muslim Sunni Law." In *Law and Society in Islam*, Ed. Devin J. Stewart, Baber Johansen and Amy Singer. Princeton: Markus Wiener Publishers, 1996. 71–112.

Jones, Jim. "Baptist pastor's words shock Muslim leaders." *Dallas-Fort Worth Star-Telegram*, http://www.dfw.com/mld/startelegram/3451104.htm?1c (last accessed 11.26.04).

Kahf, Mohja. *Western Representations of the Muslim Woman: From Termagant to Odalisque*. Austin: University of Texas Press, 1999.

Kahn, Tamam. *Untold: A History of the Wives of Prophet Muhammad*. Rhinebeck (NY): Monkfish, 2010.

Kamal, Abdul Aziz. *Everyday Fiqh*, Vol. 1. 5th edn. Lahore: Islamic Publications Ltd., 1983 [1975].

Kandiyoti, Deniz. "Islam and Patriarchy: A Comparative Perspective." In

Women in Middle Eastern History. Ed. Keddie and Baron. New Haven (CT): Yale University Press, 1993. 23–42.

Karim, Jamillah. "Between Immigrant Islam and Black Liberation: Young Muslims Inherit Global Muslim and African American Legacies." *The Muslim World* 95.4 (October 2005): 497–513.

——. *American Muslim Women: Negotiating Race, Class, and Gender Within the Ummah*. New York: New York University Press, 2009.

Kassamali, Noor J. "When Modernity Confronts Traditional Practices: Female Genital Cutting in Northeast Africa." In *Women in Muslim Societies: Diversity within Unity*. Ed. Herbert L. Bodman and Nayereh Tohidi. Boulder (CO): Lynne Rienner Publishers, 1998. 39–61.

Kassis, Hannah E. *A Concordance of the Qur'an*. Berkeley: University of California Press, 1983.

Katz, Marion. *Women in the Mosque: A History of Legal Thought and Social Practice*. New York: Columbia University Press, 2014.

Keddie, Nikki R. and Beth Baron (eds.). *Women in Middle Eastern History: Shifting Boundaries in Sex and Gender*. New Haven (CT): Yale University Press, 1991.

Khadduri, Majid. "Marriage in Islamic Law: The Modernist Viewpoints." *The American Journal of Comparative Law* 26.2 (Spring 1978): 213–18.

—— *The Islamic Conception of Justice*. Baltimore (MD): Johns Hopkins University Press, 1984.

Khan, Shahnaz. *Muslim Women: Crafting a North American Identity*. Gainesville: University Press of Florida, 2000. Republished as *Aversion and Desire: Negotiating Muslim Female Identity in the Diaspora*. Toronto: Women's Press, 2002.

Al-Khansaa Brigade. "Women of the Islamic State: A Manifesto by the Al-Khansaa Brigade," trans. Quilliam Foundation, http://www.quilliam-foundation.org/wp/wp-content/uploads/publications/free/women-of-the-islamic-state3.pdf (last accessed 05.28.15).

Korb, Scott. *Light Without Fire: The Making of America's First Muslim College*. Boston (MA): Beacon Press, 2013.

Kueny, Kathryn M. *Conceiving Identities: Maternity in Medieval Muslim Discourse and Practice*. Albany (NY): State University of New York Press, 2013.

Kugle, Scott. "Sexuality, Diversity, and Ethics in the Agenda of Progressive Muslims." In *Progressive Muslims*. Ed. O. Safi. Oxford: Oneworld Publications, 2003. 190–234.

—— "Enough with the prudes: Bring On 'Sex and the Umma'." http://www.muslimwakeup.com/main/archives/2004/04/enough_with_the.php (last accessed 05.06.04).

Kugle, Scott Siraj al-Haqq. *Homosexuality in Islam: Critical Reflections on Gay, Lesbian, and Transgender Muslims*. Oxford: Oneworld Publications, 2010.

—— *Living Out Islam: Voices of Gay, Lesbian, and Transgender Muslims*. New York: New York University Press, 2014.

—— "Sexual Diversity in Islam," in Vincent J. Cornell, ed., *Voices of Islam, vol. 5, Voices of Change*, Omid Safi volume ed. Westport (CT): Praeger, 2007, pp.131–68.

Laiou, Angeliki E. (ed.). *Consent and Coercion to Sex and Marriage in Ancient and Medieval Societies*. Washington DC: Dumbarton Oaks Research Library and Collection, 1993.

Lamptey, Jerusha Tanner. *Never Wholly Other: A Muslima Theology of Religious Pluralism*. New York: Oxford University Press, 2014.

Lane, Edward William. *Arabic-English Lexicon*. London: Williams and Norgate, 1863.

Lewis, Bernard. *Race and Slavery in the Middle East*. Oxford: Oxford University Press, 1990.

Lewis, C.S. *The Problem of Pain*. New York: Harper San Francisco, 2001 [1940].

Little, Cindy M. "Female Genital Mutilation: Medical and Cultural Considerations." *Journal of Cultural Diversity* 10.1 (Spring 2003): 30–34.

Lizzio, Celene Ayat. "Gendering Ritual: A Muslim's Reading of the Laws of Menstrual Preclusion." In *Muslima theology: The Voices of Muslim Women Theologians*. Ed. Elif Mendeni, Ednan Aslan. Frankfurt am Main: Peter Land Verlag, 2013. 167–80.

Lovejoy, Paul E. *Transformations in Slavery: A History of Slavery in Africa*. 2nd edn. Cambridge: Cambridge University Press, 2000.

Lutfi, Huda. "Manners and Customs of Fourteenth-Century Cairene Women: Female Anarchy vs. Male Shar'i Order in Muslim Prescriptive Treatises." In *Women in Middle Eastern History*. Ed. Keddie and Baron. New Haven (CT): Yale University Press, 1993. 99–121.

Mack, Beverly B. "Women and Slavery in Nineteenth-Century Hausaland." *Slavery and Abolition* 13.1 (April 1992): 89–110.

MacIntyre, Alasdair. *A Short History of Ethics: A History of Moral Philosophy from the Homeric Age to the Twentieth Century*. London: Routledge, 1998 [1966].

—— *Whose Justice? Which Rationality?* Notre Dame (IN): University of Notre Dame Press, 1988.

Maghen, Ze'ev. *Virtues of the Flesh: Passion and Purity in Early Islamic Jurisprudence*. Leiden: Brill, 2004.

Mahmood, Saba. *Politics of Piety: Islamic Revival and the Feminist Subject*. Princeton (NJ): Princeton University Press, 2004.

Mahomed, Nadeem. "Beyond Misfortune and Fault: Islam, Same-Sex Sexuality, and Liberation." MA dissertation, University of Johannesburg, 2013.

Majeed, Debra. *Polygyny: What It Means When African American Muslim Women Share Their Husbands*. Gainesville: University Press of Florida, 2015.

Malik, Iftikhar H. *Islam and Modernity: Muslims in Europe and the United States*. London: Pluto Press, 2004.

Malti-Douglas, Fedwa. "Tribadism/Lesbianism and the Sexualized Body in Medieval Arabo-Islamic Narratives." In *Same Sex Love and Desire among Women in the Middle Ages*. Ed. Francesca Sautman and Pamela Sheingorn. New York: Palgrave, 2001. 123–41.

—— *Woman's Body, Woman's Word: Gender and Discourse in Arabo-Islamic Writing*. Princeton (NJ): Princeton University Press, 1992.

Marlow, Louise. *Hierarchy and Egalitarianism in Islamic Thought*. Cambridge: Cambridge University Press, 1997.

Marmon, Shaun E. "Domestic Slavery in the Mamluk Empire: A Preliminary Sketch." In *Slavery in the Islamic Middle East*. Ed. Shaun E. Marmon. Princeton (NJ): Markus Wiener, 1999. 1–23.

Mashhour, Amira. "Islamic Law and Gender Equality – Could There be a Common Ground? A Study of Divorce and Polygamy in Sharia Law and Contemporary Legislation in Tunisia and Egypt." *Human Rights Quarterly* 27 (2005): 562–96.

Masud, Muhammad Khalid, et al. "Muftis, Fatwas, and Islamic Legal Interpretation." In *Islamic Legal Interpretation: Muftis and Their Fatwas*. Ed. Muhammad Khalid Masud et al. Cambridge (MA): Harvard University Press 1996. 3–32.

Massad, Joseph A. *Desiring Arabs.* Chicago: University of Chicago Press, 2007.

Mattson, Ingrid. *A Believing Slave is Better Than an Unbeliever: Status and Community in Early Islamic Society and Law.* University of Chicago Ph.D. dissertation, 1999.

McBride, James. "'To Make Martyrs of Their Children': 'Female Genital Mutilation,' Religious Legitimation, and the Constitution." In *God Forbid: Religion and Sex in American Life.* Ed. Kathleen M. Sands. Oxford: Oxford University Press, 2000. 219–44.

McDonough, Sheila. *Muslim Ethics and Modernity: A Comparative Study of the Ethical Thought of Sayyid Ahmad Khan and Mawlana Mawdudi.* Waterloo, Ontario: Canadian Corporation for Studies in Religion, Wilfred Laurier Press, 1984.

McLoughlin, Patrick. "Swedish Imam says Islam forbids female circumcision." Reuters, November 10, 2003, http://www.alternet.org/thenews/newsdeskL10593839.htm (last accessed 07.05.2004).

Meacham, Tirzah. "Marriage of Minor Girls in Jewish Law: A Legal and Historical Overview." In *Jewish Legal Writings by Women.* Ed. Micah D. Halpern and Chana Safrai. Brooklyn (NY): Lambda Publishers, 1998. 23–37.

Melchert, Christopher. "Traditionist-Jurisprudents and the Framing of Islamic Law." *Islamic Law and Society* 8.3 (2001): 383–406.

Mendoza, Kristin. "Debates on Personal Status Reform in Egypt: Three's a Crowd." Harvard University Center for Middle Eastern Studies M.A. thesis, 2004.

Mernissi, Fatima. *The Veil and the Male Elite: A Feminist Interpretation of Women's Rights in Islam.* Trans. Mary Jo Lakeland. Reading (MA): Addison-Wesley Publishing Company, 1991.

—— "Femininity as Subversion: Reflections on the Muslim Concept of *Nushuz.*" In *Speaking of Faith: Women, Religion, and Social Change.* Ed. Diana L. Eck. Philadelphia: New Society Publishers, 1986. Reprinted in Mernissi, *Women's Rebellion and Islamic Memory.*

—— "Morocco: The Merchant's Daughter and the Son of the Sultan." In *Sisterhood is Global: The International Women's Movement Anthology.* Ed. Robin Morgan, New York: Feminist Press at The City University of New York, 1984. Reprinted in Mernissi, *Women's Rebellion and Islamic Memory.*

—— *Women's Rebellion and Islamic Memory.* London and New York: Zed Books, 1996.

Miers, Suzanne. "Contemporary Forms of Slavery." *Slavery and Abolition* 17.3 (December 1996): 238–46.

Miller, Joseph C. "Muslim Slavery and Slaving: A Bibliography." *Slavery and Abolition* 13.1 (April 1992): 249–71.

Mir, Shabana. *Muslim American Women on Campus: Undergraduate Social Life and Identity.* Chapel Hill (NC): University of North Carolina Press, 2014.

Mir-Hosseini, Ziba. "The Construction of Gender in Islamic Legal Thought: Strategies for Reform." *Hawwa: Journal of Women in the Middle East and the Islamic World* 1.1 (2003): 1–28.

—— *Marriage on Trial: A Study of Islamic Family Law.* Revised edn. London: I.B. Tauris, 2000 [1993].

—— *Islam and Gender: The Religious Debate in Contemporary Iran.* Princeton: Princeton University Press, 1999.

Mir-Hosseini, Ziba, Mulki Al-Sharmani, and Jana Rumminger, eds. *Men in Charge: Rethinking Authority in the Muslim Legal Tradition.* Oxford: Oneworld Publications, 2015.

Moghissi, Haideh. *Feminism and Islamic Fundamentalism: The Limits of Postmodern Analysis.* London: Zed Books, 1999.

Moin, Mumtaz. *Umm al-Mu'minin 'A'ishah Siddiqah: Life and Works.* New Delhi: Idara Isha'at-e-Diniyat, 2003.

Moore, Allison and Paul Reynolds. "Feminist Approaches to Sexual Consent: A Critical Assessment." In *Making Sense of Sexual Consent.* Ed. Mark Cowling and Paul Reynolds. Aldershot (UK): Ashgate, 2004. 29–43.

Moore, Matthew and Karuni Rompies. "In the Cut." In *Sydney Morning Herald,* January 13, 2004; http://www.cirp.org/news/smh01-13-04/ (last accessed 07.05.04).

Moors, Annelies. *Women, Property, and Islam: Palestinian Experiences, 1920–1990.* New York: Cambridge University Press, 1995.

—— "Debating Islamic Family Law: Legal Texts and Social Practices." In *Social History of Women and Gender in the Modern Middle East.* Ed. Margaret L. Meriwether and Judith E. Tucker. Boulder (CO): Westview, 1999. 141–75.

Moosa, Ebrahim E.I. "Contrapuntal Readings in Muslim Thought: Translations and Transitions." *Journal of the American Academy of Religion* 74.1 (March 2006): 107–18.

—— *Al-Ghazali and the Poetics of Imagination.* Chapel Hill: University of North Carolina Press, 2005.

—— "The Debts and Burdens of Critical Islam." In *Progressive Muslims.* Ed. O. Safi. Oxford: Oneworld Publications, 2003. 111–27.

—— "'The Child belongs to the Bed': Illegitimacy and Islamic Law." In *Questionable Issue: Illegitimacy in South Africa.* Ed. Sandra Burman and Eleanor Preston-Whyte. Cape Town: Oxford University Press, 1992. 171–84.

Moosa, Ebrahim. *What is a Madrasa?* Chapel Hill (NC): University of North Carolina Press, 2015.

Moruzzi, Norma Claire. "Cutting Through Culture: The Feminist Discourse on Circumcision," Critique: *Critical Middle Eastern Studies* 14.2 (2005): 203–20.

Motzki, Harald. "Child Marriage in Seventeenth-Century Palestine." In *Islamic Law and Legal Interpretation: Muftis and Their Fatwas.* Ed. Masud, Messick, and Powers. Cambridge (MA): Harvard University Press, 1998. 129–40.

Mubashshir Majeed, Debra. "The Battle Has Been Joined: Gay and Polygynous Marriages Are Out of the Closet and in Search of Legitimacy." In *Cross Currents* 54.2 (Summer 2004); http://www.crosscurrents.org/Majeed0204.htm (last accessed 12.20.05).

Muhaddith.org. "Answers to Attacks Against Islam: Morality of marrying Aishah at an early age," www.muhaddith.org/Islam_Answers/Early_Marriage.html (last accessed 02.27.04).

Murad, Abdal-Hakim. "Fall of the Family." http://www.masud.co.uk/ISLAM/ahm/ family.htm (last accessed 05.24.05).

—— "Boys will be Boys: Gender Identity Issues," www.masud.co.uk/ISLAM/ahm.boys.htm (last accessed 05.24.05).

Murata, Sachiko. "Temporary Marriage (Mut'a) in Islamic Law." In *Alserat* 13.1 (Spring 1987).

—— *The Tao of Islam: A Sourcebook on Gender Relationships in Islamic Thought.* Albany: State University of New York Press, 1992.

Murray, Stephen O. "Woman-Woman Love in Islamic Societies." In *Islamic Homosexualities.* Ed. Murray and Roscoe. New York: NYU, 1997. 97–104.

—— "The Will Not to Know: Islamic Accommodations of Male Homosexuality." In *Islamic Homosexualities*. Ed. Murray and Roscoe. New York: NYU, 1997. 14–54.

Murray, Stephen O. and Will Roscoe (eds.). *Islamic Homosexualities: Culture, History, and Literature*. New York: New York University Press, 1997.

Musallam, B.F. *Sex and Society in Islam: Birth Control Before the Nineteenth Century*. Cambridge: Cambridge University Press, 1983.

Music, Rusmir. "Queer Visions of Islam." New York University, Graduate School of Arts and Sciences M.A. thesis, 2003.

Muslim Canadian Congress. "Human Rights for Minorities not up for Bargain: Muslim Canadian Congress endorses Same-Sex Marriage legislation." Press release dated February 1, 2005; posted at www.muslimcanadiancongress.org.

Muslim Women's League. "An Islamic Perspective on Sexuality," http://www.mwlusa. org/publications/positionpapers/sexuality.html (last accessed 08.04.04).

—— "Female Genital Mutilation," www.mwlusa.org/publications/positionpapers/ fgm.html (last accessed 08.04.04).

Mutahari, Murtadha. "The Islamic Modest Dress," http://al-islam.org/modest-dress/7.htm (part of the Ahl-ul Bayt Digital Islamic Library Project; last accessed 02.07.06).

An-Na'im, Abdullahi (ed.). *Islamic Family Law in a Changing World*. London: Zed Books, 2002.

—— "Shari'a and Islamic Family Law: Tradition and Transformation." In *Islamic Family Law*. Ed. An-Na'im. London: Zed Books, 2002.

Nadvi, Syed Suleman. *Women Companions of the Holy Prophet and Their Sacred Lives*. New Delhi: Islamic Book Service, 2001.

Nahas, Omar. "Yoesuf: An Islamic Idea with Dutch Quality." In *Community Organizing against Homophobia and Heterosexism: The World through Rainbow-Colored Glasses*. Ed. Samantha Wehbi. Binghamton (NY): Harrington Park Press, 2004. 53–64.

Najmabadi, Afsaneh. *Professing Selves: Transsexuality and Same-Sex Desire in Contemporary Iran*. Durham (NC): Duke University Press, 2014.

—— "Truth of Sex," http://www.iranian.com/Najmabadi/2005/January/Sex/index.html (last accessed 08.11.05).

Nasr, Shaikh Muhammad Musa. "Manhood in the Qur'aan and Sunnah." Originally published in *Al-Asaalah magazine* 20.19–21. Trans. Isma'eel Alarcon for the Salafi Society of North America's website Al-Manhaj.com, http://www. al-manhaj.com/Page1.cfm?ArticleID=52 (last accessed 03.29.05).

Nazer, Mende and Damien Lewis. *Slave: My True Story*. Cambridge (MA): Public Affairs, 2005.

Niazi, Kausar. *Modern Challenges to Muslim Families*. Lahore: Muhammad Ashraf, 1976.

Nomani, Asra Q. *Standing Alone in Mecca: An American Woman's Struggle for the Soul of Islam*. San Francisco: Harper San Francisco, 2005.

—— "Being the Leader I Want to See in the World." In *Living Islam Out Loud*. Ed. Abdul-Ghafur. Boston: Beacon Press, 2005. 139–52.

Nussbaum, Martha C. and Juha Sivola (eds.). "Introduction," in *The Sleep of Reason: Erotic Experience and Sexual Ethics in Ancient Greece and Rome*. Ed. idem. Chicago: University of Chicago Press, 2002. 1–20.

Open Letter to Baghdadi, "An Open Letter to Dr. Ibrahim Awwad Al-Badri, alias 'Abu Bakr Al-Baghdadi', and to the fighters and followers of the self-declared

'Islamic State'" September 19, 2014. English/Arabic PDF http://www.
lettertobaghdadi.com/pdf/Booklet-Combined.pdf (downloaded 02.03.15).

Orbach, Susie. *Bodies*. London: Profile Books, 2009.

Ormsby, Eric L. *Theodicy in Islamic Thought: The Dispute over Al-Ghazali's
"Best of all Possible Worlds."* Princeton (NJ): Princeton University Press,
1984.

Pateman, Carole. *The Sexual Contract*. Stanford (CA): Stanford University Press,
1988.

Peirce, Leslie P. *The Imperial Harem: Women and Sovereignty in the Ottoman
Empire*. New York: Oxford University Press, 1993.

—— *Morality Tales: Law and Gender in the Ottoman Court of Aintab*. Berkeley:
University of California Press, 2003.

Peletz, Michael G. *Gender Pluralism: Southeast Asia Since Early Modern Times*.
New York: Routledge, 2009.

Petry, Carl F. "Conjugal Rights versus Class Prerogatives: A Divorce Case in
Mamluk Cairo." In *Women in the Medieval Islamic World*. Ed. Gavin R.G.
Hambly. New York: St. Martin's Press, 1998. 227–40.

P., Laura. "Integrity of Heart, Peace of Soul: Finding My Path as an Asexual
Muslim," http://www.patheos.com/blogs/loveinshallah/2015/03/26/integ-
rity-heart-soul/#ixzz3VnMIhJNZ" (last accessed 03.29.15).

Plaskow, Judith. "Decentering Sex: Rethinking Jewish Ethics." In *God Forbid:
Religion and Sex in American Public Life*. Ed. Kathleen M. Sands. Oxford:
Oxford University Press, 2000. 23–41.

—— with Donna Berman (eds.). *The Coming of Lilith: Essays on Feminism,
Judaism, and Sexual Ethics, 1972–2003*. Boston: Beacon Press, 2005.

—— "Authority, Resistance, and Transformation: Jewish Feminist Reflections
on Good Sex." In *Good Sex: Feminist Perspectives from the World's Religions*.
Ed. Patricia Beattie Jung, et al. New Brunswick (NJ): Rutgers University
Press, 2002. 127–39.

—— "The Right Question is Theological." In *The Coming of Lilith*. Ed. Plaskow.
Boston: Beacon Press, 2005. 56–64.

Povinelli, Elizabeth A. *Economies of Abandonment: Social Belonging and
Endurance in Late Liberalism*. Durham (NC): Duke University Press, 2011.

Pregill, Michael. "ISIS, Eschatology, and Exegesis: The Propaganda of *Dabiq* and
the Sectarian Rhetoric of Militant Shi'ism," *Mizan: Journal of Interdisciplinary
Approaches to Muslim Societies and Civilizations* 1 (forthcoming).

Qaisi, Ghada G. "A Student Note: Religious Marriage Contracts: Judicial
Enforcement of Mahr Agreements in American Courts." *Journal of Law and
Religion* 15.1–2 (2000–2001): 67–82.

Al-Qaradawi, Yusuf. *The Lawful and the Prohibited in Islam* (Al-Halal wal
Haram fil Islam). Trans. Kamal El-Helbawy, et al.; reviewed by Ahmad Zaki
Hammad. Indianapolis (IN): American Trust Publications, n. d. [1980?].

Quraishi, Asifa. "Her Honor: An Islamic Critique of the Rape Laws of Pakistan
From a Woman Sensitive Perspective." In *Windows of Faith*. Ed. Webb.
Syracuse: Syracuse University Press, 2005. 102–35.

Quraishi-Landes, Asifa. "A Meditation on *Mahr*, Modernity, and Muslim
Marriage Contract Law." In *Feminism, Law, and Religion*. Edited by Marie
A. Failinger, Elizabeth R. Schiltz, and Susan J. Stabile. Surrey, UK: Ashgate,
2013. 173–95.

Rahman, Fazlur. "Law and Ethics in Islam." In *Ethics in Islam*. Ed. Hovannisian.
Malibu: Undenda Publications, 1985. 3–15.

—— *Major Themes of the Qur'an*. Minneapolis: Biblioteca Islamica, 1980.

—— *Islamic Methodology in History*. Islamabad, Pakistan: Islamic Research Institute, n.d. [1964?].

Rainbow Crescent. "Consider the Following: Logic and Reason," http://www. geocities.com/WestHollywood/7563/page2.html?200519   (last   accessed 04.19.05).

Raines, John C. and Daniel C. Maguire (eds.). *What Men Owe to Women: Men's Voices from World Religions*. Albany: State University of New York Press, 2001.

Ramadan, Tariq. "An International call for Moratorium on corporal punishment, stoning and the death penalty in the Islamic World," published March 30, 2005; http://www.tariqramadan.com/article.php3?id_article=264&lang=en (last accessed 04.13.06).

—— *Radical Reform: Islamic Ethics and Liberation*. Oxford: Oxford University Press, 2009.

—— "Response to the official statement of the Al-Azhar Legal Research Commission On the Call for a Moratorium published on March 30th, 2005." http://www.tariqramadan.com/article.php3?id_article=308&lang=en   (last accessed 04.13.06).

Rapoport, Yossef. *Marriage, Money, and Divorce in Medieval Islamic Society*. Cambridge: Cambridge University Press, 2005.

Reeves, Minou. *Muhammad in Europe: A Thousand Years of Western Myth-aking*. London: Garnet Publishing, 2001.

Reinhart, A. Kevin. "Impurity/No Danger." In *History of Religions* 30 (August 1990): 1–24.

—— "The Past in the Future of Islamic Ethics." In *Islamic Ethics of Life: Abortion, War, and Euthanasia*. Ed. Jonathan Brockopp. Columbia: University of South Carolina Press, 2003. 214–19.

—— "Islamic Law as Islamic Ethics." *Religious Ethics* 11 (1983): 186–203.

Reynolds, Paul. "The Quality of Consent: Sexual Consent, Culture, Communication, Knowledge and Ethics." In *Making Sense of Sexual Consent*. Ed. Mark Cowling and Paul Reynolds. Aldershot (UK), Ashgate, 2004. 93–108.

Rhouni, Raja. *Secular and Islamic Feminist Critiques in the Work of Fatima Mernissi*. Leiden, Brill, 2010.

Rispler-Chaim, Vardit. "*Nušuz* Between Medieval and Contemporary Islamic Law: The Human Rights Aspect." *Arabica* 39 (1992): 315–27.

Rizvi, Syed Aminul Hasan. "Adultery and Fornication in Islamic Jurisprudence: Dimensions and Perspectives." *Islamic and Comparative Law Quarterly* 2.4 (March 1982).

Roald, Anne Sofie. *Women in Islam: The Western Experience*. London: Routledge, 2001.

Roded, Ruth. *Women in Islamic Biographical Collections: From Ibn Sa'd to Who's Who*. Boulder and London: Lynne Reiner Publishers, 1994.

Rosenthal, Franz. "Ar-Razi on the Hidden Illness." *Bulletin of the History of Medicine* 52.1 (Spring 1978): 45–60.

—— "Male and Female: Described and Compared." In *Homoeroticism in Classical Arabic Literature*. Ed. J.W. Wright, Jr. and Everett K. Rowson. New York: New York University Press, 1997. 24–54.

Al-Rouhayeb, Khaled. *Before Homosexuality in the Arab-Islamic World, 1500–1800*. Chicago: University of Chicago Press, 2005.

Rowson, Everett K. "The Categorization of Gender and Sexual Irregularity in Medieval Arabic Vice Lists." In *Body Guards: The Cultural Politics of Gender Ambiguity.* Ed. Julia Epstein and Kristina Straub. New York: Routledge, 1991. 50–79.

―― "Gender Irregularity as Entertainment: Institutionalized Transvestitism at the Caliphal Court in Medieval Baghdad." In *Gender and Difference in the Middle Ages.* Ed. Sharon Farmer and Carol Braun Pasternack. Minneapolis: University of Minnesota Press, 2003. 45–72.

Rubin, Uri. "'Al-Walad li-l-Firash': On the Islamic Campaign against «Zina'»." In *Studia Islamica* 78 (1993): 5–26.

Ruxton, F.X. *Maliki Law: Being a Summary from French Translations of the Mukhtasar of Sidi Khalil.* Westport (CT): Hyperion, 1980 [1916].

El-Saadawi, Nawal. *The Hidden Face of Eve: Women in the Arab World.* Trans. and ed. Sherif Hetata. London: Zed Press 1980.

Sabbah, Fatna A. *Woman in the Muslim Unconscious.* New York: Pergamon Press 1984.

Sachedina, Zulie. "Islam, Procreation and the Law." *International Family Planning Perspectives* 16.3 (September 1990): 107–11.

Sachs, Susan. "Baptist Pastor Attacks Islam, Inciting Cries of Intolerance." *New York Times,* 06.15.2002, reproduced at http://www.commondreams.org/headlines02/0615-04.htm (last accessed 11.26.04).

Sadeghi, Behnam. *The Logic of Law Making in Islam: Women and Prayer in the Legal Tradition.* Cambridge: Cambridge University Press, 2013.

Al-Sadlaan, Saalih ibn Ghaanim. *Marital Discord* (al-Nushooz): *Its Definition, Cases, Causes, Means of Protection from it, and its Remedy from the Qur'an and Sunnah.* Trans. Jamaal al-Din M. Zarabozo. Boulder (CO): Al-Basheer Company for Publications and Translations, 1996.

Saed, Khalida. "On the Edge of Belonging." In *Living Islam Out Loud.* Ed. Abdul-Ghafur. Boston: Beacon Press, 2005. 86–91.

Safi, Omid (ed.). *Progressive Muslims: On Justice, Gender, and Pluralism.* Oxford: Oneworld Publications, 2003.

Salecl, Renata. "Cut in the Body: From Clitoridectomy to Body Art." In *Thinking Through Skin.* Ed. Sara Ahmed and Jackie Stacy. London: Routledge, 2001. 21–35.

Sanders, Paula. "Gendering the Ungendered Body: Hermaphrodites in Medieval Islamic Law." In *Women in Middle Eastern History.* Ed. Keddie and Baron. New Haven (CT): Yale University Press, 1993. 74–95.

Sanneh, Lamin. "*Shari'ah* Sanctions and State Enforcement: A Nigerian Islamic Debate and Intellectual Critique." In *Islam and the West Post 9/11.* Ed. Ron Geaves et al. Aldershot (UK): Ashgate, 2005.

Schmidtke, Sabine. "Homoeroticism and Homosexuality in Islam: A Review Article." *Bulletin of the School of Oriental and African Studies, University of London* 62.2 (1999): 260–66.

Schmitt, Arno. "*Liwat* im *fiqh:* männliche homosexualität?" *Journal of Arabic and Islamic Studies* 4 (2000–1): 49–110.

Schoeler, Gregor. "Foundations for a New Biography of Muhammad: The Production and Evaluation of the Corpus of Traditions from 'Urwa b. al-Zubayr." In *Method and Theory in the Study of Islamic Origins.* Ed. Herbert Berg. Leiden: Brill, 2003. 21–8.

Scott, Joan Wallach. *Gender and the Politics of History.* Rev. edn. New York: Columbia University Press, 1999.

Seedat, Fatima. "Sex and the Legal Subject: Women and Legal Capacity in Hanafi Law." Doctoral dissertation. McGill University, 2014.

Shaham, Ron. *The Expert Witness in Islamic Courts: Medicine and Crafts in the Service of the Law.* Chicago: University of Chicago Press, 2010.

—— "State, Feminists and Islamists: The Debate over Stipulations in Marriage Contracts in Egypt." *Bulletin of the School of Oriental and African Studies, University of London* 62.3 (1999): 462–83.

Shaheed, Farida. "Controlled or Autonomous: Identity and the Experience of the Network, Women Living Under Muslim Laws." *Signs* 19.4 (1994): 997–1019.

Shaikh, Sa'diyya. "Exegetical Violence: Nushuz in Qur'anic Gender Ideology." *Journal of Islamic Studies* 17 (1997): 49–73.

—— "Family Planning, Contraception, and Abortion in Islam: Undertaking *Khilafah.*" In *Sacred Rights: The Case for Contraception and Abortion in World Religions.* Ed. Daniel C. Maguire. Oxford: Oxford University Press, 2003. 105–28.

—— "Feminism, Epistemology and Experience: Critically (En)gendering the Study of Islam." *Journal for Islamic Studies* 5.33 (2013): 14–47.

—— *Sufi Narratives of Intimacy: Ibn 'Arabi, Gender, and Sexuality* Chapel Hill: University of North Carolina Press, 2012.

—— "Transforming Feminism: Islam, Women, and Gender Justice." In *Progressive Muslims.* Ed. O. Safi. Oxford: Oneworld Publications, 2003. 147–62.

Shanavas, T.O. "Ayesha's Age: The Myth of a Proverbial Wedding Exposed." http://www.irfi.org/articles/articles_151_200/ayesha_age_the_myth_of__a_ prover.htm (last accessed 11.04.04).

Shanely, Mary Lyndon with Nancy F. Cott, et al. *Just Marriage* (A Boston Review Book). New York: Oxford University Press, 2004.

Sharif-Clark, Asia. "Marrying a Believer." In *Living Islam Out Loud.* Ed. Abdul-Ghafur. Boston: Beacon Press, 2005. 67–71.

Al-Sheha, Abdul Rahman. *Woman in the Shade of Islam.* Trans. Mohammed Said Dabas. Khamis Mushait: Islamic Educational Center, 2000.

Sidahmed, Abdel Salam. "Problems in Contemporary Applications of Islamic Criminal Sanctions: The Penalty for Adultery in Relation to Women." *British Journal of Middle East Studies* 28.2 (2001): 187–204.

Siddiqi, Muhammad Iqbal. *Family Laws of Islam.* Delhi: International Islamic Publishers, 1988.

Siddiqi, Muzammil. "Would a 50-year-old 'Prophet of God' Have Sex with a 9-year-old Girl?" Fatwa, 10.22.03. http://www.islamonline.net/fatwa/english/ FatwaDisplay.asp?hFatwaID=106445 (last accessed 11.05.04).

Siddiqui, Mona. "*Mahr:* Legal Obligation or Rightful Demand?" *Journal of Islamic Studies* 6 (1995): 14–24.

—— "Law and the Desire for Social Control: An Insight into the Hanafi Concept of *Kafa'a* with Reference to the Fatawa 'Alamgiri (1664–1672)." In *Feminism and Islam: Legal and Literary Perspectives.* Ed. Mai Yamani with Andrew Allen. New York: New York University Press, 1996. 49–68.

Sikainga, Ahmal Alawad. "Slavery and Muslim Jurisprudence in Morocco." *Slavery and Abolition* 19.2 (August 1998): 57–72.

Silvers, Laury. "In the Book We have Left out Nothing": The Ethical Problem of the Existence of Verse 4:34 in the Qur'an." *Comparative Islamic Studies* 2.2 (2006): 171–80.

Sinfield, Alan. *On Sexuality and Power.* New York: Columbia, 2004.

Skinner, Marilyn B. *Sexuality in Greek and Roman Culture*. Malden (MA): Blackwell, 2005.

Skovgaard-Petersen, Jakob. *Defining Islam for the Egyptian State: Muftis and Fatwas of the Dar al-Ifta*. Leiden: Brill, 1997.

Smith, Jane I. "Women in Islam: Equity, Equality, and the Search for the Natural Order." *Journal of the American Academy of Religion* 47.4: 517–37.

Sonbol, Amira El Azhary (ed.). "Adults and Minors in Ottoman Shariah Courts and Modern Law." In *Women, the Family and Divorce Laws*. Syracuse: Syracuse University Press, 1996. 236–56.

—— *Women of Jordan: Islam, Labor, and the Law*. Syracuse (NY): Syracuse University Press, 2003.

—— (ed.) *Women, the Family, and Divorce Laws in Islamic History*. Syracuse (NY): Syracuse University Press, 1996.

Spellberg, D.A. *Politics, Gender, and the Islamic Past: The Legacy of 'A'isha bint Abi Bakr*. New York: Columbia University Press, 1994.

Squires, AbdurRahman Robert. "The Young Marriage of 'Aishah." http://www.muslim-answers.org/aishah.htm (last accessed 11.04.04).

Starnes, Todd. "Southern Baptist leaders affirm Vines in the wake of national attacks." Baptist Press, http://www.bpnews.net/bpnews.asp?ID=13645 (last accessed 02.26.04).

Stern, Gertrude H. *Marriage in Early Islam*. London: The Royal Asiatic Society, 1939.

Stern, Jessica and J. M. Berger. *ISIS: The State of Terror*. New York: Ecco/Harper Collins, 2015.

Stowasser, Barbara Freyer. *Women in the Qur'an, Traditions, and Interpretation*. New York: Oxford University Press, 1994.

—— "Women's Issues in Modern Islamic Thought." In *Arab Women*. Ed. Tucker. Bloomington: Indiana University Press, 1993. 3–28.

—— "Women and Citizenship in the Qur'an." In *Women, the Family, and Divorce Laws*. Ed. A. Sonbol. Syracuse: Syracuse University Press, 1996 23–38.

Submission.org. "Prophet Muhammed's Marriage to Aisha," at www.submission.org/women/Aisha/html (last accessed 02.26.04).

Syed, Mohammad Ali. *The Position of Women in Islam: A Progressive View*. Albany: State University of New York Press, 2004.

Taji-Farouki, Suha and Basheer M. Nafi (eds.). *Islamic Thought in the Twentieth Century*. London: I.B. Tauris, 2004.

The American Muslim. "Ayesha" in "Answers to Questions Non Muslims Ask." http://www.theamericanmuslim.org/2003nov_comments.php?id=447_0_23_0_C (last accessed 11.28.04).

The Inner Circle. http://www.theinnercircle-za.org/index_files/page0002.htm (last accessed 06.27.05).

Thompson, Ahmad. *The Wives of the Prophet Muhammad*. 3rd edn. London: Ta-Ha Publishers, 2004.

Thumma, Scott and Edward R. Gray (eds.). *Gay Religion*. Walnut Creek (CA): AltaMira Press, 2005.

Tin, Louis-George. *Invention of Heterosexual Culture*. Cambridge (MA): MIT Press, 2012.

Toledano, Ehud. "Representing the Slave's Body in Ottoman Society." In *Slavery and Abolition* 23.2 (August 2002): 57–74.

—— *Slavery and Abolition in the Ottoman Middle East*. Seattle: University of Washington Press, 1998.

Toubia, Nahid. *Female Genital Mutilation: A Call for Global Action.* New York: Rainbo/Women, Ink, 1995.

Treggiari, Susan. *Roman Marriage: Iusti Coniuges from the Time of Cicero to the Time of Ulpian.* Oxford: Oxford University Press, 1993.

Tucker, Judith E. "The Arab Family in History: 'Otherness' and the Study of the Family." In Tucker, ed., *Arab Women: Old Boundaries, New Frontiers* Bloomington: Indiana University Press, 1993. 195–207.

—— (ed.) *Arab Women: Old Boundaries, New Frontiers.* Bloomington: Indiana University Press, 1993.

—— *Gender and Islamic History,* Essays on Global and Comparative History. Washington DC: American Historical Association, 1994.

—— *In the House of the Law: Gender and Islamic Law in Ottoman Syria and Palestine.* Berkeley: University of California Press, 1998.

U.S. Department of State. Office of the Senior Coordinator for International Women's Issues, "Indonesia: Report on Female Genital Mutilation (FGM) or Female Genital Cutting (FGC)," June 2001; www.state.gov/g/wi/rls/rep/crfgm/ 10102.htm (last accessed 05.06.06).

—— Bureau of African Affairs, "Slavery, Abduction and Forced Servitude in Sudan," May 2002; http://www.state.gov/p/af/rls/rpt/10445.htm (last accessed 05.06.06).

Uebel, Michael. "Re-Orienting Desire: Writing on Gender Trouble in Fourteenth-Century Egypt." In *Gender and Difference in the Middle Ages.* Ed. Sharon Farmer and Carol Braun Pasternack. Minneapolis: University of Minnesota Press, 2002. 230–57.

Understanding-Islam.com, "What was Ayeshas (ra) Age at the Time of Her Marriage to the Prophet (pbuh)?" http://www.understanding-islam.com/related/ text.asp?type=question&qid=375 (last accessed 04.19.06).

Van Gelder, G.H.J. *Close Relationships: Incest and Inbreeding in Classical Arabic Literature.* London: I.B. Tauris, 2005.

Wadud Amina. "Alternative Qur'anic Interpretation and the Status of Muslim Women." In *Windows of Faith.* Ed. G. Webb. Syracuse: Syracuse University Press, 2000. 3–21.

—— "The Ethics of *Tawhid* over the Ethics of *Qiwamah.*" In *Men in Charge?* Ed. Mir-Hosseini, Al-Sharmani, and Rumminger. London: Oneworld Publications, 2015. 256–74.

—— *Inside the Gender Jihad: Women's Reform in Islam.* Oxford: Oneworld Publications, 2006.

—— *Qur'an and Woman.* Kuala Lumpur: Penerbit Fajar, Bakti 1992. Republished as *Qur'an and Woman: Rereading the Sacred Text from a Woman's Perspective.* 2nd edn. Oxford: Oxford University Press, 1999.

Walbridge, Linda. "Sex and the Single Shi'ite: Attitudes toward Mut'a Marriage in an American Lebanese Shiite Community." In *Family and Gender Among American Muslims: Issues Facing Middle Eastern Immigrants and Their Descendants.* Ed. Barbara C. Aswad and Barbara Bilgé. Philadelphia: Temple University Press, 1996 143–54.

Walters, Jonathan. "Invading the Roman Body: Manliness and Impenetrability in Roman Thought." In *Roman Sexualities.* Ed. Judith P. Hallett and Marilyn B. Skinner. Princeton: Princeton University Press, 1997. 29–43.

Wani, M.A. *Maintenance Rights of Muslim Women: Principles, Precedents and Trends.* New Delhi: Genuine Publications, 1987.

Webb, Gisela (ed.). *Windows of Faith: Muslim Women Scholar-Activists in North America.* Syracuse (NY): Syracuse University Press, 2000.

Weeks, Jeffrey. "The Rights and Wrongs of Sexuality." In *Sexuality Repositioned: Diversity and the Law.* Ed. Belinda Brooks-Gordon, et al. Portland (OR): Hart, 2004. 20–37.

—— *Invented Moralities: Sexual Values in an Age of Uncertainty.* New York: Columbia University Press, 1995.

Wertheimer, Alan. *Consent to Sexual Relations.* Cambridge: Cambridge University Press, 2003.

Willis, John Ralph (ed.). "The Ideology of Enslavement in Islam." In *Slaves and Slavery in Muslim Africa, Volume 1: Islam and the Ideology of Enslavement.* Ed. idem. London: Cass, 1985. 1–15.

Wingfield, Mark. "What are the facts behind Vines' words?" http://www.baptist-standard.com/2002/6_17/pages/vines.html (last accessed 05.05.06).

Wolfe, Michael and Beliefnet (eds.). *Taking Back Islam: American Muslims Reclaim Their Faith.* Emmaus (PA): Rodale Press, 2002.

Wynn, Lisa. "Marriage Contracts and Women's Rights in Saudi Arabia." In *Shifting Boundaries in Marriage and Divorce in Muslim Communities,* vol. 1 (Women Living Under Muslim Laws Special Dossier). Montpellier, France: Women Living Under Muslim Laws, 1996. 106–20.

Yalom, Marilyn. "Biblical Models: From Adam and Eve to the Bride of Christ." In *Inside the American Couple.* Ed. Yalom and Carstensen. Berkeley: University of California Press, 2002. 13–31.

—— *A History of the Wife.* New York: Harper Collins, 2001.

Yalom, Marilyn and Laura L. Carstensen (eds.). *Inside the American Couple: New Thinking, New Challenges.* Berkeley: University of California Press, 2002.

Al-Yawm al-Sa'udi: "'Al-tahjiz' wa ijbar al-mar'a 'ala al-zawaj min akbar anwa' al-zulm," April 13, 2005; http://www.alyaum.com.sa/issue/article.php?IN=11625&I=262888 (last accessed 04.16.06).

Zakaria, Rafia. "ISIS Wants You to Share This: How the Well-Meaning Public Became a Handmaiden for Terror." *The Nation,* http://www.thenation.com/article/193729/clicking-isis# (last accessed 01.15.15).

—— *The Upstairs Wife: An Intimate History of Pakistan.* Boston: Beacon Press, 2015.

Zomeño, Amalia. "Kafa'a in the Maliki School: A Fatwa from Fifteenth-Century Fes." In *Islamic Law: Theory and Practice.* Ed. R. Gleave and Eugenia Kermeli. London and New York: I.B. Tauris, 1997. 87–106.

—— *Dote y matrimonio en al-Andalus y el norte de Africa: Estudios sobre la jurisprudencia islamica medieval.* Madrid: Consejo Superior de Investigaciones Cientificas, 2000.

Index